Psychoanalytic Perspectives on Conflict

Since its inception, and throughout its history, psychoanalysis has been defined as a psychology of conflict. Freud's tripartite structure of id, ego, and superego, and then modern conflict theory, placed conflict at the center of mental life and its understanding at the heart of therapeutic action. As psychoanalysis has developed into the various schools of thought, the understanding of the importance of mental conflict has broadened and changed.

In *Psychoanalytic Perspectives on Conflict*, a highly distinguished group of authors outlines the main contemporary theoretical understandings of the role of conflict in psychoanalysis and what this can teach us for everyday psychoanalytic practice. The book fills a gap in psychoanalytic thinking as to the essence of conflict and therapeutic action, at a time when many theorists are reconceptualizing conflict in relation to aspects of mental life as an essential component across theories.

Psychoanalytic Perspectives on Conflict will be of interest to psychologists, psychoanalysts, social workers, and other students and professionals involved in the study and practice of psychoanalysis, psychotherapy, cognitive science, and neuroscience.

Christopher Christian, PhD, is Assistant Professor at the New School for Social Research, Director of the New School – Beth Israel Center for Clinical Training and Research, member of IPTAR, and Faculty at the Institute for Psychoanalytic Education, NYU Medical Center. He is Co-editor of *The Second Century of Psychoanalysis: Evolving Perspectives on Therapeutic Action* and is on the editorial board of the *Journal of the American Psychoanalytic Association* and *Psychoanalytic Psychology*.

Morris N. Eagle is Professor Emeritus, Derner Institute of Advanced Psychological Studies, Adelphi University and at York University in Toronto; Distinguished Educator in Residence at California Lutheran University. He is a former president of the Division of Psychoanalysis, American Psychological Association; is a Fellow of the Royal society of Canada; and was given the Sigourney Award for life time contribution to psychoanalysis. He is the author and co-author of over 150 journal articles and over a 100 chapters in edited books. His books include Recent Developments in Psychoanalysis: A Critical Evaluation (Harvard University Press, 1989), Psychoanalytic Therapy as Health Care: Effectiveness and Economics in the 21st Century (Analytic Press, 1999); From Classical to Contemporary Psychoanalysis: A Critique and Integration (Routledge, 2011); and Attachment and Psychoanalysis: Theory, Research, and Clinical Implications (The Guilford Press, 2013); and Core Psychoanalytic Concepts: Evidence and Conceptual Critique (2 volumes) (Routledge, in press).

David L. Wolitzky, PhD, is a faculty member in the Department of Psychology, New York University, where he held the position of Director of Clinical Training for the PhD Program in Clinical Psychology. He is a graduate of the New York Psychoanalytic Institute and is a Supervisor in the New York University Post-doctoral Program in Psychoanalysis and Psychotherapy. David is the Editor of the *Psychological Issues* book series.

In this major contribution to the field, the editors have taken the fundamental psychoanalytic premise of *conflict* as a central organizing construct for purposes of comparing and contrasting a broad array of psychoanalytic perspectives on personality development, psychopathology and therapeutic action. Their approach provides a kaleidoscopic perspective that illuminates both intriguing connections and subtle difference among diverse psychoanalytic approaches. Bringing together outstanding contributions from some of the leading figures in the field, the editors have produced a superb volume that is essential reading for anyone interested in the future of psychoanalysis.

> —**Jeremy D. Safran**, PhD, Chair & Professor of Psychology,
> The New School for Social Research

Psychoanalytic approaches differ in the way they deal with conflict—with some believing that conflict can be resolved and others rejecting such a prospect. Indeed, no psychoanalytic approach fails to conceptualize conflict, and one can reasonably conclude that conflict is fundamental to a psychoanalytic way of thinking about human beings and about treatment. Yet, it is surprising to realize that conflict has not been the subject of more focus and reflection. Until now, Christian, Eagle and Wolitzky have done an extraordinary service to the field by collecting essays from different psychoanalytic orientations—Contemporary Freudian, Object Relations, Self Psychology, Relational, Lacanian and Attachment—written by some of the most original thinkers in the field. Treatment issues are central, but the book also covers neurobiological and developmental issues as well. For psychoanalysts who long for dialogue across psychoanalytic orientations, this book is exemplary, and deserves a wide audience.

> —**Elliot Jurist**, Professor of Psychology and Philosophy, the
> Graduate Center and the City College of New York, the City
> University of New York, and Editor of *Psychoanalytic Psychology*

PSYCHOLOGICAL ISSUES BOOK SERIES

DAVID WOLITZKY
Series Editor

The basic mission of *Psychological Issues* is to contribute to the further development of psychoanalysis as a science, as a respected scholarly enterprise, as a theory of human behavior, and as a therapeutic method.

Over the past 50 years, the series has focused on fundamental aspects and foundations of psychoanalytic theory and clinical practice as well as on work in related disciplines relevant to psychoanalysis. *Psychological Issues* does not aim to represent or promote a particular point of view. The contributions cover broad and integrative topics of vital interest to all psychoanalysts as well as to colleagues in related disciplines. They cut across particular schools of thought and tackle key issues such as the philosophical underpinnings of psychoanalysis, psychoanalytic theories of motivation, conceptions of therapeutic action, the nature of unconscious mental functioning, psychoanalysis and social issues, and reports of original empirical research relevant to psychoanalysis. The authors often take a critical stance toward theories and offer a careful theoretical analysis and conceptual clarification of the complexities of theories and their clinical implications, drawing upon relevant empirical findings from psychoanalytic research as well as from research in related fields.

The Editorial Board continues to invite contributions from social/ behavioral sciences such as anthropology and sociology, from biological sciences such as physiology and the various brain sciences, and from scholarly humanistic disciplines such as philosophy, law, and esthetics.

Members of the board

Wilma Bucci
Derner Institute, Adelphi University
Diana Diamond
City University of New York
Morris Eagle
Derner Institute, Adelphi University
Peter Fonagy
University College London
Andrew Gerber
Austen Riggs Center
Robert Holt
New York University
Paolo Migone
Editor, Psicoterapia e Scienze Umane
Fred Pine
Albert Einstein College of Medicine

PSYCHOLOGICAL ISSUES BOOK SERIES

DAVID WOLITZKY
Series Editor

Published by Routledge

75. *Psychoanalytic Perspectives on Conflict,* Christopher Christian, Morris N. Eagle and David L. Wolitzky

74. *Manual of Regulation-Focused Psychotherapy for Children (RFP-C) with Externalizing Behaviors: A Psychodynamic Approach,* Leon Hoffman, Tim Rice and Tracy Prout

73. *Myths of Termination: What patients can teach psychoanalysts about endings,* Judy Leopold Kantrowitz

72. *Identity and the New Psychoanalytic Explorations of Self-organization,* Mardi Horowitz

71. *Memory, Myth, and Seduction: Unconscious Fantasy and the Interpretive Process,* Jean-Georges Schimek & Deborah L. Browning

70. *From Classical to Contemporary Psychoanalysis: A Critique and Integration,* Morris N. Eagle

Published by Jason Aronson

69. *Primary Process Thinking: Theory, Measurement, and Research,* Robert R. Holt

68. *The Embodied Subject: Minding the Body in Psychoanalysis,* John P. Muller & Jane G. Tillman

67. *Self-Organizing Complexity in Psychological Systems,* Craig Piers, John P. Muller, & Joseph Brent

66. *Help Him Make You Smile: The Development of Intersubjectivity in the Atypical Child,* Rita S. Eagle

65. *Erik Erikson and the American Psyche: Ego, Ethics, and Evolution,* Daniel Burston

Published by International Universities Press

64. *Subliminal Explorations of Perception, Dreams, and Fantasies: The Pioneering Contributions of Charles Fisher,* Howard Shevrin

62/63. *Psychoanalysis and the Philosophy of Science: Collected Papers of Benjamin B. Rubinstein, MD,* Robert R. Holt

61. *Validation in the Clinical Theory of Psychoanalysis: A Study in the Philosophy of Psychoanalysis,* Adolf Grunbaum

60. *Freud's Concept of Passivity,* Russell H. Davis

Psychoanalytic Perspectives on Conflict

Edited by Christopher Christian, Morris N. Eagle and David L. Wolitzky

LONDON AND NEW YORK

First published 2017
by Routledge
2 Park Square, Milton Park, Abingdon, Oxon OX14 4RN

and by Routledge
711 Third Avenue, New York, NY 10017

Routledge is an imprint of the Taylor & Francis Group, an informa business

© 2017 selection and editorial matter, Christopher Christian, Morris N. Eagle and David L. Wolitzky; individual chapters, the contributors

The right of the editors to be identified as the authors of the editorial material, and of the authors for their individual chapters, has been asserted in accordance with sections 77 and 78 of the Copyright, Designs and Patents Act 1988.

All rights reserved. No part of this book may be reprinted or reproduced or utilised in any form or by any electronic, mechanical, or other means, now known or hereafter invented, including photocopying and recording, or in any information storage or retrieval system, without permission in writing from the publishers.

Trademark notice: Product or corporate names may be trademarks or registered trademarks, and are used only for identification and explanation without intent to infringe.

British Library Cataloguing in Publication Data
A catalogue record for this book is available from the British Library

Library of Congress Cataloging in Publication Data
Names: Christian, Christopher, editor. | Eagle, Morris N., editor. | Wolitsky, David L., editor.
Title: Psychoanalytic perspectives on conflict / edited by Christopher Christian, Morris N. Eagle and David L. Wolitzky.
Description: 1 Edition. | New York : Routledge, 2016. | Series: Psychological issues | Includes bibliographical references.
Identifiers: LCCN 2016009963 | ISBN 9781138795204 (hardback) | ISBN 9781138795211 (pbk.) | ISBN 9781315758589 (ebook)
Subjects: LCSH: Psychoanalysis.
Classification: LCC BF173 .P77634 2016 | DDC 150.19/5—dc23
LC record available at https://lccn.loc.gov/2016009963

ISBN: 978-1-138-79520-4 (hbk)
ISBN: 978-1-138-79521-1 (pbk)
ISBN: 978-1-315-75858-9 (ebk)

Typeset in Times New Roman
by Apex CoVantage, LLC

Printed and bound by CPI Group (UK) Ltd, Croydon, CR0 4YY

Contents

Contributors		ix
Acknowledgments		xv
Introduction		xvi

1 Inner conflict in Freudian theory   1
MORRIS N. EAGLE

2 The evolution of modern conflict theory   21
CHRISTOPHER CHRISTIAN

**3 The fate of conflict and the impoverishment of
our clinical methods**   38
FRED BUSCH

4 Conflict from the perspective of free association   51
ANTON O. KRIS

5 Inner conflict in Fairbairn's theory of endopsychic structure   63
MORRIS N. EAGLE

6 Kleinian and post-Kleinian perspectives on conflict   91
NEAL VORUS

7 Analytic trust, transference, and the importance of conflict   106
STEVEN ELLMAN

**8 Emergence of conflict during the development of self:
a relational self psychology perspective**   127
JAMES L. FOSSHAGE

viii Contents

9 The phenomenological contextualism of conflict: an intersubjective perspective 146
CHRIS JAENICKE

10 Conflict and change: producer, trigger, sign, outcome 160
ADRIENNE HARRIS

11 The dialectic of desire: a view of intrapsychic conflict in the work of Jacques Lacan 177
DAVID LICHTENSTEIN

12 Forces at play in psychical conflict 195
JEAN LAPLANCHE

13 On conflict in attachment theory and research 210
HOWARD STEELE AND MIRIAM STEELE

14 Addressing defenses against painful emotions: modern conflict theory in psychotherapeutic approaches with children 223
LEON HOFFMAN, TIMOTHY R. RICE, AND TRACY A. PROUT

15 Implicit attitudes, unconscious fantasy, and conflict 242
BENJAMIN A. SAUNDERS AND PHILIP S. WONG

16 Neural basis of intrapsychic and unconscious conflict and repetition compulsion 260
HEATHER A. BERLIN AND JOHN MONTGOMERY

References 279
Index 312

Contributors

Heather A. Berlin, PhD, is a cognitive neuroscientist and Assistant Professor of Psychiatry at the Icahn School of Medicine at Mount Sinai, where she also completed her NIMH Post-doctoral Fellowship. She explores the neural mechanisms of impulsive and compulsive psychiatric disorders and is interested in the neural basis of consciousness, dynamic unconscious processes, and creativity. Dr. Berlin is a Visiting Scholar at the New York Psychoanalytic Society and was a Visiting Professor at Vassar College, the Swiss Federal Institute of Technology/ University of Zurich, and The Hebrew University of Jerusalem. She received her DPhil from the University of Oxford and Master of Public Health from Harvard University.

Christopher Christian, PhD, is Assistant Professor at the New School for Social Research, Director of the New School – Beth Israel Center for Clinical Training and Research, member of IPTAR, and Faculty at the Institute for Psychoanalytic Education, NYU Medical Center. He is Co-editor of *The Second Century of Psychoanalysis: Evolving Perspectives on Therapeutic Action* and is on the editorial board of the *Journal of the American Psychoanalytic Association* and *Psychoanalytic Psychology.*

Fred Busch, PhD, is a Training and Supervising Analyst at the Boston Psychoanalytic Society and Institute, a Geographical Supervising Analyst of the Minnesota Psychoanalytic Institute, and a Visiting Supervisor at the Vermont Psychoanalytic Institute. Dr. Busch has published over 70 articles in the psychoanalytic literature and three books, primarily on the method and theory of treatment. His work has been translated into eight languages, and he has been invited to present over 160 papers and clinical workshops nationally and internationally. His third book, *Creating a Psychoanalytic Mind: A Method and Theory of Psychoanalysis,* was published by Routledge in Fall 2014.

Morris N. Eagle is Professor Eemeritus, Derner Institute of Advanced Psychological Studies, Adelphi University and at York University in Toronto; Distinguished Educator in Residence at California Lutheran University. He is a former president of the Division of Psychoanalysis, American Psychological Association; is a Fellow of the Royal society of Canada; and was given the Sigourney Award for life time contribution to psychoanalysis. He is the author and co-author of over 150 journal articles and over a 100 chapters in edited books. His books include Recent Developments in Psychoanalysis: A Critical Evaluation (Harvard University Press, 1989), Psychoanalytic Therapy as Health Care: Effectiveness and Economics in the 21st Century (Analytic Press, 1999); From Classical to Contemporary Psychoanalysis: A Critique and Integration (Routledge, 2011); and Attachment and Psychoanalysis: Theory, Research, and Clinical Implications (The Guilford Press, 2013); and Core Psychoanalytic Concepts: Evidence and Conceptual Critique (2 volumes) (Routledge, in press).

Steven Ellman, PhD, is Professor Emeritus and past Director of the Doctoral Program in Clinical Psychology, City University; past President of IPTAR, where he is a Training Analyst; and he was the First President of Confederation of Independent Psychoanalytic Societies (CIPS). Dr. Ellman is the author of over 110 papers and chapters on psychoanalysis and sleep and brain/behavioral research. His books include *Freud's Technique Papers: A Contemporary Perspective* (Jason Aronson, 1991), *The Mind in Sleep* (John Wiley & Sons, 1991), *When Theories Touch: An Historical and Theoretical Integration of Psychoanalytic Thought* (Karnac Books, 2010), and *Enactment: Toward a New Approach to the Therapeutic Relationship* (Jason Aronson, 1998).

James L. Fosshage, PhD, is Founding President, International Association for Psychoanalytic Self Psychology and Advisory Board Member, International Association for Psychoanalysis and Psychotherapy. He is Co-founder, Board Director, and Faculty member, National Institute for the Psychotherapies (NYC); Founding Faculty Member, Institute for the Psychoanalytic Study of Subjectivity; and Clinical Professor of Psychology, New York University Post-doctoral Program in Psychotherapy and Psychoanalysis. He is on the Editorial Boards of eight psychoanalytic journals. Author of over 100 psychoanalytic publications and eight books, his most recent book, co-authored with Joseph Lichtenberg and Frank Lachmann, is entitled *Enlivening the Self* (Routledge, 2015).

Adrienne Harris, PhD, is Faculty at New York University Post-doctoral Program in Psychotherapy and Psychoanalysis and at the Psychoanalytic Institute of Northern California. In 2009, she, Lewis Aron, and Jeremy Safron established the Sándor Ferenczi Center at the New School University. With Lewis Aron she edits the Relational Book Series. She published *Gender as Soft Assembly* (Analytic Press, 2005); she edited, with Muriel Dimen, *Storms in Her Head* (Other Press, 2001), with Lewis Aron, *The Legacy of Sándor Ferenczi* (Analytic Press, 1993), with Steven Botticelli, *First Do No Harm: Psychoanalysis, Warmaking and Resistance* (Routledge, 2010) and, in 2015 with Steven Kuchuck, *The Legacy of Sándor Ferenczi: From Ghost to Ancestor* (Taylor & Francis).

Leon Hoffman, MD, is Training and Supervising Analyst in Child, Adolescent, and Adult Psychoanalysis at the New York Psychoanalytic Society and Institute. His recent publications include Hoffman, L., Rice, T. R., and Prout, T. A. (2016). *Manual of regulation-focused psychotherapy for children (RFP-C) with externalizing behaviors: A psychodynamic approach.* New York, NY: Routledge; "Mentalization, Emotion Regulation, Countertransference" in the *Journal of Infant, Child, and Adolescent Psychotherapy*; and "Emotions Influence Cognition: The Missing Ingredient in School Evaluations" in *Psychoanalytic Study of the Child*.

Jonathan House, MD, practices psychiatry and psychoanalysis in New York City. For many years he has taught at Columbia's psychoanalytic institute; currently, he also teaches courses on Freud and on Laplanche at Columbia's Institute for Comparative Literature and Society. Laplanche appointed him to, and he still serves on, the Conseil Scientifique of Fondation Laplanche. General Editor of Unconscious In Translation, a new publisher, he has translated and edited translations of Laplanche and of others. He served as Secretary of American Psychoanalytic Association and serves on the IPA's Free Association Work Group of the Committee on Conceptual Integration.

Chris Jaenicke, PhD, is a Faculty Member and Training and Supervising Analyst at the Arbeitsgemeinschaft für Psychoanalyse und Psychotherapie,e.V. Berlin. He is in private practice in Berlin, Germany, and is the author of *The Risk of Relatedness: Intersubjectivity Theory in Clinical Practice* (Jason Aronson, 2008), *Change in Psychoanalysis: An Analyst's Reflections on the Therapeutic Relationship* (Routledge,

2011) and *The Search for a Relational Home: An Intersubjective View of Therapeutic Action* (Routledge, 2015). He is an Editor of *Self Psychology: European Journal for Psychoanalytic Therapy and Research.*

Anton O. Kris, MD, Professor of Psychiatry, part time, at Harvard Medical School, has been a psychiatrist for over 55 years, a psychoanalyst for over 45 years, and a Training and Supervising Analyst at the Boston Psychoanalytic Society and Institute for over 35 years. He is the author of *Free Association: Method and Process* (Karnac Books, 1996) and numerous papers. Dr. Kris has served on the editorial boards of several of the major psychoanalytic journals and on the board of trustees of The Anna Freud Centre, The Anna Freud Foundation, and Sigmund Freud Archives, of which he was briefly Executive Director.

David Lichtenstein, PhD, is in private practice in New York. He is on the faculty at CUNY s doctoral program in clinical psychology, a founding member of Apres-Coup Psychoanalytic Association and the editor of *Division /Review*, a quarterly publication on psychoanalysis by Division 39. He has written extensively on psychoanalysis, Lacan, his clinical work with children, art, and politics.

John Montgomery, PhD, received his doctorate in neuroscience from Caltech and his BA in molecular genetics from Trinity College in Dublin, Ireland. He is the developer of Homeostasis Psychology, a new therapeutic method and theoretical model that seeks to integrate neuroscience, psychology, and Eastern and Western spiritual traditions into a unified framework that addresses nearly all psychological health and dysfunction. He is an Adjunct Professor in the Department of Psychology at New York University.

Tracy A. Prout, PhD, is Assistant Professor of Psychology at the Ferkauf Graduate School of Psychology at Yeshiva University. Her research focuses on evidence-based psychodynamic interventions for children, the interplay between defensive functioning and religious coping, and the role of religiosity and spirituality in mental health. She received post-doctoral training in psychodynamic psychotherapy at the Institute for Psychoanalytic Education at NYU Medical Center and has advanced research training through the International Psychoanalytical Association. She maintains a private practice in New York City.

Timothy R. Rice, MD, is Assistant Professor of Psychiatry in the Division of Child and Adolescent Psychiatry at the Icahn School of Medicine at Mount Sinai in New York, NY. He currently serves as an attending psychiatrist on the child and adolescent psychiatric inpatient unit at St. Luke's Hospital. His interest in conflict theory stems from his work with Leon Hoffman, MD, with whom he has written *Manual of Regulation-Focused Psychotherapy for Children (RFP-C) with Externalizing Behaviors* (Routledge, 2016), a manualized psychodynamic approach for children with oppositional defiant disorder. His interests include developing this approach in various child and adolescent populations in an academic setting.

Benjamin A. Saunders, PhD, is an Assistant Professor of Psychology at Long Island University Brooklyn. His current research investigates the role of system-justifying ideologies in predicting social and political behavior.

Howard Steele, PhD, is Professor and Director of Graduate Studies in Psychology at the New School for Social Research, where he is Co-director of the Center for Attachment Research. He is also senior and founding editor of the international bi-monthly journal, *Attachment and Human Development*. H. Steele & M. Steele are co-editors of the 2008 volume, *Clinical Applications of the Adult Attachment Interview* (Guilford Press). H. Steele is founding and current President of the Society for Emotion and Attachment Studies (SEAS). With M. Steele, H. Steele is editor of the forthcoming *Handbook of Attachment-Based Interventions* to be published by Guilford Press in 2017.

Miriam Steele, PhD, is Professor and Director of the Doctoral Program in Clinical Psychology at the New School for Social Research, where she is Co-director of the Center for Attachment Research. An Anna Freud Center trained psychoanalyst, Miriam is a member of the American Psychoanalytic Association. Miriam initiated the London Parent-Child Project, a major longitudinal study of intergenerational patterns of attachment that gave rise to the concept of Reflective Functioning. Most recently, M. Steele (with H. Steele and Anne Murphy) has pioneered the development of a Group Attachment-Based Intervention aimed at preventing child maltreatment and promoting attachment security.

xiv Contributors

Neal Vorus, PhD, is a Training and Supervising Analyst and Faculty Member at the Institute for Psychoanalytic Training and Research (IPTAR) and is an Adjunct Clinical Assistant Professor at the New York University Post-doctoral Program in Psychotherapy and Psychoanalysis. He is the author from publications on the integration of contemporary Freudian and modern Kleinian perspectives. Dr. Vorus is in private practice in New York City, where he treats both children and adults.

Philip S. Wong, PhD, is Professor of Psychology and Director of the PhD Program in Clinical Psychology at Long Island University Brooklyn. Dr. Wong's clinical-theoretical orientation combines psychodynamic and cognitive psychology, with an emphasis on contemporary ego- and self psychology. His research explores the implicit emotional and motivational dimensions of personality and psychopathology. Dr. Wong has longstanding clinical interests in ethnic minority and East Asian American experiences and is in private practice in New York City.

Acknowledgments

The idea for this book owes its origin to a series of stimulating discussions beginning at the Community Counseling and Parent Child Study Center of California Lutheran University, and later at Austen Riggs, where the editors explored the fate of a central psychoanalytic concept – conflict – and agreed that the term was overdue for a critical reevaluation. Given the importance of such a topic, it was not difficult to recruit such a distinguished group of authors. We are pleased to say that the book brings together colleagues, whose work we admire, and to these authors we owe our gratitude.

Chapter 12, "Forces at Play in Psychical Conflict," an article by Jean Laplanche, was excerpted from *Between: Seduction and Inspiration: Man*, published by Unconscious in Translation in 2015. Figure 16.1, in Chapter 16, is taken from the book, *Dreams: Disguise of Forbidden Wishes or Transparent Reflections of a Distinct Brain State?* by Robert W. McCarley, published in 2006, and is used with permission from John Wiley and Sons.

The editors would like to acknowledge the invaluable contribution of Dr. Kerri Danskin for her critical review of each chapter. We would also like to thank Christine Anderson for her careful attention to the preparation of the final manuscript. We also would like to thank Routledge and Kate Hawes for their support. We are pleased that this volume will be part of the Psychological Issues book series.

Introduction

From its beginnings psychoanalysis regarded conflict as inevitable, ubiquitous, and centrally implicated in the formation of symptoms and of character. Indeed, E. Kris (1947) described psychoanalysis as the view of mental life from the perspective of intrapsychic conflict. Kris made this comment at a time when the practice of many analysts comprised so-called classical (neurotic) patients. As we know, in the past several decades there has been a "widening scope of psychoanalysis" (L. Stone, 1954) in response to the attempt to treat patients beyond the neurotic range (e.g., borderline and narcissistic patients). This development led to new views concerning the centrality of dealing with conflict in treatment.

Much more recently, we saw an attempt to reassess the role of conflict reflected in the fact that the topic of conflict was selected as the organizing theme at the 2014 Spring meeting of the Division of Psychoanalysis in the American Psychological Association.

The program stated:

> Conflict is located at every layer of our experience – whether conceptualized with the structural or topographic models, intersubjectively determined emotional experience, the impact and constrictions of social norms and social traditions, or governments, spiritual beliefs, nations, and between factions of psychoanalysis. Conflict is a foundation of human suffering, familial in-fighting, membership and alienation, violence and war; while equally fundamental to clarification, contextualization, illumination, celebration of differences, resolution and peace.

Having decided that it was timely to survey current views of conflict, we invited authors with diverse views regarding conflict to discuss the topic in terms of their theoretical and clinical perspectives. To set the stage for the chapters that follow, we start with a list of core questions that one or more of the contributors have addressed and that are important to a contemporary psychoanalytic appraisal of the role and nature of conflict. These questions include the following: (1) Is conflict inherent in the human condition, present from birth? Or does it emerge mainly as a function of environmental failure of one sort or another? (2) What are we conflicted about? Are conflicts about sexual and aggressive wishes primary? Or are conflicts about other needs, wishes, and desires at least as important? (3) Is inner conflict at the center of psychopathology? Or are there forms of psychopathology in which inner conflict is not primary? (4) Should a focus on inner conflict be at the center of our therapeutic approach? Or are there other foci that are equally important? (5) What is the most effective way to address inner conflict in the clinical situation? (6) Is a conceptualization in terms of conflict among different structures of the personality the most useful way to understand inner conflict? (7) Are there empirical studies on conflict outside the clinical situation that broaden our understanding of the nature of conflict?

We will summarize briefly each of the chapters and for each contribution note the aforementioned issues that are addressed. Virtually all the authors seem to agree that conflict is a central aspect of psychic life and that it plays an important role in treatment. However, there are different views regarding how conflict is defined, the origins of the conflicts, their centrality in the patient's symptoms and personality style, and how they should be approached in treatment.

In this Introduction, our aim as editors is not to present a detailed summary of all the major points in each chapter. Rather, we want to identify central themes in each of the chapters in order to give readers an idea of what to expect. Readers will see how each author elaborates his or her views of conflict in the context of their particular theoretical perspective. We deliberately invited authors who would represent a wide range of views. In the concluding section of this chapter, we will offer some comments that reflect our sense of some overarching issues that emerge from the authors' contributions.

In Chapter 1, Eagle traces the evolution of Sigmund Freud's views of conflict and his formulation of the drive-defense model, a model applied to neurotic symptoms as well as to character traits, dreams, and parapraxes. As we know, according to the classical conception of the mind, sexual and aggressive wishes seek discharge and expression in consciousness.

However, whether these aims are achieved is influenced by the ego's appraisal of the relative pleasure versus potential unpleasure likely to accompany the awareness and/or expression of such wishes. Considerations of morality are also important in estimating the balance of pleasure and unpleasure in that the possibility of arousing negative affects such as guilt, shame, or humiliation might be part of the cost of attempting to fulfill a wish. Thus, there are conflicts between the id and the ego as well as between the id and the superego. This view of the mind as consisting of separate agencies was intended to account for the dynamic interplay of the person's incompatible aims. In this drive-defense model of mental functioning, the core neurotic conflict was the Oedipal conflict.

According to S. Freud (1926a), the principle anxieties defended against are what he called the "danger situations" of childhood and what Brenner (1994) referred to as the "calamities of childhood" in his presentation of modern conflict theory. The main so-called dangers or calamities are the loss of the object, loss of the object's love, castration anxiety, and superego condemnation. Signal anxiety refers to a warning that initiates the defensive processes in order to avoid a full blown traumatic anxiety.

In short, Freud saw inner conflict as due to the incompatibility between "an idea and the ego," which he early on referred to as "defense hysteria," the defense being the ego's attempt to repress the unacceptable wish. This conceptualization led to the "drive-defense" model and was applied not only to neurotic symptoms but also to dreams and personality traits and patterns.

Freud's influential theories of conflict inspired experimental research with both humans and animals. For example, the experimental induction of conflict was seen as producing an "experimental neurosis" in animals. The "experimental neurosis" induced in animals, such as that elicited by creating an approach-avoidance conflict, was considered by some to be an analog of neurosis in humans. In the 1950s, conflict was also implicated in the understanding of psychosomatic disorders. Each psychosomatic disorder was thought to be associated with a particular conflict. Hypertension, for example, was thought to result from the inhibition of aggression. As another example, according to Alexander (1950), peptic ulcers were thought to be an expression of unresolved dependency conflicts, a formulation since discredited.

The last half century has seen serious challenges to Freudian theory, including differing views of the centrality and nature of conflict. The contributors to this volume discuss many of these differences.

Introduction xix

In his contribution to the current volume, Christian (Chapter 2) reviews the development of ego psychology and presents Brenner's formulation of "modern conflict theory." In contrast to the ego psychology conception of separate agencies of the mind (id, ego, superego), Brenner advanced the notion of "compromise formation" as a substitute for Freud's structural theory. In this view, unlike Hartmann's conflict-free spheres of ego functioning, conflict is inevitable and ubiquitous. The compromises we form are the result of the dynamic interplay of sexual and aggressive wishes and fantasies; anxieties based on the "calamities of childhood" (or what Freud referred to as "danger situations"), moral standards, fear of guilt and punishment, and the appraisal of reality. On this view, all behavior is a compromise formation. Compromise formations differ with regard to how adaptive or maladaptive they are. The aim of the organism is to seek pleasure and avoid unpleasure. As implied earlier, the aim of psychoanalysis is not the elimination of conflict; it is rather to facilitate more adaptive compromise formations, that is, to enhance pleasure and reduce unpleasure. Brenner (1994) claimed that it was neither accurate nor useful to posit separate agencies of the mind because every behavior, normal as well as pathological, is a compromise formation based on various conflicting aims. At the same time, he maintained the Freudian view that the compromises formed are based on the extent to which sexual and aggressive wishes need to be contained.

In his account of Fairbairn's object relations theory, Eagle (Chapter 5) provides a detailed account of the place of conflict in that theory. Although, according to Fairbairn, splits in the ego are due to frustration and deprivation, insofar as some degree of frustration and deprivation is inevitable, it would appear that splits in the personality are also inevitable. According to Fairbairn, the primary conflict individuals have to cope with is the one between the "regressive lure of identification and the progressive urge toward separation." Fairbairn also refers to variations of this basic conflict as one between "infantile dependence" versus "mature dependence" and as "devotion" to early internal objects versus separation from them. He also describes relating to others as stand-ins for an internal object versus relating to an actual, external other. As we know, relatedness is a key theme for Fairbairn, who tells us that libido is object-seeking rather than pleasure-seeking. And, in the object-seeking is a persistent need to maintain ties to early objects. Although retaining a Freudian view, Mahler's conception of symbiosis versus separation-individuation bears some similarity to Fairbairn's view of what our basic conflict is.

In Busch's view (Chapter 3), although it can be said that traditional Freudian theory has emphasized intrapsychic conflict to the point of neglecting trauma and actual object relations, the pendulum has swung too far in the direction of neglecting unconscious conflict and fantasy. In so doing, it becomes more difficult for the patient to refind his or her mind. Analysis of unconscious conflict is seen as the path to confronting one's "devastating fears" (e.g., loss of the self, loss of the object, castration anxiety). According to Busch, one can acknowledge the importance of environmental deficits and of trauma but at the same time realize that unmet needs become enmeshed in conflict and in unconscious fantasy. For instance, a depressed mother who is emotionally unavailable to her child can make her child feel that he or she is excessively "needy." Such a feeling can readily become associated with feelings of guilt and an approach-avoidance conflict in relation to the mother.

Approaching conflict from an ego psychological perspective and stressing the importance of observing the patient's pattern of free associations, Kris (Chapter 4) makes the distinction between what he calls convergent and divergent conflicts. Convergent conflicts are those that in traditional psycho-analytic theory are conflicts between a wish and a defense against the wish or a conflict between two wishes in which one is defending against the other. Kris calls our attention to divergent conflicts which emerge in the patient's free associations when we see evidence in the transference of the alternation between wishes, neither of which is a defense against the other. For example, one might see indications of an erotic transference at one point and a wish to be taken care of as a child at another point, with neither wish being a defense against the other. The patient can also experience these two wishes as a dilemma, as an either-or situation. To illustrate this point, Kris cites a paper by Ogden (2002), which noted that in Freud's *Mourning and Melancholia* he referred to a "struggle between the wish to live with the living and the wish to be at one with the dead." Kris regards the mourning process as "the paradigm for the resolution of all divergent conflicts." Although Kris emphasizes the distinction between divergent and convergent conflicts, he states "divergent conflicts are *always accompanied* by convergent conflicts" (original italics). Kris also discusses the centrality of loss. As a consequence of choice, loss is inevitable, that is, one has to mourn the path not taken.

In Chapter 6, Vorus presents Klein's view of conflict, primarily conflicts relating to aggression. Setting aside some of Klein's oft-challenged assumptions about the young infant's mind and the early indications of the Oedipus complex, the essence of Klein's view is that the infant's and child's core conflict is between love and hate toward the caregiver. This conflict is present once one enters the "depressive position." It gives rise to anxiety and guilt about destroying the caregiver and leads the child to want to preserve a positive image of the caregiver via an internalization of a good, whole object, presumably not to jeopardize its need to be cared for. As Vorus points out, Klein viewed conflict "as ubiquitous from the start of life, as a primary condition of human existence." He then goes on to discuss some of the contributions of the post-Kleinians, noting that it was Bion, her most influential follower, who focused on the intersubjective basis for the development of the depressive position. As is well known, Bion developed his ideas with a focus on the concepts of the "container and the contained" to describe the "metabolization" of the infant's raw emotions. On this view, more fundamental than love and hate is the caregiver's failure to fulfill the role of an adequate "container." According to Vorus's description of Bion's views, "love and hatred are not bedrock. . . . Rather, the drive to know and represent brute reality in bearable form is most fundamental."

For Harris (Chapter 10), the patient experiences a conflict between strivings for growth and separation versus attempting to heal the dead or dying object. This is reminiscent of discussions of "survivor guilt" and "separation guilt." Note also the similarity to the earlier description in Kris's chapter, drawing on Ogden, of the struggle between the wish to be with the living and the wish to be at one with the dead. Harris emphasizes that the patient's difficulty of moving forward is due to the fear that if the mourning of old object ties has been completed, the result will be chaos. Harris makes the interesting point that in facilitating the patient's growth, the therapist needs to mourn the end of the caretaking process in general as well as his or her ties to the particular patient. To use Mahler's terms, we are talking about a separation-individuation process on the part of the patient and a therapist who is able to mourn the caretaking role while facilitating the patient's increasing individuation.

Ellman's chapter (Chapter 7), like Harris's, focuses on treatment and the patient-analyst relationship. With regard to conflict, he stresses the precondition that needs to be met to make it possible and productive to analyze conflict. That precondition is the development and maintenance of what Ellman calls "analytic trust." Such trust makes the patient more receptive to interpretation, including interpretation of the transference and the conflicts expressed via the transference. In other words, the patient needs to experience being "held" for interpretations to be effective. Ellman implies that "analytic trust" is itself therapeutic, even before interpretation is used. As we know, it is commonly said that the patient has to experience the analyst as an old object for the transference to flourish and as a new object for it to be resolved. How does analytic trust develop if the therapist is seen as an old object? The answer seems to be that the analyst's benevolent, therapeutic attitude and capacity to provide a safe holding environment will go a long way, even before interpretation, toward enabling the patient to experience the analyst as a new object or, perhaps we should say, "new enough" for the patient to tolerate interpretations of conflict.

Self and object relations as well as intersubjectivity theorists have in common a focus on the self in a relational matrix, that is, the interaction of two subjectivities. Therefore, it is not surprising that the chapters by Fosshage (Chapter 8) and Jaenicke (Chapter 9) take up similar themes. Fosshage combines self psychological and object relations views in offering a "relational self psychology." He begins by contrasting Freud's emphasis on instinctual drives seeking discharge with Kohut's focus on the development of a self within a self-selfobject matrix. From this perspective the central conflict is between the individual's genuine affective experience and the need to avoid "jeopardizing a needed selfobject connection." The implication is that fear of incurring parental disapproval and rejection will lead the child to suppress his or her individuality. Or, in slightly different terms, the conflict occurs between "developmental strivings and the maintenance of familiar and stable even if devitalizing, negative attitudes." Being stuck in such conflicts interferes with the person's ability to "realize its intrinsic program of action" within "selfobject" relationships in "the course of its life span." In other words, when selfobject needs are thwarted there is difficulty realizing the "nuclear self" with a resulting deficit in "self-structure." This view, as well as similar views expressed by some of the other authors, is reminiscent Winnicott's descriptions of a "true" versus a "false" self.

In a similar vein, Jaenicke (Chapter 9) presents an intersubjectivity viewpoint in which, as Stolorow put it:

> the source of conflict and disunity of the personality lies in those specific intersubjective contexts in which central affect states of the child cannot be integrated because they fail to evoke the requisite attuned responsiveness from the caregiving surround.
>
> (Stolorow et al., 1987, pp. 91–92)

The failure of "attuned responsiveness" will thwart the child's "maturational shifts." The child will then be led to "sacrifice those aspects of its agentic, authentic self that are seen as a threat to the existentially needed tie to the parents," that is, in Kohut's terms, to use the parents as selfobjects. Or, put a bit differently, the child's need to "remain in idealized connection with a caregiver will eventually conflict with the need to develop one's own sense of self and individual goals and values." An important emphasis in intersubjectivity theory is that "inner conflicts always take form in specific intersubjective contexts of developmental derailment." For example, a patient's feeling of danger in the analytic situation is seen as "emerging from the systemic interaction between the patient and the analyst."

Writing from a Lacanian perspective, Lichtenstein (Chapter 11) notes that rather than a focus on conflict per se, the emphasis is on a "divided" subject "who is never fully present at any single place or time." In this view, the idea of a coherent self is an illusion. As Lichtenstein notes, the closest Lacan gets to the idea of conflict is the inherent division between the conscious self and the unconscious subject. The result is that consciousness is inherently alienated; we always say more than we intend, we always misconstrue our actions, and we are always subverted by our desires. We are driven by our desires, which strive for complete satisfaction – an unachievable end. The aim of treatment is the realization and graceful acceptance that we must live in a divided state because conflicts are not fully resolvable, a point made by Brenner as well.

Approaching the topic of conflict from the perspective of attachment theory, the Steeles (Chapter 13) use Freud's conception of the so-called "danger situations" of childhood as their point of departure. The core anxieties are the loss of the object (being abandoned) and the loss of the object's love (being rejected). The authors consider Bowlby's notion of "internal working models," which reflect early experiences in which the core anxieties were activated. But what happens when there is no good way of coping with such anxieties? Perhaps the clearest, most extreme case is seen in "disorganized attachment." Here, the attachment figure is frightened/frightening or exhibits other anomalous behavior. However, the attachment figure is the one the child needs to seek out when distressed and in need of support. Thus, this is a conflict without a viable solution and, unsurprisingly, is associated with disorganized attachment. According to the Steeles, it helps if the child explicitly recognizes and tolerates both sides of the conflict. However, there often is a conflict between a conscious internal working model of the relationship to the caregiver, a model that tends to be idealized for defensive reasons, and unconscious working models, which more accurately reflect early traumatic experiences. Children who are considered "securely attached" appear to recognize their mixed feelings toward the attachment figure, that is, they learn to tolerate ambivalence, an achievement that is difficult for borderline patients.

With one exception, namely Chapter 14 by Hoffman, Rice, and Prout, the other authors focused on conflicts in adults. Hoffman et al. deal with conflict in children. According to these authors, a central issue for children with externalizing problems is the experience, expression, and effective regulation of negative affect. As with contemporary Freudian formulations (e.g., Brenner), they see negative affects as stemming from sexual and aggressive wishes. Noting the common distinction between "internalizing" and "externalizing" disorders in children, the authors focus on children with externalizing problems who act up; this behavior is seen as a way of avoiding negative affect. With these children, the main treatment goal is to help them develop a more adaptive way of regulating negative affect. It seems that implicit in this approach is the notion that the child will realize he or she has a conflict between expressing impulses and inhibiting them and to test behaviors that would be a realistic compromise between these two opposing tendencies.

House (in Chapter 12) presents an excerpt of Jeffrey Mehlman's translation of Laplanche's work, *Entre seduction et inspiration: l'home.* Laplanche's work, though highly influential in the field and, therefore, included in this volume, is not easy to understand, and we are not entirely confident that we are adequately summarizing House's chapter. As far as we understand Laplanche in this chapter, in the course of their ministrations to the child, parents inevitably and without conscious intention send the child an "enigmatic" message. The message is opaque to the conscious understanding of the adult and in the case of an infant it is beyond the capacity of the infant to comprehend it clearly. Nonetheless, the message conveys the unconscious sexuality of the caregiving adult. Therefore, as we understand the main thesis, all behavior, including self-preservative interactions with physical reality and interpersonal relations are "invaded by sexual conflict."

Most writings on conflict, as well as other psychoanalytic topics, are clinical and/or theoretical in nature. Rarely do we find citations of empirical research literature. We included chapters by Saunders and Wong

(Chapter 15) and by Berlin and Montgomery (Chapter 16) in order for readers to get a sense of some research that is relevant to the topic of conflict.

Saunders and Wong review empirical research that focuses on conflicts between a person's implicit and explicit attitudes. The Implicit Association Test (IAT) is an extremely popular method for assessing these differences. It has been used extensively in studies of racial prejudice and racial stereotyping by comparing responses on the IAT with subjects' conscious attitudes as tapped by self-report scales. For example, physicians' responses on the IAT predicted differences in their medical recommendations for Black versus White patients. Saunders and Wong also refer to research demonstrating that conflict between explicit, socially-desirable attitudes and implicit attitudes that are not socially acceptable is associated with self-concept, greater defensiveness, and even negative health outcomes. Their chapter demonstrates the presence and consequences of conflict in a broad social contest.

The chapter by Berlin and Montgomery (Chapter 16) focuses on the neural substrate of unconscious conflict and defenses (e.g., repression, suppression, dissociation, and repetition compulsion). For example, they review research that suggests that the dorsolateral prefrontal cortex plays an important role in inhibiting hippocampal activity, apparently in order to ward off unwanted, unconscious memories. They also present information relevant to suppression and dissociation. With regard to the latter, the evidence they refer to suggests not only a failure of psychological integration, but also neuroanatomical disconnectedness. As they note, the difficult but ultimate challenge is to accumulate a body of brain imaging research that bears on a central concept relevant to conflict, namely, the dynamic unconscious.

Concluding comments

Although couched in different theoretical terms, a common theme that emerges is the centrality of the conflict between attachment and devotion to "old objects" versus the desire to free oneself from those object ties in order to develop and express one's individual goals and desires. This view, perhaps most emphasized by object relations theories and self psychology, seems to have gained prominence in contemporary psychoanalytic theories. Another related overarching theme that emerges in these contributions is the emphasis on the role of the "danger situations" or "calamities" of childhood, the principal ones being anxieties and fears related to the potential loss of the object or loss of the object's love in the formation of conflict. Though originating during childhood, these fears and anxieties persist into adulthood. Even short of actual loss of the object or loss of the object's love are threats of such losses, threats that can be activated, for example, by the child's experience of a lapse or lack of parental attunement and empathy. In response to such threats the child can engage in a variety of reactions, for example, protecting the object (and thereby one's self) by continuing to idealize the frustrating object and taking "badness" into one's self, suppressing one's authentic emotional reactions on the assumption that to do so is the best path to safety and security.

However, we need to go further and to ask what exactly is dangerous or calamitous about the loss of the object or loss of the object's love? At first blush, there appears to be a clear difference in answers to this question on the part of Freudian theory and contemporary psychoanalytic theories, including object relations theory, self psychology, and attachment theory. From the perspective of Freudian metapsychological theory, the danger is that excitation associated with the pressure of sexual and aggressive drives will build up with no opportunity for discharge and will overwhelm the ego. From the perspective of Fairbairn's object relations theory, the ultimate danger is the "psychopathological disaster" of being without ego support from the object. From a self psychological perspective, it is the loss or absence of the object's empathic mirroring, which carries the danger of self-fragmentation. And, from an attachment theory perspective, being without the safe haven and secure base provided by the attachment figure can have dire consequences for cognitive, affective, and social development.

To be noted here is that if one is not too taken up with the different theoretical languages, it becomes clear that there is a convergence on the central idea that loss of the object's love, responsiveness, and attunement constitutes a major developmental trauma. Further, if the threat or danger of such loss is linked to the child's developmental strivings, the stage is set for an enduring conflict between these strivings and the experience of negative affects that they trigger.

One can make a case that virtually all of the contributions to this volume converge on an overarching theme, namely, that the basic human conflict is between experiencing and expressing one's true needs, including the need to actualize the self, and one's sexual and aggressive impulses, versus a fear of doing so in order to maintain a tie to the object qua object and as a selfobject. In this formulation healthy personality development is facilitated by an available, reliable, validating, and attuned caregiver. To put it in slightly different terms, the dilemma is if and how one can be one's true self without undue risk of loss of love or loss of the object. We believe all of our contributors would agree that conflict is not pathological per se but can result in pathology if not coped with effectively.

With regard to the specific questions we posed at the outset, we can say that (1) although there are perhaps some exceptions, many of the authors agree that conflict is inherent in the human condition even when environmental failures are invoked as explanatory, insofar as such failures are seen as inevitable. Individuals can be conflicted about many things, including sexual and aggressive wishes, implicit versus explicit attitudes, divergent aims, conscious intentions versus unconscious desires, and desire for individuality and autonomy versus their fear of losing connection with significant caregivers and with the protective and necessary functions the caregiver can provide; (2) Perhaps different conflicts are central for different individuals and different forms of psychopathology. Environmental failures and trauma (e.g., abuse, misattunement, and lack of responsiveness) can contribute to pathology, including developmental deficits. However, deficits often become enmeshed in conflict and unconscious fantasy; (3) Not all the contributors agree that the primary focus of treatment should be on inner conflict. Some contributors focus on issues of misattunement and deficiencies in empathy; (4) There is no singular way to address conflict in the treatment situation. For example, Busch believes that we need to approach conflict through the elicitation and interpretation of unconscious fantasy. Ellman stresses the importance of a preliminary phase of analysis aimed at establishing what he calls "analytic trust." Only then will it be productive to address the patient's conflicts. Harris writes that the therapist must deal with his or her own conflicts regarding the role of caretaker in order to be better able to deal with the patient's conflicts; (5) Traditional Freudians used the tripartite, structural model to conceptualize intersystemic and intrasystemic conflict. Brenner's modern conflict theory with its emphasis on the concept of compromise formations, and Klein's formulation of the central conflict between love and hate are views which do not necessitate a structural view of conflict; (6) In the past half century there has been an accumulating body of empirical research relevant to psychoanalytic theory, including studies relevant to conflict such as the use of the method of subliminal stimulation (e.g., see Shevrin et al., 1996; and Saunders and Wong in this volume). In recent years, this research endeavor has increasingly used neuroimaging techniques to elucidate the neural substrate of a variety of phenomena, identified in psychoanalytic theory, including conflict (see Berlin and Montgomery in this volume).

Finally, we would like to note that we asked our authors to present a conceptualization of conflict from their theoretical perspective. We did not ask them for an account of how conflict is dealt with in their particular approach to treatment or to discuss the role of conflict in a theory of therapeutic action. We offer some comments in this regard, which we believe would be generally accepted by our contributors as well as by most contemporary analysts. First, following Brenner, a criterion of a successful analysis is helping the patient toward a less maladaptive way of dealing with his or her conflicts, not the complete resolution of conflict. Second, there is no singular mechanism of therapeutic action. Thus, improved coping with conflict is not exclusively due to the generation of insights facilitated by the interpretation of unconscious conflicts. The several other therapeutic ingredients, which are more or less important for different patients, include establishing a safe atmosphere in which the patient is heard, attuned to, respected, and not judged, and in which the therapeutic alliance is maintained, and even strengthened, through its inevitable ruptures and repairs as they are experienced in the intersubjective context of the patient-analyst relationship. To these ingredients we might also add the patient's identification with the analyst and with the analytic attitude. In short, there are several, at least, implicitly supportive elements in treatment that can have therapeutic benefit and contribute to more adaptive ways of handling conflicts.

Chapter 1

Inner conflict in Freudian theory

Morris N. Eagle

E. Kris (1947) remarked that the subject matter of psychoanalysis is human behavior from the point of view of conflict. This is certainly true from both a historical and theoretical perspective. As is now a familiar account, the birth of psychoanalysis is marked by Breuer and Freud's (1893–1895) explanation of hysterical symptoms in terms of an "incompatibility" (p. 16) between certain mental contents, that is, between certain desires, wishes, and fantasies and the ego, that is, one's sense of one's self, including what one views as right or wrong. As Breuer and Freud (1893–1895) put it, "It turns out to be a sine qua non for the acquisition of hysteria that an incompatibility should develop between the ego and some idea presented to it" (p. 122). In other words, a necessary factor in the development of hysteria is the presence of *inner conflict*. In all of Freud's early cases, the individual is in the throes of a conflict between desire and reactions to that desire. In the case of Anna O, Breuer and Freud (1893–1895) write:

> She began coughing for the first time when once, as she was sitting at her father's bedside, she heard the sound of dance music coming from a neighbouring house, felt a sudden wish to be there, and was overcome with self-reproaches. Thereafter, throughout the whole length of her illness she reacted to any markedly rhythmical music with a tussis nervosa.

> (p. 40)

Elisabeth von R's conflict is between her "blissful feelings she had allowed herself to enjoy" (p. 146) with a young man and guilt at leaving her sick father. And for Lucy R, the conflict is between her desires and fantasies in relation to her employer and her reaction to the shock of reality indicating that her feelings toward him are not returned.

Although inner conflict may be a necessary condition for the development of hysterical symptoms, it is not a sufficient one. Repression must also be present. Freud was certainly aware that many people experience inner conflict without developing hysteria – just as Janet (1907) was undoubtedly aware that many people undergo traumatic experiences without developing the "splitting of consciousness" (Breuer & Freud, 1893–1895, p. 12) characteristic of hysteria. Janet's (1889) proposal was that the core predisposing factor of constitutional weakness must also be present. It is Freud's rejection of this proposal and his positing of repression, which he refers to as the "cornerstone" of psychoanalysis (S. Freud, 1893a) as a necessary factor in hysteria that marks the birth of psychoanalysis. Breuer and Freud (1893–1895) write that "before hysteria can be acquired for the first time one essential condition must be fulfilled: an idea must be intentionally repressed from consciousness" (p. 123). In short, at this early stage of his writings Freud proposes an etiological model for the development of psychopathology: the presence of inner conflict that is dealt with through repression, in Freud's words, "an occurrence of incompatibility" (i.e., inner conflict) that arouses "such a distressing affect that the subject decided to forget about it because he had no confidence in his power to resolve the contradiction between the incompatible idea and his ego by means of thought-activity" (S. Freud, 1894, p. 47). Thus, it is not conflict per se that is pathogenic, but the particular means of dealing with it.

Why, however, should the use of repression be pathogenic? Freud provides at least two reasons. One reason has to do with his assumption that every experience is accompanied by a "quota of affect" that needs to be discharged and is normally discharged through action, including talking about it (Breuer & Freud, 1893–1895, p. 166). With certain people, and in certain circumstances, particularly when an experience is accompanied by a large amount of affect, affect does not get discharged and remains in a "strangulated" state.

However, as Strachey (1955) asks in the Editor's introduction to Studies on Hysteria, "Why should affect need to be 'discharged'? And why are the consequences of its not being discharged so formidable?" The answer to these questions, as Strachey notes, is found in Freud's "principle of constancy," which was first enunciated in a 1893 lecture and more fully stated in *Beyond the Pleasure Principle* (S. Freud, 1920). According to the principle of constancy, every experience entails an increase in "the sum of excitation" (S. Freud, 1893a, p. 36) and a "quota of affect" (Breuer &

Freud, 1893–1895, p. 166) that need to be discharged. S. Freud (1893a) writes that "in every individual there exists a tendency to diminish this sum of excitation . . . in order to preserve his health" (p. 36). Indeed, according to S. Freud (1920) the mind (or nervous system) is essentially an "apparatus" designed to discharge excitation or to keep "the quantity of excitation present . . . as low as possible or at least to keep it constant" (p. 9). When the sum of excitation or quota of affect is not adequately discharged, the "quota of affect" is converted to somatic hysterical symptoms through a process that, Freud acknowledged, he did not understand.

It is not only failure to discharge excitation that Freud viewed as pathogenic but also the isolation of mental contents that repression entails. Thus, although repression enables the ego to "succeed[s] in freeing itself from the contradiction . . . it has burdened itself with a mnemic symbol which finds a lodgment in consciousness, like a sort of parasite" (S. Freud, 1894, p. 49). Freud's reference to a "sort of parasite" parallels Janet's description of "an idea excluded from personal consciousness" as "a virus, [which] develops in a corner of the personality inaccessible to the subject, works subconsciously, and brings about all disorders of hysteria" (Janet, 1889, quoted in Ellenberger, 1970, p. 149). Similarly, Charcot writes the following:

> an idea, a coherent group of associated ideas settle themselves in the mind in the fashion of parasites, remaining isolated from the rest of the mind and expressing themselves outwardly through corresponding motor phenomena. . . . The group of suggested ideas finds itself isolated and cut off from the control of that large collection of personal ideas accumulated and organized from a long time, which constitutes consciousness proper, that is the Ego.
> (Charcot, 1885, cited in Ellenberger, 1970, p. 149)

Thus, although Freud disagrees with Janet and Charcot regarding their nature and the means by which the isolation of mental contents from "personal consciousness" comes about, they agree regarding the pathogenic potential of isolated mental contents existing in the personality. I think it is accurate to say that this idea is the single most continuous idea running from pre-psychoanalytic to classical psychoanalytic to contemporary psychoanalytic theorizing.

Like a foreign body, the repressed idea is prevented from entering "the great complex of associations" (Breuer & Freud, 1893–1895, p. 37) constituting the ego and, therefore, prevents a "wearing away" process (S. Freud, 1893a, p. 37) and its "rectification by other ideas" (Breuer & Freud, 1893–1895, p. 9). One consequence is that the repressed traumatic idea retains its "freshness and affective strength" (p. 11), and the other consequence is that "psychical traumas which have not been disposed of by reaction cannot be disposed of either by being worked over by means of association" (p. 11). Thus, Freud essentially proposes two ways in which repression impairs the individual's ability to deal with traumatic ideas: one, through prevention of affective discharge, and the second, through interfering with the wearing away and associative rectification processes to which traumatic ideas are normally subjected. Freud writes that "even if [a psychical trauma] has not been abreacted," there are other methods of "dealing with the situation . . . open to a normal person" (p. 9), which, he identifies as the "rectification by other ideas" (p. 9).[1]

Although Freud repeatedly refers to traumatic ideas, unlike Janet and Charcot, who have in mind external traumas (e.g., railway accidents), Freud essentially defines trauma in terms of the individual's inability to adequately discharge the "quota of affect" or sum of excitation associated with an experience and/or inability to integrate the representation of the experience into the "great complex of associations" constituting the ego. Thus, from this newly introduced psychoanalytic perspective, the forbidden conflictual erotic desires and fantasies highlighted in the early case histories, although triggered by external events, are as much the source of trauma as the external events of primary interest to Janet and Charcot. To sum up, the birth of psychoanalysis is marked by the attribution of hysterical symptoms, not to the combination of external trauma and constitutional weakness, but to the interaction between inner conflict and the use of repressive defenses as a means of dealing with it.[2]

Freud's early formulation of the etiology of hysteria is structurally similar to his later account of neurosis and to certain aspects of his model of the mind, including the fundamental relationship between the individual and physical and social reality. With the advent of drive theory, the "incompatibility between an idea and the ego" becomes elaborated into a drive-defense or id-ego model, with instinctual wishes constituting the main source of "incompatible ideas" and undischarged "quota of affect" and excitation. However, whereas the role of inner conflict in hysteria is, so to speak, fortuitous and contingent (i.e., triggered by a set of circumstances) once drive theory is formulated as a core aspect of psychoanalytic theory, inner conflict between the id and the ego (as well as the superego) is now understood as an inevitable feature of the human condition.

At various points in his writings, Freud refers to the inevitable conflict between id and ego, in particular, the danger to the ego of instinctual demands. Thus, he states that "what it is that the ego fears from the external and the libidinal danger cannot be specified; we know that the fear is of being overwhelmed or annihilated" (S. Freud, 1923, p. 57). He also writes that "the majority of the instinctual demands of this infantile sexuality are treated by the ego as dangers and fended off as such" (S. Freud, 1926 [1925], p. 155). As another example: "In the first place, an excessive strength of instinct can damage the ego in a similar way to an excessive 'stimulus' from the external world" (S. Freud, 1940a, p. 199). Anna Freud (1966a) refers to the ego's "primary antagonism to instinct" and its "dread of the strength of instinct" (p. 157) and sums matters up by stating that "the danger which threatens the ego is that it may be submerged by the instincts; what it dreads above all is the *quantity* of instinct" (p. 165). Indeed, so fundamental is the danger that the id represents, that according to A. Freud (1966a), strength of instinct is a causal factor in psychosis. This inherent antagonism between id and ego is not so much contingent upon environmental influences (e.g., parental prohibitions)[3] but rather upon our psychobiological nature as it unfolds in society.

According to Freud, insofar as, in accord with the constancy principle, excessive and undischarged excitation constitutes the greatest threat to the ego, and insofar as instinct represents the major inner source of such excitation, it follows that undischarged tensions associated with instinct constitute an inherent potential threat to the ego – thus the fundamental antagonism between instinct and ego. The early notion that the "quota of affect" accompanying every experience needs to be discharged has now been elaborated into the ideas that instinct makes a demand upon the mind and that the tensions associated with instinctual wishes need to be discharged.[4] Given our psychobiological nature, the tensions generated by ungratified instinctual wishes do not disappear; they continue to exert pressure on the mind and "seek" various means of discharge.[5] If because of inner conflict, the forbidden instinctual wish cannot be gratified directly and an adequate discharge of instinctual tensions cannot occur, one possible consequence is disguised and partial gratification in the compromise form of a neurotic symptom. This more general formulation of the development of symptomatology has now replaced the earlier more specific proposal that undischarged "quota of affect" or sum of excitation is converted into hysterical symptoms.[6] In short, inner conflict is at the core of the neurosis.

The assumption that conflict is inevitable given our psychobiological nature is articulated by Freud in a number of other ways. There is the inevitable conflict between the pleasure principle (characterized by primary process thinking) and the reality principle (characterized by secondary process thinking). According to S. Freud (1900), early in life mental functioning is entirely dominated by the pleasure principle, that is, the demand for immediate gratification, as expressed, for example, in hallucinatory wish fulfillment. The infant and child learn over time that these methods are not successful in meeting one's needs to achieving gratification and, therefore, are forced to turn to objects in external reality and to recognize means-ends relationships in the outer world. That is, one slowly moves from the dominance of the pleasure principle to the emergence of the reality principle. However, S. Freud (1900) maintains that the influence of the pleasure principle never disappears and the tension or conflict between the pleasure principle and the reality principle remains as a permanent feature of mental functioning. That is, the demand for immediate gratification, the resort to wishful thinking, and the conflict between this mode of mental functioning and more reality-oriented cognition never disappear from mental life.

Early in life, the conflict between the pleasure principle and the reality principle is one between inner demands and wishes and the hard, unyielding nature of physical reality. That is, the sheer facts of both our biological nature and of physical reality are such that gratification of one's needs and wishes require commerce with objects in the world. Immediate gratification is not always possible, and wishing does not make it so. Learning and internalizing these facts is largely what is meant by the development of reality-testing. With the development of the ego as, among other functions, the agent of reality-testing, what early in life is essentially a conflict between wishes and the nature of external reality becomes transformed into an inner conflict – one between peremptory wishes (id) and assessments of reality (ego). Hence, from the start, there is an inevitable conflict between the id and the ego, a conclusion, as we have seen, that is repeatedly stated by both Sigmund Freud and Anna Freud.

A trajectory paralleling the relationship between the individual and physical reality also characterizes the relationship between the individual and social reality. Early in life, the conflict is between inner demands and the external social reality of prohibitions and limitations. In the course of development, societal prohibitions and values, as transmitted through the socialization agents of parents, family, and educators, become internalized in the form of a superego structure. Thus, what starts out as a conflict between inner demands and external social reality becomes transformed into an inner conflict between different aspects of oneself, namely, instinctual urges and internalized values and prohibitions.

Various forms of conflict in Freudian theory

Although there is wide agreement that the id-ego or drive-defense model captures the dominant classical view regarding the nature of inner conflict, in the corpus of his writings, Freud also refers to other forms of inner conflict. For the sake of comprehensiveness, I want to at least note their presence. They include the following:

1   The conflict between "the affectionate and sensual currents" which is implicated in sexual difficulties such as inhibition of desire and "psychical impotence" (S. Freud, 1912a), and which can be interpreted as a conflict between attachment and sexuality (Eagle, 2013).
2   The conflict between love and hate central to ambivalence and implicated in melancholia (S. Freud, 1909, pp. 236–238).
3   The conflict between heterosexuality and homosexuality, a product of our bisexual nature (S. Freud, 1937, p. 244).
4   The ego-superego conflict between seeking fulfillment of one's ambitions and fear of punishment implicated in the phenomenon of being "wrecked by success" (S. Freud, 1916, pp. 316–318).
5   The conflict within the ego between the "old peaceful ego" and the "new warlike [ego]" (p. 209) presumably central in "war neurosis" (S. Freud, 1919, pp. 208–213).[7]
6   The conflict between sexual and ego or self-preservative instincts, which S. Freud (1910b, pp. 214–215) compares to love and hunger. It is not clear why these two instincts should conflict with each other until one recognizes that according to Freudian metapsychology, the tensions inherent in the sexual instinct represent a potential threat of overwhelming the ego. In short, this is a variation of the id-ego conflict.
7   The conflict between renouncing satisfaction in the face of a danger from reality (e.g., threat of castration) and the disavowal of reality, along with the continued pursuit of satisfaction (e.g., masturbation).

What is especially interesting about this form of conflict is that according to S. Freud (1940b), both trends occur at the same time. Thus, as the title of Freud's paper makes clear, the result is "splitting of the ego in the process of defense" (a topic that will be taken up in Chapter 5 on Fairbairn's object relations theory).

8   The overarching conflict between the "two primal instincts Eros and destructiveness" (S. Freud, 1937, p. 246) (derived from Empedocles's love and strife), which Freud introduced relatively late in his writings.

I want to spend some time on this posited overarching conflict. The fundamental and irreducible nature of the conflict between Eros and destructiveness or the death instinct posited by Freud is probably the clearest expression of his views regarding the inescapable presence of conflict in psychological and biological life. Also, it seems to reflect his "final view." The conflict between Eros and destructiveness, which Freud views as fundamental to psychological and biological life, is an interinstinctual conflict between two primary instincts rather than between id and ego. Viewing intrapsychic life from the former perspective does not seem especially compatible with the id-ego model that had dominated Freudian theory. Further, there is an enormous distance between the highly abstract metapsychological formulation of a basic conflict between Eros and destructiveness or the death instinct and clinical work – a consideration that has led most analysts to essentially ignore this late version of inner conflict.

Despite this state of affairs, it is, I believe, useful to devote some discussion to Eros and the death instinct in order to gain some insight into the link between Freud's early formulations of the constancy principle and the "mental apparatus" as a discharge mechanism and the positing of a death instinct, as well as the conceptual difficulties to which these early formulations lead. S. Freud's (1937) description of the aim of the death instinct as "the urge . . . to return to an inanimate state" (p. 246) reflects the continuing influence of the constancy principle in Freud's thinking. Recall that in accord with the constancy principle, the primary function of the "mental apparatus" is to discharge excitation and thus keep the level of excitation at a zero level or as low as possible. As S. Freud (1924) puts it,

We have taken the view that the principle which governs all mental processes is a special case of Fechner's 'tendency toward stability,' and have accordingly attributed to the mental apparatus, the purpose of *reducing to nothing* (my emphasis), or at least keeping as low as possible, the sums of excitation which flow in upon it.

(p. 159)

S. Freud (1924) borrows the term *Nirvana principle* from Low (1920) to describe this tendency and, taking his formulation to its logical conclusion, notes that the "Nirvana principle" "[belongs] . . . to the death instinct" (p. 160). For, reducing the sum of excitation to zero is, of course, equivalent to returning to an inanimate state, that is, death. Freud also recognizes that, pushed to its logical extreme, the metapsychological equation of unpleasure with increases in excitation and pleasure with reduction of excitation also aligns the pleasure principle with the death instinct and grapples with what is to him the mysterious facts that increases in excitation can be pleasurable and that experiences of pleasure are not only a function of a "quantifiable factor," but also of a "qualitative characteristic" (p. 160) about which, he states, we know little. He also writes that although the Nirvana principle belongs to the death instinct, it "has undergone a modification in living organisms through which it has become the pleasure principle" (p. 160). And, S. Freud (1924) goes on to say, "the source of the modification" of the Nirvana principle "can only be the life instinct, the libido" (p. 160).

All this, in my view, is Freudian metapsychology at its most questionable and its most confused and confusing. What seems to be required is a thorough overhaul of the general conception of pleasure and unpleasure defined in terms of decreases and increases in excitation, and then linked to the constancy principle, the Nirvana principle, and a conception of the primary function of the mental apparatus as discharge of excitation. As things now stand, from a Freudian perspective, right from the start, a primary function of the "mental apparatus" and the aim of the death instinct converge. That is, insofar as both the primary function of the "mental apparatus" and the aim of the death instinct is discharge of excitation, the latter to the zero point, the two converge. Further, if one keeps in mind that, according to Freud, the essence of gratification of instinctual wishes and needs entails discharge of excitation, one is forced to also recognize the odd link between gratification and the death instinct in Freud's formulations. Further, on this view, the individual is, so to speak, damned if he or she does and damned if he or she does not. That is, the failure to discharge excitation confronts the individual with the danger of excessive excitation and, carried to its extreme, the discharge of excitation entailed in gratification becomes equivalent to a return to an inanimate state, that is, the state that is the aim of the death instinct.

These odd convergences suggest still another reason (others have been presented) that there is something profoundly amiss with the fundamental formulations of the constancy principle, the notion of the mind or nervous system as a discharge "apparatus," and the posited equivalence of gratification with discharge of excitation. Many of these odd implications and links would disappear with the relatively simple steps of getting rid of the Nirvana principle and redefining the constancy principle entirely in terms of homeostasis rather than zero excitation.

Finally, Freud's conceptualization of Eros as a unifying force in psychic life, which does not appear to be compatible with the idea that instincts, including the sexual instinct – which is surely at least a distant cousin of Eros – are an implacable enemy of the ego. If, as Freud maintains, Eros is an instinct, then, along with other instinctual forces, it too should carry with it the threat of excessive excitation. However, it is clear that Freud does not view Eros as *that* kind of instinct. But, if that is so, the fundamental nature of at least some instincts is altered, now understood by Freud as a unifying force rather than one that is inherently in conflict with the ego.

Inner conflict and post-Freudian developments

Throughout its many developments and modifications, inner conflict has remained at the center of Freudian theory. For example, according to ego psychology, a critical criterion of mental health is the extent of conflict-free ego functioning (H. Hartmann, 1939). Inner conflict has also remained at the center of post-Freudian conceptions of psychopathology and mental functioning despite radical rejection of key Freudian propositions and despite differences regarding their content. For example, for Horney (1946), inner conflicts remain at the core of neuroses despite the fact that her identification of core inner conflicts in terms of attitudes of "moving toward," "moving away from," and "moving against" people is radically different from Freud's conceptualization of inner conflicts. As another example, despite his rejection of Freudian personality theory and his very different understanding of its nature, inner conflict remains at the center of Fairbairn's (1952) formulation of psychopathology. Fairbairn's (1952) emphasis on the fundamental conflict between "the regressive lure of identification and the progressive urge toward separations" (p. 43) calls to mind the conflict between symbiosis and separation-individuation at the center of Mahler's (1968) and Mahler's et al. (1975) conceptualization of personality development and psychopathology; aspects of which Mitchell (1988) refers to as the "relational/conflictual model," particularly, the conflict between different "relational configurations" and the conflict between "safety and autonomy" emphasized by J. Greenberg (1993).

One can also point to the enduring role of inner conflict among French analysts. For example, Widlöcher (2002b) writes that clinical psychoanalysis is concerned primarily with the conflict between auto-erotic fantasies associated with infantile sexuality and object love. One can also note the implicit conflict in Lacan's (e.g., Widlöcher, 2002b) theorizing between living one's life in accord with the desire of the Other and the release of one's own subjectivity and desire.

Inner conflict and psychoanalytic treatment

As noted earlier, according to Freudian theory it is not inner conflict per se that is pathogenic. Indeed, inner conflict is assumed to be inherent in the human condition. What renders inner conflict pathogenic is mainly how one deals with it, namely, through repression. Thus, as discussed earlier, coping with inner conflict through repressive defenses is a critical mediating factor in the pathogenic consequences of inner conflict. As we have seen, this is so for at least three main reasons: (1) repression prevents the adequate discharge of the "quota of affect" associated with conflictual desires and experiences, (2) repression prevents the assimilation and integration of conflictual mental contents that have been rendered isolated through repression into the rest of the personality, and (3) essentially equivalent to (2), but stated at a different level of discourse, repression keeps the individual from confronting and attempting to resolve his or her conflicts in the light of reality considerations. It should be noted that all three consequences of repression serve to weaken the personality: through the build up of excessive excitation and its conversion into somatic symptoms, through burdening the personality with isolated mental contents that function like a "parasite," through requiring a "permanent expenditure of energy" (S. Freud, 1925, p. 30) that could be directed toward more constructive activities, and through the prevention of resolutions of conflict that would allow the individual to pursue developmental goals (see Eagle, 2000, Part I).

Given the aforementioned conception of psychopathology, it would follow that therapeutic interventions would be directed to (1) facilitating adequate discharge of affect surrounding the repressed mental contents – in short, *abreaction*; (2) bringing the repressed mental contents to consciousness so that they can be integrated into the "great complex of associations known as the ego" (Breuer & Freud, 1893–1895, p. 9) – in short, can be integrated into the rest of the personality; and (3) also as a function of being brought to consciousness, evaluating repressed mental contents in the light of reality consideration.[8]

There is little point in repeating the familiar story of the evolution of Freud's techniques from the use of hypnosis and abreaction to what came to a commonly agreed upon method, in particular the use of free association and interpretation. My interest is in demonstrating the logical links between Freud's conception of the factors involved in psychopathology and the nature of psychoanalytic treatment. I also want to call attention to two observations: one, abreaction was dropped from the psychoanalytic repertoire of techniques and process goals despite the fact that its theoretical justification embedded in the constancy principle had not been relinquished;[9] two, what remained at the core of the theory of psychoanalytic treatment were the goals of enhancing conscious awareness and integrating hitherto unintegrated mental contents into the personality structure or, in more experience-near terms, into one's more expanded and realistic sense of who one is – and perhaps, into one's more expanded, integrated, and realistic sense of who one wants to be.

One important clinical reason that Freud gave up the use of hypnosis lies in the fact that although hypnosis might succeed in bringing a hitherto unconscious mental contents into conscious awareness, these content were likely to remain *unintegrated* into the individual's personality and his or her sense of who he or she is. And yet, that did not deter Freud from identifying as an essential goal of psychoanalysis "making conscious what has so far been unconscious" (S. Freud, 1896, p. 164), which, in itself, does not necessarily entail integration of what has been made conscious. Freud was obviously aware of this possibility, but attributed it to resistance and invoked the concept of *working through* (e.g., S. Freud, 1926 [1925], p. 158) as a means to dealing with such resistance. He writes:

> One must allow the patient time to become more conversant with this resistance with which he has now become acquainted, to *work through*

it, to overcome it, by continuing, in defiance of it, the analytic work according to the fundamental rule of analysis.

(Freud, 1926 [1925], p. 158)

However, what is actually involved in working through is not at all made clear by Freud.

Although the therapeutic primacy of integrating isolated (repressed) mental contents into the rest of the personality is clearly implied in Freud's early emphasis on bringing these contents into contact with the "great complex of associations," one can easily lose sight of this aim in the context of identifying making the unconscious conscious as a primary therapeutic goal. For, as noted, unconscious material can be made conscious without being integrated into one's sense of who one is and what one is doing. This outcome is not limited to hypnosis but would apply to any means of making the unconscious conscious, including the use of interpretation. Further, the Freud who emphasizes the renunciation of unconscious wishes once they are made conscious seems to suggest that certain wishes cannot be readily integrated into the rest of the personality.

With the exception of sublimation, which does suggest successful integration, renunciation is the patient's only realistic and healthy option. This is so, I believe, because inherent in the id-ego model as well as the formulation of the theory of the Oedipus complex is the implication that at least certain instinctual wishes cannot be realistically integrated into the personality. With regard to the former, in view of the posited primary antagonism between the id and the ego and the danger that excessive strength of instinct represents, integration of certain infantile instinctual wishes into the rest of the personality would not appear to be very possible nor desirable. As for the theory of the Oedipus complex, it is the *relinquishment* of incestuous and hostile wishes, not their integration, which enables normal development to proceed. In both cases, renunciation and sublimation are the only realistic options.

It was not until 1933 that Freud articulated as the overarching goal of psychoanalytic treatment, "where id was, there shall ego be" (p. 80). Understood in a particular way, this aphorism has important implications for the possibility of integration and for one's conception of the goal of psychoanalytic treatment. One can understand "where id was, there shall ego be" in a number of ways. As Apfelbaum (1966) has pointed out in a classic paper, from a traditional ego psychological perspective, it can be

14   Morris N. Eagle

understood as where infantile instinctual wishes were, there shall *greater ego control be*. This interpretation is compatible with an emphasis on renunciation of infantile wishes as a therapeutic goal. From this perspective, infantile wishes are kept in check by a strengthened ego.

However, there is a different way of understanding the aphorism, particularly if one keeps in mind that the original German "wo Es war, soll Ich werdern" (S. Freud, 1933, p. 80). One can now read the aphorism as where impersonal *it* was, there shall *I* be, which conveys the extremely important idea that an ideal outcome of psychoanalytic treatment is one in which the I (self) is expanded to now include and integrate hitherto unintegrated aspects of oneself that had been defensively excluded and rendered as an impersonal it, as a sort of foreign alien body (see Brandt, 1961).

The possibility of integration between id and ego runs counter to the assumption of primary antagonism between the two, and as such, suggests the possibility of treatment (and developmental) outcomes that are not envisaged by the usual conception of id-ego relationship. On the traditional view, given the inherent antagonism between the two, the timelessness of the unconsciousness and, therefore, the inevitable "frozen in time" unchangeable nature of infantile instinctual impulses, the best one can expect from even highly successful treatment are renunciation, sublimation, and greater ego control of impulses. In contrast, in the interpretation of where id was, there shall ego be that I am proposing (and as proposed in Apfelbaum's 1966 paper), developmental maturation of id impulses themselves can occur, which renders greater ego control less of an issue, and which permits the possibility of integration of id and ego as developmental and treatment goals.

Freud himself discussed the possibility of the latter developments at various points in his writings. For example, at one point, S. Freud (1915d) suggests that it is the repressed status rather than their inherent nature that renders instinctual wishes so formidable a threat. He writes that the "repressed instinct-presentation . . . develops in a more unchecked and luxuriant fashion. It ramifies, like a fungus, so to speak, in the dark and takes on extreme forms of expression" that are alien to and terrify the individual because of "the way in which they reflect an extraordinary strength of instinct. This illusory strength of instinct is the result of an uninhibited development of it in phantasy and of the damming-up consequent on lack of real satisfaction" (p. 149). This passage is unique in the corpus of Freud's writings in suggesting that the formidable strength of instinct and the threat it represents to the ego to which S. Freud and A. Freud repeatedly refer, is not, as suggested by the constancy principle, an *inherent* one, but is rather a *fantasy* fed by the circumstance that repressed impulses do not see the light of day and take on fantastic proportions.

In a relatively late paper, S. Freud (1926b) writes that "there is no natural opposition between ego and id; they belong together, and under healthy conditions cannot in practice be distinguished from each other" (p. 201) – a formulation that utterly contradicts the idea of an inherent and necessary antagonism between id and ego. Indeed, Freud's statement suggests that a necessary antagonism between id and ego is more descriptive of psychopathology than of healthy functioning[10] and also implies that the main task of psychoanalytic treatment is to restore or contribute to an increasing unity between id and ego – a task that is implicit in the goal of where id was, there shall ego be when that is understood as where "it" was, there shall "I" be.

If, because it is based on fantasy and allowed to ramify in the dark, the strength of instinct is partly illusory, it is not clear why renunciation is always or frequently necessary. Once the repressed wishful fantasy "sees the light of day," it may become modulated, more susceptible to integration and, therefore, not require renunciation. However, although this possibility is clearly implicit in Freud's previous statements, it is not compatible with a whole set of Freudian assumptions regarding the nature of instinctual wishes, including assumptions that the sheer quantitative demand made by the id that renders it an inherent threat to the ego, that the id is immune to influences from the external world (see H. Hartmann, 1939), and that sequestered instinctual wishes, including infantile wishes, cannot themselves mature. As Apfelbaum (1966) noted, given these assumptions, it is understandable that the options for development and therapeutic change are limited to renunciation, sublimation and, more generally, greater ego control over timeless and unchangeable instinctual impulses. When these assumptions are relinquished, therapeutic change can include the maturing and modulation of instinctual impulses themselves and, therefore, the reduction of their demand on the mind. Also, one does not have to confront the puzzle of what it means to renounce instinctually based impulses.

There are, in effect, two Freuds in regard to the origins and fundamental nature of inner conflict as well as its consequences and its fate in treatment. There is, as we have seen, the metapsychological Freud who ultimately locates inner conflict in the constancy principle and the inherent relationship between the id and the ego. And then there is the Freud who locates the source of inner conflict more contingently in interpersonal experiences, that is, in parental prohibitions and punishments in relation to instinctual wishes and the "danger situations" of loss of the object, loss of the object's love, castration threats, and superego condemnation that certain parental behaviors generate.

According to the logic of the latter Freud, were parental behaviors (and, more generally, society) less punitive, conflict surrounding instinctual wishes would diminish – a state of affairs Freud thinks is possible in so-called "primitive" societies. In contrast, according to the logic of the former Freud, because it is a function of our psychobiological nature, inner conflict between instinctual wishes and the ego is inevitable and is relatively independent of parental (and societal) behavior and demands. For this Freud, treatment aims for renunciation and/or sublimation of instinctual wishes. For the Freud who understands inner conflict as largely contingent upon environmental influences, the treatment aims of id-ego integration and unity of the personality can be more readily envisaged.

This latter position, the more optimistic one, places Freud in a broad historical spiritual-philosophical context in which unity of the personality is an overriding and lifelong quest, for example, reflected in Kierkegaard's (1847) definition of purity of heart as willing one thing and Confucius's (translated by Lau, 1979) pronouncement that at 70, I could follow what my heart desired, without transgressing what was right. This latter Freud also belongs to a conception of an overriding goal of psychoanalytic treatment as discovering what A. Stone (1997) refers to as the "otherness of oneself" (p. 36), avowing this discovered otherness as one's own and integrating it into an expanded and more unified concept of oneself. What is especially interesting is that this goal of unity and integration is essentially a return to the early Freud who viewed isolated mental contents as pathogens and who essentially identified as a treatment goal the restoration of the unity of the personality that obtained before the patient was beset by an "incompatibility" between an idea and the ego. Recall that for Freud repressed mental contents are pathogenic because they are isolated and unintegrated into the rest of the personality. Hence, an overriding goal of treatment is restoration of unity of the personality through integration of the isolated conflictual content.

Epilogue

Although, as noted, inner conflict remains central in post-Freudian theoretical developments, it no longer has a monolithic status in psychoanalysis. As early as 1963, Gitelson remarked that the use of repression as a primary defense no longer characterized many contemporary patients – which, if true, certainly has implications for the role of inner conflict in the psychopathology of those patients.[11] Over the last 30 to 40 years, psychopathology has been conceptualized in terms of deficits and defects (e.g., Kohut, 1984), developmental arrests (e.g., Stolorow & Lachmann, 1980), and maladaptive schemas and representations (e.g., Eagle, 2013). Further, different conceptions of the nature and aims of treatment have accompanied these different conceptions of the nature of psychopathology.

For example, Kohut (1984) replaces the primacy of insight and the expansion of awareness that it entails with the aim of "repair" of self-defects and accretions in self-cohesiveness through the analyst's empathic understanding and through such process as "optimal failure" and" transmuting internalization." As another example, a conception of psychopathology in terms of maladaptive schemas and representations (e.g., pathogenic beliefs, insecure attachment patterns) has been associated with an emphasis on the "corrective emotional experiences" (Alexander & French, 1946) inherent in the therapeutic relationship as the primary means of altering these maladaptive schemas and representations. And as a final example, one that emphasizes defects in the capacity for mentalization as a hallmark of psychopathology, the primary focus of psychotherapy is not on uncovering repressed memories or impulses or gaining insight into unconscious conflicts, but on the "rekindling of mentalization" (Fonagy et al., 2001, p. 368).

It is interesting to note that S. Freud (1911, p. 191) describes a type of illness which, as the following passage makes clear (particularly, if one overlooks the language of infantile fixation of libido), is quite similar to what is described in the contemporary literature as "developmental arrest":

> We are here concerned with people who fall ill as soon as they get beyond the irresponsible age of childhood, and who have thus never reached a phase of health a phase, that is, of capacity for achievement and enjoyment which is on the whole unrestricted. The essential feature of the dispositional process is in these cases quite plain. Their libido has never left its infantile fixations; the demands of reality are not suddenly made upon a wholly or partly mature person, but arise from the very fact of growing older, since it is obvious that they constantly alter with the subject's increasing age. *Thus, conflict falls into the background in comparison with insufficiency.* But here, too, all our other experience leads us to postulate an effort at overcoming the

fixations of childhood; for otherwise, the outcome of the process could never be neurosis, but only a stationary infantilism.

(p. 235)

Especially interesting is the final sentence of the previous passage in which Freud suggests that despite an "inhibition of development" (p. 235), the patient can be treated psychoanalytically so long as one sees as part of the clinical presentation "an effort at overcoming the fixations of childhood" (p. 235). When that effort is not present, "the process could never be neurosis, but only a stationary infantilism" (p. 235). What Freud is clearly suggesting here is that even when the primacy of "insufficiency" (defects or developmental arrests) relative to conflict is present, psychoanalytic treatment remains possible so long as some element of inner conflict is present. That is, there must be some degree of inner conflict between infantile fixations and normal developmental strivings. Or, to put it in a somewhat different way, the patient's "insufficiency" must be accompanied by some sense of inner conflict regarding his or her "insufficiency." Without the sense of inner conflict, Freud suggests, there would be little motivation or "effort at overcoming" (p. 235) the infantile fixation or "insufficiency."

I think that Freud's perspective has much validity and applicability to the psychoanalytic treatment of patients whose primary pathology is described in terms of self-defects or developmental arrests (see Eagle, 1984, Chapter 12). Finally, it is worth noting that Freud's comments can be read as suggesting, not only resolution of conflict, but developmental growth, as an aim of psychoanalytic treatment.

The metaphor of unity of the personality as an overriding therapeutic goal makes sense only when one conceives of pathology as entailing disunity, that is, inner conflict. When psychopathology is understood differently, other metaphors become more apt. For example, when pathology is understood in terms of self-defects, the therapeutic metaphor employed is one of "repair" (Kohut, 1984). When pathology is understood in terms of developmental arrest, the metaphor is one of resumption of developmental growth (e.g., Winnicott, 1965). And when psychopathology is understood in terms of maladaptive schemas and representations, the dominant therapeutic metaphor is one of replacing old schemas and representations with new more adaptive ones. Although they are often presented as such in the literature, these different formulations are not mutually exclusive.

Although conflict may no longer have a privileged status in psycho-analytic theory, its centrality did not end with Freud (e.g., see Horney [1946], *Our Inner Conflicts*). The importance of inner conflict remains at the core of different attempts to understand human nature and psychological functioning from a psychoanalytic perspective. It seems to me that when inner conflict is understood broadly as being at war with oneself, it will remain critical to our understanding of the human condition – even if it is not viewed as central to this or that specific form of psychopathology (e.g., self-defects or developmental arrest). And, accordingly, the striving for greater awareness and greater unity of the personality as vital human quests will, I believe, remain a core aim and value for many people. It is in this sense that the goal of where id was, there shall ego be – when it is understood as where impersonal or alien it was, there shall I be – is central to any theory that attempts to grasp the nature of human nature.

Notes

1 It is interesting to observe that whereas the therapeutic role of abreaction soon faded, associative rectification essentially can be understood as a precursor of the role of insight and working through in psychoanalytic treatment.
2 Despite S. Freud's rejection of Janet's (1907) emphasis on constitutional weakness, the fact is that as early as in his "Early Drafts on Hysteria," S. Freud (1940 [1892]) already refers to a "hysterical disposition" (p. 149). In his subsequent writings, S. Freud (1898) acknowledges that "heredity is no doubt an important factor" (p. 271) in neurasthenia but should not be given primary importance. He suggests further that because heredity is inaccessible to the physician's influence, the therapeutic forces must necessarily be on factors we can change. More generally, S. Freud (1939 [1934–1938]) attempts to deal with the role of constitutional factors with his concept of "complemental series" (p. 73).
3 I will return to this issue later in the chapter.
4 I have wondered whether the idea that sexual tensions need to be discharged if one is to preserve one's health is partly rooted in folk beliefs. I recall hearing on a number of occasions when I grew up the comment accompanied by a knowing look that a particular woman's problems, ranging from acne to "nervousness," would be ameliorated once she married. On one occasion, during my teenage years, the father of a friend of ours who had returned home after being hospitalized during a psychotic episode approached a group of us with the request that we find a prostitute for his son. It was clear that he thought that this would be curative. I do not know of any literature that links Freud's hydraulic model to folk beliefs.
5 Because of this continual pressure on the mind, repression of instinctual impulses "demands a persistent expenditure of force" (S. Freud, 1915d, p. 151) – another aspect of the pathogenic consequences of repression.

6 Other more "normal" means of discharging instinctual tensions in a disguised and compromised way include dreams, humor, parapraxes, and fantasy. Thus, Freud formulated a, so to speak, "unified" theory in which a single process is hypothesized to underlie phenomena as different on the surface as neurotic symptoms, dreams, humor, parapraxes, and fantasy.

7 I cannot refrain from noting here that Freud's jargon of conflict between "peaceful ego" and "warlike ego" simply amounts to the statement that the soldier is conflicted between wanting to save his life and not wanting to view himself and be viewed by others as cowardly and unpatriotic.

8 In "translating" Freudian theory into the terms and concepts of neo-Hullian learning theory, Dollard and Miller (1950) refer to the therapeutic function of making the unconscious conscious in terms of bringing to bear the individual's problem-solving functions as a means of resolving conflict.

9 Abreaction remained at the center of Janov's (1970) primal scream therapy, the core rationale of which is Freud's early formulations of the role of the failure to discharge affect in hysteria and the therapeutic importance of achieving adequate discharge in treatment.

10 Ironically, the idea that instinctual impulses are inherently dangerous and antagonistic to the ego parallels and appears to confirm the patient's fearful and anxious fantasies in relation to his conflictual wishes and desires.

11 Christian (personal communication, December, 2013) traced the frequency of references to the term *conflict* from 1953 to the 2009 issue of the *Journal of the American Psychoanalytic Association* and found a steady decline from about 1985 to 2009.

Chapter 2

The evolution of modern conflict theory

Christopher Christian

E. Kris (1947) famously asserted that psychoanalysis is the study of human behavior from the viewpoint of conflict. With the development of modern conflict theory, Brenner would take this adage to its natural conclusion. In fact, when one mentions conflict in psychoanalysis, it is the work of Brenner (as well as Arlow) that immediately come to mind. Like no other contemporary theory in psychoanalysis, modern conflict theory[1] placed conflict and compromise formation at the heart of how the mind is understood and defined the elucidation of compromise formations as the central task of the analyst. In this chapter, I will briefly review a set of key publications that were critical to the development of modern conflict theory and discuss their influence on Brenner's thinking, and then I will discuss the critical revisions of ego psychology that culminated in modern conflict theory – a theory that in important respects departs from ego psychology.

The history of ego psychology is perhaps a familiar one and its beginning is often traced to Freud's publication in 1923 of *The Ego and the Id*. In this monograph, Freud presents his second theory of the mind, referred to as the structural theory, in the form of the id, ego, and superego. This revised theory was meant to supplant[2] the topographic model that Freud introduced in the *Interpretation of Dreams* in which the mind was divided into Unconscious (Ucs), Pre-conscious (Pcs) and Conscious (Cs). The problem that Freud observed prompting him to introduce the structural theory can be briefly stated as follows: in the topographic model, the unconscious was hypothesized to contain instinctual wishes that met opposition from, and were subsequently repressed by, the ego based on moral grounds. A problem challenging this model was Freud's growing recognition that not everything that is unconscious is instinctual in nature. The moral prohibitions that make the instinctual wishes objectionable and dangerous, for

22 Christopher Christian

example, could be unconscious, and the operations by which the ego seeks to decrease anxiety also could be unconscious. In addition, the unconscious in the topographic model was thought to be characterized by a type of mental functioning labeled *primary process*. However, it became clear that highly organized fantasies with stable verbal narratives could be unconscious. That is to say, there were fantasies in the unconscious that were defined by secondary process. These contradictions ultimately lead to the revisions that culminated in the structural theory.

Shortly thereafter, in 1926, with the publication of *Inhibitions, Symptoms and Anxiety*, Freud makes another important theoretical revision, introducing the concept of *signal anxiety*. Earlier, Freud had understood anxiety in biological terms and as the result of undischarged or inadequately discharged tension resulting from the accumulation of libido, which was transformed and given outlet in the form of anxiety. Repression thus was thought to precede and cause anxiety. Among other reasons for revising this theory was the recognition that repression and other forms of defense were *precipitated* by anxiety. In these situations, the ego would perceive a danger and send a signal to itself to mobilize some kind of self-protection against the dangerous impulse. S. Freud (1926a) concluded, "We may legitimately hold firmly to the idea that the ego is the actual seat of anxiety and give up our earlier view that the cathectic energy of the repressed impulse is automatically turned into anxiety" (p. 93).

The ego was thought to be capable of not only detecting an impulse but also anticipating the consequences of the impulse, taking into account subsequent self-reproaches and condemnation, as well as external dangers. The fate of that impulse, therefore, was altered by the ego's anticipation of what might ensue upon its expression. Signal anxiety was meant to avoid a fuller emergence of anxiety related to the impulse that was seeking discharge. Signal anxiety was the equivalent of a small taste that prompts one to reject the whole bowl of soup. With the concept of signal anxiety we see a blurring between id and ego such that a biologically-driven impulse has to be given shape and articulated as a wish in order for the ego to determine its fate. That is, to determine how much of the wish needs to be defended against, how much can be gratified, and at what cost. Readers will note the level of anthropomorphism with which the ego was being described. It was a *homunculus* acting as a signal operator directing traffic, interpreting sensations and experience, subjecting its own mental

The evolution of modern conflict theory 23

processes to *reality-testing*, determining the potential consequences of specific thoughts and impulses, and facilitating or postponing motor action.

These two papers, *The Ego and the Id* (1923) and *Inhibitions, Symptoms and Anxiety* (1926a), signaled a shift in, or at the very least a broadening of, the analyst's attention from the contents of the unconscious to include the role of the ego and the modes by which the ego managed to achieve some intrapsychic balance between the different demands that it confronted. Soon after the publication of Freud's *Inhibition* paper, Robert Waelder (1936)[3] elaborated on the monumental balancing act that the ego faced and introduced the concept of *multiple function*. According to Waelder, the ego was a task-solving agency of the mind, facing problems and seeking their solutions. The number of problems faced by the ego was determined by the number of agencies placing demands upon it: the id and the superego as well as by the outside world, with its external dangers. To these three demands, Waelder would add a fourth: the compulsion to repeat. When presented with demands by these different forces, the ego could choose to overcome or join each agency. That is, defend against them or integrate the demands of each agency by active assimilation into the ego. An example of active assimilation is when the ego, during the Oedipal phase, identifies with the father and the father's moral strictures – a process that culminates in the development of a psychic structure in the shape of the superego. With the principle of multiple function, Waelder postulated that in every act the ego sought to satisfy *all of its constituents*. No attempt at a solution for one problem, was not at the same time a solution for other problems. The character of each psychic act "is a *compromise* between instinct and the defense against it" (Waelder 1936, p. 49). The organism, as Waelder saw it, always acts in its entirety and as a whole. Every psychic activity sought to provide some degree of instinctual gratification and defense against the instinct, taking into account moral consideration and external dangers. At first glance, it may seem that Waelder was restating what S. Freud (1900) had already described with the concept of over-determination as detailed in the *Interpretation of Dreams*. That is, when, through the process of condensation, a single dream image manages to express and/or gratify more than one disguised wish. But Waelder was postulating something more radical. Rather than multiple wishes represented or gratified in one image, all of the agencies of the mind were being addressed in each and every psychic act.

24 Christopher Christian

From Waelder's paper emerged a critical question about the ego as an agency of the mind. According to Waelder, the ego sets tasks for itself, deciding between "overcoming the other agencies or joining them to its organization by active assimilation" (Waelder, 1930, p. 78). As Friedman (2007) has pointed out, it was always a controversial issue to talk about the ego as having its own source of energy and drive. This would become the conundrum that H. Hartmann (1939) would need to address, and he would do so by developing a new metapsychology with concepts such as a *conflict-free sphere*, *neutralized energy*, and an *autonomous ego*. With these concepts, Hartmann sought to define an ego that operated independent of instinctual drives, and whose activities included making decisions, the pursuit of mastery, intelligence, and other cognitive functions. For Hartmann, the ego was not simply tied to conflict and pathological functioning, with a role circumscribed to mobilizing defenses but, in addition, the ego could have at its disposal energy that was independent of conflict beginning at birth (primary autonomy). There were also ego functions that may have become tied to conflicts stemming from aggressive and sexual drives but could be *de-sexualized* and de-aggresivized and develop secondary autonomy by a process that he would describe as *neutralization*. According to Hartmann, the ego could operate within a *conflict-free sphere*. In this way, Hartmann sought to define psychoanalysis as a general psychology and not just a theory of psychopathology and its treatment. H. Hartmann (1939) would also introduce the term *average expectable environment* to emphasize the relevance of reality in facilitating or hindering adaptation. Thus, the ego was not limited to its role in conflict vis-à-vis the id and the superego, warding off impulses and avoiding guilt and self-punishment, but would also operate to find ways to gratify impulses, as made possible by the opportunities afforded by the person's social milieu.

In the same year that the English translation of Waelder's *Principle of Multiple Function* was published, and predating Hartmann's publication by three years, Anna Freud (1936) published her groundbreaking monograph, *The Ego and the Mechanisms of Defense*. With a series of clearly written and evocative case studies, Anna Freud would illustrate the mechanisms that the ego had at its disposal to reduce anxiety in the face of the intrapsychic dangers that Sigmund Freud had detailed in *Inhibition, Symptoms and Anxiety.*

According to Young-Bruehl (2002), Anna Freud's monograph was one of two "systematic works of the 1930s [that] were understood by all

Freudians to be the key elaborations of the structural theory" (p. 757) – the other one was Hartmann's *Ego Psychology and the Problem of Adaptation*. And, Wallerstein (1984) considered *The Ego and the Mechanisms of Defense* as "the foundation piece of the whole of the modern era of ego psychology and of how we collectively understand and practice psychoanalysis" and "perhaps the single most widely read book in our professional literature" (p. 66).

Finally, around this same period, Fenichel, drawing on the new emphasis placed on the ego, would stress the importance of what he described as a *theory of practice* (Fenichel, 1938, p. 423). At the heart of his theory of practice were therapeutic techniques focused on the ego and its defensive operations. A number of well-accepted precepts emerged from Fenichel's work, including the axiom of focusing on defenses before content. When interpreting clinical material, Fenichel explained, it was no longer sufficient for the analyst to show the nature of an impulse to the patient: Equally important was to show the patient the defenses marshaled to address the impulse. As an analysis progressed, the content being defended against, the means by which it was defended, and the motivation for doing so, ideally should be interpreted together. For Fenichel, psychoanalysis was defense analysis, entailing a lengthy process of working through that required the analyst to show the patient, again and again, the manifestation of his or her typical modes of self-protection.

In all, by the 1940s, the era of ego psychology had begun in earnest, launching, according to Bergman (1997), "one of the most productive periods in the history of psychoanalysis" (p. 71). This period, spanning 40 years, marked what has been referred to as the hegemony of ego psychology in American psychoanalysis. Through these groundbreaking contributions, psychoanalysis changed from so-called *id analysis* or *depth psychology* to ego psychology and the analysis of defense. Modern conflict theory would strive to push psychoanalysis from being focused on the analysis of defense to an analysis of the total personality.

Modern conflict theory can be defined by the influence that these seminal publications had on Brenner's theoretical developments and in terms of the critical challenges, revisions, amendments and, in some cases, ultimate renunciations of basic ego psychological constructs that Brenner proposed. Beginning with a reconsideration of the concept of signal anxiety, I will now detail the critical revisions that culminated in modern conflict theory.

Signal anxiety revisited

In three critical papers, Brenner (1974, 1975, 1979a) would make the case that anxiety was not the only signal that the ego would use to instantiate defense. Unpleasure of any sort, such as depressive affects (Brenner, 1992), could also serve as a signal to mobilize defenses. Brenner (1974) defined affects as a sensation of unpleasure or pleasure accompanied by mental ideation and temporality, where anxiety is a sensation of unpleasure accompanied by the idea that something bad *will* happen, whereas depressive affects are the sensation of unpleasure accompanied by the idea that something bad *has* happened. In either case, the unpleasure and the ideation, may be conscious or unconscious. Brenner considered his revision of signal anxiety as one of the two most important revisions that he would make to psychoanalysis (Brenner, 1988 interview with Parcell), the second one being his views on the ubiquity of conflict and compromise formations.

One might ask why this revision of the concept of signal anxiety was so important? Well, for one thing, it challenged some precepts about the types of affects that were thought to be associated with different stages of development, such as pre-Oedipal and Oedipal periods. Castration fears and fantasies, for instance, were typically thought to trigger signal anxiety, whereas ideas related to the experience of loss were typically thought to trigger depressive affects. Dating back to Abraham (1911), unconscious conflicts that were linked to depressive affects were typically understood as pre-Oedipal and belonging to the oral stage. Brenner now proposed that ideation related to the Oedipal period, such as castration thoughts and fantasies, could also be linked to depressive affects. "There are instances," Brenner (1979a) wrote, "when reality and fantasy combine to convince an Oedipal boy that castration has actually happened, that it is a fact, not a danger" (p. 185). The same is true in some cases with girls. Clinical evidence did not support the notion that, in patients with depressive affect, experiences of object loss and oral conflicts were automatically of primary importance.

Whereas Freud made reference to the typical *dangers* of childhood (loss of the object, loss of the object's love, physical harm, and fear of superego condemnation), Brenner, in keeping with his views regarding depressive affects, preferred the term *calamities of childhood*, to indicate not only ideas about something bad happening in the future, as the word *danger* implies, but also to account for ideas or fantasies about something bad having already transpired.

The particular type of unpleasurable affect, in turn, had important implications for the understanding of the particular types of defenses mobilized to mitigate them. So, for instance, while some defenses may be aimed at reducing anxiety attendant to something in the future (e.g., avoidance, repression of a wish), other defenses are aimed at diminishing or changing unpleasurable affects associated with ideas that something bad has already happened, such as undoing or reparation. The fantasies of *undoing* and *reparation* and their relationship to depressive affects had already figured prominently in Melanie Klein's (1935a) description of the depressive position. Other defenses were aimed at diminishing the awareness that something bad has already transpired (denial) or changing how one feels about ideas that something bad has happened (e.g., rationalization).

The relevance to adult psychoanalysis is that the childhood wishes and the sources of unpleasure during infancy become the sources of anxiety and depression in adulthood. In all, an awareness of the origins of the unpleasure in light of a person's past history, wishes, and thoughts (both libidinal and aggressive), the variation of affects to which these gave rise, and the accompanying defenses were all critical to arriving at a more accurate understanding of one's patient. Brenner (1975) believed that in order to understand a symptom, "One must reconstruct, as far as possible, not only what dangers were and unconsciously still are, the part of the patient's anxiety, but also what calamities were, and unconsciously still are, a part of his depressive affect" (p. 26).

"Mechanisms" of defense

Another major challenge that modern conflict theory posed to ego psychology related to the notion of *mechanisms of defense*, as articulated most clearly by Anna Freud (1936) in her monograph, *The Ego and the Mechanisms of Defense*. Specifically, the idea of mechanisms posed problems because the term *mechanisms* gave the false impression that there were mental activities and processes of the mind that worked solely and exclusively in the service of defense. Projection, for example, was a mental activity that could operate in the service of defense, just as well as it did in the service of gratifying libidinal wishes, such as when a person projects onto another his or her feelings of love in the service of a sexual fantasy. It was more accurate and less confusing to appreciate the fact that any mental activity or "ego functioning can be used defensively" (Brenner,

28 Christopher Christian

1992, p. 373). Throughout a series of writings spanning over five decades, Brenner would convincingly illustrate (1959, 1982b, 2008) how defenses were as varied and extensive as the range of mental activities and could be defined only in terms of their mitigating effects on unpleasurable affects.

Hartmann's conflict-free sphere

A prevalent idea in psychoanalysis in general, and in Hartmann's work in particular, was that conflict characterized mental illness and that non-pathological or *normal* functioning operated outside the realm of conflict. So-called normal functioning was not only free of conflict but also was assumed to be independent of the drives and drive derivatives, including infantile wishes. Modern conflict theory, with its focus on the ubiquity of conflict and compromise formation, challenged these ideas with the understanding that so-called "normal behaviors" are also the product of conflict and compromise formation. Using detailed clinical examples, which were for the most part absent in Hartmann's writings, Brenner would go on to show how so-called normal behaviors, like vocational choices, hobbies, and selection of spouse, among other things, were also the products of conflict and compromise formation. He noted, "there is no sharp line that separates what is normal from what is pathological in psychic life" (Brenner, 1982b, p. 150). The aim of psychoanalysis was not the removal of conflict but rather the alteration of compromise formations. Furthermore, what defined so-called *normal* behavior from pathological was not the absence of conflict but rather the achievement of better compromise formations, such that the person could obtain as much pleasure without undue unpleasure. In cases of psychopathology the person's compromise formations were deficient, insofar as the person incurred too much inhibition of pleasurable thoughts and activities or incurred too much of an intrapsychic cost for pleasure in the form of self-punishment. In this way, Brenner's ideas rejected H. Hartmann's (1939) most accepted tenet of "a conflict-free sphere." Brenner (1992) would write, "There is no conflict-free sphere of mental functioning. There are only more or less satisfactory compromise formations" p. 378).

Principle of multiple function

Waelder's principle of multiple function, that is, the idea that in every act the ego attempts to address all of the agencies of the mind, figured prominently in the development of modern conflict theory with its emphasis

The evolution of modern conflict theory   29

on compromise formation. In agreement with Waelder's notions, Brenner wrote that when we consider a symptom we do not wonder, "Is this a disguised drive derivative? Is it some displaced form of anxiety? Is it a hidden defense? Is it a superego manifestation?" We don't ask any of those questions because we know in advance that it must be all of them in one way or another (Brenner, 1992, p. 376).

Brenner's idea of compromise formation, however, differed from Waelder's view. As Smith (2003) made clear, for Waelder, compromise formation was more a consequence of the problem-solving-tasks that the ego sets for itself and less a consequence of conflict. In Waelder's account, the ego is attending to different demands stemming from different pressures placed upon it by the id, external reality, the superego, and by a compulsion to repeat. Whichever way the ego manages to respond to this predicament is inevitably a compromised solution simply because all the agencies can never be fully satisfied to the same degree. Here, this compromise formation is not the result of an attempt at balancing pleasure and unpleasure but rather it is the result of the limitations of the ego in ever meeting the insurmountable tasks it faces. Thus, Waelder notes, the perpetual sense of dissatisfaction that is common to everyone. In an Editor's comment to Brenner's (2009) "Memoir," Smith points out "the difference between Waelder's view and that of Brenner becomes even sharper when Brenner suggests eliminating the concept of the ego altogether" (Brenner, 2009, Editor's note, p. 659).

Structural theory redacted

In 1994, Brenner introduced his most radical revision to psychoanalysis after what he himself described as intensely conflicted feelings about doing so. He would develop a paper in which he concluded that it was time, as Boesky (1994) summarized it, to "seriously consider abandoning the concepts of id, ego, and superego because these terms erroneously separate and disconnect the components of conflict in the human mind" (p. 509). In Brenner's (1994) words, his doubts concern whether the facts support the theory that

> there is a structure or agency of the mind, the id, that consists of drive derivatives; that is separate from another agency of the mind, the ego, which has other functions, including defense; and that both are separate from another structure, the superego.

(p. 474)

Ultimately, modern conflict theory would be defined by its emphasis on the ubiquity of intrapsychic conflict and compromise formations. The components of a compromise formation are (1) an *objectionable wish or thought* that is challenged on moral grounds; moreover, these frustrated wishes or thoughts are derivatives of sexual and aggressive wishes originating from childhood; (2) *unpleasure* originating from the strictures that oppose the wish, and a fear of punishment *that results in conflict*; and, (3) *attempts at an intrapsychic compromise*, whereby the person attempts to gratify these derivatives of childhood wishes, without incurring too much cost in the form of unpleasure.

By describing a personal wish, rather than alluding to the term *drives*, and by using the term *person*, rather than an *ego*, Brenner was developing a theory that was closer to clinical experience. Much like Schafer (1973), he was calling for an *action language* that was devoid of metapsychological abstractions, which were *experience-far* (as opposed to *experience-near*), and lent themselves to misconception about how the mind works.

Boesky (1994), notwithstanding his cogent challenge to Brenner's revisions, explains in his critique some of the confusion attendant to the structural theory in his summary of what is problematic with the concept of the id. The id on the one hand is seen as a pure biological drive, a cauldron of energy. And yet in the id we find structured ideation in the form of wishes. Does the id energy stop being "id" once it is articulated into a wish by the ego? Boesky quotes Schur (1966) who said that "since the id was supposed to contain repressed ideational content it was necessary to view it as structured in some way. It was not just a seething caldron of bodily drive energies" (Boesky, 1994, p. 514). Boesky acknowledges that to divide the mind into structures, such that impulses are located in one structure the id; defenses located in the ego; and guilt and self-punishment in the superego is problematic because in doing so, we fail to account for the fluidity between the function of these structures.

However, Boesky argued that these structures were best understood as metaphors that served to connote a set of functions which operated in some kind of predictable configuration and according to some developmental timeline. The terms *id*, *ego*, and *superego* separate some of these functions for the sake of convenience.

> One of the advantages of the terms *id*, *ego*, and *superego* has been that it has allowed us to artificially but conveniently separate these

The evolution of modern conflict theory   31

functional organizations for purposes of discussion and investigation of the developmental fate of each of the three major functional components.

(Boesky, 1994, p. 512)

The critical question becomes, at what cost do we abandon the concepts of id, ego, and superego and is the cost offset by any gains in doing so? Brenner's answer was that whatever we gain in convenience is offset by the lack of accuracy.

The relational turn

Another major challenge to conflict theory came from the relational turn in psychoanalysis. Over time, the focus on intrapsychic conflict gave way to concerns with interpersonal processes. By the late 1980s and early 1990s, the concept of intersubjectivity, and a so-called two-person psychology, began to take hold in American psychoanalysis with the works of Benjamin (1988, 2005), Aron (1991), Stolorow and Atwood (1992), L. Hoffman (1995), Orange et al. (1997), and Mitchell (1998). As Hafter-Gray (1986) put it, the new focus was on "the difficult doctor-patient relationship, rather than the difficult patient" (p. 201). Subjectivity, like countertransference, became a term that cut across theoretical paradigms.

Brenner gave little importance to the role of countertransference, and much less to the concept of subjectivity or intersubjectivity, in the therapeutic process. The term *countertransference* comes up only in 5 of over 90 publications in Brenner's corpus. What Brenner had to say about countertransference was contained in a brief but incisive paper titled, "Countertransference as compromise formation" (Brenner, 1985). The central argument in this paper, which emanates directly from Brenner's ideas on transference, can be summarized as follows: compromise formation is a ubiquitous part of mental functioning. Like the patient, an analyst's thoughts, behaviors, and even choice of profession are the products of conflict and compromise formations.

When the balance in the components of the analyst's compromise formations become disturbed in his or her work with a patient, we refer to it as countertransference. As one might expect, some patients will upset this balance, at which point the analyst benefits from trying to understand how and why, using introspection, consultation with colleagues, and/or

32   Christopher Christian

personal analysis. We see, perhaps to our surprise, that Brenner's ideas about countertransference as the product of conflict and compromise formation have much in common with contemporary views on subjectivity as purported, for example, by Renik (1993, 2006). According to both Renik as well as Brenner, the analyst can never escape from his or her subjective perspective. Put differently, the analyst can never escape from the fact that everything the analyst thinks or does is the product of his or her own conflicts and compromise formations.

The critical question is to what extent, and in what ways, does the analyst make use of his or her subjectivity for understanding the analysand? Arlow (1979), for instance, was explicit about the importance of the analyst lending an ear to his or her inner experience as a way of arriving at an understanding of the analysand's unconscious fantasies and conflicts and developing interpretations to communicate such understanding. Arlow posited that as the analyst follows the flow of the patient's material, a change occurs whereby the analyst's attention is directed to something going on within himself. Arlow (1979) writes, "The thought that first appears in the analyst's mind rarely comes in the form of a well-formulated, logically consistent, theoretically articulated interpretation" (p. 200). Regardless of the thought, Arlow continues,

> Either immediately or shortly thereafter, a connection can be and is made between what the analyst has been thinking and feeling and what the patient has been saying. It is at that point that the analyst's inner experience is transformed into an interpretation.
>
> (p. 200)

Arlow (1979) contends that unless there is some marked countertransference interference, such as when the analyst is ill, in pain, or overwhelmed by personal problems of his own, the analyst's associations *always* represent a commentary to himself about the analysand's unconscious thought process.

In later writings, and perhaps in reaction to implications for technique attendant to the relational turn in psychoanalysis, Arlow (1995) would temper this view and warn of what he saw as a danger in the recommendations of Jacobs (1986), Schwaber (1992), and Renik (1993) that the analyst deliberately turn his attention during the session to his own experience as a way of understanding the analysand. The danger here, as Arlow saw it, was that by focusing on the analyst's "transient, personal anxieties" the analyst would be distracted from following the patient's flow of associations. "Under such circumstances, listening may become confused, overly theoretical, and intellectual in orientation" (Arlow, 1995, pp. 226–227). In a posthumously published paper entitled "Some Notes on Intersubjectivity," Arlow (2002) reiterated that the analyst's associations "serve as *signposts* leading to the direction of insight into the patient's difficulties and the insight so achieved may be correct" (p. 2). But he cautioned against the idea that "simply by virtue of the fact that it occurred to the analyst's mind, that fact alone was sufficient to substantiate the interpretation" (p. 2). According to Rothstein (2005), "Brenner's (1982b) description of the interminable irrationality of analyst and patient as manifest in part in the transference and countertransference emphasizes a *ubiquitous subjective* perspective" (italics added, p. 418)." To acknowledge that the analyst's subjective experience can help him or her understand something about the patient, and to recognize that our subjectivity makes our observations fallible, was only one dimension of the challenge posed by relationists. The more profound claims that some relationists, such as Benjamin (1998, 2004) and Mitchell (1998), made had to do with a view of the mind as co-created and co-determined. According to Benjamin (2010), for example, the patient's mind cannot be understood as a unitary entity, separate from that of the analyst. It was the relational dynamics, and not the analysand's mind, that needed to be the focus of observation and clinical inquiry. This became and remains a dividing line between modern conflict theory and some contemporary views of psychoanalysis. For many conflict theorists, to conceptualize the patient's difficulties as mainly co-constructed by the interpersonal field is to diminish the role of the intrapsychic dimension and to discard the role that intrapsychic conflict and unconscious fantasy play in our patients' lives.

Another common criticism of modern conflict theory has to do with its focus on childhood instinctual and aggressive wishes as the sources of conflict in adulthood. Does it really make sense to say that pleasure in adulthood is somehow a derivative of childhood sexual and/or aggressive wishes? The notion that everything is a derivative of such wishes is too broad a conceptualization, in the opinion of some. Perhaps the concept of compromise formation is limited to clinical work with patients dealing with sexual and aggressive wishes, and with superego considerations. When we are not talking about neurotic patients who have conflicts regarding sexual and/or aggressive wishes, is it a stretch to claim that such wishes are always motivating behavior?

To this line of reasoning, I believe that Brenner's response can be summarized as follows: the organism operates along the pleasure-unpleasure principle such that it seeks to maximize pleasure without undue unpleasure. A person's assessment of what is pleasurable and unpleasurable has been influenced by early experiences of childhood regarding the pursuit of pleasure and its attendant consequences. The pleasure-seeking wishes from childhood, which become associated with impending calamities, and elicit the strongest defenses, tend to be of a sexual and aggressive nature. And, the biggest calamity from which the child must protect himself or herself entails some kind of loss. The child will strive to avoid such loss at all cost – a notion that became a fundamental premise of attachment theory. These experiences, real and fantasied, and the assessments that the child makes regarding them, leave a permanent mark on how the person determines what is pleasurable, at what cost, and what is dangerous. Every subsequent psychic act undergoes this unconscious assessment.

However, Brenner ultimately believed that it was best to attribute motivation to the broader category of the pleasure-unpleasure principle rather than to reduce motivation to a pair of drives (libidinal and aggressive). He, thus, in the end concluded that "what is important is what are the pleasure-seeking memories and fantasies and what are the unpleasure-avoiding memories and fantasies that together are causing that particular patient's conflicts" (Brenner, 2008, p. 717).

Modern conflict theory is aimed at parsimony, developing an internally consistent theory of how the mind works based on, and supported by, clinical observation. It sought to define a clear theory of practice, to use Fenichel's term. Both Arlow and Brenner sought to pare psychoanalysis from unsupported or contradictory terms and, in doing so, developed "a spare and lean theoretical vocabulary" (Smith, 2007, p. 1060). The term *modern* or *modernity* has been used to denote a historical period marked by a break from tradition and an embracing of the enlightenment. In this respect the term is apt in defining the new theory that Brenner forged. It became axiomatic in New York psychoanalytic circles that when Brenner wrote a paper, psychoanalysis lost a term. As Friedman (2011) so vividly put it, by the time Brenner was done with his so-called *addendums* and revisions, there would be no diagrams left on the chalkboard – that is, no topographic theory, no structural theory, no so-called defense "mechanisms," and no primary and/or secondary process.

The evolution of modern conflict theory   35

In the end what was left can be summarized as follows: first and foremost is the explicit understanding of the ubiquity of conflict as part of both normal and so-called pathological functioning. These conflicts have their origins in the calamities of childhood, marked as they are by early relationships with parents, events, childhood wishes, fantasies, and fears. Second, there is the awareness that defenses can be triggered by any unpleasurable affect. Then there is the recognition that there is no such thing as special mechanisms of defense but rather that any activity of the mind can be used for the purpose of achieving pleasure or reducing unpleasure. And, finally, in place of an *ego* is the less confusing term *person* when referring to the agent of mental activities. To this list we might add a growing appreciation of the role that countertransference or subjectivity plays in understanding a mind in conflict.

By way of illustrating how an analyst's own conflicts and compromise formations, or one's subjectivity, if you will, informs treatment, I will briefly describe a short segment of the beginning of a psychoanalytic treatment. A single woman in her late 20s sought treatment for marked inhibitions, particularly around her aggression, which became most evident in her difficulties in advancing her career. The patient was offered psychoanalysis, which she accepted in principle but refused to use the couch for the first two months of the treatment. Within a two-week period, the patient produced a number of interesting dreams. In one dream, she is in a doctor's office for a checkup: *"I am sitting on the examination table and the doctor says that she (referring to the patient) needs that injection that they have been discussing. He's holding a syringe. It is red and it looks like it's made of plastic."* She added that she was trying to postpone the procedure but that the doctor was only half listening. In her associations, she saw the dream as a comment on her refusing the couch. She said that the examination table must be a disguised reference to the couch; she related the color of the syringe to the color of my couch and then thought about how the syringe also represented "something phallic." She then spoke of worries about sexual feelings that were associated with using the couch and revealed that part of her fear of letting go in an analysis was that she would fall in love and suffer when the analysis ended.

I commented on her experience of me, as the doctor in the dream, not listening to her protests. She did not elaborate on this aspect of the dream and instead proceeded to assure me that, in fact, I listened carefully.

In my associations to her dream, I likened my analysand to Irma, that famous recalcitrant patient of Freud, who refused his recommendations. It was this particular association, a joke to myself, with its underlying hubris, that made me aware of a particular type of pleasure that I was taking in my work. This represented a particular countertransference response, albeit one devoid of the storms that we tend to associate with countertransference. Through its recognition I came to realize how hard the patient was working to please me by the production of so many dreams; how much she wished to be the ideal patient even in defiance of the couch. Her dreams, which were like gifts, made for work that was going a little too well. And, yet, another part of my countertransference was to pay a blind eye to this aspect of her character that influenced her *need* to produce such rich material. It was the *smooth sailing* experience that alerted me to what I was overlooking and that once recognized would take up the rest of her analysis. As a bit of context, the patient had a sibling who died when she was very young, after which point she took it upon herself to become a replacement child, working doubly hard to please her grieving parents.

In many respects, this short and simple illustration represents the mundane, almost imperceptible, influence of my countertransference in my understanding of a patient. The frequency with which these moments of *recognition* occur almost renders them unremarkable – particularly when the feelings that are evoked in the analyst are ego-syntonic, such as feelings of pleasure, warmth, humor, hopefulness, and excitement, as opposed to more upsetting feelings that we typically associate with a countertransference response. In agreement with Arlow (2002), I believe that there is no need to adopt too vigilant of a stance for evidence of how the patient's material relates to the analyst's own conflicts and compromise formations. The analyst need not go in search of countertransference. The fact is that countertransference, insofar as it represents an unconscious process, should catch us by surprise. Stepping into each session with a vigilant stance toward one's reactions becomes a willful attitude that is contrived and restrains the fluidity that I believe is necessary in the analyst that allows him or her to go in and out of different states of mind in relation to oneself and the other. A capacity to suspend a willful attitude facilitates a *receptivity* to communications from the patient as well as from within oneself. Arlow (1979), in *The Genesis of an Interpretation*, has described the process by which we encourage the patient to relax a vigilant stance and dream during the session. At times, the analyst calls the analysand's attention to something in the analysand's material, as if waking the patient from his sleep to say "look what you just said," "look what just happened." A similar process takes place in the analyst, where he relaxes his attention and allows for messages to come from within, at which point he rouses himself from his semi-somber state to say "look what just happened" and from there, develops some kind of interpretation. I believe that potentially damaging enactments result when the analyst does not wake up in time, either to his own or the patient's dream, so that patient and therapist play something out over an extended period of time without full conscious awareness.

Conclusion

For quite some time the analysis of intrapsychic conflict was seen as the defining feature of psychoanalysis. Today, it is safe to say that this is no longer the case. In fact, a contextual analysis of papers published in the *Journal of the American Psychoanalytic Association* from 1953 to 2010 (Dent & Christian, 2014) that examined the use of the word *conflict* and any derivatives, such as *conflictual, conflicting*, and so forth, shows a clear decline in the usage of *conflict* beginning in the mid-1980s, which roughly corresponds to the beginning of the relational turn in American psychoanalysis. Yet, as we have seen, and something that is most evident in the chapters of this volume, conflict remains relevant to a wide range of clinical approaches. However, the term *conflict*, and the components of conflict, are often defined and understood very differently. In this chapter, I have sought to define how conflict is understood from the perspective of modern conflict theory. In my own practice, I have found this approach most helpful in understating patients with a wide range of problems, who have presented for both psychoanalysis and psychotherapy.

Notes

1 Brenner (2008) attributed the term *modern conflict theory* to Sandor Abend in a personal communication.
2 The topographic model, in fact, was never fully discarded by Freud or subsequent analysts who often made use of, and reference to, both models of the mind.
3 *The Principle of Multiple Function: Observations on Over-determination* was originally published by Waelder in German in 1930 and then translated into English for publication in *The Psychoanalytic Quarterly* in 1936.

Chapter 3

The fate of conflict and the impoverishment of our clinical methods

Fred Busch

Although the epic discovery of unconscious conflicts within the mind and their connection to human illness were the very basis of the development of psychoanalysis, we seem to have gradually forsaken the role of conflict as a causative factor in the difficulties our patients bring to us. The question is why? It is my impression there were a number of catalysts that played a central role.

The seeds for radical discontent with the role of intrapsychic conflict lie, in part, within our own history. S. Freud's (1897) move from the seduction hypothesis, to the theory of unconscious fantasies based on intrapsychic conflict as causative in psychopathology, sealed over the role of early object relations for some time, eventually leading to discontent with singular reliance on the conflict model. This continued with the rejection of extra-analytic data showing the centrality of environmental circumstances on mental and physical development, starting with Spitz (1945, 1946), resistance to their single-mindedness grew stronger. In short, the inflexibility of those in charge of "official" theory played a role in the rejection of key elements of that theory.

The resulting gaps in understanding were filled by newer theories that should have been welcome additions but instead became separate schools of thought in opposition to Freudian theory and the role of unconscious conflict. In fact, the very role of the unconscious has been redefined or diminished in most of the newer theories.

Eagle et al. (2001) captured the position of new view theorists well, stating that according to these theorists the mind interpretively and interpersonally constructed:

> Because mind is accorded no factuality independent of interpretive construction, nothing is held to be uncovered or discovered in

the psychoanalytic process. According to this view, mind is not pre-organized but rather awaits organization and the articulation of mental contents through interpersonal interaction.

(p. 459)[1]

The metapsychology debates of the 1970s and 1980s (Schmidt-Hellerau, 2005) involved the rejection of drive theory, which further de-emphasized conflict theory. Freud's theory had proposed that drive and repression (defense) were closely wedded and that this marriage was the paradigm for conflict. In moving away from the drive concept, we lost the sense of the brute force of instinctual demands, and delivered the self to a more benign idea of wishes, leading to an encouragement of these wishes rather than understanding the inhibitions that stem from conflict between opposing forces.[2]

While the importance of early trauma has been a central part of our growing understanding of patients, the "bad object" has become for many the primary explanation of our patients' problems. However, as I've shown (Busch, 2005), the mind's relentless need to make sense of what happened leads to fantasies of cause and effect, which have become intertwined with the trauma. To appreciate the trauma while still being alert to the fantasies and guilt associated with it gives our patients the best chance of working through.

In other words, it is not only the trauma itself that remains traumatic. Inevitably, the feelings and fantasies the trauma stimulates become part of a dangerous intrapsychic field making it part of intrapsychic conflict (Busch, 2005, pp. 27–28)

Psychoanalytic technique

The trends noted earlier have led to an emphasis on what seems necessary but not sufficient for psychoanalysis to occur. For example, empathy and relatedness have become sufficient for many. As Lichtenberg (1998) stated,

Are we, through a perceived empathic failure, the source of the aversive response, or are we a listener sensitive to the patient's aversive stance? . . . Many instances of antagonism and withdrawal that I had been taught to regard as resistance I now consider a patient's trusting response to an ambiance of safety.

(p. 26)

This raises the question: if psychoanalysis is nothing more than a form of relating,[3] what have we to offer beyond what many therapies, friends, or religions do? Bolognini (1997) is critical of psychoanalysts who confuse empathy with being kindhearted. Too often, he believes, empathy is confused with a superficial analytic atmosphere that is blissful and fusional. If we ignore unconscious conflicts, we deprive analysands of the opportunity to build more structure such that the patient is less anxious, less inhibited, less defended, and able to arrive at more satisfying compromise formations.

Psychoanalysis began as a curative process for unconscious conflict, and for most of the international community it remains so. Aisenstein (2007) elegantly captures the essence of the psychoanalytic task from its inception forward and points to a main goal of analyzing unconscious conflict:

> Analysis is uncompromising in relation to other therapies because it alone aims . . . at aiding our patients to become, or to become again, the principal agents in their own history and thought. Am I too bold in insisting that this is the sole inalienable freedom a human being possesses?
>
> (p. 1459)

Aisenstein emphasizes here that the curative power of psychoanalysis lies in the goal of helping the patient re-find his mind, in part through the analysis of unconscious conflict. This can be referred to as "creating a psychoanalytic mind" (Busch, 2013), a process through which we help patients understand that they have a mind, that this mind leads them to think and do things in a particular way, and that they can understand it by seeing what comes to mind, reflecting on it and playing with it (Busch, 2007). This is the essence of the gift of psychoanalysis. When patients come to us, we hope to show them that the curative process may be gleaned by consultations with one's mind, so that the inevitability of repetitious actions is replaced by the possibility of reflection.

While one might wish for empirical evidence to show the superiority of one method over another, this has proven to be complicated.[4] However, there is empirical research that informs a theoretical position that shows why the representation of unconscious conflicts are necessary for changing pathological patterns. Since 1914, when Freud first showed how unconscious conflicts were expressed as repetitions, we have learned more about why the mind works in this way, mainly in two areas. First, as has been shown by myself (Busch, 1995, 2009), and many others, the earliest forms of thought are actions or are encoded in action determinants. Further, unconscious mentation is "pre-symbolic" (Basch, 1981), "pre-conceptual" (Frosch, 1995), or "concrete" (Bass, 1997), so that what is repressed is stored in thoughts closer to action (an impulse to do). In short, what is unconscious is under-represented in language and thought. Second, in a highly simplified version of the findings from neuroscience, we can say that information processing involves the activation of multiple nodes in a network at once, in a series of patterns. In conflict we find simple structures, leading every lover to become the same lover; one can posit that this is likewise a result of a simple pattern of node activation in the brain. By building new representations we change simple networks into more complex ones, leading to information processing slowing down, making reflection possible (see Westen & Gabbard, 2002).[5] This is why there has been a paradigm shift across certain psychoanalytic cultures, labeled by LeCours (2007) as moving toward a paradigm of transformation. Rather than primarily searching for buried memories, we attempt to transform that which is under-represented into ideas that are representable in language and thought. For example, we attempt to build representations as a way of helping the patient build structure and thus contain previously threatening thoughts and feelings so that he can move toward deeper levels of meaning. As noted by LeCours (2007), what is represented can continue to build structure and enhance the ability to contain. This leads to what Green (1975) called "binding the inchoate" (p. 9) and containing it, thus giving a container to the patient's content and "content to his container" (p. 7).

In short, what I'm suggesting is that by ignoring unconscious conflict as a source of the problems that bring patients to our offices, we rob them of the chance to build more complex representations via understanding the fears and wishes that keep conflicts in place. What makes this process so difficult is that what has been repressed is kept out of awareness because it connects to the most devastating fears known to humans (e.g., loss of self, fears of disintegrations, loss of the object, castration anxiety). This is at the heart of unconscious conflict and must be taken into consideration if we think knowing thyself is an integral part of the curative process. S. Freud (1914a) articulated the centrality of this process to working through when he stated: "This working through of the resistances . . . is a part of the work which effects the greatest changes in the patient and which distinguishes analytic treatment from any kind of treatment by suggestion" (p. 155). However, Freud himself had difficulty holding to this position (Busch, 1992, 1993). P. Gray (1982) highlighted what he generously called our "developmental lag" in using resistance analysis in practice. This has led analysts to try various methods to overcome resistances rather than analyzing them. As Bolognini (1997) warned, empathy has "become the analyst's ideal goal, a kind of all-purpose philosopher's stone, potentially capable of resolving any clinical difficulty" (p. 279).

Unconscious fantasies and their role in conflict

In this example we find a number of developmental interferences that played a role in the patient's symptoms. It was clear the patient felt narcissistically vulnerable as he described various ways that he felt his parents didn't understand or appreciate him. However, only empathizing with the pain this caused him (which was also threatening) led only to a partial representation of his problem. Discovering his unconscious fantasy added another important element to his capacity for representing, and the increasing distance he was able to obtain from, his crippling symptoms.

Jeremy

Jeremy came for treatment soon after taking his first job following graduation from a prestigious college. Crippling anxiety when meeting new people in his job left him exhausted and overwhelmed in the work situation. He had similar experiences starting when he was in high school but eventually found friends with whom he was comfortable. However, outside of this immediate group he still experienced anxiety. Medication was somewhat helpful, but at the urging of his prescribing psychiatrist he sought individual treatment.

While Jeremy felt his parents were generally kind and giving, he complained that they couldn't or wouldn't try to understand him. He felt they never saw him, in contrast to his two brothers who were considerably older. However, in trying to appreciate how painful this might have been for Jeremy, he would immediately follow this with protestations that it wasn't that bad. In this we see we have to be empathic with all sides of a patient, even those where accepting empathy causes conflict. Over time I could understand that for Jeremy,

The fate of conflict   43

hearing my appreciation for the pain he had that his parents couldn't or wouldn't hear him, made him feel even more endangered of being outside the family.

In fits and starts Jeremy became more comfortable in the sessions, and I found him an engaging if cautious person. He said that for the first time in his life he felt *heard*.

In this session Jeremy began talking about how it was hard to forget about his ex-girlfriend as many of his friends had connections to her. He then talked about how self-centered she was. When she called he knew she was going to want something from him, like to help her move or drive her somewhere. As I was puzzling about this I had the sense that with this woman, Jeremy knew he should never expect anything from her, and he felt safe in this way. She could never disappoint him. Yet he was also constantly feeling like an outsider with her. In this I thought I could see Jeremy protecting himself from ever feeling dropped by her, and yet never feeling wanted.

I then said, "I've had a growing sense recently that you often feel like you don't *belong, and with this woman you both repeat this and protect yourself at the same time.*" Jeremy then said, "I've felt like I don't belong forever!" and immediately fell silent. After a while he said, "I found myself focusing on this one spot on your carpet, where the pattern is different than the rest." He showed it to me. I said, "Something that doesn't belong." He fell silent again and then noticed that he wanted to say, "Can we talk about something else?" After a brief pause he said, this reminded him of the time, he thought he was four or five, and his mother was starting to read him a book, designed for children, that talked about how babies were born. After the first few pages he remembered saying, "Can we talk about something else?" Jeremy's memory at the time was that his mother seemed so different when she started reading the book. He didn't remember exactly how he saw her as different, but he now thought she seemed anxious. He recalled growing up in his very Catholic family where sex was a taboo topic. In school, when they showed a sex education film, he was the only one in his class who wasn't allowed to see it. He then remembered that recently he was watching a movie on TV with his parents, and when the main couple started to kiss passionately his mother left the room, making up an excuse about getting some water.

I then said, "When your feeling of being an outsider becomes clear, your thoughts go to sexual issues and what you experienced as your mother's discomfort with sexuality." Jeremy then said,

"I think I realized that from that first time, around four or five, but could never say it because it would have made her feel more uncomfortable. Then when I started getting interested in girls, and started having fantasies about them, I felt like I was a pervert. In fact, it was about that time I became so anxious when around people, but it was really mainly with the women."

Later in the treatment Jeremy went on to describe how he felt he was always noticing things that made him feel different in the family but couldn't figure out why. An example that came to mind was when his mother introduced him to her Catholic friends; she seemed uncomfortable, but she didn't seem that way with his brother.

At some point in the treatment I suggested the possibility to Jeremy that he developed a fantasy that his mother was ashamed of his birth because she was older, and it was a sign of her continued sexual activity, which she felt would be disapproved of in her strict Catholic community. Jeremy couldn't remember having such an idea (and I didn't expect him to at that moment), but many more memories came to mind of his mother's shame around his birth.

Discovering Jeremy's unconscious fantasy was not the solution to his problems. Rather it was another piece in building a more complex representation of the reason for his symptom, and in this way building structure so that containment of his anxiety is more possible.

In summary, patients come to our offices caught up in unconscious conflicts driven by highly saturated simple structures (e.g., boss=angry father, leading to inhibition). By building increasingly complex representations of meaning of unconscious conflicts, we give our patients the opportunity to reflect rather than act. One might imagine an empty room with two doors. Entering this room through one door, there would be nothing to impede a person from quickly moving through to the next door. Then one might imagine the same room with lots of furniture. Upon entering the room one has to spend more time in it before going through the other door. This is the situation with someone in a successful analysis. At first they can't help but enact unconscious conflict. However, via analysis, actions based on unconscious conflict become contained, and reflective space is opened so that thoughts are no longer dominated by the push to act.

The search for a new definition of psychoanalysis

It is my impression that in the United States colleagues seem to career from one theory to another[6] or work to show that "old" theory is so flawed that only the shiny, new model has the answers. At times there has been a "take no prisoners" approach with the introduction of new theories, especially in the United States, while in most other countries new versions of theory (e.g., the Kleinians, French, and Bionions) ground their theories in the Freudian unconscious. As Sugarman (1995) noted, J. Greenberg and Mitchell (1983) were adamant about the essential incompatibility between the theoretical underpinnings of relational and drive-conflict models. He also suggested that a similar problem could be seen with modern-day self psychology. Although Kohut (1971, 1977) originally formulated self psychology to complement structural thinking, his later work and its development by other self psychologists replaces the classical-structural model with the self psychological one (see Eagle, 1984 for more on this concept). Sugarman unearthed the following comment by Levenson (1988), which characterizes the view of those seeing no value in the Freudian conflict model: "The flabbiest intellectual position is, as I've said, 'So what? You just move back and forth between these polarities'" (p. 562).

In general I have found it crucial to my continued development as an analyst to try to understand perspectives that are different from those in which I was trained.[7] I see these other views as important, sophisticated contributions to Freud's theory of conflict rather than as the replacement. For example, I cannot imagine practicing psychoanalysis without incorporating some of Kohut's concepts of narcissistic development or Ogden's views on thinking as dreaming. However, so many important ideas lead to splits rather than energizing the theory as a whole. So we argue over whether case material is better understood from a Freudian, Kohutian, Relational, or other perspective, rather than where and when each perspective might be useful.

While I have no doubt most patients who come for analysis have experienced narcissistic deprivations of a serious degree, to understand an individual only in these terms robs them of the opportunity to overcome conflict-driven restrictions in the rich experience associated with an inner life. In the past (Busch, 2005) I have criticized the increasing domination of a traumatocentric view of patients' problems. In fact, I have never seen a patient in psychoanalysis in whom there has not been some form of interference in healthy narcissistic development that has led to unconscious fantasies of causation and solution, resulting in intrapsychic conflict. For example, a child's egocentric view of the world leads him to experience his depressed mother's inability to nurture and mirror his healthy demands as due to his excessive needs. Thus, the ongoing trauma of a lack of mirroring leads to his needs becoming associated with unconscious fears of deadness, abandonment, and guilt. In analysis, when he begins to feel needful toward the analyst, these internal dangers pull him back to an inhibited emotional stance. In short, it is not only the trauma itself that remains traumatic. Inevitably, the feelings and fantasies the trauma stimulates become part of a dangerous intrapsychic field. In this way, a trauma also becomes part of an intrapsychic conflict. Thus, it seems that analytic work has to be informed by attunement to empathic breakdowns, past and present, and their effects on the patient's psychic life both inside and outside of the analysis, while we also listen for the resultant unconscious fantasies and intrapsychic conflict.

Looked at from another perspective, A. Kris (1983) presented an excellent argument for the role of an unconscious sense of guilt (from any one of a number of sources) in patients with narcissistic difficulties. Such patients may show the narcissist's inability to feel valued or appreciated, while raging at those around for not providing enough mirroring or inadequately serving as idealizing others. However, with some of these patients it is not primarily inadequate or damaging caretakers that drive their narcissistic difficulties but an unconscious sense of guilt. Therefore, with these patients their state of deprivation is due to the conflicts caused by feeling they are getting too much. To treat it otherwise may be temporarily gratifying but unsatisfying for a long-term understanding. That is, many patients feel gratified and understood when we show them that part of the difficulties they have lived through are the result of early trauma, neglect, emotional abandonment, abuse, and so forth. However, the rich but conflicted fantasy life one develops as a result of these events cannot be used for creative dreaming if they remain unanalyzed as part of the curative process. Further, certain patients with a history of depression can be led into a malignant regression if they see themselves only as victims.

Narcissistic slights as a defense against conflict

Here I will present a case from my own practice in order to demonstrate how exploring conflict with patients can help them increase their experience of choice. The patient to be presented, Anna, is in her third year of analysis. While Anna unconsciously invites me to engage in a narcissistically hurtful act that has an erotic quality, this is a wish/defense against her growing awareness of lovingly erotic feelings with me, and the feelings of great sadness it arouses. The unconscious conflict over the wish to be loved, and the painful feelings of sadness it brings, first emerging in a dream and the feelings it brings, leads to feeling "fucked," which is a defense against and the enactment of the unconscious conflict.

Anna flies into her analytic session. Before she even lies down on the couch Anna states, "I couldn't wait to tell you about this weekend." In a rush she begins to tell me, at great length, of the various ways her husband mistreated her. It was not told in any great distress, but more in the form of conspiratorial togetherness. It was a story I heard many times from Anna, so her feeling that "she couldn't wait to tell me" struck me as an important indicator of some way she was viewing the analysis and/or our relationship. When Anna paused for a breath, I expressed my empathy about how distressing this seemed to be and also wondered about this "couldn't wait to tell me" feeling. She cut me off saying, "Yes, yes, but let me tell you about this other incident that happened." Anna then proceeded to tell me a lengthy story where she visited her parents, and her mother spent a long time on the phone with her sister. There were many other slights as well.

While I considered the stories of being mistreated by others as a displacement from something she felt with me, I also had a familiar feeling of irritation about being interrupted, and had the thought of confronting Anna with her lack of consideration of others, thus suggesting her use of projection. However, I could see how this would be experienced by Anna as an attack, an unconsciously wished for enactment on my part. My thoughts went back to how propelled she was to tell me these stories, blotting out any other possible thoughts, that is, hers or mine.

Another story of a similar nature quickly followed, presented in this same breathless manner. Listening to this story, I sensed an excited quality in her breathlessness. After a brief silence, I said to Anna that again, she seemed in a rush to tell me what happened, so much so that it seemed difficult to register what I said. After a brief pause Anna said, "I hate your voice." Puzzled and intrigued I waited. She then said, "I had a sexual dream about you last night. It wasn't you in the dream, but it was a tall guy with a beard. I thought of you as soon as I woke up. We made love in the most tender and exciting way. When we finished I cried. I didn't want to tell you. It makes me so sad when I think of being loved instead of fucked. Better to go on feeling angry about being fucked than this overwhelming sadness. It's really scary. But maybe the dream indicates it's not as scary as it was."

In this vignette, we see how throughout most of the session Anna's feelings of being fucked in life drown out any other possible thoughts. In fact, Anna had experienced various narcissistic injuries in growing up, which she hadn't recognized coming into treatment. Her initial presentation of her "calm, boring family" served to cover over a benign neglect, except for the mother's occasional outbursts of anger. Being yelled at, accused, and criticized became the sustenance of human relationships. This emerged over time and, indeed, Anna had married a man who seemed to criticize her, which she reported on at length.

We had spent a large part of these first years of Anna's analysis uncovering and understanding these interferences in healthy narcissism and their effects. However, over time, I had the impression that Anna focused on her history and certain realities to stop thinking rather than freeing her to dream her thoughts as Bion (1962b) put it. Put another way, she could not allow herself the freedom to think of her thoughts in multiple ways. We had been working on this in various ways, which allowed her to represent her frightening feelings in a dream. My observation on what I understood as her enacted conflict expressed in both her excited way of talking and the inhibition of what she was able to talk about in the session, allowed her to talk about her dream, the fears it aroused, and the hope she found in representing these conflicted feelings.

Concluding thoughts

In 2001 Martin Bergmann wrote "if the value of 'know thyself', first articulated in the city of Delphi in Ancient Greece, is still important, psychoanalysis has no rival among other forms of psychotherapy" (p. 15). In our current psychoanalytic culture, especially in the United States, we increasingly distance ourselves from what is at the heart of know thyself, and the centrality of unconscious conflicts in preventing self-knowledge while these same conflicts direct our actions. The claims of the "newer" ideas of what is curative in psychoanalysis have added to our understanding, but at the same time they seem to reject this idea, which has been the very essence of psychoanalysis since Freud.

This raises the important question Blass (2010) explored in her carefully titled and reasoned article, "Affirming 'That's not Psycho-Analysis!' On the Value of the Politically Incorrect Act of Attempting to Define the Limits of Our Field." She writes, "in recent years it seems the act of defining psychoanalysis has come to be considered illegitimate. We are now encouraged to describe what analysts *do*, but to refrain from judging what analysis *is*" (pp. 82–83).

When we reject what has been basic to psychoanalysis, namely, the critical role of conflict theory, and develop new models of the mind and new treatment methods, can we still say these "new" theories are psychoanalytic? To say that these " new" theories are not psychoanalytic doesn't devalue their therapeutic value but rather that their value is in another area, the field of therapy. Why would someone who rejects most of what has been identified with psychoanalysis still want to be called a psychoanalyst, unless, as Blass (2010) asserted, it is a matter of personal and professional identity? As she noted, a clinician who identifies with the therapeutic definition of psychoanalysis, but does not relate to the basic concepts held throughout most of the analytic world, may simply enjoy the positive evaluation and cache of being a psychoanalyst. Thus we have the odd situation of those who want to be identified as psychoanalysts while rejecting much that has been basic to it.

Notes

1 Eagle (2003) elaborated on this "new view" further when he noted, "in trying to understand another, one is only addressing one's own subjectivity – in all this, there is the danger that the very existence of the patient's mind structured independently of the analyst is called into question" (p. 422).
2 Schmidt-Hellerau (2005) showed how in the aftermath of metapsychology debates we were left with slogan-like headlines. Question: "Two theories or one?" (G. Klein, 1973). Answer: "Metapsychology is not psychology" (Gill, 1976); therefore, one theory – clinical theory – is enough (Gill, 1977, p. 582). Question: "Drive or wish?" (Holt, 1976), and the answer, given in the same source, is: "Drive is dead, long live wish!" (p. 194).
3 For example, in a PEP search, the word *authenticity* appeared approximately 100 times in the period from 1900 to 1970. From 1970 to 2013 it appeared approximately 2,000 times.

4 While Eagle and Wolitzky (2011) express that, "findings of empirical research are not always clear-cut and are not often of immediate and concrete use in clinical work" (p. 793), they do not agree with critics who dismiss this type of research.
5 The mind works in thousandths of a second, so we are not thinking of an obsessional process here.
6 See Rangell (2004, pp. 130–134) for an example.
7 My psychoanalytic training was an interesting combination of Arlow/Brenner, and Merton Gill (especially his views on transference). My training as a psychologist was in the Rapaport-Schafer school, which had a profound influence on my thinking about the structure of the mind.

Chapter 4

Conflict from the perspective of free association

Anton O. Kris

The editors' invitation to present my approach to conflict – "We are familiar with your writings on free association and the role of distinguishing between convergent and divergent conflicts" – offers me an opportunity to review work that began 40 years ago and occupied my attention for 20 years (1976, 1977, 1982, 1985, 1988, 1990a, 1990b, 1992). Those ideas about conflict remain essential to my clinical work, although I have been fortunate to learn a great deal from the advances in psychoanalysis in recent decades. My theoretical formulations developed as a consequence of my focus on free association rather than the prevailing focus on a model of the mind. I made an attempt to formulate the phenomena of psychoanalysis in terms of free association (1982). For some readers, the assumption that they could readily translate my formulations into formulations based on their theory of mind (e.g., Smith, 2003), though I warned against it, led to a failure to find these association-based formulations helpful. The next few paragraphs are intended to orient the reader to the background and source of my way of formulating associative data.

The centrality of inferred unconscious conflict seemed obvious to Freud and his successors. Early in the work with my second analytic patient I encountered a succession of associative patterns that intrigued me. They did not follow the course I had been taught to expect, in which analytic pursuit of the defenses would lead to a lifting of repression. For this young woman, a relatively mature, often erotic transference would increase in intensity and surprisingly vanish, to be replaced by one in which wishes to be taken care of predominated. These alternations in the transference appeared to me to be the expression of opposing wishes in alternation, pulling my patient in opposite directions rather than, as prevailing theory held, the use of the second to defend against the first. Too often that sort of formulation referred to one wish as "real" and the other as (mere) "defense." The two transferences appeared to me, however, to reflect two wishes in conflict, in which the patient perceived the expression and satisfaction of one wish as preventing the expression and satisfaction of the other, that is, as either-or dilemmas (A. Kris, 1977).[1] In my view, analytic thinking had unwarrantedly turned *reaction formation* into the universal model of conflict.

Writing a review of psychoanalytic propositions in regard to divergences (A. Kris, 1985) bolstered my views. The earliest of these divergences was to be found in *The Interpretation of Dreams* (S. Freud, 1900), in which Freud distinguished between the *push-component* of repression, from above, and the *pull-component*, from below (p. 547). In a footnote added in 1914 he clarified his view:

> In any account of the theory of repression it would have to be laid down that a thought becomes repressed as a result of the combined influence upon it of *two* factors. It is pushed from the one side (by the censorship of the Cs.) and pulled from the other (by the Ucs).
>
> (p. 547, f. 2)

The pull-component was, in fact, Freud's unique contribution to the widely accepted concept of repression, espoused by Wilhelm Griesinger (1845) in his influential textbook of psychiatry, in which the ego was thought to be a group of ideas that pushed away other ideas. For Freud, repressed ideas, in tandem with the push-component, exerted a pull on dream elements that prevented them from rising into consciousness.

Many other bipolarities populated psychoanalytic formulations, for example: pleasure principle and reality principle; primary and secondary process; progression and regression; homosexuality and heterosexuality; love and hate; sadism and masochism; self and other; ego and outside world (A. Kris, 1985, 1988). Freud, however, did not describe these polarities as conflicts: to him, *conflict* meant repression.

An error in S. Freud's (1920) thinking at this time, however, when he had come to view the ego as the locus of defense and resistance, led him to write: "The unconscious – that is to say, the 'repressed' – offers no resistance whatever to the efforts of the treatment" (p. 19). This contradicted the views he had expressed on many occasions over the previous two decades. The pull-component of repression had been silently relegated to the concept of fixation, which, like the bipolarities, now was no longer thought of as an element of conflict. Even though S. Freud (1926a) explicitly corrected this error six years later by including the resistance of the id

From the perspective of free association   53

as the source of the repetition compulsion, it left analysts with a focus on repression as push without pull. As Edward Weinshel (1984) put it:

> The workings of the resistances of the id are even more mysterious . . . and more impervious to our direction and control. It is very difficult – perhaps impossible – to formulate meaningful interpretations dealing with such phenomena as the repetition compulsion, the adhesiveness of the libido, or the channelization of various instinctual discharge patterns.
> (p. 77)

The concept of divergent conflicts[2] restored the potential for understanding and interpreting those phenomena, although for me it is formulated first as an associative pattern and, only secondarily, as an inferred conflict in the mind. Searching for precedent, the concept of *intrasystemic conflict* that accompanied the development of the theory of the ego had seemed to me to refer to bipolar conflict. Later, however, I discovered that in every instance that I could find in the psychoanalytic literature, the model (often implicit) had reverted to the idea that one element *pushes* another out rather than the idea that two wishes may pull in opposite directions.

Many authors believe that Freud's formulations of conflict were substantially improved once they came to be considered as compromise formations among four elements of mind (Brenner, 1982b, 2006) in what has come to be known as "modern conflict theory." In this way of thinking, unencumbered by structural considerations, all mental elements are conceived of as vectors, composed of convergent forces. In my view this welcome simplification in theoretical formulation nonetheless excludes the direct recognition of divergences in the free associations and in patients' experience.

For clinical purposes, I find formulation in terms of the free associations (A. Kris, 1982) a formidable advantage.[3] It offers the immediate recognition that divergent wishes (forces, tendencies) pull *apart*, which necessarily means they are felt to pull the individual (person, self) apart. Divergence, as in two teams engaged in a tug of war, seemed to me more useful in describing many kinds of ambivalent wishes, especially those associated with development and other either-or phenomena (A. Kris, 1977), than the concept of reaction formation. I do believe that conflicts seen in associative phenomena reflect mental conflicts, but any formulation that neglects divergent tendencies seems to me to miss a crucial dimension of conflict.

Why all this matters can be illustrated by the very common error of looking for the "real" conflict *behind* a divergent one. That way of looking at

54   Anton O. Kris

things will necessarily fail to appreciate a patient's experience. Divergent conflicts are never found in pure culture, not even in adolescence or in the rapprochement phase of early development where they appear so starkly. They are *always accompanied* by convergent conflicts, in which the associations can be seen as two football teams meeting at the line of scrimmage, their forces moving toward each other. The two kinds of conflict correspond to the pull-component and the push-component of S. Freud's (1900) concept of repression. I see no objection to viewing them as two aspects of conflict.

To illustrate my way of working with these concepts, I want to focus on mourning. Convention links mourning with the loss created by death, yet it is a commonplace of everyone's awareness that all manner of losses over a lifetime require mourning. It is only a little less evident that all *decisions* require a confrontation with loss and, hence, a process akin to mourning.

Many psychoanalytic authors, beginning with S. Freud (1917), have described the alternating quality of mourning. Anyone who has lost a beloved person recognizes the bittersweet experience of remembering the one who has been lost. The pleasure in the moment of greatest closeness in remembering, however, is destroyed by the recognition of loss, that the person is no more. The extent to which that painful recognition is diminished provides one measure of the completeness of mourning. Mourning takes place in precisely the alternations between closeness and the sense of loss. It is the paradigm for resolution of all divergent conflicts. The either-or quality of these dilemma conflicts regularly implies the loss of one side or the other, and only a process akin to mourning can lead to a new solution.

Thomas Ogden (2002), in a profoundly creative essay, noted:

> In 'Mourning and melancholia' Freud uses the term ambivalence in a strikingly different way; he uses it to refer to a struggle between the wish to live with the living and the wish to be at one with the dead.
>
> (p. 778)

That is not far from describing the mourner's plight as divergent conflict. It was much less "different" for Freud, five years after adopting Bleuler's term *ambivalence*, which he used in a variety of contexts (see A. Kris, 1985), than to analysts, 85 years later, for whom ambivalence refers mainly to simultaneous love and hate of one object.[4]

Despite the enormously innovative and fruitful ideas in *Mourning and Melancholia* (1917), especially those on internalization and identification elaborated in *The Ego and the Id* (1923, e.g., p. 28), Freud (1917) mistakenly held that "Reality-testing has shown that the loved object no longer exists, and it proceeds to demand that all libido shall be withdrawn from its attachments to that object" (p. 244).[5] This view, which correctly describes the expectations of those who suffer from *pathological*, interrupted mourning, implies that mourning *creates* loss – by the "demand that all libido shall be withdrawn." So, one of my patients, who wanted analysis, feared that it would take away the few memories he had of his father, who had died when he was young. Mourning, in my experience, far from creating loss, makes it possible to remember the lost loved one without reviving the painful recognition of acute loss or an anxious expectation of it. From another viewpoint, the process of mourning restores a portion of oneself that is bound to the lost object.

Although normal mourning does not require detachment of love (libidinal cathexis in the language of an earlier era) from the lost object, it does require *acknowledgment* that that person will not be actively present. Generally, we continue to love those we loved before they died. What was difficult to explain in terms of *economics* is easier to understand with the concept of psychic reality. In my view, the pain of mourning derives from the requirement that loss be *acknowledged*. That need to acknowledge is in conflict with a wish to deny the loss, a wish to keep things seeming to be as they were – a divergent conflict. That is, mourning requires one to relinquish an illusion of unaltered continuity. But the surrender of that illusion, however painful, does not *create* loss; it may permit the first full experience of a loss that has already occurred. Patients whose mourning is impaired find it helpful to recognize, through interpretation, the distinction between creation of loss and a process that leads to tolerable acknowledgment of loss.

The problem of interrupted mourning illustrates for me the interaction of divergent conflicts and convergent conflicts. The view of mourning as divergent conflict immediately alerts us to the problem of how mourning may be interrupted. The interruption of mourning stops the necessary alternation between the recognition of loss and the illusion of continuity. The most common basis of interruption, in my experience, is punitive, unconscious self-criticism,[6] especially self-reproach for unconscious hostility to the lost object (A. Kris, 1990a). Here Freud had it right, although his formulations were heavily laced with economic propositions that no longer speak to analysts.

When the mourner's thoughts and feelings are not allowed expression (or the silent expression of reflection), and alternation between loving memory and painful recognition of loss is interrupted, mourning fails. Unconscious hostility and self-criticism are not the only influences, however, that may interrupt the process. For example, terror at being alone and helpless may be sufficient. A need to avoid the recognition of the kind or intensity of love for the lost object – unconsciously loving someone too much or too sexually – can also interrupt the process.

A Roman Catholic man in his 40s in analysis had several intense nightmares of drowning in the course of a few days. His associations led to grief over the abortion of a fetus some 20 years earlier, in a relationship before marriage. Although a sense of guilt (one form of punitive, unconscious self-criticism) for murder surely contributed to his interrupted mourning, he had not been able to allow himself to know how intensely he had already loved the fetus. In his nightmares his forbidden love emerged as identification.

Ordinarily, where love for the lost object remains in awareness, the divergent conflict between the wish to perpetuate the lost person's life and the wish to accept reality interacts with unconscious convergent conflicts between desire (including hostility) and self-criticism. The mourner is keenly aware of the divergent conflict but mostly unaware of the convergent conflicts that prevent its resolution. This does not, however, mean that the unconscious, convergent conflict is any more real than the conscious, divergent one.

A 14-year-old boy was brought by his mother, some 6 months after the death of his much-loved and admired father. He was clearly the most secure of her three highly intelligent children – I had referred both of his older siblings for treatment earlier – but he was falling asleep in school and, in general, had not recovered his natural liveliness. A gloomy dream, after some months of treatment, represented the state of affairs. He was lying down in a snow bank, possibly some sort of tunnel. Associations did not come readily, so I suggested that he draw the dream image. To his amazement he drew a picture that we both recognized at once as Piglet, with an immediate connection to the lament about the snow and nobody knowing how cold his toes were growing. Warm memories of *Winnie-the-Pooh* being read to him in childhood reflected another side, which we recognized. This was a step along the way to recovery of a memory of a moment a few months before his father died. His father was in the hospital, receiving a final diagnosis of untreatable cancer. As was their wont, my patient read his current book report to his father over the phone. As he read: "Lord Jim's triumph is in death," he had felt he was saying that his own triumph was in his father's death. The painful self-critical reaction to this thought kept him at some emotional distance from his father in the remaining months and prevented the necessary mourning after his father died. Relief followed recollection relatively quickly, as mourning was able to proceed.

In this case it was not a matter of lifelong ambivalence preceding a depressive reaction. Here, I believe, the upsurge of Oedipal wishes in early adolescence overwhelmed his ordinary balance and led to the self-interpretation of hostility and death wishes and punitive, unconscious self-criticism.[7]

For me, the process of mourning is the paradigm for the resolution of all divergent conflicts. Divergent conflicts occur with great frequency, most significantly in the perpetual tension between progression and regression in the course of normal development. Freedom to remember the lost object without pain is not the whole story of mourning. Most prominently we think of internalization and identification as a part or product of the mourning process (S. Freud, 1923). How the free associative process leads to that sort of change and to what extent mourning and the processes akin to mourning require the assistance of another person for their completion exceed the bounds of this attempt to delineate the divergent conflicts.

Among the many advances that followed Freud's structural hypothesis and the subsequent shift in his theory of anxiety, the work of Melanie Klein (1935a, 1940) expanded on some developmental implications of Freud's ideas on mourning. For her, the depressive position – a concept which some thought to be her greatest contribution – comes about with the increasing recognition and acknowledgment of the infant's separateness from mother and with the recognition of whole objects rather than part objects. It thereby becomes the defining developmental achievement that makes mourning possible. It is a structural concept, as Hanna Segal (1979) pointed out, that implies movement in both directions between positions.

Some 50 years ago, Anna Freud (1965) revised the psychoanalytic view of regression by describing it as a principle of *normal* development, not merely as pathology. Mental development, unlike somatic development, requires backward motion as well as forward motion, regression and progression. She did not describe it as developmental conflict, although in regard to regression in drive development she noted the longstanding psychoanalytic association between regression and fixation. In my view, Anna Freud's description of regression and progression in normal development bears a close resemblance to the process of mourning though it does not generally relate to the loss of a loved one; hence I have referred to it as a process *akin* to mourning (A. Kris, 1985, 1987). Both mourning and progression-regression have appeared to me to be prototypes of divergent conflicts.

On several occasions I have worked with patients who have been caught between two loves and found that they were helped by my attention to promoting the alternate expressions of desire for the two loves. As love and obligation were expressed, first for one, then for the other, a variety of internal objections (convergent conflicts) appeared. Where convergent conflicts can be usefully tracked down, pursued until they yield their secret, divergent conflicts require tolerance for the alternating, repetitive process, like the tides going in and out, that is their hallmark. If divergent conflicts are viewed as convergent ones, in an attempt to lift repression, the natural rhythm of alternation is interrupted by the analyst's interventions. This can lead to patients feeling misunderstood and, worse, to impasses in treatment.

I want to focus now on punitive, unconscious self-criticism, which plays a very large role in the *convergent conflicts* of nearly all my patients. Where I had been taught to see anxiety as ubiquitous, I had not recognized that unconscious self-critical attitudes are equally prevalent. It has been useful for me to view the painful affects (shame, guilt, embarrassment, humiliation, mortification, and depression) as a combination of punitive, unconscious self-criticism and various attitudes to oneself. Tell-tale signs appear regularly in the associations as *should* and *ought*, and occasionally a dream reveals the punitive, unconscious self-criticism quite openly. The consequent self-abrogation of ordinary rights occurs in a variety of forms, often only hinted at in the associations. Although, in general, analysts can afford to allow the associations to affect them without special scrutiny, they must be alert for punitive, unconscious self-criticism. For, if the patient perceives even a subtle criticism on the part of the analyst, the associations can shut down dramatically.

Forty years ago, in trying to understand "narcissism," which was so variously defined and described, I observed what seemed a regular pattern of unconscious self-criticism leading to unconscious self-deprivation, and a sense of entitlement to make excessive demands, justified by the deprivation. I came to view this as a vicious cycle, in which the entitlement was the cause of further unconscious self-criticism (A. Kris, 1976). In the treatment of narcissistic patients – which for me means patients who suffer from self-inflicted repetition of past injuries – it has been helpful to recognize this vicious cycle (A. Kris, 1990a). For those patients whose projections lead them to experience any reference to unconscious self-criticism as a criticism coming from me, I have learned to focus first on the self-deprivation. Eventually it becomes possible to help the patients recognize their unconscious self-criticism. My experience has taught me that then, when they have come to recognize the connection between their self-criticism and their self-deprivation, they can make sense of the connection between entitlement and further self-criticism. Moving too fast can lead to an interruption in the free associative process, which may come to a halt or, worse, become distorted by the patient's misunderstanding of where the criticism comes from. This has led me, often, to say "one of us is critical of you." In some instances, gilding the philosophic pill, I offer a second guess.

This view of narcissistic patients requires a considerable tolerance of the patient's entitlement,[8] which may appear as *demands* for special treatment from the analyst, or from others outside the analysis, where one must stand by as the patient is repeatedly rebuffed. Heinz Kohut's (1972) *affirmative* analytic stance, aiming to permit the patient to develop a comforting, self-object transference seemed to me, 40 years ago, to be enormously helpful. I viewed it, however, in different theoretical terms. His explicit rejection of a concept of conflict seemed untenable.

Kohut's (1984) view that what he called "the penetration-to-the-unconscious-via-the-overcoming-of-resistances model" (p. 113) is insufficient to guide our therapeutic approach seems right to me, but I believe it is based on an unnecessarily narrow concept of conflict. The addition of a concept of divergent conflicts to the convergent ones (repression in this case), which combines mourning with therapeutic remembering, seems to me to solve that problem.

The most important observation of punitive, unconscious self-criticism for my personal psychoanalytic development was the recognition that patients took silence on the analyst's part as agreement with the patient's self-critical attitude (A. Kris, 1990a). This observation led me increasingly to adopt an actively affirmative attitude to counter those, often silent, projections of self-criticism. Such affirmative interventions facilitate the associative process but do not generally provide lasting effects by themselves. A subsequent process is required. This change in stance, which caused me great concern at first, because I believed that it was a retreat from neutrality, led me to conclude that in the presence of punitive, unconscious self-criticism the set point of neutrality must be adjusted (A. Kris, 1990a). The way the patient hears the analyst chiefly determines what is neutral.

In the development of my own analytic stance (A. Kris, 1990b), my change to an affirmative attitude has led to a far less austere position with my patients. Could it lead to less intense transference reactions, particularly negative transference reactions? This has not seemed to be the case. On the contrary, just as feeding the Rat-man brought Freud intense hostility, so too with my experience. I have discussed this elsewhere (A. Kris, 2013).

The relationship between trauma and punitive, unconscious self-criticism provides another complicated illustration of interrupted mourning. It is clear enough that trauma acts as a fixation point to which the traumatized individual must return again and again without relief. By trauma I mean the consequences of a noxious influence that breaks through the ordinary means of warding off painful or frightening events. Trauma may come from an external source or from the person's body and, occasionally, from the person's mind, as when the prospect of repetition of a painful mental state or illness becomes a source of continuing anxiety. In every example I have seen, trauma produces punitive self-critical attitudes, both conscious and unconscious (A. Kris, 1987). Edward Bibring's (1953) theory of depression as a reaction to helplessness seems to me to arrive at the same conclusion. Guilt as a response to trauma appears to occur very early in childhood, according to many observers. Why this should be so remains an unsettled matter, I believe. One factor may be a need to gain control over helplessness. Punitive, unconscious self-critical attitudes are, in any case, an essential part of all narcissistic reactions, as I have tried to demonstrate. However they come about, the interference by self-critical attitudes prevents the resolution through mourning of the conflict between the fixation created by trauma and the wish to live in the present and move on into the future. A focus on the self-critical tendency, first, rather than an attempt to promote recollection of the trauma directly, is apt to be helpful in the promotion of a process of mourning.

As a concluding example, another aspect of the interaction of the two types of conflict may be seen in the termination of psychoanalysis. Mourning at the end of a long, intense relationship holds no particular surprise. Some 20 years ago, however, I tried to show that for some men, whose early experience with their anxious, depressed mothers had required greater than usual dependence on their fathers, it was correspondingly harder to develop the necessary independence from me to engage in a competitive, Oedipal relationship (A. Kris, 1992). The threat of loss seemed regularly to interrupt such a development. I described the arduous process of helping these patients with the interaction between self-critical attitudes to their competitive and hostile wishes and their fears of losing their father and of losing me. These fears also impeded the conclusion of the analytic work. The unsatisfactory measure used by Freud, in the forced termination of the analysis of the Wolf Man (S. Freud, 1918), seemed to me to accept the patient's pathological belief that mourning is impossible, because the mourner believes it creates the loss it seeks to make tolerable. I chose another course by pointing out to these patients that they did not include termination of analysis in their thinking. That is, by interpreting the reluctance to *consider* termination, I helped them initiate the very slow process of mourning required to resolve the stalemate. The initial reaction to my making this kind of intervention is not always one of warm appreciation. Often the first response is to dismiss me summarily – a defensive threat to stop the analysis at once. A more subtle version appeared in the analysis of a man who was very familiar with the analytic literature: "But we haven't gotten to my Oedipus complex," he complained. "And we never will," I replied, "unless you include termination in your thinking." To some extent we were successful.

In this chapter I have tried to show that formulation of psychoanalytic phenomena in terms of the method of free association permits a distinction between divergent conflicts and convergent conflicts relevant to a number of aspects of psychoanalytic therapy. It requires the "willing suspension of disbelief" to refrain from immediate translation into theories of mind in order to make it useful.

Notes

1 Leo Rangell (1963a, 1963b) had earlier suggested the distinction between defense conflicts and dilemma conflicts. His ideas gained little traction.
2 I found it necessary to employ the ungainly term *divergent conflicts* (A. Kris, 1985) to replace the term I had used earlier, *conflicts of ambivalence* (A. Kris,

1982, 1984), when I became aware that for most analysts ambivalence brought to mind only love and hate for the same object. (I take this matter up, further, in the following.)

3 It may well be that theories of mind may be much better suited for other purposes.

4 Even now, however, analysts may speak of an adolescent as ambivalent about growing up or an adult as ambivalent about gender identification or sexual object choice. These are examples of divergent conflict.

5 Elsewhere in his writings, Freud does not make that error, but its presence in his seminal discussion of mourning created a considerable problem for analytic understanding (Siggins, 1966). Fifty years after the publication of "Mourning and Melancholia," Brodsky (1967), focusing on mastery of affects in a discussion of working through, noted, at last: "After the work of mourning is completed, the lost object may still be loved but is no longer painfully longed for" (p. 491).

6 I find it useful to distinguish punitive, unconscious self-criticism, which produces pain and deprivation, from constructive self-criticism, which helps us navigate our world and learn from experience.

7 S. Freud (1911) described a very similar dream dynamic in "Formulations on the two principles of mental functioning."

8 The publication of the Freud-Jones correspondence (Paskauskas, 1993) revealed that Freud held an (unpublished) view of the importance of self-criticism in narcissistic disorders similar to mine (A. Kris, 1994).

Chapter 5

Inner conflict in Fairbairn's theory of endopsychic structure

Morris N. Eagle

This chapter deals with the place of inner conflict in Fairbairn's object relations theory of personality structure. Insofar as Fairbairn proposes his object relations theory as an alternative to Freudian theory, it would be useful to provide a context for Fairbairn's ideas by starting with a brief outline of the Freudian view of object relations, against which Fairbairn was reacting and which constitute the point of departure not only for Fairbairn's theory of the endopsychic structure of the personality, but also for the theoretical precursors of Fairbairn's formulations. Hence, the outline of the Freudian view of object relations will be followed by a brief discussion of the precursors of Fairbairn's theory. The remaining and majority part of the chapter will be devoted to a discussion of Fairbairn's theory of the endopsychic structure of the personality, including the implications of that theory for his conceptions of psychopathology and treatment.

Freudian view of object relations

There are four highly interrelated components of the Freudian theory of object relations. One is that the aim of drives is discharge and the object is primarily a means for the achievement of that aim. Indeed, S. Freud (1915a) defines the object as "the thing in regard to which the instinct achieves its aim" (p. 122). The second major posit is that drive and object are originally unconnected. As Freud puts it: "[the object of an instinct] is what is most variable about an instinct and is *not originally connected with it*" (p. 122) (my italics). The third major posit is that our original relation to objects is one of hate. Freud writes that,

> It cannot be denied that hating, too, originally characterized the relation
> of the ego to the alien external world with the stimuli it introduces. . . .

At the beginning, it seems the external world, objects, and what is being hated are identical. If later on an object turns out to be a source of pleasure, it is loved, but it is also incorporated into the ego; so that for the purified pleasure-ego once again objects coincide with what is extraneous and hated.

(p. 136)

S. Freud (1915a) also states that "the ego-subject coincides with pleasure, and the external world with unpleasure" (p. 136). When "the object is a source of unpleasurable feelings," it only "repeat[s] in relation to the object the original attempt at flight from the external world with its emission of stimuli. We feel the 'repulsion' of the object and hate it" (p. 137). In other words – and Freud could not be clearer – our original relation to objects is one of "repulsion" and "hate" largely because, in accord with the constancy principle, they confront the mind with unwanted excitation and tension that need to be discharged.

The fourth major Freudian assumption is that object relations develop primarily because objects are necessary for drive gratification. As S. Freud (1915a) puts it, "[the object] becomes assigned to it [i.e., the instinct] only in consequence of being particularly fitted to make satisfaction possible" (p. 122). On this view, it would follow that were satisfaction possible without the need to turn to objects, we would never develop an interest in objects, let alone object relations. As a clear expression of this point of view, S. Freud (1900) writes that the primary reason that the infant turns to the actual object is that the infant's initial attempt to gratify the hunger drive through hallucination of the breast does not succeed in removing the tensions of hunger. As Freud puts it, "satisfaction does not follow, the need persists" (p. 605). Hence, the infant has no choice but to turn to the actual breast, if satisfaction of the hunger drive is to occur. Thus, over time and with experience, the initial hatred of objects is gradually replaced by attachment to the object.

As one can see from the foregoing, from a Freudian perspective, from the very start of life, the infant is confronted with conflict, one between the drives pushing for immediate gratification through hallucinatory wish fulfillment and the hard reality that objects are necessary for gratification. The latter generates another equally stubborn fact of reality, namely, that delay of gratification is often inevitable. The conflict between the inner push for immediate discharge and the hard facts of external reality – early on, a conflict between the individual and physical reality – is a precursor of the *inner conflict* between the id and the ego, the fundamental Freudian model of personality structure. The emphasis now is no longer limited to the conflict between inner drives and external reality but now includes conflict between two inner structures, namely, the drives and the ego as the agent of reality-testing, that is, as the psychic structure that has internalized (i.e., learned) the lessons of reality.

A similar developmental trajectory describes the relationship between instinctual wishes and *social reality*. Early in life, the primary focus of conflict is between the child's instinctual wishes and prohibitions and values emanating from parents, society's socialization agents. Over time, parental prohibitions and values become internalized as a personality structure, namely, the superego. Thus, just as is the case with regard to the conflict between instinctual demands and external psychical reality, so similarly, does the conflict between instinctual wishes and external social reality becomes transformed into *an inner conflict* between two structures of the personality. This, in short, is the set of formulations against which Fairbairn and precursors of object relations theory were reacting.

Precursors to and influences on the development of Fairbairn's object relations theory

The formulation of a distinctive object relations theory is marked by rejection of one or more of the aforementioned Freudian posits regarding the development of object relations. An initial important theoretical step in developing an object relations theory is represented by Klein's (1975) insistence, contrary to Freudian theory, that drive and object are, from the very beginning, inextricably linked – that is, there is no drive without an object. Other important contributions to object relations theory originating in the Hungarian school[1] include Ferenczi's (1933) concept of "passive object love," (as cited in Bowlby, 1969, p. 371); Hermann's (1933, 1976) postulation of a primary component instinct to cling; Balints's (1937) concept of primary object relation which "is not linked to any of the erotic zones; it is not oral, oral-sucking, anal, genital, etc.; love but something on its own" (as cited in Bowlby, 1969, p. 372). Benedek's (1956) reference to "post-partum symbiosis" to describe the bond between infant and mother (as cited in Bowlby, 1969, p. 374); Ribble's (1943) observation that "infants have an innate need for contact with the mother" (as cited in Bowlby, 1969, p. 373); and Suttie's (1935) postulation of a primary and inherent "need for company" (as cited in Bowlby, 1969, p. 376). Finally, as Bowlby (1969) observes, Winnicott (1938) assigns greater weight to mother's provision of contact, warmth, movement, and quiet as components of mothering than her provision of food (see Bowlby [1958/1969] for an excellent review of psychoanalytic formulations of the child's tie to mother).

Even S. Freud (1912d) himself anticipated the primacy of object relations when he writes that in comparison to the "sensual current,"

> the affectionate current is the older of the two. It springs from the years of childhood; it is formed on the basis of the self-preservative instinct and is directed to the members of the family and those who look after the child.
>
> (p. 180)

He also writes that the affectionate current "corresponds to *the child's primary object-choice*" (original emphasis) and that "the sexual instincts find their first objects by attaching themselves to the valuations made by the ego-instincts" (p. 180). In other words, Freud seems to be referring here to a "primary object-choice" that is not originally based on drive gratification and pleasures from the erogenous zones. However, Freud does not further develop the implications of this formulation and, indeed, replaces this version of his dual instinct theory with sex and aggression as the primary instinctual drives (see Eagle, 2007).

Although, as noted, the formulations of a distinctive object relations theory is marked by rejection of core aspects of Freudian theory, the fact nevertheless remains that Freud's description of internal objects and his discussion of splits in the ego also need to be viewed as precursors of object relations theory.

Although Freud did not use the term *internal object*, as Ogden (1983) makes clear, he essentially refers to internal objects in a number of contexts. In *Mourning and Melancholia*, in the course of discussing identification, Freud describes, in Ogden's words, the replacement of "a lost external object with an aspect of oneself that has been modeled after the lost external object" (p. 228). The taking in and modeling of oneself after an external object is apparent in the concept of the superego. Indeed, Fairbairn (1952) writes that the model for his theory of endopsychic structure was based on Freud's concept of the superego. S. Freud (1940a) writes with regard to the formation of the superego that a part of the external world is abandoned and has instead,

> by identification, been taken into the ego and thus become an integral part of the internal world. This new psychical agency continues to carry on the functions which have hitherto been performed by the people [the abandoned objects] in the external world.
>
> (p. 205)

To be noted in this account is that like Fairbairn's split-off ego structures, the superego, a sub-structure of the personality, is endowed with the capacities to assess, think, judge, punish, approve and disapprove, and so forth – all capacities that the external object, which is now internalized, has.

S. Freud (1894) also partly anticipated Fairbairn's formulation of split-off ego structures both in his early acceptance of Janet's emphasis on "splitting of consciousness" (p. 46) and, in one of his last papers, his discussion of "splitting of the ego in the process of defense" (S. Freud, 1940b). In this paper, he discusses a phenomenon in which different parts of the ego operate in very different ways in relation to understanding of reality.

Fairbairn's object relations theory: we are inherently object-seeking

Despite all the above flirtations and fits and starts, hinting at the development of a theory of object relations that does not rest on drive theory, no coherent and comprehensive theory was developed prior to Fairbairn's theory of endopsychic structure of the personality, which rejects virtually every one of the aforementioned four Freudian posits regarding the nature of object relations, as well as the overarching id-ego model. Fairbairn's (1952) point of view is captured by his insistence that "libido is primarily object-seeking (rather than pleasure-seeking, as in the classic theory)" (p. 82). He also puts it more succinctly: "The ultimate goal of libido is the object" (Fairbairn, 1952, p. 31). As Ernest Jones puts it in his preface to Fairbairn's (1952) book, that instead of beginning, as Freud did,

> from stimulation of the nervous system proceeding from excitation of various erotogenous zones and internal tension arising from gonadic

activity, Dr. Fairbairn starts at the centre of the personality, the ego, and depicts its strivings and difficulties in its endeavor to reach an object where it may find support.

(p. v)

The integrity and intactness of the ego depends upon object relations rather than drive satisfaction and the discharge of excessive excitation. Thus not only are we object-seeking creatures from birth on, but throughout life ego intactness depends on cognitive affective ties to objects. Given that loss of ego integrity is the "ultimate psychological disaster" (Fairbairn, 1952, p. 52), we are willing to endure much suffering in order to preserve some kind of tie to the object.

THE ENDOPSYCHIC STRUCTURE OF THE PERSONALITY

Splitting of the ego and of the object

According to Fairbairn, we are all born with a unitary ego. As Fairbairn (1954) puts it, "the pristine personality of the child consists of a unitary dynamic ego" (p. 107). Under the impact of deprivation, the unitary ego is split into the libidinal ego and the anti-libidinal ego. The central ego is what remains of the original unitary ego. As far as I understand Fairbairn's metapsychological scheme, the splitting of the unitary ego and the multiplicity of subsidiary ego structures comes about in the following way: because mother is both gratifying and frustrating, she becomes an ambivalent object for the infant.

> Since it proves intolerable [to the infant] to have a good object which is also bad, he seeks to alleviate the situation by splitting the figure of his mother into two objects. Then, insofar as she satisfies him libidinally, she is a good 'object' and, insofar as she fails to satisfy him libidinally, she is a 'bad' object.
>
> (Fairbairn, 1952, p. 110)[2]

The "bad" object, Fairbairn goes on to observe, has two facets: it frustrates as well as tempts. Indeed, it is this very combination of frustration and allurement that renders the object "bad." In order to deal with this intolerable situation, the "bad" object is split into the alluring and exciting object and the rejecting and frustrating object. Both the exciting and frustrating objects are then repressed.[3] Because the ego "maintains libidinal attachment to the objects undergoing repression" (Fairbairn, 1952, p. 112), it, too, suffers the fate of division and is split into the libidinal ego and the anti-libidinal ego or internal saboteur. The central ego rejects these attachments to the internal "bad" object, with the consequence that along with the internal exciting and frustrating objects, the subsidiary egos share the fate of repression. Stating this in less metapsychological language, one can say that a particular aspect of the self or ego is in an "affective relationship with a particular aspect of the object world" (Rubens, 1994, p. 157). Thus, one aspect of the ego (the libidinal ego) is in an affective relationship with one aspect of the object (its exciting and alluring quality) and another aspect of the ego (the anti-libidinal ego) is in an affective relationship with another aspect of the object (its rejecting quality).

Fairbairn suggests that were it not for deprivation and frustration, the ego would remain a unitary one. However, under the impact of these experiences, splits in both the ego and the object occur, forming what Fairbairn (1952) refers to the "endopsychic structure of the personality" (p. 82). Thus, instead of assuming, as Freud did, that it is inherent in the human condition, Fairbairn appears to maintain that inner conflict in the form of splits in the ego arises as a consequence of parental rejection, deprivation, and frustration. Whereas for Fairbairn, in a utopian world devoid of frustration and deprivation, conflict would play a minor role in psychological life, for Freud, conflict would remain an inherent and essential aspect of the human condition.

However, an important caveat must be introduced. Although the aforementioned contrast between Freud's and Fairbairn's views of conflict may be valid in the context of imagining a utopia, it is much narrowed when one considers Fairbairn's acknowledgment that because some degree of frustration and deprivation is inevitable, it, therefore, follows that some degree of conflict and splits in the ego is also inevitable. Hence, as is the case in Freudian theory, for all practical purposes, conflict is also inevitable in Fairbairn's theory – although, of course, Freud and Fairbairn differ regarding the nature of conflict. Indeed, the inevitability of some degree of frustration and deprivation itself would appear to reflect something important about the human condition rather than constituting a contingent happenstance fact. In short, although Fairbairn's theory seems to provide an environmental failure account of psychopathology, it is, to an equal degree, an account of the inevitability of splits in the ego in the real world. In that sense, it parallels Freud's conclusion regarding the inevitability of neurosis given human nature and the nature of social reality.[4]

From a Freudian perspective, it would appear that if one sets aside the metapsychological formulation of an inherent antagonism between the id and the ego, the development of inner conflict would be contingent upon the occurrence of the "danger situations." But this would be a misleading conclusion. For, implicit in Freudian theory is the idea that the mere fact of being embedded in civilization exposes one to the prohibitions, punishments, and threats of parents as socializing agents that constitute the "danger situation." In effect, this is the Freudian version of the inevitable parental deprivation and frustration to which Fairbairn refers. In both cases, save for a fantasied utopia, some degree of deprivation and frustration – Fairbairn's language – and some degree of exposure to the "danger situations" – in Freud's language – are inevitable. The consequence is that some aspect of the child's experiences of his or her desires and needs will inevitably be associated with some degree of anxiety and/or guilt, and will, therefore, become implicated in inner conflict and rifts in the personality. As Mitchell (1988) puts it, everyone growing up in a family is "bent out of shape" in some way. In my reading of Mitchell, this is not to be understood as psychopathology. For it is the various idiosyncratic ways in which we are bent out of shape that defines our individuality and contributes to the richness of character.

The internal object

The crucial step in the formation of the endopsychic structures is the internalization of the depriving and frustrating experiences as an internal "bad" object. And here we need to pause and try to elucidate what Fairbairn means by the crucial concept of internal object.[5] Generally speaking, internalization refers to the process of taking in experiences and making them part of oneself. However, certain highly negative experiences cannot be fully assimilated and are internalized as introjects, that is, as representations that are not fully integrated into one's self-organization. As Schafer (1968) observes, they are often experienced as felt presences. It is not surprising to learn that Fairbairn based his concept of internal object on Freud's concept of the superego, which is often experienced as both part of oneself and, at the same time, as a parental voice standing on one's shoulder lodged in one's mind. As Guntrip (1969) notes, in contrast to internalization in the form of an introject, internalization of positive experiences are more fully assimilated and serve as what one might refer to as psychic aliment for the building of psychic structure. When, however, experiences are intolerable, they are split off from the central ego and become organized as crystallized endopsychic structures or, one can say, split-off subsystems with their own aims and motivations that are unintegrated into the rest of the personality. As I have described elsewhere (Eagle, 1984), borrowing from Piaget (1976), the contrast between the internalization of good versus bad experiences can be analogized to ingesting edible food versus a non-edible object. Edible foods are digested and metabolized, that is, become part of one's body, and serve as aliment to energize and build. In contrast, indigestible substances (e.g., a piece of plastic) cannot be metabolized and retain their identity as a foreign body. A similar contrast, Guntrip tells us, characterizes the difference between the internalization of good metabolizable experiences and bad unassimilable experiences. The latter experiences get "stuck in one's craw."

As Guntrip points out, experiences that are capable of being integrated into the personality result in memory, learning, and gradual alteration of the whole self. That is, they are fully assimilated and, as such, serve as "aliment" for the growth of memory, learning, and self. When, however, experiences are intolerable, they are not permitted to reach full consciousness and are split off from the central self. They become crystallized as endopsychic structures or, one can say, split off subsystems with their own aims and motivations that are not integrated into the rest of the personality.

At another level of discourse, Fairbairn (1952) writes that the child internalizes the "bad" object in order to control it better (I am not at all certain that I truly understand this formulation). More understandably, he writes that the child takes the badness of the object into himself or herself in the hope that by reversing the badness and being good, he or she will earn the parent's love. To believe that one is not loved because of one's badness, a conditional fact, Fairbairn (1952) notes, is preferable to feeling unloved unconditionally. The latter offers no hope that there is anything that one can do to earn parental love. As Fairbairn (1952) puts it, "it is better to be a sinner in a world ruled by God than to live in a world ruled by the devil" (pp. 66–67).

However the internalization of the object comes about, the result is that once internalized, it is now part of the personality, a component of the endopsychic structure of the personality. This means that the attitudes, goals, aims, and motivations of an originally external object have now become part of one's personality structure. Although one can perhaps understand this kind of internalization as ordinary identification, Fairbairn (1952) makes it clear that for him the term *identification* is a shorthand for "primary identification," by which he means to signify that "the cathexis of an object which has not yet been differentiated from the cathecting object" (p. 14, fn. 1). In other words, for Fairbairn, primary identification means lack of differentiation between self and other and implies the presence of a symbiotic relationship with the object.

Repression and dissociation

Starting with the debate between Janet and Freud regarding the etiology of hysteria, a sharp and continuing distinction has been made between dissociation and repression, leading to a focus on different forms of psychopathology. Freudian theory developed in relation to inner conflict and neurosis, whereas followers of Janet, such as Prince (1906) pursued an interest in dissociative phenomena, including fugue states and multiple personality. In its emphasis on splits in the ego, Fairbairn's theory of endopsychic structure seems to harken back to pre-repression early S. Freud's (1894) emphasis on "splitting of consciousness" (p. 46), which, at that point in his thinking, was in essential agreement with Charcot's and Janet's view of hysteria as largely a dissociative phenomenon. No wonder that Fairbairn (1952) calls for a return to early Freud – "back to hysteria" (p. 92), as he puts it. An emphasis on splits in consciousness and splits in the ego reflects a dissociation perspective, the replacement of which with a conflict-repression model marked the birth of psychoanalysis. And, indeed, the focus in the non-psychoanalytic theorizing of Janet and his followers was mainly on splitting and dissociation in response to external trauma rather than on inner conflict and, as noted, ultimately culminating in an emphasis on such clinical phenomena as multiple personality found in the work of Prince (1906) and others. In short, the dissociation and repression theories went off in quite different directions.

A question that arises is whether Fairbairn's theory of endopsychic structure should be viewed as a dissociation theory or a theory of repression, the latter intimately linked to an inner conflict model. As noted, historically, the emphasis on the former has been associated with non-psychoanalytic theories, whereas an emphasis on inner conflict has been the hallmark of psychoanalytic theory. Fairbairn's emphasis on external trauma and splits in the ego as its consequences does, indeed, seem to align itself with Charcot's and Janet's similar emphasis on external trauma and splits in consciousness. However, unlike Charcot's and Janet's formulations and closer to Freud's perspective, the external trauma with which Fairbairn is concerned are not in the realm of entirely external events (e.g., railway accidents), but in the realm of frustration and deprivation of one's needs and desires. And although such deprivation and frustration refer to external environmental trauma, they lead to important consequences regarding how one experiences and what one does with these needs and desires.

Before pursuing further the question of where Fairbairn's theory is to be located, let me briefly elaborate on the distinction between repression and dissociation. For many years, there were few references to dissociation in the psychoanalytic literature. Interest in dissociative phenomena was reserved for relatively exotic phenomena such as amnesia and fugue states and particularly multiple personality, the latter evoking much skepticism. However, outside the psychoanalytic context, interest in dissociation was revived, as seen, for example, in the "neo-dissociation" theory of Hilgard (e.g., 1991) and in the work of Kihlstrom (e.g., 1992a, b). During the last number of years, partly motivated by a renewed interest in trauma, in particular, physical and sexual abuse, there has been an increasing interest within the psychoanalytic community in dissociative phenomena, as expressed, for example, in the work of Bromberg (e.g., 1996, 2003), Chefetz (e.g., 2004) and as implicit in Kernberg's emphasis on splitting in borderline conditions.[6]

The distinction between splitting and repression continues to be made, with splitting viewed as a more primitive phenomenon associated with personality defects and more severe psychopathology such as borderline conditions, and repression viewed as a more mature defense associated with inner conflict and neurosis. For example, Kernberg (1995) proposes that the personality development of individuals with borderline conditions has either been arrested at the developmental level of splitting or represents a defensive regression to that level.[7] An example of such splitting provided by Kernberg is the borderline patient's alternation between idealization and denigration of the therapist. Further, according to Kernberg, it is not the case that the borderline patient represses, say, memory of the idealization at the time that he or she is denigrating the therapist or repressing the memory of denigration at the time of idealizing the therapist. Both sets of memories may be available to consciousness. It is, rather, that different sub-structures of the personality or different ego states organized by different affects alternate with each other in an unintegrated manner. The result is that there is no relatively singly dominant personality structure that organizes psychological life but rather alternating sub-structures that are dissociated from each other.

In contrast, in repression, although certain conflictual mental contents are repressed and, therefore, unconscious, there is a relatively stable and dominant personality structure. This distinction has also been described in terms of horizontal splitting in repression – that is, a single and stable personality structure split into consciousness and unconsciousness, and vertical splitting in dissociation – that is, the absence of a single stable and dominant personality structure but rather different and dissociated personality structures.[8]

From an experience-near perspective, one can say that the individual who resorts to repression, that is, who is able to push conflictual material out of awareness, experiences a relatively unified conscious state, whereas the individual who resorts to splitting experiences different conscious or ego states that alternate over time and that are dissociated from each other (see Bromberg, 1996, 2004). A hypothesis implicit in this distinction is that individuals who resort to repression should show fewer problems with issues of identity than those who resort to splitting, where problems with identity should be dominant.

Although, as noted, the replacement of splitting and dissociation by repression marked the birth of psychoanalysis, a concern with splitting and dissociation has re-entered the psychoanalytic literature. Indeed, this step was already taken by S. Freud (1940b) in one of his last papers, "Splitting of the Ego in the Process of Defense." Although one of his main concerns in that paper is fetishism, his observations are relevant to a wide range of clinical dissociative phenomena. In his paper, Freud describes a psychological state in which the individual appears to know and not know at the same time. In other words, in this state, it is not that a unitary ego represses certain mental contents so that they are not available to conscious experience. It is, rather, that the ego itself, as well as consciousness, are split so that two conscious states – knowing and not knowing – are present at the same time (or perhaps rapidly alternating times), as well as two split-off ego structures that are associated with these different conscious states.[9] In short, the individual is in a dissociated state.

And now we return to Fairbairn's theory of endopsychic structure. I would suggest that it should be viewed as a hybrid theory that includes an emphasis on both dissociative processes (splits in egos structures and accompanying internal objects) as well as on repression and conflict. Thus, split-off ego structures are not only dissociated from each other but are also in conflict with each other, that is, are associated with conflicting aims and motives (the libidinal ego and the anti-libidinal egos pursue conflicting aims and are engaged in conflicting object relations) and are in conflict with the central ego. Hence, although, as noted, like Janet, Fairbairn also proposes that splits in the ego occur as a reaction to external trauma, he veers off in a direction quite different from the Janet tradition. The external trauma of interest to Fairbairn are inevitable ones, hardly similar to something like railway accidents. Paralleling Freud's formulation of the fate of unacceptable impulses, the aims and motives associated with the libidinal and anti-libidinal ego are repressed by the central ego. The result is that in the case with the repressed impulses of Freudian theory, the individual pursues object relational aims and motives of which he or she is unaware.

One can sum up Fairbairn's formulation of the consequences of trauma by noting that unlike other, including non-psychoanalytic, theories of trauma, his emphasis is on the conflicting aims and motives that are generated by the trauma. In Janet's theory, the "automatic" (i.e., relatively unmotivated) consequences of trauma are "splits in consciousness." Similarly, in self psychology theory, the "automatic'" consequences of the traumatic absence of empathic mirroring are self-defects. That is, the individual is not *motivated* to deal with trauma by developing self-defects. Rather, the self-defects are an "automatic" effect of the trauma (Kohut, 1984). In contrast, in Fairbairn's theory of endopsychic structure, the splits in the object and the ego are not simply "automatic" consequences of the trauma of parental frustration and deprivation but constitute motivated attempts to deal with the conflicts generated by the trauma.

A fundamental conflict posited in Fairbairn's theory of endopsychic structure is the one between accepting the reality of the trauma, that is, the conflict between accepting and not accepting the reality that the object is not and will not be loving. As we have seen, the "solution" to this kind of conflict is to internalize as well as split the object into its exciting (or alluring) and rejecting aspects along with the ego structures (libidinal and anti-libidinal ego) that are in an object relationship with these two aspects of the object. A major consequence of this internalization and splitting is that an "internal saboteur" is now lodged in the personality and the original conflict between accepting and not accepting an external traumatic reality has now been transformed into an inner conflict characterized by attitudes and feelings of contempt and shame in relation to one's own needs. Further, according to Fairbairn, because the central ego represses these conflictual internalized object relationships they are played out outside the individual's awareness. Thus, to sum up, in Fairbairn's theory of endopsychic structure, there is no hard and fast distinction between a conflict-repression and a trauma-dissociation model. It invokes both dissociation (i.e., splitting) in response to external trauma and inner conflict between the dissociated elements of the personality.

The distinction between repression and dissociation becomes somewhat blurred in Freud's own work, particularly in his formulation of the superego and his discussion of the vicissitudes of repression and the return of the repressed. With regard to the former, the superego is often experienced as an introject (what Schafer [1968] describes as a "felt presence") that is part of the self and yet, not fully part of the self, often popularly described as an external homunculus standing on one's shoulder and uttering injunctions to oneself – a sort of partly ego-alien quasi aspect of oneself. It is no wonder that the superego served as a model for Fairbairn's concept of internal object.

With regard to the latter, according to Freudian theory, in instances of massive return of the repressed, hitherto repressed mental contents become conscious with the result that ego-alien material, that is, material alien to one's sense of who one is, invades consciousness. According to the logic of Freudian theory, this massive return of the repressed (in contrast to a titrated pace under conditions of safety) not only elicits intense anxiety but also constitutes a threat to one's experience of oneself as familiar and unified. In the language of Sullivanian theory (Sullivan, 1955), a massive return of the repressed would be experienced as "not me" (rather than "bad me"), a dissociative experience that threatens the very integrity and unity of the self.

As discussed earlier, both Sigmund Freud and Anna Freud viewed as an ultimate danger the overwhelming of the ego by the strength of instinct, which they understood in the quantitative terms of the ego being overwhelmed by excessive excitation. However, from a more clinical and experience-near perspective, this can be more meaningfully understood as one's sense of self having great difficulty in withstanding the onslaught of ego-alien "not me" experiences. In classical theory, the source of the onslaught is taken to be the eruption into consciousness of infantile sexual and aggressive mental contents. However, as Sullivan's (1955) concept of "not me" suggests, any set of intense ego-alien experiences constitute trauma that can threaten ego integrity. Indeed, the essence of traumatic experience is that it cannot be assimilated by existing structures and, therefore, threatens their integrity. This is the case whether the trauma is triggered by external events or by "return of the repressed." I recall hearing a poignant account of a patient, who today would be diagnosed as dissociative identity disorder, who described her dissociative reaction to repeated and lifelong traumas by saying: "If it did happen, it probably happened to someone else. I dreamt it. Someone else dreamt it. That's what happens. It's not mastery, but it is survival. How much can one person take?" (Finnegan, 1993, p. 8).

If that patient were to describe her experience employing the language of Fairbairn's theory of endopsychic structure, she might say in reaction to her experiences of deprivation and rejection: "It is too much for one ego to bear" – hence, the splitting of the ego. However, unlike what one might refer to as straightforward dissociation, in Fairbairn's account, the individual does not have conscious access to the experiences and internal object relations associated with each of the slit-off subsidiary egos. Unlike Kernberg's borderline patients, who engage in splitting, but who have conscious access to each ego state, idealizing at one time and denigrating at another time, in Fairbairn's account, the patient not only splits but also represses the experiences and aims of each of the subsidiary egos. Indeed, according to Fairbairn (1952), paralleling classical theory, successful treatment requires that repression be lifted. However, unlike classical theory, it is not the repression of impulses that need to be lifted, but rather the traumatic experiences – what Fairbairn (1952) refers to as the "bad object situation" (p. 69) – that led to splitting in the first place. In short, once again, reflecting a hybrid theory, the mending of dissociation requires the prior step of lifting repression.

Various forms of conflict in Fairbairn's object relations theory

I have discussed the conflicts between the aims, motives, and different object relations characteristic of the libidinal ego and the anti-libidinal ego. There are other forms of conflict discussed by Fairbairn in more clinical and experience-near terms. One such conflict is the one between, on the one hand, the individual's "devotion to his repressed object" (Fairbairn, 1952, p. 72) and, on the other hand, the individual's strivings to free himself or herself from these powerful ties to internal objects and find and relate to a real external object in the world. One can, in broad terms, see this as a conflict between fantasy and reality and, in more specific terms, as a variant of symbiosis – separation-individuation conflict (Mahler, 1974); and in Fairbairn's (1952, p. 43) words as a conflict between "the regressive lure of identification [read "primary identification"] and the progressive urge toward separation" (p. 43). It is important to note that from the perspective of Fairbairn's object relations theory, separation-individuation or the progressive urge toward separation, is not simply a matter of increasing independence from the object, but of "mature dependence" rather than "infantile dependence" on the object (Fairbairn, 1952, p. 34). That is, healthy functioning always entails an object relational component, that is a self in relation to another (Rubens, 1994).

Fairbairn has a good deal to say regarding the dynamics involved in the individual's "devotion" and "obstinate attachment" to internal objects. Recall Ernest Jones's preface to Fairbairn's 1952 book in which he states that "Dr. Fairbairn starts at the centre of the personality, the ego, and depicts its strivings and difficulties in its endeavor to reach an object where it may find support" (p. v). As we have seen, according to Fairbairn, we are object-seeking creatures who cannot function or survive psychologically without a relationship to objects, internal and external. As Fairbairn makes clear, the ego cannot survive in such a world; and the "loss of the ego is the ultimate psychopathological disaster" (Fairbairn, 1952, p. 52). Hence, we cling to our internal "bad" objects as preferable to an empty inner world devoid of object relations. Even "bad" object relations are preferable to no object relations. The latter is experienced as unsustainable. This is critical in the maintenance of psychopathology and is a major clinical challenge in the treatment of certain patients.

Illustrative clinical phenomena

As Armstrong-Perlman (1994) observes, some patients spend their lives "pursuing alluring but rejecting objects . . . [who] have remained elusive objects of desire" (p. 223). Despite the unsatisfying nature of these

Inner conflict in Fairbairn's theory 79

relationships – often not merely unsatisfying, but abusive and cruel – the patient cannot relinquish them. The loss of the relationship and of the vital connection it provides are experienced as catastrophic, leading to the disintegration of the personality. Many of these patients experience an intense conflict between, on the one hand, the recognition that they should leave the relationship and even the desire to do so and, on the other hand, the unbearable fear of the psychological consequences of loss of a connection to external and internal objects. As Armstrong-Perlman (1994) writes: "The fear is that loss will lead either to the disintegration of the self, or to a reclusive emptiness to which any state of connectedness, no matter how infused with suffering, is preferable" (p. 224).

My own clinical experiences, particularly with women in abusive relationships, are entirely in accord with Armstrong-Perlman's description. For a number of years, as part of a university community service program, I have been working with women who have been subjected to domestic violence. Whatever the differences among the life circumstances and life trajectories of these women, there is a set of dynamics that many of them share that illustrate Fairbairn's formulations with remarkable clarity. These dynamics include[10] the following:

(1) An abiding and chronic conflict between the conviction that they need to leave the relationship and the profound fear of inner emptiness and lack of connection that, they are convinced, leaving the relationship would bring about. That this fear is not merely a fantasy is made evident when even successful (and frequently short-lived) attempts to leave the relationship often result in profound depression, anxiety, suicidal impulses, and utter despair. In one case, after exiting the relationship, one of the woman in the group became utterly dysfunctional and could not even manage to get out of bed. Not surprisingly, she returned to the abusive relationship. Frequent returns to the abusive relationship are, indeed, the norm in domestic violence. It is important to reiterate that for many abused women, leaving the relationship is experienced as giving up not only an actual external relationship, but also an internal affective connection, the loss of which is psychologically equivalent to inner emptiness and void and loss of the ego. In accord with Fairbairn's formulation, many of the women in the group reported their experience of their partner not only as abusive and rejecting but also as exciting and alluring. They often experienced

this excitement in their sexual experiences as part of their "reunion" following one of the break-ups in the relationship.

In understanding the experience of many of these women, we have found it useful to think in terms of addiction and affect regulation. That is, just as the individual with a drug addiction becomes dysregulated when the drug is not available, so similarly do many of the abused women become dysregulated when they experience loss of connection to the object or, at times, even when they anticipate such loss. Although I have been focusing on abused women, where the dynamics I have described are strikingly clear, they are also present in other maladaptive relationships.

(2) Despite knowing otherwise at the rational cognitive level, many abused women are generally unable to give up the fantasy that the abuser will, at some point, meet their needs, and are unable to accept at an emotional level the hopelessness of the relationship in this regard. When, at times, this reality becomes too emotionally evident, it is often followed by the same kind of depression and despair that is brought about by attempting to leave the relationship. Thus, the conflict between a realistic recognition of the need to leave the relationship and the intense fears that even the serious thought of such an action brings about is paralleled by the conflict between the wan fantasy that love and caring will eventually be forthcoming and the reality that this will not happen. In both cases, real emotional engagement with these realities is likely to bring about despair and depression. Hence, such emotional engagement is either avoided or, if it does occur, is followed by a retreat from it. This becomes a very thorny issue with patients for whom this dynamic is central.

(3) It is not uncommon for many abused women to respond with rage to the experience of humiliation and frustration of their needs. It is also not uncommon for such rage to be followed by ruefulness and shame, self-contempt, attempts to undo, and the conviction that the abuser's negative and contemptuous characterization of them is accurate.

(4) Expressions of rage are often followed by attempts to be "good" in the hope that by being good, even saintly, they will earn the abuser's love. This dynamic can be seen as paralleling, at the adult level, of Fairbairn's (1952) earlier noted description of the child taking the badness

Inner conflict in Fairbairn's theory 81

into himself or herself in the hope that by reversing the badness and being good, he or she will earn the parent's love.

(5) The attempt to be unqualifiedly "good" does not last, and episodes of rage, of course, recur. This triggers the vicious cycle of shame, self-recrimination, attempts to be good, failure, more rage, and so on.

(6) In his discussion of "obstinate" ties to early objects, Fairbairn does not appear to take up the issue of object choice. It is, however, a common theme that emerges in work with abused women, often expressed as puzzlement regarding their attractions and preferences. That is, they question why they are so frequently attracted to men who turn out to be abusive and, more generally, are unable to be loving and caring. What is striking in the pattern of victims of domestic violence and more generally, in the pattern seen in the kind of sado-masochistic relationships in which my patient was involved is the predictability of object choice. Thus, many victims of domestic violence get involved with the same type of abusive partner over and over again.

Why is this the case? As noted earlier, this is often a question posed by the victims of domestic violence themselves. I am not suggesting that this question can be answered in a definitive way. However, I think that some answers, implicit in Fairbairn's theorizing, are more useful and insightful than the vague and essentially non-explanatory concept of repetition compulsion. First, one must recall that, according to the perspective of Fairbairn's object relations theory, not only are we object-seeking creatures, but the kind of cognitive and affective connections we form with objects, including internal objects, define our very identity. Hence, to a significant extent, to paraphrase Rubens (1994), a particularized relation of specific aspects of the self in a relationship with specific aspects of the object would define our identity and our way of being with an other. To put it another way, the template or schema based on early experience of the subsidiary ego structures in a particular relationship to internal objects is experienced as a vital aspect of one's identity that, whatever suffering it may bring, is not readily relinquished. In short, object choice contributes to maintenance of one's identity.

(7) Another issue that emerges is the fantasy of transforming the "bad" object into a "good" object. Fairbairn attributes the persistence of the tie – the "devotion" and "obstinate attachment" – to the "bad" object

largely in terms of fear of confronting a void if that tie were to be relinquished. Thus, the conflict almost exclusively emphasized by Fairbairn (1952) is between clinging to that tie and freeing oneself from that tie, that is, the conflict between "the regressive lure of identification and the progressive urge toward separation" (p. 43).

However, there is another kind of conflict one can observe that is also implicated in object choice, but goes beyond that factor. Earlier, I have discussed the futility of the patient's hope to transform the "bad" object into a "good" object, with the implication that this is a futile and unrealistic hope because of the reality of who the object is (e.g., an abuser), that is, because of an unfortunate object choice. This is, of course, true. Thus, many of the abused women we have seen report not being at all attracted to or interested in men who are "nice guys" and not likely to be abusive. However, there is often more subtle clinical evidence that the lack of interest in the "nice guy" and the attraction to the potentially "bad" object are also motivated by conflicts pertaining to intimacy and the accompanying fear of engulfment. Thus, although my patient did appear to be subject to a great deal of abusive behavior and suffered greatly under its impact, on the occasions when her partner seemed to make an effort to behave more positively toward her, she would frequently become provocative and behave in a way that was virtually certain to sooner or later reinstitute the usual interactional pattern.

So the issue was not entirely one of object choice but also of my patient actively contributing to the constant re-creation of an interactional scenario that matched the template of her well established inner world of object relationships. Thus, side by side with her fantasy that her partner could be transformed into a "good" object and that they would live happily ever after was her actual behavior that served to repeatedly re-create and maintain the "bad" object situation. My patient's further fantasy of intimacy and closeness and living happily ever after were far more powerful in organizing her psychological life and sustaining her than any possibility of intimacy in the actual relationship. Indeed, the latter was repeatedly sabotaged.

Fairbairn attributes this gap between fantasy and reality to the patient's "devotion" and "obstinate attachment" to early object ties. That is, the patient needs to maintain her connection to internal objects. I think he is largely correct. However, I would suggest that the "devotion" to early objects and object relationship is also in the service of avoiding the dangers represented by actual intimacy and an actual "good" object. Indeed, some of the women in our domestic violence program described the experience of a "normal" (i.e., non-abusive) relationship as boring and dead. Thus, we have already come to the third issue, namely, either the avoidance or lack of interest in a potentially "good" object and/or the seeming persistent unconscious efforts at transforming a potentially "good" or "good enough" object into the familiar "bad" object.

The previous dynamics are not limited to domestic violence and outright abusive relationships but are also present in other relationships. Consider individuals involved in affairs in which one individual is not fully available because he or she is married. The relationship is often sustained by the excitement of an illicit affair, but also, in some cases, by the fantasy of intimacy and love that will be forthcoming when the hitherto unavailable individual becomes fully available. It is not uncommon, however, in such cases for the excitement and intimacy to disappear once the situation changes and the unavailable individual becomes available. It becomes clear in these instances that the excitement and intimacy are sustained not only by the illicitness of the relationship but also by fantasy and cannot survive the reality of the object's actual availability. The degree of relatedness and intimacy activated in fantasy cannot be matched by the degree of relatedness and intimacy experienced in the actual relationship.

I recall a remarkable scene of a film I saw some years ago. The film is set in a small Israeli village. One of the characters in the film comes out into the street every night when the moon appears and in a poignant lamentation, cries loudly "Rachel. My Rachel." One, of course, has the immediate image of a terrible loss in the life of this poor soul. A few scenes later, we find our character in the grassy field of a mental hospital at dusk behind a metal fence. A woman walks up to the fence and our poor soul also approaches the fence to greet her. The woman is none other but Rachel. They chat for a while in a mundane, relatively affectless way: "How are you? How have you been?" and so on. Soon the moon emerges in the sky and our character excuses himself, walks to the center of the field and bays at the moon: "Rachel. My Rachel." The scene brilliantly demonstrates that the object in our character's object relationship is an internal object, that his passion and affect are directed to the internal object, and that he is living in an inner fantasy world that has little or nothing to do with the actual Rachel. (The scene can be seen as a dramatic depiction of the distinction made by Lacan [2006] between the object that triggers desire and the object desired.)

I am also reminded of the intense love affair between Fermina and Florentino in Gabriel Garcia Márquez's (1985) *Love in the Time of Cholera*. The love affair was conducted solely via letters. When Fermina actually encountered Florentino in person, "She asked herself, appalled how she could have nurtured such a chimera in her heart for so long with so much ferocity." In responding to the question, "What can literature teach us about love?", in the February 9, 2014, *New York Times* Book Review section, after citing the previous passage from Márquez's novel, the reviewer David Levithan (2014) writes: "I have always been more in love with my fantasies of the woman I was with, not the beautiful and complicated human beings they actually were . . . true love . . . asks us . . . to truly see the people we love" (p. 18). I would add that from a Fairbairnian perspective, true object relationships with actual others make the same demand. It is interesting to observe the continuum – rather than a radical discontinuity – between the psychotic character in the Israeli film and both the literary character of Fermina and the actual character of David Levithan, along with the rest of us.

In and out program

Guntrip (1969) has described a pattern that he refers to as an "in and out program" (p. 36) that some individuals adopt as a means of dealing with the conflict between the need for object relationships and the fear of being engulfed by them. Although his main focus is on schizoid phenomena, the dynamics he describes are more widely applicable. The dilemma to which the "in and out" pattern is a solution is the chronic conflict between desire and longing for closeness in a relationship with another and fear of being swallowed up and engulfed in the relationship. On the one hand, the individual cannot survive psychologically without some connection to the object, the absence of which produces the terror of isolation, and on the other hand, every object relationship is experienced as carrying the risk of engulfment and the loss of individuality. The risk is particularly intense when the object relationship is a symbiotic one, established on the basis of what Fairbairn (1952) refers to as primary identification. Thus, the individual is damned if she or he does and damned if she or he does not.

The compromise solution to this seemingly unresolvable conflict that the individual often reaches is the in-out program described by Guntrip (1969), which can be expressed in various ways and can take various forms. One form is alternating periods of literally being in and out of the relationship, that is, separations and reunions. This pattern is frequently seen in domestic violence couples – repeated break-ups and reunions. Another in-out pattern is remaining in the relationship, but without full commitment, with, emotionally speaking, one foot always out the door. Still another in-out pattern is chronically maintaining an optimal degree of distance that avoids both the terror of isolation and the fear of engulfment. This is probably the most stable form of the in-out pattern.

Implications for treatment

The goals of psychoanalytic treatment from the perspective of Fairbairn's object relations theory can be stated in a number of ways. One primary goal is the implementation of

> a process whereby infantile dependence upon the object gradually gives place to mature dependence upon the object. This process of development is characterized (a) by the gradual abandonment of an original object-relationship based upon primary identification; and (b) by the gradual adoption of an object-relationship based upon the differentiation of the object.
>
> (Fairbairn, 1952, p. 34)

What Fairbairn has in mind here is not an amelioration of "over-dependency" as it is generally understood but rather the gradual replacement of object relationships in which one is relating to an internal object with object relationships in which one is relating to the real "differentiated" objects in the external world. As Ogden (1983) writes, from a Fairbairnian perspective, "one measure of psychological health is the degree to which internal object relations can be modified in the light of current experience" (Fn. 6, p. 238).

The goal of "gradual abandonment" of ties to the internal object is met with many difficulties and barriers. These barriers include the patient's resistance against re-experiencing the "bad object situation" once repression is relaxed and perhaps most important, the patient's fear of experiencing the catastrophe of an empty objectless inner world were the patient to relinquish his or her "devotions" and "obstinate attachment" to internal object.

As noted earlier, another related formidable barrier is the difficulty of abandoning the hope or fantasy that one can transform the "bad" object into a "good" object that one wants and needs the object to be – similar to the child's hope that he or she can earn the object's love. I worked with a woman who consistently reacted to the realization that this hope or fantasy in relation to her partner would not be fulfilled with the experience of depression, despair, and suicidal thoughts and feelings. She repeatedly dealt with these intolerable feelings by re-instating the hope and fantasy that the "bad" object could be transformed into a "good" one, only to be severely disillusioned through her experience of her partner's abusive and demeaning behavior – with the terrible reality that her fantasy and hope were futile. This would then lead once again to despair and suicidal impulses, a cycle that would be repeated again and again. My patient would both recognize the reality of the futility of her hope and fantasy and, at the same time, disavow that terrible reality and continue to nurture the hope and fantasy that she could transform the "bad" object into the "good" object who would love her. As S. Freud (1940b) describes in his essay on "Splitting the Ego in the Process of Defense," her behavior and her psychic life reflected, at one and the same time, both the recognition and the disavowal of reality.

According to Fairbairn, the patient comes to treatment with an inner world that is a closed system in which a relationship with external objects "is only possible in terms of transference" (Fairbairn, 1958, p. 381), that is, in which the external object is experienced as a stand-in for an internal object. A central aim of treatment is to enable the patient to experience and relate to external objects more fully in terms of who they are. One can partly understand this aim as attempting to tilt the conflict between a fantasy-saturated inner world and an inner world directed toward reality in the direction of the latter. In an important sense, implicit in Fairbairn's view of treatment is the aim of enhancing reality-testing when that is understood and expanded to include the domains of affect and object relations. Another way to put it is to say that an overarching aim of treatment is to transform the patient's solipsistic inner world in which object relationships are essentially relationships among different aspects of himself or herself to object relationships with actual objects in the world. As

Christian (personal communication, June 2015) observes, such a transformation often requires a process of mourning of the loss of the idealized internal object.

Another overarching aim of treatment from a Fairbairnian perspective is to enhance and enlarge the province of the central ego. This means lifting repression of internal objects and split-off ego structures and integrating them into the central ego, that is, achieving greater unity of the personality. However, the accomplishment of this aim runs up against strong barriers. These include the patient's resistance against re-experiencing the "bad object situation" once repression is relaxed and, perhaps most important, the patient's fear of experiencing the catastrophe of an empty objectless inner world were the patient to relinquish his or her "devotion" and "obstinate attachment" to internal objects.

According to Fairbairn, in order to risk the confrontation with these dangers, the patient must experience the therapist as a "good" object. Given the closed system with which the patient comes to treatment, it is not clear from Fairbairn's writings how the therapist gets to be experienced as a "good" object nor even what it means, specifically, for the therapist to be a "good" object. What kind of characteristics, interventions, interactions constitute being a "good" object from Fairbairn's perspective?

Although perhaps obscured by different language, as one can see from the previous, there are many parallels between Freud and Fairbairn regarding the aims of treatment. However, there is one important process aim stated by Fairbairn that highlights an important difference between Freud and Fairbairn. I refer to Fairbairn's (1952) statement that an important goal of treatment is to "exorcise" the "bad" internal object. In effect, Fairbairn is stating that the patient needs to rid himself or herself of what under the impact of trauma, he or she defensively made part of the self. That is, he or she must re-externalize what was originally external and defensively internalized. In striking contrast, an important aim of treatment from a Freudian perspective Freud – as expressed in the adage, where id was, there shall ego be – is the re-internalizing (and integrating) aspects of one's psychobiological nature (e.g., instinctual wishes and urges) that were defensively rendered external. These differences reflect two sharply different views of human nature.

What does Fairbairn have to say about resolution or amelioration of inner conflict as a goal of treatment? First, let us review what Fairbairn identifies as core inner conflicts. These include the conflict between infantile dependence and mature dependence, the conflict between "the regressive lure of identification and the progressive urge toward separation" (Fairbairn, 1952, p. 43), and the conflict between the individual's "devotion" and "obstinate attachment" to internal objects and the freedom to relate to new external objects, which is essentially a conflict between relating to others as stand-ins for internal objects and relating to others in terms of who they actually are, that is, as actual others with their own characteristics, interests, aims, needs, and so on.

These different expressions of conflict are not only interrelated but, in an important sense, are essentially different aspects of the same fundamental conflict. Or perhaps one can say that they are different ways of describing the same general fundamental conflict. Thus, infantile dependence, the regressive lure of identification, the individual's "devotion" and "obstinate attachment" to internal objects, and the relating to others as stand-ins for internal objects, all have in common the individual's powerful tendency to live in a fantasy inner world in which one is relating to early objects that have been internalized and thereby have become aspects of oneself. Thus, the individual lives in an inner world in which the rejecting and alluring aspects of the object have been internalized and become part of a personality that is characterized by unintegrated and conflictual parts and in which one responds to one's needs and longings with self-contempt and shame – affects that reflect the internalization of the experience of attitudes of the object.

For Fairbairn, the resolution of conflicts between infantile dependence and mature dependence, between the regressive lure of identification and the progressive urge toward separation, between the "devotion" and "obstinate attachment" to early internal objects and object relationships to actual objects, and the conflict between pursuing one's needs and self-contempt and shame in response to one's needs all rest on the success of the treatment in facilitating the patient's ability to experience the therapist as a "good" object. As Fairbairn (1952) puts it, therapeutic success is a "function of establishing a special kind of object relationship with the therapist" (p. 87); two, this, in turn, makes it safe for the patient to lift repression and re-experience the "bad object situation"; three, it makes it safe to "exorcise" the internal "bad" object without the fear of living in an empty inner world; and four, enables the patient to engage in object relationships with actual objects in the external world. As noted earlier, what is not made very clear in Fairbairn's writings are the specific routes to and processes involved in these achievements. For example, how does the patient come to be capable of experiencing the therapist as an actual "good" object rather than largely as a transference stand-in for an internal object? In classical theory, the answer to this question lies in the analysis of the transference; in Control-Mastery theory, it lies in the therapist's test-passing; in Alexander and Freud's (1946) theory, it lies in corrective emotional experiences; and in Kohut's (1984) self psychology, it lies in empathic understanding and "optimal failure." Fairbairn's answer to this question is not entirely clear or specific. More generally, his writings are more concerned with descriptions of the nature of personality structure, particularly in psychopathology, than with specifics of therapeutic process and outcome.

Notes

1 Of course, Melanie Klein can be included in this school.
2 See Kernberg's (1967) discussion of the object relational unit consisting of self-representation, object representation, and affect, which is clearly influenced by Fairbairn's formulation.
3 In trying to understand Fairbairn's often convoluted formulation and place it in a language that is more comprehensible, I take Fairbairn to be saying that through a motivated process, the individual lacks conscious access to certain representations of the object.
4 As has been noted by M. T. Hoffman and L. Hoffman (2014), Fairbairn's account of the child's original "pristine personality" and "unitary ego" giving way to splits in the ego under the impact of the reality of the world evokes the biblical image of the fall from grace, an image quite in line with Fairbairn's early interest in theology and his early plans to become a minister (see Eagle [in press] for further discussion).
5 Fairbairn (1952) observes that "it is always the 'bad' object . . . that is internalized in the first instance, for . . . I find it difficult to attach any meaning to the primary internalization of a 'good' object which is both satisfying and amenable from the infant's point of view" (pp. 110–111). However, at a later point in his writings, Fairbairn allows for the possibility of the internalization of the "good" object based on a complex and turgid argument that, I must confess, I do not fully understand.
6 Unlike most theorists who emphasize splitting and dissociation, Kernberg does not emphasize the role of external trauma but instead focuses on constitutional factors such as the presumed strength of the aggressive drive in borderline patients.
7 Although Kernberg assumes that there is a normal developmental stage characterized by splitting (between "good" and "bad" object and self-representations), there is no evidence for this assumption.
8 An interesting question that arises is the nature of unconscious processes and contents in individuals who engage in splitting and do not resort to repression. If the dynamic unconscious is the "storehouse" of repressed mental contents,

and if certain individuals are not capable of carrying out repression but rather employ splitting and dissociation, does this mean that there is no dynamic unconscious in these individuals, but rather unintegrated and dissociated conscious states? This is a very different model of mental functioning than the one implicit in the "cornerstone" concept of repression.

9 The most striking example of a state of both knowing and not knowing, avowing and disavowing, is seen in the reactions to death of a loved one. The bereaved individual knows that his or her partner is dead, and at the same time, hears his or her footsteps or expects him or her to be home at the usual time. It is as if there is a terrible conflict between avowing and disavowing and as if the bereaved individual needs to titrate the impact of the trauma in small doses in order to integrate it and fully avow the loss in incremental steps over time. As is also implicit in S. Freud's (1940a) paper, one can meaningfully view these reactions in terms of a conflict between accepting the reality of an event and not accepting it.

10 Although our work has been done with women, one may find a similar pattern with others regardless of gender.

Chapter 6

Kleinian and post-Kleinian perspectives on conflict

Neal Vorus

Psychoanalysis has traditionally been defined as the quintessential science of human conflict or, in E. Kris's (1947) words, "human behavior viewed as conflict" (p. 6). However, along with the proliferation of schools of psychoanalytic thought and practice has emerged considerable diversity of opinion regarding how analysts conceptualize conflict and on the precise role, if any, that conflict plays in the development of psychopathology (see Smith, 2003). For example, when speaking of the kinds of conflict that matter to psychoanalysts, are we referring only to unconscious conflict, or do we also mean the everyday conflicts that are subject to conscious introspection? To what extent do we now conceive of the origin of psychopathology in terms of fundamental conflicts, whether between internal structures, internal objects, or instincts, or to what extent do we see conflict as a secondary phenomenon, a by-product of environmental failure?

In this chapter I aim to address these questions from the perspective of Kleinian and post-Kleinian thought, first by following the evolution of Klein's views of conflict throughout her writings, then by describing the theoretical reformulation that follows from the work of Wilfred Bion. I will begin by taking up the early Kleinian period, with its clinical focus on the primacy of aggression, but mainly holding to traditional Freudian interstructural notions of conflict. Second, I will review the period beginning with Klein's integration of Freud's dual instinct theory and proceeding through the introduction of the paranoid-schizoid and depressive positions. During this second phase Klein had begun to posit the elemental conflict between love and hate as a kind of psychological bedrock and saw psychological development as a difficult path toward whole object relations in the face of this very painful constitutionally-determined given. Finally, I will address the work of Bion and his influence on a post-Kleinian view of conflict in mental life. In a word, Bion dethrones conflict as the prime mover of psychological existence, replacing it with an initially pre-conflictual primary drive toward truth, which, in its earliest form, is directed at finding the means to represent and bearably know reality, via the relationship of container to contained. It is the thesis of this chapter that, while some aspects of Bion's late theorizing were repudiated by post-Kleinians, his view of an initially pre-conflictual drive toward representation that propels both development and therapeutic action underlies the clinical approach of many contemporary Kleinians.

Early Klein (1921–1929) and the emerging clinical importance of aggression

The Kleinian perspective on conflict begins with understandings that emerged from Klein's treatment of young children early in her career, at a time when there were no real precedents for her to follow. As others have noted (e.g., J. Greenberg & Mitchell, 1983), Klein's earliest writings are, in broad outline, "ultra-Freudian" in their depiction of ubiquitous Oedipal conflicts pervading all aspects of children's behavior and mental functioning. However, a careful reading of Klein's early writing reveals the extent to which, from the beginning, her clinical focus was less on conflict between *structures* on the constant interplay of loving and hating impulses toward the *object* from the beginning of life.

For example, in her first paper, entitled "Development of a Child," M. Klein (1921) presents the case of Fritz, who was actually (in disguised form) her 5-year-old son Erich, who had become inhibited in both his curiosity about the world and in his imaginative play. In working to free him from these inhibitions, Klein developed a technique that involved the facilitation of free imaginative expression through play, which yielded a wealth of phantasies involving "extraordinary aggressiveness" alternating with tender fondness toward both of his parents, an early example of *splitting*. As she demonstrates in this paper, it is the extreme sadism that frightens Fritz, and the opportunity to express his destructive phantasies through play that releases him from his inhibitions.

Klein's papers throughout the 1920s document the work with her first child patients, and what stands out above all else in these case examples is the extent to which all of these children suffered from crippling anxieties due to unrelenting sadism. Klein's distinctive clinical approach with her patients was to recognize and articulate the psychic reality of these frightening phantasies. For example, her patient Ruth's opposition to using a large sponge to wash a baby doll yielded the following interpretation from M. Klein (1932):

> I showed her in every detail how she envied and hated her mother because the latter incorporated her father's penis during coitus, and how she wanted to steal his penis and the children out of her mother's inside and kill her mother.
>
> (p. 38)

As in this example, Klein's interpretations tended to focus nearly exclusively on the hateful and aggressive dimension of Oedipal conflict rather than on the libidinal, except insofar as such impulses are infused with sadism. The child's guilt is specifically linked to the hatred felt toward a loved object.

Although Klein's early clinical examples differed from traditional Freudian accounts in the ways described earlier, her theoretical account adhered largely to the Freudian assumption that conflict originated *between structures* and was, therefore, necessarily of Oedipal origin. That is, insofar as the tripartite structure was a developmental achievement only completed around the age of 5, intrapsychic conflict as such was similarly envisioned as only arising after the first few years of life. Because Klein saw conflict as originating prior to that age, she began to account for differences in her perspective by making several theoretical modifications. First, she dated the Oedipus complex earlier, to the second year of life.[1] This change was consistent with a view emphasizing the emergence of a severe, primitive superego marked by a predominance of pre-genital (oral- and anal-sadistic) characteristics. This early superego is described by Klein less as a structure and more as a relationship with a monstrous, hateful entity that issues retaliatory attacks from within; rather than issuing pangs of guilt, "the superego becomes something which bites, devours, and cuts" (M. Klein, 1928, p. 187). Intrapsychic conflict is seen here as taking place between this terrifying internal presence and the often overwhelmed and overpowered ego of the child.

Dual instinct theory and the ubiquity of conflict from the beginning of life

An important evolution in Klein's thinking begins to take place in 1932, with her first use of Freud's dual instinct theory. The integration of this conception of motivation changes her view of conflict in several important ways. First, and most important, she henceforth views conflict as ubiquitous from the start of life, as a primary condition of human existence. Following S. Freud (1920), she sees the primary task of the neonate as one of defending itself against the death instinct, initially by directing destructive impulses outside of the self. As Klein (1932) describes, introjective mechanisms soon ensue, which alternate with projection in building up the internal and external world. Just as the initial projections create good and bad external objects, so do primal incorporations build up good and bad internal objects that form the basis of the superego, initially by facilitating a split in the id whereby libido becomes mobilized against the destructive drive. In this way, the primal superego (in identification with the split infantile id) becomes "the vehicle of defence against the destructive impulses within the organism" (p. 127). This is a radical departure from Freud's more limited conception of the superego. For Klein, the superego is not merely an identification structure providing a defensive resolution of the Oedipus complex; rather, it is the instantiation of a primal battle between forces of life and death waged from the beginning of life. While it makes sense to describe the ego's confrontation with a sadistic superego as a site of conflict, both internally and (via projection) externally, the more fundamental conflict is now explicitly viewed as that between Eros and the death instinct, love and hate.

As Klein had demonstrated clinically from the beginning, the young child not only faces anxiogenic impulses but also deals with an agglomeration of hostile and sadistic elements generated by his or her own projected sadism. The initial defense against such objects is to launch further destructive attacks, which engender additional phantasies of retaliation in kind, described by M. Klein (1993) as a sadistic vicious circle. At this point in her theorizing, Klein is increasingly cognizant of the importance of Eros, of libidinal impulses, in moderating destructiveness. However, it isn't until her introduction of the "depressive position" in 1935 that Klein is able to fully describe the essential nature of the conflict between love and hate toward the object and the fundamental importance of the secure internalization of the whole, good object in the face of this conflict. What Klein needed was a theoretical framework that would allow her to describe the relationship between love and destructiveness not as unfolding on a developmental timetable (e.g., genital love surpassing pre-genital sadism) but in terms of the opposing forces of integration and disintegration (fundamentally rooted in life and death instincts) that are ubiquitously present throughout life.

In her paper "The Psychogenesis of Manic-Depressive States," M. Klein (1935b) introduces a new developmental perspective wherein the etiology of various forms of psychopathology is no longer understood in terms of psychosexual fixation points, but instead "by changes in the relation of the subject to the object" (p. 263).[2] The changes she has in mind are those that involve degrees of integration of both subject and object and of loving and destructive impulses. In Klein's view, the very young child in the first few months of life is necessarily unintegrated and capable of relating only to "part objects." With cognitive maturation the child gradually becomes able to apprehend a more integrated sense of himself or herself and external objects. Reality-testing improves, and internal objects grow more realistic. The ego is now capable of identifying more fully with good objects. However, this growing integration brings with it a new form of anxiety due to the child's growing recognition of dependence on the good object. As Klein puts it, "The dread of persecution, which was at first felt on the ego's account, now relates to the good object as well and from now on preservation of the good object is regarded as synonymous with survival of the ego" (p. 264). This marks the beginning of the depressive position, wherein the child begins to develop awareness that the bad object attacked in phantasy is also the good, loved, and needed object. This results in renewed splitting, now motivated more by a desire to preserve than a wish to destroy, and consequently operating on "planes which gradually become nearer and nearer to reality" (p. 288). Other defenses also emerge that are more integrative than destructive in nature. The use of projection begins to lose value and the ego makes greater use of introjection of the good object as a mode of defense. The child attempts to restore the good object from sadistic attacks, via reparative phantasies. At a theoretical level, as the ego and its objects become more unified, Eros begins to dominate in the psychic economy, and as constructive impulses grow, divisive forces start to give way to constructive impulses and activities.

However, the emergence of the depressive position does not immediately result in a diminished experience of conflict. Rather, quite the opposite. The child is now confronted with a new level of awareness of the consequences of his or her own sadistic impulses, which continue unabated, as Klein describes in the following:

> Only when the ego has introjected the object as a whole and has established a better relationship to the external world and to real people is it able fully to realize the disaster created through its sadism and especially through its cannibalism, and to feel distressed about it.
>
> (p. 269)

From an external perspective one might say that with the advent of the depressive position the conflicted nature of the mind diminishes due to the emergence of integrative tendencies, which facilitate awareness of the object and of oneself in totality. The world is less split and divided. However, from the standpoint of the child's subjective experience, conflict *increases* due to this growing awareness. The child now "realizes the disaster" created through its sadism and feels "overwhelming guilt," which may initiate a defensive retreat to the paranoid-schizoid position as a way of obliterating this scope of awareness. Alternatively, the child may utilize the manic defenses of omnipotence and denial as a way of holding onto good objects while denying their importance or the danger to which they are subjected (thus reducing the subjective experience of conflict). Obsessional mechanisms represent an advance over manic defenses, as the sadism involved in manic states of triumph and contempt for the object are lessened and a desire to control predominates, resulting in a strengthening of reparative tendencies.

Throughout her writings, Klein believed that the depressive position, marked by an often overwhelming experience of ambivalence, is ultimately overcome in infancy, although it can be reactivated in adult life. In Klein's words:

> The more the child can at this stage develop a happy relationship to its real mother, the more will it be able to *overcome the depressive position*. But all depends on how it is able to find its way out of the conflict between love and uncontrollable hatred and sadism.
>
> (p. 287, italics added)

As Likierman (2001) has pointed out, this notion of *overcoming* the depressive position was superseded by Klein's followers, who describe this position as a progressive developmental phenomenon, characterized less by the crisis of overwhelming ambivalence than by the emerging capacity to tolerate states of conflict. It represents the beginning of intersubjective awareness, the growing capacity for consideration and concern for others, and ultimately the shift from an "ego-centered to an object-centered state" (p. 115). Stated in terms of these newly emerging capacities, the post-Kleinian view of the depressive position envisions it as a more permanent feature of mental life, albeit one that continues to fluctuate with a more primitive, ego-centered paranoid-schizoid one. And, in a significant departure from her writings, Klein's followers have begun to describe the intersubjective foundation of the development of the depressive position, which ushers in a new formulation of *pathogenic* conflict.

Bion and the post-Kleinians: containment and the truth drive

The thinker most associated with the new intersubjective dimension in Kleinian thought is Wilfred Bion, arguably Klein's most prolific and influential follower. He is perhaps most known for his concepts of the "container and the contained," which injected an interactive dimension into Kleinian thought. In Bion's (1959, 1962a) formulation, the infant gains the capacity to become aware of, and begin to tolerate and mitigate, unbearable experiences through a particular mode of interaction with the mother, in which the child projects into the mother raw proto-emotions (beta elements), which the latter contains and metabolizes through maternal reverie. In her interactions with the infant the mother returns these bits of experience to the infant, now detoxified ("metabolized") and thereby made bearable. In effect, the infant begins to experience psychically its own emotions as they are embodied in the mother's responses – her facial expressions, body posture, vocalizations, movements. Bion is describing an unconscious process whereby the mother is impacted by the infant's as-yet-unthinkable experiences, and her capacity to psychically register and be affected by those experiences (rather than defend against them) results in her serving as a vehicle of representation. These transformed elements (alpha elements) are now capable of being mentalized and provide the foundation for thinking. Over time the infant internalizes the mother's containing function, which makes possible continued emotional growth and the capacity to learn from experience.

As it relates to the question of conflict, post-Kleinian thought is characterized by an important (and often unacknowledged) pivot from foundational Kleinian assumptions. Whereas Klein arguably saw the conflict between Eros and death instinct, love and hate, as fundamental, Bion (1965) described the most essential, foundational aspect of human life as arising prior to the emergence of conflict. For the infant, finding a means of representing experience, in Grotstein's (2004) words a "truth drive," is the most fundamental need in early life. This drive ushers the infant into intersubjective relating from the start and makes the mother's capacity to receive, metabolize, and translate the child's unmediated emotional experience the fundamental psychological requirement. What the mother takes in and processes for the infant is *not* a by-product of conflict, but rather, it is the primal sense impression of unmediated reality itself, "O," in Bion's (1962b) nomenclature. Love and hate, principle conflictual ingredients in Klein's view of the mind, arise secondarily, as emotional forms of knowing and relating to objects ("L" and "H"). The more fundamental motivation is that toward truth and knowledge ("K"), manifest initially in the drive to transform raw sensory impressions into thoughts and, eventually, the capacity for thinking.

In Bion's framework, the forms of intense early conflict so fundamental for Klein are reinterpreted in terms of the basic need to give tolerable form to the chaotic, overwhelming experience of brute reality. In Grotstein's (2007) words, "with O as the centerpiece of this new metapsychology, P-S [paranoid-schizoid position] and D [depressive position] can then be understood as adaptive (normal) paranoid, manic, and/or depressive defenses against the intolerable emergence of O" (p. 130). The content of these positions, as described by M. Klein (1935b, 1940), involves conflict between primary love and hatred felt toward an object, first experienced in part-object terms, then later as a whole object. From Bion's standpoint, love and hate are relegated to forms of knowledge about an object; one "knows (K) an object by how one feels (L and/or H) about it" (Grotstein, 2007, p. 137). Love and hate are the emotional categories by which one comes to know objects, and thus the paranoid-schizoid and depressive positions represent modes of organization of this knowledge. Initially, reality is beyond categorization and, in unfiltered form, psychically unbearable. When mediated by maternal containment the capacity for binary categories is achieved (P-S), in the form of unconscious phantasies of good and bad internal objects. A further evolution in knowing is achieved with integration and the capacity for objectification (D). This sequence is simultaneously the evolution of the process of thinking and the development of increasingly mature modes of object relations – for Bion, these are one and the same, motivated by the fundamental drive toward truth and knowledge.

While for Bion conflict is not an inherent feature of psychic life at the start as it was for Freud and Klein, he certainly saw many of the basic modes of conflict described by the latter as part of the normal unfolding of P-S and D, in their function of triangulating O (i.e., giving representational form to an initially overwhelming and chaotic confrontation with brute reality). However, his clinical focus was less on these conflicts as they would be typically understood in Klein's writing than on their role in the transformation in O, or more appositely, as reflecting difficulties related to what, for Bion, constitutes the more *essential* conflict, that which results from inadequate containment.

It was his clinical encounter with such difficulties that led Bion toward his distinctively interpersonalized version of Kleinian thought through his introduction of the process of maternal containment. In a series of papers in the 1950s on his work with psychotic patients Bion (1956, 1957a,b, 1959) began to describe the idea of a "negative container" in the transference with such patients, wherein they experienced him as an impermeable mother, hostile to their emotional outpourings, and hateful toward them for their emotionality. In his description, this object is both attacked by the infant and internalized, resulting in an "obstructive object" or "negative container" that ushers attacks internally against the child's desire for knowledge and wish to form links with objects. The attacks emanating from the negative container represent the most primal form of conflict in Bion's writings and are clearly a *response to environmental failure* on the part of the infant.

While contemporary Kleinians have not universally taken up all aspects of Bion's theory[3] and do not tend to explicitly differ with Klein's view of the primacy of mental conflict, a close reading of prominent writers in this tradition reveals the extent to which (a) their clinical attention is most often focused on breakdowns in certain mental functions – symbolization, self-reflection, mature communication, affect tolerance, reality-testing; and (b) they tend to attribute these difficulties to some form of failed maternal containment. Moreover, contemporary Kleinians tend to account for the process by which they achieve therapeutic gains with their patients in terms of a re-establishment of the container-contained relationship vis-à-vis the analyst. As Schafer (1997) has pointed out, while contemporary Kleinians do not overtly repudiate the content-focused interpretive approach of Klein (i.e., extensive use of part-object language), the shift from interpreting content to interpreting process and function reflects a fundamental realignment of the theory. From my point of view, this realignment also reveals a changed view of the place of conflict in Kleinian thought.

Although paranoid-schizoid and depressive positions remain central organizers of clinical material in contemporary Kleinian writing, the latter now tend to distinguish the *normal* mode of these positions from pathological forms. For example, in Steiner's (1987) writings on psychic retreats, he describes a common, pathological defensive structure composed of an organized set of perverse, split, internal object relationships that serve the function of providing a refuge from the pain associated with either paranoid-schizoid or depressive position. Thus, psychic retreats offer a kind of third position wherein emotional contact is averted in favor of an avoidance of pain or anxiety. Psychopathology, in this formulation, is not reducible to the normal conflict endemic to the positions, but rather to the inability to bear mental pain – itself explicable by a breakdown in the container-contained relationship.

In Betty Joseph's (1983) classic paper, "On Understanding and Not Understanding," she describes a frequently encountered problem wherein patients appear to seek understanding through analysis but actually engage in a repudiation of understanding by unconsciously splitting-off and projecting the aspect of themselves that seeks understanding into the analyst, who is then warded off. While Joseph explains the difficulties experienced by these patients in traditional Kleinian terms – as manifesting an inability to tolerate the pain of the depressive position, wherein real understanding becomes possible – this formulation does not, in itself, constitute her explanation of the pathology per se. Instead, this is explicable in relation to the quality of parental understanding, as illustrated by two of Joseph's clinical examples. In the first, a child patient projects experiences of stupidity, desperation, and immobility into the analyst through various non-verbal actions (tying the analyst up, smearing glue on his trousers, wrapping him in tape, etc.). Joseph explains that the child had previously suffered traumatic separations from parents, who appear to have had no conception or concern regarding the impact of these separations. Because of their complete inability to register the child's experience, it remains "outside his verbal range," communicable only in primitive form in the paranoid-schizoid mode. Similarly, an adult patient who repeatedly and systematically undermines real understanding through pseudo-explanation suffers, in Joseph's view, from the aftereffects of "having had no real belief in her world, in her emotional surroundings, as if deep sincerity was lacking between her parents and herself" (p. 294). While adhering to Klein's dynamic formulations, Joseph, like other post-Bionian Kleinians, offers a fundamentally transformed view of psychogenesis, wherein the conflicts that are pathogenic (as opposed to merely ordinary) are those that take place in relation to the child's natural drive for representation, for understanding via maternal containment (i.e., Grotstein's [2004] "truth drive"). It is as a result of failed containment that the desire to be understood is subject to attack, which results in a failure to fully traverse the depressive position.

Contemporary Kleinian views of conflict

The contemporary Kleinian literature can be read as a catalog of the many ways that containment fails and the patient has suffered from a failure to internalize a whole, good (i.e., containing) object. The place of conflict in these formulations is somewhat complex. While the fundamental problem of psychic functioning is often characterized theoretically as the struggle to maintain the good object in the face of a primordial struggle between Eros and the death instinct (or, more typically, love and hatred toward the object), at an experiential level the majority of patients described by contemporary Kleinians are barely capable of registering conflict, as their psychological functioning has often been drastically reduced by a predominance of splitting. These are patients not yet able to sustain depressive position functioning, in which conflict between love and hate becomes bearable. Because of failure of adequate containment, these patients have failed to internalize a whole, good, and containing object, but instead are inhabited by a destructive and envious superego that distorts their object relationships and emotional capacities. Their psychological functioning is often characterized as paranoid-schizoid in nature, and they tend to rely on primitive defenses, many of which are aimed at maintaining psychic equilibrium at the cost of emotional growth and change.

Analytic treatment with such patients is primarily oriented toward restoring the capacity for growth through interpretive interventions aimed at re-establishing the possibility of a containing object relationship with the analyst. In a sense, these patients suffer from the overwhelming effects of inadequate maternal containment, which has nearly eliminated the capacity to tolerate any experience of internal conflict, as the experience of difference itself has been extruded through processes of splitting and projective identification.

One contemporary Kleinian who exemplifies this current trend of thought is Ronald Britton. In his now well-known paper, "The Missing Link: Parental Sexuality in the Oedipus Complex," Britton (1989) describes a number of patients who suffer from a failure to develop what he refers to as "triangular space," which involves the integration of subjective and objective points of view of the self so that the child becomes capable of self-reflection and tolerance of various, at times conflicting, points of view. In Britton's formulation, triangular space is achieved when a child has come to tolerate and accept the conflictual nature of their relationship with *both* Oedipal objects following an earlier tendency to toggle back and forth between positive and negative Oedipal positions:

> The evasive use of this switch is halted by the full recognition of the parents' sexual relationship, their different anatomy, and the child's own nature. This involves the realization that the same parent who is the object of oedipal desire in one version is the hated rival in the other.
>
> (Britton, 1989, p. 86)

For Britton, this realization on the part of the child not only entails the recognition of limitations and generational boundaries but also establishes a new functional capacity to shift between different modes of relating and between subjective and objective vantage points: "The acknowledgment by the child of the parents' relationship with each other unites his psychic world, limiting it to one world shared with his two parents in which different object relationships can exist" (Britton, 1989, p. 86). This is a world in which conflict is tolerated.

In contrast, for many patients the development of triangular space is aborted because of their intolerance of the link between the parents. In his formulation, the intolerance results from a fundamental failure of containment by the mother, and consequently, the experience of the mother is split, with the frustrating/non-containing aspect defensively projected into the father. In order to maintain this defensively purified good object, mother and father must not connect. Any hint of a different perspective on the part of the analyst is felt to be an indicator of parental intercourse, and with it, the reconstitution of the non-receptive deadly mother:

> In the early years of her analysis I found that any move of mine toward that which by another person would have been objectivity could not be tolerated. We were to move along a *single line* and meet at a single point. There was to be no lateral movement.
>
> (Britton, 1989, p. 88; italics added)

With the patients that Britton describes, splitting of the non-permeable aspect of the containing mother prevents the recognition of the Oedipal relationship and the development of triangular space. As a result, only a singular perspective is tolerated within the analytic couple, and within the patient's mind. The capacity to register and tolerate internal conflict or different points of view would be seen as an analytic achievement, resulting from a growing recognition and tolerance of the Oedipal situation. However, the conflict from which these patients suffer is not simply Oedipal, but more fundamentally, involves pathology of containment itself. As such, effective treatment requires the therapeutic restoration of containment in relation to the analyst; the latter must provide effective containment, in which the patient's experience can be thought about, and this thinking conveyed to the patient in tolerable form:

> The only way I found of finding a place to think that was helpful and not disruptive was to allow the evolution within myself of my own experience and *to articulate this to myself* whilst communicating to her my *understanding of her point of view*.
>
> (Britton, 1989, p. 89, italics in the original)

Here conflict is present (as a pathogenic agent) as a by-product of a failure of containment, and treatment requires that the process of containment be re-established in a manner tolerable to the patient, ultimately leading to the re-establishment of the capacity for thought (alpha function) in the patient.

Conclusion

In this chapter I have summarized the evolution of Kleinian and post-Kleinian perspectives on conflict that began with Klein's early observation that her child patients suffered from intense conflicts related to hateful, destructive phantasies about their loved objects. This observation led her to a technique and a way of listening that allowed her to see the ubiquity of such conflicts in both children and adults. She posited this fundamental conflict between love and hatred as a kind of psychological bedrock, and because this involves our relation to the object world at its most basic level, Klein shifted her primary focus from the more interpersonally-based conflicts of the 5-year-old Oedipal child to the experiences taking place at the inception of object relatedness in the first year. The familiar Freudian concept of Oedipus complex moved accordingly to the first year, as did the primal origins of the superego. Klein ultimately envisioned the capacity to internalize a whole good object, despite overwhelming feelings of hatred and anxiety, as the most essential psychological achievement, the key determinant of the ongoing capacity for emotional growth.

While contemporary Kleinians write in ways that appear to suggest essential continuity with Klein's basic vision of human conflict, it is my view that their reliance on Bion's concept of the container-contained relationship points to the predominance of his vision of human conflict, which is fundamentally at odds with Klein's. In Bion's view, the kinds of conflicts first described by Klein – those that are involved in pathology, not the quotidian stuff of normal consciousness – tend to result from an environmental failure on the part of the mother in her role as the container that filters and metabolizes the child's initial experience of reality. Love and hatred are not bedrock, in his view. Rather, the drive to know and represent brute reality in bearable form is most fundamental. Children may alternate between affectionate and angry feelings toward parents as a matter of course; this is part of the ordinary flow of life and not, essentially, pathogenic. The breach in psychic experience that results in illness is dyadic in nature and not simply internal to the child. Contrary feelings of love and hate result in illness when the essential equipment for processing emotional experience – a product of early maternal containment – is already broken.

What are the implications of this perspective? I believe they can be found in examining the clinical focus of most contemporary Kleinian writers. As Schafer (1997) has so clearly described, those Kleinians who came of age after Bion began to shift away from a content-focused approach and toward more processive listening and interpreting. They tend to focus preferentially on the transference and, in particular, on the patient's perception of the analyst's experience of their mind. To what extent do they sense the analyst as truly thinking about their thinking? To what extent is a link to the analyst's mind even tolerated? In many of their writings, the fundamental clinical task is revealed to be the re-establishment and internalization of the analyst as a containing object in the face of implacable resistances to this process. With these patients, the basic conflict does not involve hatred of a loved object per se, but rather, hatred of the link to an object experienced as non-containing, and as hatefully rejecting or distorting one's own emotional experience. It is this very specific kind of conflict that is addressed in an analytic treatment, the primary focus of which involves the intersubjective process of knowing and being known.

Notes

1 Eventually M. Klein (1929) will move it even earlier, to the middle of the first year.
2 This sentence arguably represents the beginning of object relations theory as a distinct school of psychoanalysis.
3 According to O'Shaughnessy (2005), London post-Kleinians think highly of Bion's work in the early and middle phases, but part company with him when it comes to his writings about the transformation of O, which they regard as overly mystical. However, as Grotstein (2007) has observed, close examination of the work of Betty Joseph and her followers reveals the extent to which they make use of Bion's notion of transformation, even if the concept of O remains unmentioned.

Chapter 7

Analytic trust, transference, and the importance of conflict

Steven Ellman

The present chapter attempts to provide an explanation for the decreased interest in the concept of conflict in contemporary psychoanalytic thought. In particular, the concept of unconscious conflict is perhaps the greatest recipient of criticism. Perhaps even more fatally than criticism, the concept suffers from neglect in current psychoanalytic theories. My explanation for this neglect proposes that the interest in the "real" relationship occluded interest in pursuing the analysis of conflict. This in part occurred as a reaction to the "American" classical position that derided any aspect of analysis that went beyond the interpretation of unconscious conflict. Classical analysts' restrictive view of analysis produced opposing views that paradoxically led to a widening scope of psychoanalysis by Freudians, such as Zetzel and L. Stone, and by independents in Britain, such as Winnicott (1960b) and Balint (1958, 1968). In the United States, interpersonal and self psychological positions also widened the scope and, in turn, increased the importance of the therapeutic relationship in analysis. All of these analysts led contemporary relational analysts to shift the emphasis on the therapeutic relationship from being an important factor to virtually the only factor in clinical analysis. In what follows I will try to show that this too is a restrictive view of analysis. I will argue that a good enough analysis includes aspects of the therapeutic relationship as well as the interpretation and understanding of unconscious conflict.

In the chapter I will first give a historical view of the difficulties analysts have faced in including both relational and conflictual elements in an ongoing analysis. In the next section I will try to discuss how to reach the point in an analysis where conflict can be usefully interpreted. Here, I define and try to illustrate how one establishes analytic trust. What I have termed *analytic trust* is an important factor in determining the analysand's readiness to utilize interpretive interventions, particularly those interpretive interventions that relate to the ongoing transference. The establishment of analytic trust will then occupy this section of the chapter leading to the following section where the importance of interpretation of conflict will be discussed. In most analyses, conflict is most usefully (meaningfully) interpreted in terms of the ongoing transference. Thus, interpretation of conflict will be discussed most fully in terms of the efflorescence of transference manifestations. The termination phase of analysis will be briefly discussed in terms of analytic trust and the analyst's ability to trust that it is the patient who is eventually his or her own analyst and has to continue the treatment. There will also be an attempt intermittently throughout this chapter to demonstrate how many (most) of the concepts presented can be understood from the theoretical perspective that Bion and Winnicott have put forth.

Historical review

In the heyday of analysis when patients were abundant and the American Psychoanalytic Association was attempting to limit the number of analysts in the United States (Keiser, 1969; Richards,1998), it was usual for analytic institutes to be very careful in their selection of patients who were deemed fit for analysis. This selection process presupposed that analysts knew who benefited from analysis and what actually occurred in and through the analytic process. Perhaps because of these doubtful assumptions and despite the careful selection of patients, the task of determining analyzability was frequently judged more difficult than it appeared in various publications. For Freud, a major criteria for analyzability was the patient's ability to utilize an interpretation (Ellman, 1991). Greenson's (1965) version of the working alliance attempted to judge the patient's ability (willingness) to adhere to analytic prescriptions, that is, free association. In my view compliance was often mistaken for analyzability. In addition, many clinicians did not share the fantasy of being able to assess analyzability or necessarily believe that the criteria that either Freud or Greenson put forth were entirely helpful. It was, therefore, not surprising that L. Stone's (1954, 1961) and Zetzel's (1956, 1971) concepts of the therapeutic alliance were immediately popular; they gave clinicians a method of reaching patients that went beyond the "boundaries of classical analysis."[1] It may be that these "boundaries" prohibited patients who might most benefit from analysis from receiving these benefits (Moskowitz, 1996; Ellman & Moskowitz, 2008). Stone's attempt at widening the scope of analysis in part through concepts like the therapeutic alliance was rejected by Brenner (1979b) and M. H. Stein (1981) as promoting the acceptance of residues of unanalyzed transference. Despite these objections, the gates were opened by these concepts as well as many other concepts straining at the boundaries of the classical position.

As I have tried to show (Ellman, 1991), Freud implicitly recognized that elements that might be considered suggestion were important determinants of his therapeutic results and he, therefore, labeled these elements as *unobjectionable* in different senses of the term. For example, when he labeled certain forms of transference as unobjectionable, he maintained that this form of transference only aided the patient to endure analysis but that the therapeutic results he obtained were derived from the results of his interpretive efforts. He also recognized that the "attitude" of the analyst entered into the patient's ability to be helped in analysis but he avoided fully discussing the factors that might today be called the real relationship (or the relationship depending on one's view of the importance of transference). Although I have stated two seemingly separate factors, Brenner (1979b, 1982b) and M. H. Stein (1981) maintained that despite his protests Freud, to some extent, avoided analyzing the patient's transference manifestations. This was particularly clear in Freud's (1912b) concept of the unobjectionable transference.

In contrast to authors like Stein and Brenner, who have advocated interpreting the transference more fully, at the other end of the continuum some relational analysts have maintained that interpretation of unconscious fantasy is virtually anti-relational (Levenson, 1983; Bromberg, 2008). Thus Bromberg (2008), a relational analyst, states the following:

> Traditionally, thinking in terms of unconscious fantasy demands from an analyst at least implicit loyalty to the belief that the therapeutic action of psychoanalysis is tied to the process of interpretation, and that a patient must be analyzable as a prerequisite.

(p. 139)

Bromberg's comments are illustrative of one end of the analytic spectrum. To develop a differentiated position one must sort out the varied components of this type of position. At this end of the spectrum (relational) analysts tend to deny or downplay the importance of analyzing unconscious fantasy or perhaps deny the existence of unconscious fantasy. Clearly in either alternative the analysis of unconscious fantasy is not an aspect of an analysis. However, the concept of conflict is not coincident with unconscious fantasy. One might see consciousness as divided (split) by conflict. Yet it is possible that even if one sees consciousness as split, one needn't assume that the split is a result of conflict. Thus while it is possible to view splitting as a sign of conflict, concepts like developmental deficit allow one to hypothesize that developmental processes failed to occur and thus structures were never achieved. Adhering to this position one might state that aspects of the therapeutic relationship might be able to facilitate a developmental line that allows the patient to mend or repair this deficit. In the position that I am outlining an analyst downplays the concept of conflict (conscious or unconscious) and, in turn, elevates the importance of the therapeutic relationship.

One might view Bromberg's statements and the assumptions they imply as either a sign of progress in finally understanding the myth of unconscious conflict and unconscious fantasy or as a retreat by psychoanalysts who are unable to deal with unconscious conflict in the psychoanalytic situation. The view that I will present is a compromise suggesting that Bromberg's statement represents a reasonable condensation of the experience of some clinicians attempting to enter the world of patients, particularly patients who are examples of the widening scope of the psychoanalytic world.[2] I will suggest that what is particularly successful in entering the world of patients (who are labeled *narcissistic* or *borderline*) involves some aspect of a focus on the "real" relationship. It is not until one enters the patient's world that the analysis of unconscious conflict is possible (at least most of the time).

The shift in focus naturally moves the clinician away from immediately interpreting conflict and, therefore, for a period of time, necessarily away from the interpretation of unconscious conflict. This "real relationship" focus is frequently considered "good enough" and the treatment is ended before there is a shifting focus on unconscious conflict or any aspect of conflict. Although the treatment may not end abruptly, it may plateau in this way for a period of time. When this occurs, the clinician continues to turn away from the idea of interpreting or even conceptualizing the patient in conflict. Thus, in the treatments that I am imagining, there may be a good deal of progress that both analyst and analysand experience, and an interpretation or the recognition of conflict in any substantial way may seem like an unwelcome intrusion in an ongoing useful analysis. Given this view, one might ask: even if one conceives of unconscious fantasy as important in the person's development, if a treatment can progress without significantly encountering conflict, why would one advocate analyzing conflict, particularly what the analyst believes is unconscious conflict? In the remainder of this chapter I hope to answer this question and maintain that if the analytic pair is truly able to separate, unconscious conflict is a necessary component of an analytic treatment. Here, I must digress regarding the phrase *truly separate*: I don't truly believe that the analytic pair ever fully *separate*, rather there are degrees of autonomy and learning to be comfortable in one's own voice that I am calling separating. More completely, I will elsewhere try to specify how the analytic pair can endure and mourn separation and separateness but this can happen only if the capacity for object love is developed to a reasonable extent.

The establishment of analytic trust

The first task in analysis is to help the patient begin to create a new object relationship in the therapeutic situation (Loewald, 1960; Ellman, 1991, 1997; Bach, 1994). For a utilizable analytic relationship, the patient must penetrate the analyst's psychological world and the analyst must facilitate and be receptive to this penetration. The analyst must also gradually allow this penetration to be perceptible to the patient. This process is at the heart of analytic trust and eventually an utilizable analytic relationship.

The initial phase of analytic trust, then, can be defined as the patient's realistic view of the analyst who can feel their states and, in turn, the patient can experience a place in the analyst's subjective world. (The patient always will have more reactions than the one that I am describing.) This understanding is not communicated primarily in intellectual terms but by the analyst feeling the intensity of the patient's responses and being able to communicate this to the patient. The interpenetration is a necessary condition for the patient to feel held (Winnicott, 1960b). In Bionian terms, it facilitates beta elements being translated into alpha elements. As I will point out in more detail later in the chapter the movement from beta to alpha elements involves what Bion has described as linking.

These experiences and, usually, an experience of containment, are necessary concomitants of trust being built in the analytic situation. Analytic trust is not synonymous with the concept of therapeutic alliance. Therapeutic alliance refers to the patient being allied to the analyst's way of proceeding in the analytic situation. The patient complies with analytic instructions and, as Brenner (1976, 1982b) has stated, this compliance is often related to the patient's transference state. Analytic trust may be established whether the patient is willing to comply with the analyst's instructions.[3] It involves a penetration of subjective states and a communication of this interpenetration. Undoubtedly, analysts can communicate this understanding in different ways and through different theoretical lenses. What follows are examples of pathways to the establishment of analytic trust.

A patient enters a treatment and complains of not being able to use her mind. As soon as she feels she understands something, it changes. She is anxious if the weather changes or if her employer seems to be looking at her in a different way (positive or negative). This woman has just left a treatment where her analyst terminated the treatment. This occurred after she had left various phone messages over a period of months saying that she felt there was something wrong with the treatment. In a phone message, he finally agreed with her and suggested that she see another therapist who could also provide her with help through medication. She saw this therapist for a brief period of time and then found another referring analyst who sent her to me. After weeks of reflecting her bewilderment about these changes, including the change in her previous analyst (who was initially confident of being able to help her), we begin to understand that she wants me to remain the same whatever she may say to me or do in our sessions. She wants to be able to change and have me remain the same. The next two years are spent in my remaining relatively consistent and stable while she attempts in various ways to provoke me and destroy my stability. She is constantly testing to see if she can trust my stability. If I attempt to interpret her provocations she becomes irate and tells me in one form or another that she cannot stand me in this position (an interpretative position). Gradually, she shares her thoughts with me, and at first relates that I hate people.

She goes on to say that I am an analyst because I can be secretly contemptuous of her difficulties. It is only when she can consider and feel that there may be more to me than my hatred and the hatred she has put in me that her transference has reached an interpretable form. Before that, I can only reflect her pain at having to "bare her soul" to someone who is secretly contemptuous of her plight.

In this example, there had to be sufficient holding and containment before her transference manifestations were in interpretable form. During the initial periods, I was limited to reflecting her frightening, horrifying, and enraged states. The earlier sentence is a previous description that I put forth (Ellman, 2010a), but here one might say that the reflection of her states was a way of facilitating the development of alpha elements (see following), which can potentially provide links between patient and analyst. When her hatred was at a high level and threatened to overwhelm her, she frequently evacuated her mind and utilized projective identification as a main defense. Projective identification enabled her to temporarily rid herself of her destructive thoughts, and when they reappeared in her object world they appeared as part of the object's (my) destructive tendencies.

Bion interlude-analytic trust in Bionian terms

In Bion's conceptualization (1963, 1967a,b) thinking (through linking) occurs when alpha elements emerge through a joining of pre-existing perceptual tendencies that create an anticipation, which is met with a realization in external reality (linking). He refers to this as having thoughts that can be used for thinking. However, before we can fully understand linking, we have to realize that for Bion the most primitive experiences are characterized by beta elements that he describes as "thoughts without a thinker" (Bion, 1970). One might say that Bion's concept of beta elements (1967a) is similar to Freud's (1915a, b) "thing" as opposed to "word" representation. For Bion, raw sensory-emotional elements stimulated by the environment are referred to as beta elements, and he maintains that they exist in and of themselves (the thing-in-itself, Bion, 1962a) and prior to thinking. By superimposing the Kantian Ding-an-sich on Freudian and Kleinian theory, Bion posits that pure thoughts have an existence of their own, an existence which is older than the mind which thinks those thoughts – they exist independently of any particular individual. If Kantian thinking isn't your cup of tea one might say that "thoughts without a thinker" is a way of describing a universal genetic tendency that governs primitive or early perceptual states (more accurately sensory states). These universal tendencies are triggered by the environment and form beta elements. The transformation of beta elements into alpha elements allows for linking and thinking (Bion, 1965, 1967a,b, 1977).

The transformation takes place through a containing object; one might consider an infant as the "contained" and a mother as the container. V. Stevens (2010) has described the container as "the mother in a state of reverie" being "capable of withstanding the infant's terror and nameless dread of annihilation in the face of absence, physical, emotional, or cognitive" (p. 521). "This safe place shares many qualities with Winnicott's (1960b) 'maternal holding environment' but adds the notion of a 'thinking couple,' with the emphasis on the mother's capacity to withstand raw emotions and transform them into digestible bits of meaning which can be added to other bits" (V. Stevens, 2010, p. 521). Bion utilizes Klein's concept of evacuation; thus, beta elements that are experienced as concrete[4] can be expelled or projected into other objects. While Klein conceptualized projective identification[5] as an important early means of communication between mother and infant, Bion has extended this concept and emphasized the communicative role of projective identification. Thus beta elements are not simply evacuated but, more important, projected into and re-introjected in a transformed representation or state. The container provides the transformational element and the contained/container is a key aspect of Bionian theory.

Winnicott's (1960b) holding environment provides interesting ideas about how the mother is able to transform beta into alpha elements. His views on object presenting and object utilization describe a maternal figure in a state of reverie that is able to sense the infant's states and respond slightly before or after the infant begins to experience various sensory and physiological conditions. Winnicott's view of illusion might be profitably included in Bion's view of the transformation of elements. Just as I view Freud's bifurcation of thing and word representation as mistaking a dichotomous function for one that is continuous, I would suggest that there are various steps between beta and alpha elements (Ellman, 2010b).

To return more directly to the analytic situation, for affective interpenetration to occur the analyst has to be in state of reverie that is similar to the one Bion has described.[6] His famous phrase to be "without memory or desire" (1967a, p. 17) is an admonition to the analyst to be as much in the present as possible. His suggesting this impossible ideal is one way of placing an end point on a scale. The state of reverie is an important ideal and similar to other ideals that have been put forth. Spillius (1988), an important Neo-Kleinian, has maintained that Bion, in stating this conceptualization, was giving his interpretation of Freud's (1912a) position of the analyst maintaining "evenly hovering attention." If one combined both statements we might conclude that the analyst in reverie puts aside previous conceptualizations and is attendant to internal and external experiences as they arise in the analytic session. From this position, appropriate reflective comments allow the patient to feel present in the analyst's mind. More important when the analyst can return the patient's evacuations in a transformed manner, the possibility of building links is enhanced. The same is true for synthetic comments that start to show how the patient has similar reactions to various people (objects if you prefer) in their present or past experience. Thus reflective, synthetic and containing interventions, all help to build the capacity for linking. Without sufficient capacity for linking, sustained analytic trust is not possible. Put in other terms, linking signifies the emergence of alpha function which, as V. Stevens (2010) puts it, "allows a relationship to be fully experienced. This relationship, then, becomes the verb which links objects, leading eventually to such feelings as envy and jealousy" (p. 525). Although envy and jealousy are featured in this sentence, alpha function allows for linking in a variety of ways and significantly allows for dreaming to take place. If Bion were aware of contemporary sleep research (Ellman, 1991, 2010b) he might revise his statement about dreaming, although his views about dreaming need only little revision. The quality of dreaming in schizophrenic patients has mostly concrete form (Ellman, 1991, 2010b) when compared to dreams elicited from other patients or subjects. Bion in my view is stating that there is a difference in dreams containing mostly beta elements that conform to the differences that Cassirer (1923, 1925) describes in different forms of thinking and Langer (1942) describes when talking about signs and symbols. Both Langer and Cassirer are talking about the difference between thinking that is purely denotative (sign) and thinking that is symbolic and rich with connotative meaning.

To relate Bion's ideas more fully to affective interpenetration it is important to emphasize that affective interpenetration often is more difficult with patients who have a need to destroy the analytic relationship (as well as other relationships in their life). Some patients, before utilizing an analytic treatment, frequently have to survive a sense of betrayal or, in a less dramatic but more continuous manner, the patient has to tolerate a sense of being misunderstood. Bion's ideas about containment are implicitly present in various forms of both Winnicott's and Balint's (1968) formulation about treating the patient who, in Winnicott's (1960b) terms, is "Not well chosen for classical psychoanalysis" (p. 38). Paraphrasing Winnicott, surviving rather than sidestepping or avoiding the destructive aspects of the analysand is a necessary condition for a successful analysis to take place. One has to survive the patient's negative affect but, in the course of survival, it is crucial to be able to return the affect in a manner that is receptively metabolized (Bion, 1977). In more ordinary language, it is important to survive and talk about, for example, the patient's rage without moving away from it or being retaliatory. Of course, this is easily said, not always easily accomplished. In addition "metabolized" rage should include the adaptive aspect of this response.

As vertical splitting becomes more prominent in what many analysts would characterize as borderline experiences, containment becomes the central facet in the beginning phases of treatment. In the treatments that I am alluding to, ruptures are externalized and frequently enacted, and the first rupture that must be endured is one that threatens to break apart the analytic couple. More dramatic splitting presents at least two different issues that lead to difficulties in the analytic situation. Frequently, affect is quickly disposed of in some form of action or in a rapid negation, projection (for me, the correct term is *projective identification*), or rapid oscillation (evacuation) to another state or sense of self and other. Here, the interpenetration of affect is even more important, with the analyst being able to not only experience the affect, but also gradually present it to a patient who has already left the affective state and clearly wants no part of this experience. Frequently, this type of patient kills the affect with action that, at times, involves substance abuse, and it is particularly important to re-experience with the patient, the affective state. This has to be done gradually and in successive approximations. With patients who utilize splitting, dissociative states are common. Gradually, the analyst has to unite these states with reflective comments that show how the patient transitions from one state to another. I have previously given an example of a patient (Ellman, 2010b) who frequently oscillated between states with the aid of drugs.

Clinical examples

This patient, Mr. X, woke up in the morning and snorted cocaine; then, when his agitation grew he would take alcohol to reduce his agitation. Gradually in treatment he could tolerate my bringing him back to situations where he felt slighted or wounded by a colleague or a woman whom he was dating. Mild disagreements were experienced as slights and at times fatal slights. The fatality often involved a relationship or a movement in business where despite his addictions he was financially successful. This was the case because of certain technical abilities that allowed him to function and alternatively feel like one of the princes of the city or, alternatively, part of the city's refuse. His views of his success were so disparate that here we could at times tie together states that were disparate or even contradictory. When talking about a friend who had turned to being perceived as an enemy at times, we first could explore a feeling of being betrayed by someone holding a view that differed from his, particularly if it was around an issue that he felt strongly about.

He might state that he never knew that John was a budding liberal and at first I could only respond and reflect his disappointment or his anger. At a later time I might comment on how he needed a friend to be at one with his political ideas. Even later we talked about an elementary view that it might be possible for one to be a loyal friend and have somewhat (very) different views. "I know that, and you are treating me like an idiot," he said when I would make this elementary point. Here, I responded "Perhaps, but at times you act as if you don't know this elementary perspective. For instance, I remember you telling me how loyal John is and how you liked that about him." This was said to Mr. X at a midpoint toward the end of what I consider to be the opening phase of treatment. Mr. X surprisingly said that this reminded him of times when he would get angry at subordinates' views even when he elicited their views via reports. It was strange, he said, because, "I would ask Betty to write a report on a company and I might resent her for doing it. I don't get it." I said, "Perhaps Betty was thinking for herself – ". He interrupted me and said, "You're right, but there are other things I want to talk about." It was several sessions later when I asked him about Betty's report and why he thought I was right. He told me he felt "a queasy feeling as if things were slipping away," and I said it was difficult for him to stay with that feeling. What was slipping away was the sense that he wanted to have all knowledge in his group residing in his mind and no one else's, but this was a thought that was clarified later in the treatment.

Gradually Mr. X could tolerate divergent thoughts of an elementary kind and when this was true, interpretive interventions started entering my mind. I began to link various aspects of his life that went beyond the here and now of the session and while I was suspicious of this movement, it was here that in retrospect I would say that an analytic third was truly developing.[7] Here, when I mention interpretive comments, I imagine that I am making a comment that involves an unconscious, conflictual element of the patient's functioning. At this point in time I was clearly with both *memory and desire*, and the desire was to help the patient become conscious of conflict that he had defended against for most of his life. His grandiose fantasies were a manifestation of an unconscious desire to possess everything that he needed to be completely self-sustaining. It was an attempt to block out his need for others or to have others as his slaves whom he could sadistically control. At the same time other people's statements that presented contradictory views were seen as aggressive attempts to subdue him and control him. Both elements of this conflict were mostly unconscious in terms of the developmental conditions that led to his conflicted state. However, elements of his conflict frequently moved into consciousness, and when this occurred, splitting and projection (projective identification) became his primary defenses. Thus he could much more easily see others as assaulting him as opposed to his being viewed as the aggressor or sadist.

I am assuming that if my interpretation were good enough, I would be speaking to a process that was also active in him and would activate aspects of his defended-against psyche that would lead us to a new aspect of his mental life. A good interpretation does not gain immediate conscious acceptance but rather leads to new materials or new insights. Thus, although he could not directly (or immediately) accept my intervention (if I was truly relating to an unconscious aspect of his mental life), his subsequent associations might convince him that we had arrived at something important. Frequently with patients like Mr. X a good interpretation is taken over by the patient after a short period of time. It is either something they said or something they always knew. In the process I am trying to describe, analytic trust is strengthened and an emerging third is developing. My assumption about the analytic third is that it is dependent on the patient's being able to see and value others who are separate from his needs and desires. He was beginning to be able to be in that state of mind.

The strengthening of trust gradually leads to two interrelated, somewhat "paradoxical" results; at the same time that the analyst is trusted and included in the analysand's world, both members of the dyad are more comfortable in being separate and both are more comfortable in maintaining separate perspectives. If this separation can be tolerated, it is the birth (or a strengthening) of a reflective self-representation within the analytic situation (and the third). When the patient begins to include me as a separate object in his or her object world, it is then that the possibility opens up to include aspects of the other within what may be the final part of the initial phase of analytic trust.

To more clearly delineate some of the earlier I will remind readers that I am using the term *interpretive* or *interpretation* in a specific manner. Here I mean only those interventions that are designed to delineate or facilitate aspects of the patient's functioning that are defended against in terms of conscious or unconscious processes.[8] The assumption is that unconscious processes are ones that will lead to some initial difficulty in terms of the therapeutic relationship. If the intervention truly speaks to an unconscious process, then at least to some extent the patient will initially (and perhaps for a while) seek to reject some aspect of the communication. The assumption is that interpreting an unconscious process always involves conflict. Trust will be strengthened only if the interpretation leads to some new material that is of interest to the analytic pair. I will leave Mr. X and turn to Dr. A for a clinical example that illustrates the strengthening of trust when an interpretive process occurs, particularly when an aspect of the transference is the subject of the interpretive process. We will then return to the Bionian analysis of the process.

Dr. A was a surgical resident when a senior colleague first referred him to me. He came for a consultation because of an "embarrassing incident" that he did not want to relate to me in his first consultation session. He mentioned to me that he had discussed this event with a previous analyst and the analyst began to question him and began to take a history. In short, the first analyst began to treat Dr. A like a patient and this was clearly a humiliating experience for Dr. A. During our first meeting, he mentioned that he was having some difficulties with his fiancée and with his chief resident. It was important for him to tell me that, despite these difficulties, he was probably going to be chief resident next year and that he already had several excellent job offers.

At the end of our first meeting, he thanked me for my time and told me that I had been of "good value" to him. He said that he thought that he had cleared up his difficulties. Given this somewhat rapid departure, I was surprised when, a week later, he called and asked if he could meet with me another time. When we met he wondered if I had any questions and I wondered what he would like to talk about. After several moments of awkward silence he began to tell me about the "incident." He knew a famous actor from his homeland and he, the actor, and his fiancée went out together one night. For the rest of the session Dr. A described some of his feelings about the fact that the three of them had sex together. His fiancée was very upset that he had agreed to this arrangement. Dr. A was upset that he had been so influenced by this famous man. He began to tell me that famous people had always fascinated him, and that his father is considered a famous patriot in his country. After he told me this the session was almost over, and I asked him whether he wanted to schedule another session. At that point he again rose and thanked me for my help and said that he thought that he was feeling better.

After several consultations, he agreed to try twice-a-week psychotherapy. After eight months, he began a four-times-a-week analytic treatment. He needed no coaxing to use the couch, since he preferred not to see my face. Whenever there was a break that was longer than our normal weekend break, Dr. A would, at the beginning of the session, thank me and tell me that he had decided to end the treatment. He always included the idea that I had been of help to him. Thus, one might say that, for him, every out of the ordinary variation in schedule was experienced as a difficult separation and tended to produce a conflict state that led to a feeling of a rupture in our relationship. Why this was true was one of the central questions in our eight-year treatment.

As the treatment progressed, Dr. A began an idealizing transference where he considered me not only a good analyst but also an outstanding scientist. Most of our sessions had an intermingling of his pain in contemporary relationships and a description of his family life and why he felt that it had been necessary for him to leave his birthplace. It took him a while to begin to tell me about his alcoholism (his alcoholic blackouts) and how, at times, his feelings of humiliation were so strong that he needed to "black" (block) them out. In my mind, although he certainly experienced humiliation, his depressive feelings were much more difficult for him to acknowledge.

At the same time that his idealizing transference was forming, he also began to talk about the alteration of states that would at times overtake him; when he performed a successful operation, for a period of time he fantasized that he was or would be the greatest surgeon in the world. He felt that none of the faculty or attendings had anything to teach him and that soon he would be recognized for his unrivaled talent. If he felt that he made a mistake, he would be extremely worried that he would be demoted to becoming a scrub nurse. It took a period of time for him to talk about why his perceived failures were usually accompanied by the fantasy of

120 Steven Ellman

his becoming a scrub nurse. His mother had been a scrub nurse, and in his move to the US he at first worked as a scrub nurse since he "felt" he could not get any job as an MD until he was licensed. In my mind, his move to the US had some aspect of an identification with his mother, but it was not at all clear as to why I felt this was true. He talked about how his mother had been independent and how both she and his father had affairs. He mentioned a number of things about his past, but none of them seemed to touch his extreme sensitivity to our separations.

Gradually, as the treatment progressed, he began to improve; he broke up with his fiancée and met a woman who eventually became his wife. His alcoholic bouts (and blackouts) were mostly a thing of the past, and his relationships with his peers and supervisors (now partners) had greatly improved. However, he still quit analysis at each separation, and this was something that did not seem to be able to be interpreted away.

After a long period in treatment I began to note his selfobject transference where we were both famous clinicians and scientists. Slowly, we began to understand some of the early roots of his grandiosity and how he used it to bolster his oscillating self-esteem. His real accomplishments now seemed more genuine to him, and at times he was genuinely proud of his successes. His ability to endure transference interpretations increased his trust in the process, since he now could feel that he could tolerate something that was distressing that did not accord with his conscious thoughts. Other thoughts could be of value to him, and the therapeutic relationship could survive the crisis of differences. The differences were that, at the time of the interpretations, we had different views about the nature of our interaction. It was previously quite difficult for him to tolerate opinions that were different from his opinions.

After his residency (his third year in treatment) he was offered a professorship at a good medical school, and there he did both clinical work and research. At the end of the fourth year of the analysis, the patient decided to get married. At this same time, he was offered a job in another state. Accepting the post meant that he would have to stop analysis. It was not clear to him (or to me) that this opportunity was one that would be of benefit to him. Nevertheless, he seemed compelled to take this job with what seemed like diminished clinical and research possibilities compared to the position he held in the New York area. I, of course, wondered about my reaction to the idea of what I considered to be his unilateral termination (or premature termination). He seemed determined to go forward on this

Analytic trust, transference, and conflict   121

path until a long separation (two weeks) occurred and he had the following dream:

> You were giving a lecture and it seemed to me – at least I thought that
> you were doing well – I was in the audience and watching you. For
> some reason I was watching your face and your expressions seemed
> vacant [he said a version of vacuous] . . . The audience was enthusias-
> tic but you still seemed not to respond and then suddenly . . . I was in
> Moscow [his home city] and I thought this is the most beautiful city
> in the world.

Although by that time he was someone who found value in dreams, he
began to say how this dream was meaningless and how this time he was
serious and that "analysis had gone as far as it could go." I said to him that
he talked about analysis as if it was person or a thing separate from us,
and he belittled my remark. I could feel that I was annoyed with Dr. A. I
said that if he wanted to leave it was certainly his right and there was nothing that I could do about it (I said some other things that must have been
angrier because I did not write them down). After this clipped, enacted
interchange, things in the session shifted and Dr. A began to talk about an
operation he had just performed, then he said that it seemed to him that I
looked sick. He said that he was not sure why he thought that, but it came
to his mind that when he came into the office that I looked sick. It seemed
to me that we were back in the dream, and I commented that, in the dream,
even though things seemed to be going well for me, I seemed sick or at
least non-responsive. He, at that point, became quite sad and said that he
really felt that I had helped him a great deal and that he wanted to know
in reality, not in the dream, whether I was sick. I said to him that dream
was very real to him and it was beginning to feel real to both of us. Perhaps
he thought that I was ill because he was planning to leave me or perhaps
because we had just separated? He was somewhat disoriented, and the session ended with my feeling that something important had happened, but I
was not sure what it was.

In the next session, he began by saying that he was disappointed that I
did not answer his question and that he never seems to have my full attention. This seemed odd to me, and again I was reminded of the dream from
the session the night before. I said that this time it seems that his reaction
to our separation was where he felt that I was unresponsive to him and

then excused me by saying that I must be sick. He said that he thought that I was sick even though he knew (sort of) that perhaps I wasn't. I mentioned that he never talked about how he felt when our separations occurred. He began to talk about an event in his life when he said that he had a dream about his mother and she was there but not really moving. He described this dream and some of his thoughts for a long while and then paused. The thought that occurred to me seemed far-fetched, but I said to him that I thought that at some point in his life his mother was sick or depressed and that no matter how good an audience he was for her he couldn't please her. Moreover, in the dream about me, he was also the audience and wondered if he could really please me; if he could, perhaps I would never leave him. This led to a string of thoughts (some were memories) about how he remembered and was told how precocious he was as a child. He also remembered how he was unable to tolerate criticism when he went to school. He would begin to cry if he made a mistake. We began to realize that with his (maternal) teachers he needed always to please them, and if he was told that he was wrong, or did not understand something, the fear of (maternal-derived) separation surfaced. Over a period of several sessions we put together a reconstruction where his mother was taken away ill (I thought depressed), and that he fantasized that he had not been delightful enough (his word from another language). In my terms, he had not delighted her enough and so he thought that she left him for others.

Later that year, his mother visited him (for the first time in several years) and he asked her about this and she told him that she had been depressed after the birth of his sister and was hospitalized for at first a month, and when that was ineffective, she was hospitalized for several additional months after being home for only two or three weeks between hospitalizations.

This transference-countertransference sequence, which led to a reconstruction, was a turning point in the treatment. A number of issues around sibling and Oedipal rivalry gradually emerged and, as they emerged in different contexts, they occurred in an increasingly object related manner. His somatic delusion (that he had chronic syphilis from the age of 17 to the present, a delusion that, even though he knew it was an impossibility, he held on to until 4½ years into the treatment) gradually was understood as a damaged penis unable to really delight his mother or any other woman in a continuous manner. It was also seen as a punishment for his desire to be delighted by or receive pleasure from a woman. His homosexual concerns were, in part, a wish to be willing to tolerate assistance from a man who would help him navigate the difficulties of keeping a woman happy. His idealizing transference had largely homosexual underpinnings, both in the sense of Freud's use of the term in normal narcissistic development, and in his conflict about submitting to the powerful male (the famous male). Repair of the maternal rupture that was continuously reproduced in the treatment situation was, nevertheless, key to allowing other issues to effloresce in the transference.

I have presented the case of Dr. A for two overlapping reasons:

(1) To try to illustrate that the analysis of conflict at times requires a good deal of preparation;
(2) To illustrate how my therapeutic actions can be described in Bionian terms.

I have tried to spell out how the development of analytic trust was necessary for Dr. A to dream and then subsequently utilize a transference interpretation. I would consider the years of reflection, synthesis, and containment as helping move beta to alpha elements and then allowing linking to occur. In this case linking occurred at one point dramatically through dreaming. This dream encapsulated his desire to have his mother's complete attention and his anger and depression that others captivated her. This trauma was embedded in his conflicted wish to be the center of all of the groups in which he participated. At the same time that he wished to be central he was at times overwhelmingly guilty about wanting and needing this attention. He was also quite ashamed of his sense of mortification if he was not sufficiently acknowledged. His underlying masochism was evidenced early in the treatment when he had to submit to his famous compatriot and offer him his fiancée. Of course, there are more conflicted components to this action but for present purposes it is important to state that unless conflicts are analyzed the patient will not really be able to be his or her own analyst in the years subsequent to the completion of the analysis.

Here with Dr. A as well as the other patients that I have used to illustrate the different components of analytic trust, the eventual analysis of conflict was important to completing a fuller analytic process. Dr. A's conflicted desire for his mother's attention was importantly experienced in the transference. This allowed for Oedipal conflicts to emerge and become the central aspect of the continuing analysis. Each of the components of the subsequent analysis dealt with the Oedipal conflicts with which he has lived and enacted. Thus the early achieving of analytic trust is sometimes

124 Steven Ellman

taken as a full therapeutic result. This is understandable for while the patient is in a usable selfobject transference their functioning is considerably improved. However, in my view, analysis of conflict leads to a higher probability of a lasting analytic result. It also widens the patient's ability to continue the analytic process after the actual analysis has finished.

Whether the analysis is continued after the treatment is finished is in part determined by how the analytic pair traverses the termination phase of the treatment. Here the shift is that the analyst begins to trust that the analysand is able to conduct the treatment and utilize what the analytic pair has discovered. This is not meant to imply that the analyst is totally passive but rather that he or she allows the shift toward the patient becoming to a greater extent the interpreting member of the analytic pair. To the extent that this can occur it strengthens the bonds of analytic trust while at the same time allowing for the pair to separate (Ellman & Moskowitz, 2008).

Concluding comments

A compelling aspect of Bion's thought is movingly (and clearly) described by Birksted-Breen (2012) where she maintains that the theory of reverie is the analytic third of the treatment situation. She looks at what she calls *here-and-now* interventions and maintains that "so called 'here and now' interpretations cover a . . . range of types of interpretations. I speak of . . . technique . . . that is characterized by frequent interventions aimed at describing the patient's experience . . . toward the analyst throughout the session." She describes these interventions as "a particular way of conceiving of the transference interpretation" (p. 820). In my view she notes with implicit and mildly stated alarm the "frequent interventions aimed at describing the patient's experience towards the analyst throughout the session" (p. 820). She then argues that the rise of interest in using an approach that utilizes the frequent interventions as described by Busch (2011) and Blass (2011) makes it "particularly essential that analytic attention be rooted in the kind of temporality engendered by the analyst's evenly suspended attention," or reverie.

Birksted-Breen in her critique tries to show that a variety of authors have indicated the need for space in the analytic situation (Winnicott, 1967; Britton, 1989). She as well as Spillius (1988) note that Bion's concept of reverie is an outgrowth or at least strongly related to Freud's (1912b) idea of evenly suspended attention. Both concepts put the analyst in a state of allowing interpenetration of affect and attempting to feel and understand the meaning of interpenetration. Birksten-Breen sees the type of technique exemplified by Busch (2011) as not allowing for a true interpenetration of affect. Rather this type of over-engaging analyst makes it difficult for the patient to truly experience his or her own endogenous, or internal, states. I would perhaps go a step further and maintain that the technique that requires frequent interventions in the manner described by Busch (2011) makes evenly suspended attention or reverie difficult, perhaps impossible to achieve. This is also true for Arlow's mode of listening for continuity of themes. Now this may seem like a surprising statement since I have tried to show that reflection, synthesis, and containment are necessary for the development of analytic trust. One might say that Busch uses some of the same types of interventions. Here the difference could be described in the frequency of intervention but, more important, in the type of analytic theory that is carried as your third (a third in Birksted-Breen's terms). In my view, Kohut (1971, 1977; Bach, 1994) or a version of defense analysis (Gray, 1964) is a way of entering the patient's world, creating a world of intersubjectivity. This is not an end point but rather a way station that helps the patient become able to tolerate interpretations of conflict and utilize the interpretation of consistent transference states. The analyst moving in and out with frequent interventions interferes with these states. There are, of course, times when frequent interventions seem like the only way to preserve the analysis, but this is different from the analytic third that Birksted-Breen is relating to the analytic community. Her third is an attempt to relate an analytic attitude that allows an analysis to continue even when the process seems extremely difficult. I find her use of the analytic third interesting and although I have used the term in a different manner (Ellman, 2010b), it may be that her concept is a more enduring use of the term. I include Birksted-Breen's analysis to emphasize that the development of analytic trust at the beginning part of treatment is not an end of treatment but rather a way of allowing the analyst to enter the patient's world so that conflict can be usefully interpreted. Moreover, it is not a theory that advocates frequent interventions but rather interventions that can be felt and shared by the analytic couple. Usually at the beginning of treatment or when moving to a new transference state the emphasis is not on the patient's reaction to the analyst. This typically takes some time to accept and utilize.

In conclusion, an interesting aspect of Bion's thought is both his emphasis on the truth and paradoxically on the unknowable aspect of the truth

126   Steven Ellman

(O). Here again it is hard to follow Bion as he leaps off the cliff, but watching his ride is exhilarating and at the same time instructive. His admonition is always to open one's mind and leave behind the well-worn "truths" that theory proclaims must be correct. Now this may seem to contradict Birksted-Breen's third. I would argue that, in fact, it is the opposite. Her third argues not for theoretical answers but an analytic attitude that is derived from, in my opinion, the best of Freud and Bion. My view of the concept of analytic trust is hopefully derived from Bion, Freud, Winnicott, and a variety of other analysts who have helped me understand that entering the world of the patient is necessary but not sufficient for a full analysis. The interpretation of conflict (unconscious conflict) allows for both the understanding and working through of internalized struggles and also strengthens analytic trust. Of course, Bion's ideas of linking and containment are crucial for this process to occur.

Notes

1 Unfortunately even an eminent analyst such as Akhtar (2009) has equated the working alliance and the therapeutic alliance. Greenson was proposing a way of gaining the patient's acceptance while at the same time evaluating the patient. Zetzel and L. Stone, on the other hand, were attempting to talk about a state of the patient that might be induced by the appropriate analytic attitude. Unfortunately neither Stone or Zetzel made this point with enough clarity.
2 Or, in other terms, patients who would not have been considered analyzable in the past.
3 Christian (personal communication) has suggested that one could argue that a sign of analytic trust is the patient's willingness to disagree with the analyst's instructions. I agree with this point.
4 Here the meaning of *concrete* is similar to Susan K. Langer's concept of sign as opposed to a symbol (1942). She uses Cassirer's (1923, 1925) concepts of symbols having multiple connotative connections as opposed to a sign which stands only for the thing itself. Clearly Cassirer was in many ways presenting a theory (in Bion's terms) of linking.
5 Klein's main emphasis was projective identification as an early defensive process.
6 Many contemporary authors such as Ogden (1997) and Ferro (2009) have movingly described the state of reverie in the analytic situation.
7 In this chapter I am unfortunately doing something that I railed against in a recent publication (Ellman, 2010a). I do not have the latitude to discuss my views on intersubjectivity and the analytic third except to say that from my theoretical lens both concepts imply a development in the analytic situation as well as in terms of theories about childhood development. I rail against the idea of inserting a term without clearly defining the term.
8 I am using the term *defended* and the defense may be seen as either separating conscious states (splitting) or keeping an aspect of the person's representational unconscious. In either case the person is not conscious of the defensive process and so I will use the term *unconscious processes*.

Chapter 8

Emergence of conflict during the development of self

A relational self psychology perspective

James L. Fosshage

Since its inception, Freudian psychoanalysis has held that inner conflict is central to psychological life.[1] In S. Freud's (1923) tripartite model the primary constituents of conflict are the instinctual drives pushing for discharge, the social and, subsequently, the superego's prohibitions against expression of these instinctual wishes, and the ego's defensive regulatory efforts. This ego psychological model has remained the most prominent model in American Psychoanalytic Association's Institutes to the present day.

On a descriptive level, most psychoanalysts would agree with H. Hartmann's (1939) statement, "conflicts are part of the human condition" (p. 12); yet differences abound when considering sources of conflict, its primary constituents, and its centrality in psychological life and therapeutic action.

Kohut (1982) took strong exception to Freud's view of man's lifelong conflict between "the drives that spring from the biological bedrock . . . and the civilizing influences emanating from the social environment as embodied in the superego" (p. 402). He proposed an alternative model that "man's essence is defined when seen as a self . . . attempting, and never quite succeeding, to realize the program laid down in his depth during the span of his life" (p. 402). Whereas Freud believed that intergenerational strife and conflict, as manifest in the Oedipus complex, is fundamental to man, Kohut declared, "It is the primacy of the support for the succeeding generation . . . which is normal and human, and not intergenerational strife and mutual wishes to kill and to destroy" (p. 404). A father is "committed to the next generation, to the son in whose unfolding and growth he joyfully participates – thus experiencing man's deepest and most central joy, that of being a link in the chain of generations" (p. 403). Whereas Freud viewed intrapsychic and intergenerational conflict to be central, Kohut asserted that development of the self within a self-selfobject (relational) matrix and intergenerational support was primary.

The topic of this chapter is to address how the primary sources and constituents of conflict as well as its role are understood within self psychology. I will briefly delineate the self psychological model and track its evolution in order to establish a context for understanding the conceptualization of conflict, its sources, and role. I will organize my discussion around the following topics: primary elements of conflict, development of self, organization of experience, motivation, and theory of therapeutic action. Throughout my discussion I will especially highlight clinical implications and close with a clinical vignette for illustrative purposes.

Primary elements of conflict

At the most general level, intrapsychic conflict in ego psychology is theoretically and clinically central; modern conflict theory (Brenner, 1982b, 2006) has further emphasized the omnipresence of conflict in life and the analytic situation.

In contrast, development and maintenance of the self within a self-selfobject matrix is theoretically and clinically central in the self psychology model. Kohut's (1971, 1977) early conceptualization of the self-selfobject matrix provided the foundational structural framework of a relational model that has subsequently evolved more fully into what I (Fosshage, 1992) and others (including Bacal, 1998a; Shane et al., 1998) have called relational self psychology. Relational approaches in general propose that conflict primarily emerges out of relational experience that subsequently becomes internalized. Relational experience is composed of the interaction of two or more subjectivities (Atwood & Stolorow, 1984), each bringing to the interaction motivations, perceptions, affects, and previously established patterns of organizations of experience or implicit procedural knowledge.

While unlimited possibilities for conflict exist, the primary elements of *conflict* in Kohut's (1982) self psychology are posited to be the individual's striving "to unfold his innermost self, battling against external and internal obstacles to its unfolding" (p. 403). Emerging within relational systems, the principal source of conflict involves a relational thwarting or obstruction of a child's needs and strivings to develop and maintain the self. For example, when a child's affective experience is not met with a relational "home" (Socarides & Stolorow, 1984) – that is, recognized, understood, and related to – a child is deeply conflicted between what is experienced as required abdication of her (or his) affective experience to maintain a self-object tie and remaining connected to her affective experience, potentially jeopardizing a needed selfobject connection. Similarly, if a parent mistakenly attributes an intention to a child, the child is placed in a conflictual situation of either asserting or abandoning her experience. In another conflictual situation, an adult patient of mine described how as a boy he had submitted to his father's angry, brutal spankings for fear that any objection on his part would exacerbate his father's rage and intensify the beatings. While deeply conflictual, submission was experienced as a self-protective adaptation. Once conflictual relational experience becomes internally organized (structuralized), conflict can emerge primarily intrapsychically as well as contribute to its repetition in future relational encounters including, of course, the analytic relationship (to be further discussed under the rubric "Organization of Experience").

Development of the self within a self-selfobject matrix

Kohut (1977, 1984) placed at the center of psychological development *"the self"* striving "to realize its intrinsic program of action" within "self-selfobject" relationships "in the course of its life span" (p. 42). The self refers to an experiential center of initiative, personal agency, organization, and action. His conception of the self emphasized both constitutional and relational origins. The "intrinsic program of action" refers to hard-wired factors – some are universal (e.g., mirroring, idealizing, and twinship selfobject needs) and some are unique to the individual (e.g., talents, temperament, and capacities). When Kohut referred to the development of the self, he did not mean development of any self, but rather development of the individual's unique self in keeping with its intrinsic program.

The realization of the self requires relationships, called self-selfobject relationships (Kohut, 1984). Kohut defined selfobjects as the use of the other to provide certain functions pertaining to the development and maintenance of the self. "Self psychology holds that self-selfobject relationships form the essence of psychological life from birth to death" (p. 47). They are so crucial in the psychological sphere to the development and maintenance of the self throughout the life span that they are likened to oxygen in the biological sphere (Kohut, 1984). Thus, "The developments that characterize normal psychological life must, in our view, be seen in the changing nature of the relationship between the self and its selfobjects, but not in the self's relinquishment of selfobjects" (p. 47). This conceptualization of self and selfobject relationships thus addresses a pivotal dimension of relational experience that is central to normal and pathological development, transference, and therapeutic action. The origins of the most significant conflicts from a self psychological perspective involve self and selfobject relationships. Correspondingly, infant research has illuminated the powerful impact of the mother's responsive attunement or misattunement to the infant (Beebe & Lachmann, 2002).

Kohut (1984) postulated that the fundamental motivation is a striving to "realize the nuclear self and its program of action" (p. 42). A child needs to be seen, acknowledged, recognized, and affirmed by parents or parental surrogates to feel worthwhile and capable, which are referred to as mirroring selfobject needs. To feel capable, in turn, promotes ambitions. A child also needs from a parent a sense of protection, security, and safety, called idealizing selfobject needs. Selfobject needs gradually mature throughout a lifetime. A child's idealizing selfobject needs, for example, mature from a requirement for an all-powerful, all-protective parent to a parent who has admirable qualities that become a source for formation of ideals. In his last book, Kohut (1984) identified twinship selfobject needs, that is, an experience of essential likeness, whether it be a part of a family, peer group, or community, that contributes to the development of the self. Arrests in the development of the self occur when selfobject needs are significantly thwarted, resulting in deficits in self-structure.

The impact of trauma on psychological development, for Kohut (1984), depended on its frequency and severity, the responsiveness of the selfobject surround, and on the "ability of the self" (p. 42) to maintain itself in the face of adversity, also called resilience (Fajardo, 1991; DiAmbrosio, 2006). Kohut (1984) believed that "in the presence of a firm self, conflict per se is by no means deleterious" (p. 45). Conflict can challenge and stretch a person with a sufficiently firm self to find creative solutions that, in turn, contribute to the development of further capacities and strengthening of the self. Lachmann (1986) has identified what he called an "adversarial selfobject" that challenges and stretches a person in a manner that is self-enhancing. And from an evolutionary perspective, Slavin and Kriegman

(1992) posit that conflict between people's self-interests is a basic constituent of human existence.

From a self psychological perspective patients seek psychoanalytic treatment with a fundamental striving to overcome internal and external encumbrances and to further self-development. In the beginning of treatment, Kohut (1984) found that patients are often defensive or protective as they anticipate that past hurts will likely be repeated in the analytic relationship. Developmental strivings are in conflict with expectations of hurt and undermining responses based on past experience, expectations that require (defensive) self-protection. These dynamics are typically operative at an unconscious level, requiring an interpretive lifting of these "transference resistances" that, in turn, enable emergence of selfobject needs and the formation of selfobject transferences. Once a selfobject transference had been established Kohut (1977, 1984) focused on the subsequent rupture/ repair cycles that became the mainstay of his theory of therapeutic action. He understood that ruptures are triggered by the analyst's empathic failures and that the restoration of understanding and explanation will repair the ruptures and the selfobject connection. During "optimal" ruptures Kohut hypothesized that the patient internalizes the selfobject functions of the analyst, expanding the capacity for self-regulation, and simultaneously learns that ruptures are reparable, facilitating the development of the self, its resilience and elasticity. Later, Kohut (1984) added that ongoing selfobject experience in the psychoanalytic situation creates a second avenue of therapeutic action, what we refer to today as new relational experience.

Kohut posited that the thwarting of selfobject needs principally interfered with the development of the self and created deficits in self-structure, limiting a person's capacity to self-regulate and thrive. Subsequently, the question emerged as to what happens to these negative experiences of selfobject failure. Do they simply disappear, leaving deficits in their wake, or are they registered in memory and organized into a different sort of self-structure? While consistent thwarting of selfobject needs can arrest the development of "the self," creating deficits in self-structure, it simultaneously is organized into negative self and self-with-other schemas (see Atwood & Stolorow, 1997). For example, when a child expresses her feelings and is met with her father's domineering response, "That's not what you feel!" the child can easily feel undermined, questioning her feelings as well as experiencing shame for having such feelings. To capture these repetitive negative as well as positive experiences of self, contemporary or relational self psychologists gradually shifted to the use of a more phenomenological term – *sense of self* – and spoke of its affective coloration, cohesiveness, and continuity (Stolorow et al., 1987). Thus, clinically, relational self psychologically oriented analysts recognized that they must identify these negative or devitalizing self organizations and interaction patterns and their relational experiential origins, facilitating a patient's reflective awareness and gradual extrication from them in order to co-create, integrate, and consolidate a more positive, vitalized cohesive sense of self. Whereas Brandchaft (Brandchaft et al., 2010) noted that "Kohut establishes a basis for a developmental psychology of the self that encompasses both deficit and conflict" (p. 54), relational self psychologists (and intersubjectivists) have added these devitalizing self and self-with-other organizations as a primary source of conflict with developmental strivings (to be discussed further under the rubric "Organizations of Experience").

While the term *sense of self* more comprehensively captures the range of self-experience, it fails to address directly the potentially unique hard-wired aspects of self-experience that were an integral part of Kohut's original vision (Fosshage, 2003a, 2011a; Summers, 2011). The nature/nurture issue is far from resolved and I (Fosshage, 1992, 2003a, 2011a) especially emphasize the importance of addressing constitutional issues, supported by more sophisticated, detailed research, to sensitize us in identifying and respecting the core uniqueness of each individual in our analytic work.

In a further development of what we call relational self psychology, the term *selfobject* has also been gradually redefined. Stolorow et al. (1987) re-conceptualized the selfobject relationship as not a separate type of relationship but as a dimension of all relationships, called the *selfobject dimension of relationships* that oscillates between foreground and background of experience depending on the self-needs of an individual. Furthering a phenomenological emphasis (Lichtenberg, 1991; Lichtenberg et al., 1992), re-conceptualized "selfobject" as "selfobject experience," referring essentially to vitalizing experience. Selfobject experience addresses a wider range of experience, from solitary (e.g., exercise, writing a paper) to more immediate relational experience. Essentially we refer to the vitalizing and devitalizing dimension of experience, a dimension of experience that is crucially important for the development and maintenance of a positive, thriving sense of self.

The development of a vitalized, cohesive sense of self involves a number of developmental processes. Recently, on the basis of infant research Lichtenberg et al. (2015) have delineated 12 developmental processes that begin during the first year of life and continue to be relevant throughout the life span. They include emergence of a sense of self as a feeling, embodied doer – doing with others and self (a sense of personal agency); sensing that one's self and significant others have a positive identity based on affirming attributions; a capacity to feeling known and recognized for one's authentic qualities; gaining confidence that disruptions in relationships and pursuits will be repaired and a more optimal context restored; and a capacity for forming and sharing narratives.

Organization of experience

It is commonly accepted that human beings, among other animals, learn from and organize experience to negotiate and adapt to future experience and changing contexts. A host of variables contribute to our moment-to-moment experience, including shifting motivations, perceptions, affects, thoughts, meanings, actions, past learning, established organizations, temperament, events, relational interactions, and context. Organization of experience, occurring throughout waking and sleeping, is primary in the formation and transformation of selfhood.

Learning and memory processes are principle organizers of experience. Psychoanalysts have tended to be averse to the term *learning*, equating it with explanations of behavior in terms of learned stimulus/response connections. Earlier studies of classical and operant conditioning viewed the animal as a black box and failed to include how the animal mediated these connections. Now, the mediating black box has been opened up, and animals are seen as having affects, motivations, and organizing and memory processes (Panksepp, 1998), all of which variously affect learning. Cognitive scientists now view operant and classical conditioning as complex learning processes.

Most revolutionary is the empirical finding that perceptual/cognitive/affective processing occurs simultaneously at two levels of awareness, an unconscious (implicit) as well as conscious (explicit) level. Discovery of the implicit level has expanded the realm of unconscious affective/cognitive processing far beyond Freud's dynamic unconscious. "Contemporary researchers," Drew Westen (2006) writes, "recognize that most processing occurs outside of awareness, as the brain processes multiple pieces of information in parallel" (p. 444). In addition to waking cognition, REM and dream research has amply demonstrated that REM and non-REM and corresponding dream activity continue cognitive/affective processing during sleep (Palombo, 1978; Fosshage, 1983, 1997a, 2007; Winson, 1985; R. Greenberg, 1987; Fiss, 1989, 1990; Kramer, 1993; E. Hartmann, 1998; Hobson, 1999, 2013; among others). Recognition of implicit and dream, in addition to explicit, processing creates a picture of a fluid, plastic brain always processing, integrating, and organizing experience through multiple pathways.

We refer to implicit and explicit thematic experiential learning that variably shapes current and future perceptions, reactions, affects, meanings, and actions as organizing patterns (Piaget, 1954; Wachtel, 1980; Stolorow & Lachmann, 1984/85; Fosshage, 1994), expectancies (Lichtenberg et al., 1996, 2002, 2011), attitudes (Fosshage, 2013; Coburn, 2014), and interaction patterns (Fosshage, 1995; D.N. Stern et al., 1998; Beebe & Lachmann, 2002). How do organizing patterns function? We establish expectancies on the basis of lived experience that, in turn, dispose us to attend selectively to cues that correspond with those expectancies, to attribute meanings to those cues that correspond with the expectancies, and to interact, often implicitly, in a manner that confirms the original expectancies (Fosshage, 1994). Organizing patterns are essential for adaptively negotiating our lives in ever-changing relational contexts and fundamentally contribute to a sense of self, a sense of others, and a sense of being in the world.

Learning processes, implicit and explicit, are primary in all relational models of development and pathogenesis. Learning involves organization of experience much of which is used for purposes of negotiation and adaptation. A range of motivations and affects, of course, is variously activated and influence interaction and learning processes. For example, a frequently rageful parent can trigger fear and aversion that impacts the interaction, what is learned, the establishment of expectancies, and constructions of future experience. Learning processes, in my view, are generally underappreciated and even viewed pejoratively, perhaps especially by psychoanalysts who hold a "drive/structure model" (J. Greenberg & Mitchell, 1983), for the latter assumes intrapsychically-generated drive-driven fantasies that distort the child's experience of parents and others. Positing the ubiquity of conflict, defensive processes, and compromise formations, modern conflict theory positions the analyst to question the veracity or actuality of the patient's reported experience and requires that the analyst get behind the defenses – contributing to an aura of distrust or "suspicion" in the analytic relationship (Wachtel, 2008). In contrast, self psychologists with their emphasis on the empathic listening/experiencing perspective attest to the importance of believing patients' reported experiences at least as an aspect of *their* experience, to be further explored in understanding its various constituents and etiology – contributing to an aura of "trust" in the analytic relationship (Orange, 2011) (an analytic attitude of distrust is still maintained by many proponents of relational/ structure models, what Wachtel, 2008, calls a default position). These differences, of course, are sharply portrayed in the Freud/Ferenczi controversy over fantasy or seduction as the primary explanation of the genesis of sexual-abuse trauma.

Traumatic and/or repetitive learning offers an easily accessible, parsimonious explanation of how certain attitudes become intractable. In contrast to the common assumptions of ego psychology, object relations and self psychology that the patient, respectively, is "resisting change," "holding on to object ties," or "holding on to selfobject ties," to explain to a patient that the intractability of a particularly problematic self-percept is related to learning based on, for example, endless repetitions throughout childhood, makes for an easily understood and palatable explanation. Additional understandings that a patient is "holding on" to the attitude to maintain an object or selfobject tie might also be revealed through further exploration.

In addition to disruption or arrests of developmental processes (Kohut's emphasis), recognizing that developmental arrest experience also forms unconscious and conscious devitalizing attitudes of self and self-with-other has increased the complexity of the analytic task. Psychoanalytic treatment from a relational self psychological perspective must identify and bring to reflective awareness those devitalizing organizing themes or attitudes and their relational origins to undermine their felt reality. Increased reflective awareness can gradually enable a person to intercede consciously to deactivate a devitalizing attitude. This process, however, is formidable. Devitalizing psychological organizations are established on the basis of lived experience that involves thousands of repetitions over the childhood years and/or are traumatically based affectively-peak experiences. When a child does not feel seen or does not feel heard, selfobject needs motivate the child to try again and again to obtain the needed mirroring parental response; yet with established expectations that the parent will be unresponsive and fail, the need to protect oneself from further trauma directly conflicts with developmental strivings. The child could feel angry yet conflicted about expressing anger for fear of further jeopardizing hope for a selfobject connection. In the face of further thwarting, the child could deflate and protectively withdraw. Conflict is an integral part of this experience. The ingredients of conflict involve a fundamental striving to seek the needed nutrients for development and regulation of self in tension with previous or current relational thwarting of these needs, the establishment and activation of expectancies that the past will repeat itself, potentially exposing a person to a frightening re-traumatization that requires self-protection. Within this model defenses function to protect the self. Defenses are not viewed as resistances but rather as important self protectors. The primacy of self-protection tends to elicit an analyst's understanding and acceptance during the exploration and understanding of the relational origins of the patient's experienced threat.

For example, a number of years ago a man in his mid-forties came to me shortly after leaving a previous analysis during which he had become more depressed and on the verge of losing his business. During the second session he was disparaging himself for not going out to sell his business – how could he expect to survive if he didn't go out and knock on doors? I asked him what his fantasy was if he knocked on a door. He immediately exclaimed, "They would shut the door on my foot!" I responded, "With a fantasy like that it is only prudent to stay home!" He laughed and with a sigh of relief replied, "No one ever said that!" I was making clear that his expectancies, not his self-protection, was the problem. We then focused on the origins of his expectations.

When parents' responses consistently undermine implicitly and explicitly a child's perceptual, affective, and cognitive experience, a child's need for mirroring increases. In the face of parents' insistent agendas, a child will ultimately abdicate his or her own experience and "pathologically accommodate" (Brandchaft, 1994, Brandchaft et al., 2010) to parents in attempts to secure the needed attachment/selfobject tie – accommodation in service of adaptation. It is tantamount to selling one's soul in an effort to save it. To call the accommodation "pathological" is unfortunate, for accommodation occurs to assure survival. From an object relations perspective, Winnicott (1960a) described a similar conflictual process resulting in the development of the "false self."

Different attitudes learned, for example, from mother and father, parents and teachers, or parents and peers can easily conflict. Or, for example, different attitudes communicated explicitly in content and implicitly in tone create conflict. These conflicts and their origins must be brought to reflective awareness for understanding, assessment, and conscious resolution.

An analysand working to free herself from negative self-attitudes, negative attitudes toward others, and problematic interaction patterns requires giving up the stabilizing influence of these familiar, well-learned, and reinforced psychological organizations and, in some instances, attachment to the parent to whom the analysand, as a child, had accommodated – frightening and conflictual processes. To the degree that patients have needed to forfeit themselves and have lost touch with themselves, the therapeutic task is to help patients reconnect to their own experience through close tracking of their intentions, affects, perceptions, and meanings, all of which contribute to a developing sense of self as a center of initiative, personal agency, and control.

Motivation

Motivation plays a central role in our lives, for motives are primary in directing and giving meaning to our thoughts and actions. *Motives* or *intentions* (equivalent terms) refer to an experiential sense of desiring and choosing goals and taking action to achieve these goals (Lichtenberg, 1989, 2002; Boston Change Process Study Group (BCPSG), 2008). Successful action evokes positive affect, contributing to a sense of personal agency. In our daily lives we experience a kaleidoscope of shifting desires, urges, aims, and strivings.

Cognitive scientists (e.g., Bruner, 1986, 1990, 2002) and infant researchers (Meltzoff, 1995; BCPSG, 2008; among others) suggest that motives are the "basic mental unit" for understanding human behavior. To understand one another and ourselves we constantly assess each other's motives. To be in touch with our intentions is basic in defining a sense of self. Lichtenberg (1989), first alone and, subsequently, with Lachmann and myself (Lichtenberg et al., 1992, 1996, 2002, 2011) proposed that sensing and identifying a patient's motivational priorities moment-to-moment is pivotal in both gaining empathic entry into a patient's experiential world and helping patients anchor themselves in their inner experience of shifting motivations, primary in establishing a sense of self. The Boston Group (BCPSG, 2008) refers to this as tracking the "intention unfolding process" (p. 131).

Kohut's (1984) postulation of a fundamental motivation "to realize the nuclear self and its program of action" (p. 42) was central to his model. In an effort to integrate aspects of psychological and cognitive developmental theory, neuroscience, and non-linear dynamic systems theory, I (Fosshage, 2011a) have recently attempted to update the formulation of what I call a *developmental motivation* and refer to it as "an inherent tendency in human beings to grow or develop, meaning to expand in function, to self-organize with increasing complexity in keeping with basic and evolving motivational values or preferences" (p. 96). This inherent tendency has been variously conceptualized as a striving to self-actualize (Jung, 1953; Winnicott, 1965; Maslow, 1968/2011; Kohut, 1984), effectance drive (White, 1959; J. Greenberg, 1991), destiny drive (Bollas, 1989), and expansion of function (Ghent, 2002). Whether conceptualized as an inherent tendency or as an overarching developmental motivation, it, in my view, is central in our lives and provides the motivational momentum and overall direction for psychoanalytic work (Fosshage, 2013).

In the clinical encounter Kohut (J. Miller, 1985) noted that picking up on a patient's developmental strivings – that is, sensing and articulating what a patient is striving toward – increases understanding and implicitly supports these strivings. In contrast to the ego psychological emphasis on resistance and defense, this self psychological focus has become referred to as picking up on the "leading" or "forward edge" (Tolpin, 2002; Lachmann, 2008) of the material. Where conflict is focal in an ego psychological analysis, developmental strivings and developmental processes and related conflicts emergent within relational systems are central in a self psychologically oriented analytic process.

Kohut (1984) postulated a "program of action" unique for each person, what might be referred to as a developmental direction. How might we understand the origins of developmental direction? Among the various approaches to this issue (e.g., Jung, 1953; Bollas, 1989), I (Fosshage, 2011a) have recently proposed,

> The shifting priorities and strengths of motivational values and preferences, using Edelman's (1987, 1989, 1992) terms, substantially contribute on a moment-to-moment basis to an individual's developmental direction . . . each momentary actualization of intention or motivational preference within an affirming relational context contributes incrementally to a sense of agency and vitality.
>
> (p. 95)

Close tracking of motivations with those patients who have "lost" a sense of who they are especially contributes to the consolidation of a vitalized sense of self, to "finding" oneself again.

Theory of therapeutic action

While initially emphasizing the interpretation of selfobject needs, Kohut (1984) concluded that change does not occur in the "cognitive sphere per se" but in the relational experience that requires analysts and patients to sufficiently co-create needed selfobject experience. The subsequent "relational turn" and recognition of "implicit relational knowing" (D. N. Stern et al., 1998; Fosshage, 2005, 2011b; BCPSG, 2008) has additionally emphasized both the complexity of the change process and the importance of the patient/analyst co-creation of new relational experience.

The rupture/repair cycles, central in Kohut's theory of therapeutic action, have in relational self psychology become more complex. While Kohut proposed that ruptures were caused by the analyst's failure to understand, Stolorow and Brandchaft (1987) noted that some failures of understanding are easily rectified without disturbance, while others create a significant rupture, eliciting rage or states of deflation – called empathic failures and selfobject ruptures, respectively. Subsequently we have learned that selfobject ruptures involve activation of traumatically based experiential themes or organizing patterns of the patient (Fosshage, 1994). Reparation requires exploration, discovery, and understanding of the activated organizing pattern and the analyst's identification and acknowledgement of his or her contribution. A cycle of rupture and repair, thus, both increases reflective awareness and understanding as well as co-creates a new relational experience – in this instance, mutually understanding the contributions of each to the rupture.

Therapeutic action, in my view, occurs along two fundamental pathways. (Fosshage, 2003a,b, 2005, 2011b). The first is the explicit mutually exploratory, reflective avenue to therapeutic change. While this corresponds with the traditional psychoanalytic focus on interpretation and insight, relational approaches at large emphasize a more collaborative exploratory process and the analyst's exploratory suggestions, instead of interpretations, that expand reflective awareness. An analyst engenders reflective awareness of unconscious and conscious devitalizing self and self-with-other images and their relational origins (including conflictual processes previously described). This process, in turn, gradually empowers patients to reflectively intercede and deactivate problematic patterns.

Most persons presenting for treatment have not been sufficiently seen, heard, or believed in the emotional depths. Self psychologists have learned how important understanding from within the patient's experiential world is. To quote Kohut (1984), "The patient, as I finally grasped, insisted – and had a right to insist – that I learn to see things exclusively in *his* way and not at all in *my* way" (p. 182). He elaborated that all of his explanations were only from the outside, "that I did not fully feel what he felt, that I gave him words but not real understanding, and that I thereby repeated the essential trauma of his early life" (p. 182). Kohut is quite explicit here of the importance of the analyst's affective presence and empathic capability of feeling the patient's experience in the process of understanding the patient. While this initial task is paramount, especially in the early phases of treatment, we, in my view, cannot and do not remain "exclusively" within the patient's perspective. To increase reflective awareness of organizing patterns requires input from us that falls outside the patient's perspective. For example, asking initial exploratory questions like "Have you felt that way before in your life?" and "When did you begin to feel that way about yourself?" implicitly introduce a developmental, learning perspective that gradually undermines the "felt reality" of a negative percept.

In addition, responses do vary widely depending on what is optimal (Bacal, 1985, 1998b) or facilitative (Fosshage, 1997b) and what can require various listening perspectives (Fosshage, 1995, 2003a, 2011c). For example, in contrast to an empathic listening/experiencing perspective where we attempt to understand from within a patient's experiential world, to listen to/experience the patient as an other within a relationship, what I call the other-centered listening/experiencing perspective, provides us with information about the impact patients have on others, about interaction patterns that expand our view of a patient and potentially increase a patient's understanding of his or her relationships. And last, when a patient asks an analyst directly if the analyst was angry or disapproving, the analyst must reflect on his experience, what I call the analyst's self-perspective, to identify his experience and be able to respond to the patient in the overall experience of trying to understand who is contributing what to the dyadic field, the analytic relationship.

Conflict during the development of self 141

These processes of exploration and understanding of the patient-analyst experience simultaneously contribute to the second fundamental avenue of change – new relational experience. Exploration and understanding is of paramount importance, yet it is but one of many types of new relational experience. Others range, for example, from co-created moments when a patient feels heard, known, affirmed, (Kohut, 1984) challenged, and inspired (I. Hoffman, 2009) with moments of camaraderie and mutual reciprocity (see Teicholz, 1999; Bacal & Carlton, 2011; Fosshage, 2011b,c). New vitalizing experience often occurs at an implicit procedural level; yet explicit focus amplifies and integrates new experience. New relational experience gradually establishes new percepts, a vitalized sense of self, and more effective relational procedures.

Clinical illustration

Samantha, a 37-year-old woman, was well-spoken, quite attractive, dressed in a casual trendy manner, and demonstrated a charm and outspokenness.[2] Her outspokenness carried a tension that I learned was part of her battle to overcome squelching influences.

She said that she was conflicted "between what I was bred to be and my inner integral self. . . . My inner self has been squashed and wants out or I will die. . . . I was the perfect child – forget it – I am not the repressed, elegant Swiss-German girl." She had been taught "to control cerebrally" her feelings. As a result, she felt "an Amazon woman in me emerging that was previously smashed."

Samantha emphatically described how her parents had not seen or known her "inner integral self." Instead, they had imposed upon her their image of a "repressed, elegant Swiss-German girl." To maintain the attachment and secure affirmation Samantha had to pathologically accommodate her parents' requirements and became "the perfect child," yet she was quite aware of an intense defiance and aggressively-tinged reassertion of herself, that is, "an Amazon woman," was emerging within her.

In the ensuing analytic process Samantha began to access and explore memories and her affective life that had been frozen. Her dreams, which made clear that she was quite imagistically gifted, were excruciatingly long and painful.

As she wrote them, painful memories emerged. I have selected portions of one dream that occurred approximately 14 months into treatment. The dream opens with Samantha on the beach watching the surfers play in the late afternoon. She must pick up her father and begins to worry that she will be late and accused of being irresponsible. She writes:

> I am on my way again to my destination. However, I am angry and feel I am 'behaving' obstreperously. The surfers have gone, but have left their surfboards behind, standing in tumbles next to the pier. I can see the fish hooks in the sand and the fishing poles beside them. The hooks stick out from the surface of the sand. I sit and look at them first, and then very decidedly walk towards them, all the do's and don'ts and restrictions, regulations, controls, musts, have to's, should's, always, never to, and will now do's, given to me by my parents are ringing in my ears as I walk across the beach. I want to touch this dark blue surfboard, it sits, fin facing me, the underbelly of it slightly worn down, the color rubbed slightly away from being pulled across the sand after being in the water. It's like a blue finned whale. I walk across the fish hooks and feel and hear the hooks puncturing my skin, and curving into it, and out on the other side. I don't care. I must reach out and touch that blue board. I feel the pain of the hooks, but am disembodied from it at the same time.

In her determined, undaunted effort to touch the blue surfboard, she initially found it necessary to "disembody" herself from the pain of the impaling fish hooks. Later, in the dream she begins to feel the excruciating pain as she tries to free herself from the hooks. She knows that her parents will reprimand her. There is a concert that night, and she realizes that she has ruined their evening for they will need to take her to the hospital to have the hooks extracted. What stood out for us in our discussion was how her parents would be furious with her – re-igniting the desperate struggle to find, in spite of the danger and in defiant reaction against her parent's dictates, some beauty, some freedom, some peace as symbolized in the image of the dark blue surfboard. The blue surfboard was a powerful image for Samantha, capturing her desire for freedom of movement, gliding with nature, peaceful existence, beauty, and strength like a "blue fin whale" – a powerfully enlivening experience.

As Samantha wrote this dream, traumatic memories burst into her awareness – having been hit by a car and then having been hit by her enraged mother; being called to dinner, forcing her to leave her cat to die alone; her broken arm which her parents did not immediately take care of; her not being told the truth before she underwent dental surgery; her not being told of her brother's death for eight hours after he was killed in a car accident; and her father's screaming at her when she saw him naked when she was 11, "the shame he made me feel."

Her intention and determination to reach the freedom of the surfboard, "her destination," still required painful, even dangerous, defiance of her parents' agenda. With emotional thawing, she was able to feel the pain as she recalled the traumatic memories (see Davies & Frawley, 1994; Bromberg, 1998; Brothers, 2008).

These intense conflicts involve traumatic abuse and thwarting of mirroring and idealizing selfobject needs, imposition of her parents' agenda, her partial accommodation and loss of her self, and her determined attempt and resilient effort to reassert herself and be her. The essential elements of conflict were the relational thwarting of selfobject needs and strivings, the imposition of parental agendas, and Samantha's attempt to negotiate between her developmental strivings and the need to maintain selfobject or attachment ties.

Conclusion

While conflict is clearly a part of the "human condition," differences abound in psychoanalytic theories when considering sources of conflict, its primary constituents, and its centrality in psychological life and therapeutic action. The interpretation and resolution of conflict are central in the ego psychological model based on Freud's drive theory; modern conflict theory, with its emphasis on the ubiquity of conflict in life and the analytic situation, amplifies its centrality.

In contrast to the assumptions of ubiquity and centrality of conflict, Kohut's self-psychology regards the development and maintenance of the self to be central in life and in the analytic situation. Kohut postulated the interplay both of nurture – emergence of the self within a relational, self-selfobject matrix – and nature – selfobject needs, the individual's uniqueness and the fundamental striving to "realize" the self, what I call a developmental motivation.

Kohut's conceptualization of self and selfobject relationships addresses a pivotal dimension of self and relational experience that is central to normal and pathological development, transference, and therapeutic action. Within relational models, conflicts are viewed as emergent properties of relationships. Self psychology proposes that the most emotionally potent conflicts involve the selfobject dimension of relationships, that is, the thwarting of developmental strivings and selfobject needs. Expanding on the scaffolding of Kohut's psychology of the self, relational self psychologists have noted that relational experience that thwarts development of the individual's unique self simultaneously forms negative, devitalizing attitudes and images of self and self-with-other. Conflict subsequently can occur between developmental strivings and the maintenance of familiar and stable, even if devitalizing, negative attitudes.

In relational self psychology, conflict, when emergent and in the forefront, is addressed. Developmental processes, however, remain in view. Attuned to the patient's developmental striving, the analyst, using the empathic perspective of listening and experiencing, picks up on the "leading edge" of the clinical material to facilitate the developmental process and fortify the patient's strivings. The challenge to the analyst/patient dyad becomes apparent when the patient's devitalizing organizing patterns, procedures, and attitudes, based on thwarted and conflictual relational lived experience, subsequently become, even by seemingly "small" triggers, repeatedly played out in the patient's relationships, including the analytic relationship. Activation of problematic organizing patterns in the analytic relationship can trigger selfobject ruptures, eliciting the "darker emotions" of fury or deflation that, along with the relational origins of the evoked pattern, must be reflectively understood to be deactivated. Often this requires the additional use of other-centered and analyst's self-listening/ experiencing perspectives to facilitate a reflective awareness of a patient's interaction patterns or impact on others as well as more open detailed examination of the contributions of each participant in a problematic or conflictual analytic encounter. Through these and other processes, patient/ analyst co-create new relational experience, establishing new vitalizing attitudes toward self and other.

Whether encountering conflict, analytic change, I believe, occurs along two fundamental, interrelated pathways: explicit reflective exploratory work and new implicit and explicit relational experience. Rather than change taking place primarily through exploration, the traditional focus, or primarily through implicit relational learning, a more recent proposal, I emphasize the interplay between the implicit and explicit systems for therapeutic change.

Notes

1 I wish to express my appreciation to Sandra Hershberg, MD and Christopher Christian, PhD for their very helpful editorial questions and suggestions.
2 This clinical illustration is borrowed from a larger case study: Fosshage, J. (1999). "Different forms of intimacy: The case of Samantha," presented at The 22nd Annual International Conference on the Psychology of the Self, Toronto, Canada. (Unpublished manuscript). It is used more extensively in a new book, *Enlivening the Self* (Routledge, 2015), by Lichtenberg, J., Lachmann, F. and Fosshage, J.

Chapter 9

The phenomenological contextualism of conflict

An intersubjective perspective

Chris Jaenicke

The contributors of this book about the role of conflict in contemporary theories of psychoanalysis have been asked to address two fundamental questions from their particular theoretical perspective: Can psychoanalysis still be considered the study of conflict, and if so, what are we conflicted about, or which aspects of mental life are in conflict? Before describing conflict from an intersubjective viewpoint, I will briefly reiterate the traditional psychoanalytic view in order to help clarify how the theories diverge. Stolorow (2006) has provided us with a point of convergence between the traditional and a contemporary view of conflict in a paper entitled "The Relevance of Freud's Concept of Danger-Situations for an Intersubjective-Systems Perspective." By reformulating Freud's concept of danger situation through a post-Cartesian, Heideggerian lens he was able to find a "nice bridge to an intersubjective-systems perspective on the analysis of resistance" (Stolorow, 2006, p. 419). The contextualization of experiences of endangerment, in particular in the conflictual and resistive aspects of the transference, provides us both with points of convergence and divergence between Freud's view of conflict and our own. In a clinical vignette in which I attempt to demonstrate the intersubjective nature of resistance I would like to highlight what I believe to be the most salient clinical contribution of an intersubjective understanding of conflict.

Another purpose of discussing how the traditional and the intersubjective views of conflict diverge and converge is to demonstrate that psychoanalysis, no matter which viewpoint one might take, is embedded in a long, passionate, and formidable tradition of struggling with the experience of being human.[1] As Eagle (2011) writes, central to the conception of psychopathology in classical theory is the

> presence of inner conflicts between anxiety-laden wishes and desires and defenses erected against them. This can be described as a

drive-defense or id-ego model and is another way of saying that it is neurosis that is the main arena for the classical psychoanalytic theory of psychopathology.

(pp. 265–266)

Furthermore, given the fact that in the drive-defense model functioning is understood in terms of a conflict between two *structures* of the personality, the id and the ego, and that inner conflict has to do with repressed and unacceptable *universal* sexual and aggressive impulses, it is not only implicated in neurosis, but also seen as a model for general psychic functioning. The prime example about what we are conflicted about in Freudian theory is, of course, "the oedipal one, consisting of incestuous wishes toward the opposite-sex parent and hostile wishes toward the same-sex parent" (Eagle, 2011, p. 65). In the Freudian view, the goal of treatment is to resolve conflict and thus "to restore the unity and integrity of the personality" (p. 65). In intersubjectivity theory, the source of conflict and disunity of the personality lies in those specific intersubjective contexts

> in which central affect states of the child cannot be integrated because they fail to evoke the requisite attuned responsiveness from the caregiving surround. Such unintegrated affect states become the source of lifelong inner conflict, because they are experienced as threats both to the person's established psychological organization and to the maintenance of vitally needed ties.
>
> (Stolorow et al., 1987, pp. 91–92)

Thus, from an intersubjective perspective we can already surmise at this point that psychoanalysis can still be considered the study of conflict. A detailed account of the intersubjective view of conflict will begin to answer the second question regarding the aspects of mental life which are seen to be in conflict and will show how the theories differ.

Conflict in intersubjective-systems theory

We can pursue these questions by first examining the general theoretical antithesis assumed to exist between Kohut's self psychology and conflict psychoanalytic psychologies (G. Klein, 1976; Kohut, 1977; Stolorow, 1978). From an intersubjective perspective "inner conflict always takes form in specific intersubjective contexts of developmental derailment" (Stolorow et al., 1987, p. 88). This view has the advantage of relieving us of a reductionistic necessity to index classical theory to the neuroses and relationalists to what Mitchell (1988) has termed the *developmental tilt* toward non-conflictual, pre-Oedipal issues; rather, we can understand the relationship between various developmental origins and prerequisites that lead to the experience of a self-in-conflict. One major difference, however, between classical and intersubjectivity theory is that as phenomenological contextualists we do not assume that we are motivated by universal, endogenous drives, nor is mental functioning seen predominantly in terms of a conflict between ubiquitous intrapsychic structures. Rather, we are concerned with understanding the highly idiosyncratic subjective experiential worlds and the unique intersubjective fields in which these individual worlds originated, are upheld, and are in-conflict about. While inner human conflict has retained its central importance in intersubjectivity theory, the nature and origin of conflict is not seen in terms of the presumed vicissitudes of drives, rather

> it is our contention that from a psychoanalytic perspective conflict is always and only a subjective state of the individual person and that it is the task of psychoanalytic inquiry to illuminate the specific contexts of meaning in which such conflicts take form.[2]
>
> (Stolorow et al., 1987, p. 88)

Conflicts may arise at various points in a developmental progression, depending on whether the caregiving surround is able to respond to a child's evolving states and needs and thus to be attuned to the child's maturational shifts. In order for an experience of the self-in-conflict to occur, a minimal degree of structuralization of the sense of self has to have been achieved. If the cohesion of self-experience is threatened or lost, the imperative need to re-establish an archaic selfobject tie in order to restore self-integrity will be in the foreground. Once the tie has been restored, inner conflict can emerge as figure, while the tie serves as the ground. However, as soon as central strivings or affective states are experienced as threats to the maintenance of the bond, the need for an immersion in an archaic selfobject tie may once again become pre-eminent. These shifts in the figure-ground of developmental needs and the experience of self-in-conflict may occur within one analytic hour or within the course of the structuralization processes throughout treatment (Stolorow & Lachmann, 1980). Instead of viewing conflict as inevitably structuralized or predetermined by drives, intersubjectivity theory focuses on the specific developmental origins and intersubjective fields from which such conflicts arise and seeks its resolution in an understanding of the intersubjective field in treatment in which it re-emerges. If the parents of a child are not able to follow the maturational shifts in development, the child will sacrifice those aspects of its agentic, authentic self that are seen as a threat to the existentially needed tie to the parents. Analogously, patients will adapt themselves to their therapists to uphold the required bond.

This contextualized view of the self-in-conflict does not, however, suggest a purely constructivist view of structuralization because it takes into account the developmental prerequisites of conflict and the invariant principles that unconsciously organize a person's patterns of expectations and experiential worlds. The fact that these experiential worlds are dynamic, fluid, messy, and subject to change depending on the responses of the current intersubjective fields does not justify a dichotomous, bifurcated view of invariant versus variant organizing principles, outside versus inside, unconscious versus conscious experiences. The experiential world of an individual in intersubjectivity theory is seen both in terms of pre-organized stable organizing principles[3] and as being highly context-sensitive. The supposed antithesis between pre-organized and fluid states is not seen as incompatible but is understood as interrelated: what we may or may not experience is seen as fluid and flexible, both as a product of a person's invariant organizing principles and the intersubjective fields which allow or disallow specific experiences to occur. Experiential worlds and intersubjective fields constitute one another in a circular manner (Eagle, 2011; Stolorow, 2013). I will return to this point later in my discussion of danger situations.

The development of an intersubjective view of conflict began with an elaboration of Kohutian theory (1977) by postulating two overlapping processes in self-development: "(1) the consolidation of a nuclear sense of coherence and well-being, and (2) the differentiation of self from other and the corresponding establishment of an individualized array of guiding aspirations and ideals" (Stolorow et al., 1987, p. 89). According to this position, conflicts arose and were structuralized around a caregiver's response to the child's needs at any point in the development of self-consolidation and self-differentiation. The need to remain in idealized connection with a caregiver will eventually conflict with the need to develop one's own sense of self and individual goals and values (Stolorow et al., 1987).

A prime example of the connection between developmental failure and conflict that exemplified the thesis that a child will adapt himself to the needs of the parents in order to maintain an existentially needed tie was the experiential configuration previously conceptualized as a "superego conflict." Stolorow (1985) argued that once a child has structuralized parental requirements as invariant organizing principles of his or her subjective world, he or she will be subject to feelings of guilt, shame, and anxiety whenever his or her own emotional states or strivings differ. If a child's need for self-demarcation threatens a parent's need for an archaic state of oneness, the child's strivings for self-differentiation will become enduring sources of conflict and guilt. The child will thus experience acts of self-demarcation as destructive and the parental need for an archaic selfobject will result in the child's perception of himself or herself as a cruel destroyer. The developmental process of self-boundary formation will become a constant source of guilt and self-punishment and will result in the formation of a "harsh-superego."

In a shift from the motivational primacy of drive to the motivational primacy of affect, intersubjective-systems theory postulates that "emotional experience is inseparable from the intersubjective contexts of attunement and malattunement in which it is felt. Therefore, locating affect at its motivational center automatically entails a radical contextualization of virtually all aspects of human life" (Stolorow, 2013, p. 385). Thus, in a further elaboration of conflict formation, the *failure of affect integration* became central in understanding the genesis and structuralization of inner conflict. When a child is faced with an ongoing absence of affective attunement, he or she will begin to dissociate and disavow his or her own emotional reactions and will ultimately perceive affectivity itself as dangerous, necessitating defenses against affects to maintain a brittle self-structure. The constant derailment of affect integration will lead to an enfeebled sense of self and previous structuralizations will be felt as vulnerable to self-fragmentation. The child will begin to develop a "defensive self-ideal" purified of those emotions that were felt to threaten the early surround. In treatment, a patient's inability to feel and name affects serves the defensive purpose of warding off a re-traumatization, as well as an attempt to uphold the defensive self-ideal. Conflict arises in those moments when affective states threaten to break through and the failure in maintaining a purified ideal once again becomes a source of shame and self-loathing.

From an intersubjective perspective, the resistance to affect cannot be conceptualized or interpreted solely in terms of intrapsychic processes within the patient. Rather, it is the patient's expectation that his or her emotions will once again meet with faulty responsiveness due to some quality in the therapist's reactions that lend themselves to heralding a possible re-traumatization (Ornstein, 1974). While resistance can be seen as the continuing hold of pre-established organizing principles, it also directs our attention to the specific intersubjective field co-constituted by the therapist that either maintains or loosens the grip of dissociated affect: "It is in the defensive walling off of central affect states, rooted in early derailments of affect integration, that the origins of what has traditionally been called the 'dynamic unconscious' can be found" (Stolorow et al., 1987, p. 92). Thus the previously mentioned antithesis between pre-organized and fluid states, as well as between the unconscious and conscious, vanishes and is replaced by a focus on the intersubjective systems that allow different psychological phenomena to arise or recede. The repression barrier, that is the boundary between conscious and unconscious, has become contextualized. The extent to which we are able to express the entire depth of our inner experience can be understood only in the context of what the intersubjective fields – past and present – have encouraged or prohibited.

Whatever a patient feels to be tolerable or unacceptable will originally be a consequence of developmental trauma. Whatever a patient feels he may be allowed to express now will also depend on his or her experience of the therapist.

Conflict can be viewed as central to psychoanalysis inasmuch as the possibility of the re-integration of affect and the working through of the resistances play a central role in our understanding of the essence of therapeutic change: the naming of the previously repressed, dissociated, or unformulated affects allows a re-integration which strengthens the sense of who we are.

Finally, before turning to the concept of danger situation and an intersubjective system's view of resistance and conflict in a case vignette, two broad classes of affect states must be distinguished that often may lead to the structuralization of conflict in the context of selfobject failure and affective derailment. When *developmental strivings* such as "feelings of pride, expansiveness, efficacy, and pleasure in oneself, as well as willful rebelliousness, emergent sexuality, and competitive aggressiveness" (Stolorow et al., 1987, p. 93) are not met with phase-appropriate mirroring because

152   Chris Jaenicke

they are felt to be harmful to the caregiving surround, such affect states will become the source of conflict and guilt. Self-cohesion, self-esteem, and ambition will be weakened, leading to a lack of self-consolidation. The second source of structuralized conflict are those painful emotions that occur in reaction to experiences of an endangered self and/or a threatened selfobject bond.

If a child is not helped to integrate painful feelings because they are felt to threaten a parent's self-organization, then these unintegrated *reactive feeling states* will become a lifelong source of conflict. In analysis, experiencing pain will be resisted as this may herald a traumatic vulnerability in face of an anticipated faulty responsiveness.

A bridge between theories: the danger situation

In reviewing Freud's concept of danger situation, Stolorow (2006) came to the conclusion that there is an ambiguity or shifting status in conceptualizing these situations as internal versus external, thus creating a intrapsychic versus interpersonal dichotomy. One can see how in Freud's ontogenetic sequence of danger situations – helplessness due to overwhelming instinctual tensions, loss of the love object, loss of the object's love, castration, and attack by the superego – endangerment moves from totally internal (overwhelming instinctual tension) to interpersonal (loss of the object, loss of the object's love) to a mixture of internal and external (hostile wish and fear of castration) to once again become wholly internal (the dread of the superego). In Stolorow's view Descartes' (1641/1989) metaphysics dividing the finite world into thinking substances (mind) and material substances had a profound influence on the evolution of the scientific worldview. The Cartesian metaphysical dualism led to a number of interrelated bifurcations, such as mind-body, cognition versus affect, reason versus desire, subject versus object, and internal versus external, pervading Western folk and academic psychology, as well as psychoanalysis. Stolorow credits Heidegger (1927/1962) with challenging the subject-object bifurcation generally and for the view that "human life was primordially engaged and contextually embedded" (Stolorow, 2006, p. 418). From this perspective, a patient's experience of endangerment must, therefore, be seen as emerging from the systemic interaction between the patient and analyst (Stolorow, 2006). In other words, those bifurcations that were previously seen as dichotomous or contradictory collapse when understood from within the more inclusive framework of an intersubjective-systems perspective. For instance, the false dichotomy of subject-object, internal-external in regard to a patient's experience of endangerment can now be applied to an intersubjective-systems approach to the analysis of resistance. The question of whether the danger is internal or external does not pose itself from a post-Cartesian, intersubjective viewpoint. When danger is seen as an emergent property of an intersubjective field, then the analytic task will be to investigate both the activities of the analyst that lend themselves to a patient's fear of possible re-traumatization – thus eliciting resistance – and to the meanings that are guiding the patient's understanding of those activities. Therefore, resistance itself becomes contextualized and its meaning is revealed both in terms of internality and externality. Thus the investigation of the patient's experiences of endangerment within the specific intersubjective field of treatment also opens the pathway to analyzing the interrelationship between resistance and the self-in-conflict. Thus in both Freudian and intersubjective-systems theory danger situations evoke resistance. The intersubjective perspective, however, emphasizes the contextuality of resistance. In our view, resistance is a co-construction, an emergent property of each unique intersubjective field.

One of the major differences between the classical and intersubjective-systems theories is that Freudian theory is a hybrid theory attempting to describe psychological phenomena on two different levels of discourse: the level of meaning and the level of mechanism (Eagle, 2011). One level uses the language of meaning, intentions, desires, and beliefs, and the other level uses the language of energy transformations. As also noted by G. Klein (1976) Freud actually had two theories, one (the level of meaning) which he applied in his clinical case studies, and the other (the level of mechanism) with which he formulated his metapsychological theories. Intersubjectivity theory has taken a different approach. In an attempt to expand Kohut's idea of a pure psychology, psychoanalysis is conceptualized as a phenomenological contextualism. The danger situation provides a good example in order to demonstrate how the theories diverge and converge according to the aforementioned different levels of discourse. In Freud's (1923) view defenses were erected against those danger situations that were seen as largely external – loss of the object, loss of the object's love, and the threat of castration – because they are associated not only with inherent threats to the ego (mechanistic level), but also because, as Eagle (2011) proposed, the individual associates them with "prohibitions,

154   Chris Jaenicke

punishments and threats," from caregivers (p. 68). However, as Eagle (2011) further notes, Freud does not provide a great deal of information about what caregivers might be doing to make a child anxious about the danger situations (meaning level). Primarily danger situations are discussed in the "mechanistic imagery of a mental apparatus disposing of drive energies" (Stolorow et al., 1987, p. 88). In Stolorow's (2006) view the ambiguity of internality versus externality in regard to Freud's theories can also be ascribed to his unacknowledged adherence to Cartesian philosophy. In summary, the theories converge in their agreement that danger situations exist and elicit defenses and resistances based on internal conflicts. They diverge in that in intersubjectivity theory "inner conflict always take form in specific intersubjective contexts of developmental derailment" (Stolorow et al., 1987, p. 88), whereas "this contemporary emphasis on early parental failure can be contrasted with Freud's relative de-emphasis on the role of parental behavior in the development of psychopathology" (Eagle, 2011, p. 267). The bridge is in viewing the patient's experience of endangerment in terms of not only inner conflict, but also the specific intersubjective field in which conflicts arise in the repetitive, conflictual, *resistive* dimension of transference. A vignette will illustrate the clinical contribution of an intersubjective-systems theory understanding of conflict, resistance, and the danger situation.

I would like to preface the case vignette that follows with some remarks regarding what I consider an expansion, or radicalized version, of intersubjective-systems theory. In my view, therapeutic action is "soft-assembled" within the patient-analyst system. In the intersubjective field, the emotional worlds of both participants play a constitutive role, as do the successes and failure of the therapeutic process. Through the enmeshments of life-themes that occur in any therapeutic process, the conflicts in each of the participants will be mobilized, if not necessarily in an equal way or on the same structural level. Initially they will be played out silently on the bi-directional level of therapeutic action. In the course of time, the analyst's internal reflections and comprehension of what is occurring on the level of mutual influencing will gradually increase and will serve as an important source of his interventions on the asymmetric level of therapeutic action. Thus, one can postulate that an intersubjective understanding of conflict as applied to treatment consists of two individual, subjective experiences which were formed in a matrix of differing degrees of developmental failure, and which, after having undergone transformations in later intersubjective fields, will ultimately become crystallized in the meeting of two differently organized, colliding experiential worlds in the therapeutic process. Just as conflict cannot be viewed as a purely intrapsychic struggle but rather as a psychological phenomenon that originates, arises, and recedes in specific intersubjective systems, so must conflict also be seen as a product of the intersubjective field created by patient and analyst and fueled by both experiential worlds, including those affects that are conflictual and which incur resistance in each participant. To address in advance the possible critique, "Whose treatment is it anyway?" the answer, of course, in terms of the goal, the focus, and the asymmetric level of therapeutic action of treatment remains the patient. We have already noted that a patient's "transference expectations, unwittingly confirmed by the analyst, are a powerful source of resistance to the experience and articulation of affect" (Stolorow, 2007, p. 4).

In the case to be discussed, an intractable repetitive transference occurred, which from a systems view can be conceptualized in terms of a rigidly stable "attractor state" (Thelen & Smith, 1994). In attractor states a lock occurs between the analyst's expectations – his stance – and the patient's worst fears of disappointment and failure. This can lead to a protracted impasse, or, if allowed to continue, even result in termination of the therapeutic process. Previously such immovable attractor states were often conceptualized as negative therapeutic reactions. From an intersubjective perspective, impasses can be understood only systemically. A disturbance in the locked system must occur in order to bring movement into the process. While both participants can instigate such a disturbance, the analyst's self-reflection and increased awareness of the effects of his stance on the patient can provide the needed impetus for the therapy to proceed. Nonetheless, even the provision of such an impetus by the analyst cannot be understood as occurring outside of the influence of the bi-directional field.

While our main concern and task remains in illuminating how the patient has assimilated us and the entire patient-analyst interaction, and while we cannot predict how we unwittingly contribute to confirm the invariant organizing principles of the patient by even the minutest perceptions of us, our "stance" is nonetheless composed of our entire experiential world, including our own conflicts, resistances, and fears. Thus, as I have attempted to show throughout my work (Jaenicke, 2008, 2011, 2014) the process of change, while remaining concentrated on the patient by definition of the therapeutic task, will not occur without a process of transformation in both the participants.

Case illustration: Daniel[4]

Daniel is the youngest of four children. He grew up in a family that was mainly preoccupied with the running and the survival of the family business. At the age of 6, Daniel already had the responsibility of the packaging and expedition of the firm's products. Daniel described himself as an "employee" of a father who tyrannically drove him to ever-increasing levels of work and achievement by denigrating his contributions, calling him a "wimp" or "loser" whenever he did not meet harsh demands. He experienced his mother as helpful in practical matters but became enmeshed with her in a sexually-connotated narcissistic need to sustain her in the face of his father's neglect. Thus one of Daniel's organizing principles was that he became "Mr. Never-Enough." In the face of a severe lack of affective attunement, Daniel developed a defensive self-ideal in which his own agenda not only became a threat to his relationships, but also served as a defense against affectivity in general, as he had come to expect that his affect states would be met with disdain, disgust, exploitation, and disinterest. He avoided experiencing and showing his emotions, as that would only reveal a deep sense of an inner defect. Daniel developed into a lone fighter, a "Shadow Man" whose mode of relating to the world was organized by becoming an expert in solving other people's problems, while his own needs and desires became increasingly foreign to him. Without any support from his family, Daniel obtained two university degrees and now works as an IT trouble-shooter, traveling the country solving seemingly unsolvable computer problems. Although Daniel was very successful in his work, his relationships were brief. Once the initial sexual attraction waned, there was not enough basis to sustain a relationship which was characterized by Daniel's preoccupation with his partner's needs and, therefore, ultimately led to a feeling of emptiness and exploitation. Thus when Daniel came into treatment he was suffering from burnout and a deep sense of isolation.

In our sessions, Daniel inundated me with rapid-fire, detailed accounts of his life. Initially, I mostly just listened. When I did make a comment, these interventions embarrassed Daniel. He felt that he should already have come to any perception of himself that I offered. He organized my intended empathic responses as instances of being shamed and exposed. In the father-transference he experienced himself as too slow on the uptake and me as someone who enjoyed proving that to him with my therapeutic expertise. Thus a subtle battle of the experts ensued and, actually, the town didn't seem big enough for both of us. An intractable attractor state developed in which I felt thwarted in my expectation to be able to help Daniel, and Daniel was driven by a fear to fail in what he grasped as his task to achieve therapeutic success. I wanted Daniel to accept my empathy, to understand that I understood him. He, on the other hand, wanted me to understand that he basically didn't need me to understand him. Unconsciously, of course, he did want me to understand him, however, as this was linked to painful feelings of inadequacy, he had no choice initially but to resist a dialogic form of understanding. He was conflicted because he felt that to accept my interventions would be tantamount to revealing his defects – chiefly in the form of painful feelings – and thus that his felt inadequacies would be met with my disgust and disdain, much as in the past with his father. This eventually led to a stalemate, in which my listening silence led Daniel to offer me an ever-increasing cascade of material.

As I came to eventually understand, my analytic stance dovetailed with my brother-transference. My close relationship with my older brother, whom I admired, was also based on the premise that in order to maintain our bond, I was not allowed to win in any game or competition with him. This was physically enforced until I grew larger than my brother. Interestingly, Daniel is of slight and small stature. In a reverse identification – I was my brother, Daniel was me – I felt my interventions to be like hammer blows for Daniel and my very size to be like a bull in a china shop. Daniel later supported this view, as he felt that at the end of his tremendous efforts to make himself understood, my "one-sentence responses" seemed to him like "blows of a baseball bat." Thus I had an organizing principle quite analogous to Daniel's. We both were conflicted insofar as we had learned that a direct expression of our needs, feelings, and aggressive assertiveness led to severe opposition and loss of the object's love. Both of us were used to the role of the eminence gris, experts who worked behind the lines and then vanished. As a child I identified with Lash Larue, a masked avenger of bad deeds by night, equipped with a whip. Daniel was the expert "Shadow Man," dropping into trouble-spots, fixing problems, and leaving. Our conflicts were rooted in different forms of developmental failure leading to the same conclusions: neither of us expected to be heard unless it was at the price of accommodation. In the repetitive, resistive, conflictual pole of the transference he expected to be shamed by me and thus warded off my attempts to understand him. His unconscious conflict

158 Chris Jaenicke

was fueled by the expectation of exploitation. Admitting that I understood him would only lead to my making further demands on him. He, therefore, upheld a defensive self-ideal cleansed of any need. As these life-themes became enmeshed through the deepening of the therapeutic process, our individual intrapsychic conflicts became exacerbated. As stated earlier, internal conflicts cannot be understood apart either from the pre-existent invariant organizing principles, or from the intersubjective fields in which they arise or recede. In systemic terms, our conflicts were brought forth in such a manner as to create an attractor state in which we became locked into a state of immobilization. In dynamic systems theory such stagnation can be changed only through a perturbation.

Finally the perturbation came in the form of my increasingly feeling irritated, antsy, and left out by the wall of sound created by Daniel's monologues. In one session I interrupted him after 40 minutes and quite bluntly blurted out that I felt excluded. I had left the safe haven of analytically-endorsed silence, which had masked my accommodation. In the next hour, I felt that I had perhaps over-stepped my bounds. I felt awkward and crude about my intervention. Daniel responded that it had initially angered him, but he had then read one of my books and now felt he understood more about what I was trying to achieve in tracking his various emotional states. We laughed about how he had once again tried to be the expert, to solve the problem of our relatedness on his own. At the same time, it had been *my book* that he had read, and the implicit relatedness became explicitly expressed. Thus, a shift occurred in our communication. Daniel now felt he could communicate with me, and I felt less restrained in my reactions to him.

Concluding remarks

I would like to stress several points here. I did not recognize my brother countertransference until much later when I first wrote about Daniel. Nonetheless I had had inklings in my feelings about the difference in our sizes, in my awkwardness toward someone smaller than me, and through my eventual irritation with myself about remaining mesmerized in an accommodating stance. Certainly, I had also had aggravated and impatient feelings about Daniel, but what released me and re-opened the path of empathy was the fact that I was able to overcome my own conflict in regard to showing myself and expressing a need. Both Daniel and I had felt excluded and both needed to come out of the shadows. What I am emphasizing is that conflict, resistance, and danger situations all have to be grasped as to how they occur in both of the therapeutic participants and how they are upheld or resolved as a function of our understanding of their co-constitution in the intersubjective system. In my view, we need to pay much more attention to how the bi-directional level of discourse is intertwined with whatever we may do or not do on the asymmetric level of discourse. Finally, it bears repeating that nothing will change for our patients unless we have the courage to expand our abilities of reflection to include ourselves and how we are implicated in everything that occurs in treatment. Transformations, like all psychological phenomena, are contextual. In this sense, I agree with Mitchell's (1988) view: "Conflict is inherent in relatedness" (p. 160).

Notes

1 I am endebted to Morris Eagle's (2011) book *From Classical to Contemporary Psychoanalysis: A Critique and Integration* for an in-depth contextualization of the differences and similarities in the theories of psychoanalysis and for providing a renewed appreciation for our profession.
2 The following account is based on Chapter 6, "Developmental Failure and Psychic Conflict, " in *Psychoanalytic Treatment.An Intersubjective Approach*, Stolorow et al., 1987.
3 Invariant emotional organizing priciples are understood to refer to those unconscious conclusions a person has drawn from the repetition of interactions with the significant surround about the nature of self, other, and the world. In sum, they are the building blocks of which a personalty consists.
4 For a detailed account of the therapeutic process with Daniel see Chapter 4 in: Jaenicke, C. (2014), *The Search for a Relational Home: An Intersubjective-Systems View of Therapeutic Action*, Routledge, New York/London.

Chapter 10

Conflict and change

Producer, trigger, sign, outcome

Adrienne Harris

There are many ways and many situations within the analytic setting in which to find conflict. I think this is increasingly true across a number of different theoretical orientations and over our changing history. At its origins and for much of its history, the power of psychoanalysis emanated from the conviction that great psychic labor and deep fundamentals of character emerged from the impact of intrapsychic conflict over inherent biological drives and the attendant anxieties around sexuality and aggression. Now we are attentive to the presence and function of conflicts that may be intersubjective and interrelational, internally and externally derived and, in certain instances, transgenerational.

We find the potency of conflict in the individual's encounter with the culture at many levels. Conflicts are particularly likely to emerge as individuals are engaged by, become subject to, or resist the cultural surround when that individual inhabits or is inhabited by any of the many forms of non-normative identity and personhood (race, class, sexuality, disability, culture, and gender). Contested forms of identification are at the forefront of many clinical concerns encountered with patients and manifest with anguish and with difficulty in the transference-countertransference matrix.

In this chapter I want to examine conflict (intersubjective, intrapsychic, and enacted), attendant on the process of change itself. I am thinking of conflict as an inherent aspect of developmental movement and that such movements (macro or micro) are charged with powerful experiences of disequilibrium. I see these conflicts around change as complex, multidirectional, and unstable. Conflicts that emerge in conditions of psychic or relational transformations are produced by many different affect states and relational vertices.

In the clinical material from several patients, I am particularly going to focus on the presence and function of despair and terror in conflictual transactions that precede and accompany and sometimes sabotage change and mutative action. I think it is striking that in the complex scenes that can emerge around change (often at very unconscious levels), many patients' fear of their own aggression plays a potent role, alongside their very active aggression.

In 2005, I wrote an essay on conflict in relational theory which focused on the sites of conflict in the divided states in the internal world, the forms of conflict underlying motivational theories that were what Ghent (2002) described as small *d* drive theories in which motivational systems (like sex or aggression) were *emergent* from more primitive procedures (turning to light and warmth, orienting to objects, etc.) (Harris, 2005). It was an essay, however, in which I did not problematize change but only set it within a two-person system.

The theoretical home for *this* essay is relational and a relational space where object relations and internal worlds are the site of conflict just as trenchantly as conflicts played out in intersubjective interactions. While there are many ways to think about conflicts from a relational perspective and in different degrees and contexts, I still subscribe to all these forms of conflict developed in my 2005 essay as key sites for change or for entrapment and stasis. Here I am addressing more specifically the role of conflict in change itself.

One central idea is that the person in conflict feels in the grips of two impossible errands (Apprey, 2015). Growth will entail separation, and separation from dead or dying objects can feel or be intolerable. It is thinking of change as the moment when a conflict over psychic tasks and mental freedom creates a dangerous point of struggle or even impasse. Whether we call this the abyss or the edge of chaos, or a dramatic fear-laden journey of separation, for some, perhaps in some way for all patients, this is a point, I believe, of maximal conflict and danger. One sees this in the wax and wane of progress in analysis and the reversals and panics when psychic shifts begin or catch momentum.

In this essay, therefore, I draw on the field theory aspects of relational theory and specifically both Bion's (1962b, 1970) notions of the catastrophe of change (Goldberg, 2008) for a strong discussion of this aspect of Bionian theory and W. Baranger's (2009b) concept of a spiral process. I see these forms of movement and psychic shift both as the site of mourning and the site of impasses in mourning. These ideas connect to a powerful set of concepts that I find extremely useful, which have been developed by J. Henri Rey (1988), in an influential yet not so well-known paper, "That which Patients Bring to

Analysis". In that paper, Rey argues that patients may arrive in treatment with a hidden agenda – an errand as Apprey (2015) might say – which is to repair the damaged objects in their history now part of a dying or damaged internal world. Heal the object and then the patient can change. This is the impossible bind in which a treatment may be enfolded.

In the spirit of relational theorizing about the potent role of counter-transference and the analyst's subjectivity, I want to turn Rey's lens on the analyst's unconscious task as well. Approaching the question of anxious resistance to change and the conflict-tinged determination to spoil growth, one must ask the same questions about the presence of such fears in the analyst's countertransference. Relational analysts have made a very strong focus on the instrumentality of countertransference and the powerful ways the analyst's process disrupts and/or facilitates psychic change in the patient.

Thinking then of what fears of change the analyst may bring to treatment leads me to think about what "errands," as Apprey calls them, the analyst may bring to the work. To put this in Rey's terms, we can ask, what do analysts bring to analysis? I have pursued some of these ideas in the context of trying to think about the analyst's melancholy, the difficulties in self-care, and the force of hidden omnipotences in what the analyst brings to the dyad (Harris, 2009, 2010, 2014).

As part of a project on looking at how analysts do or don't take care of themselves, I have come to focus more and more on omnipotence and melancholy as one of many points of countertransference tension or conflict and vulnerability. It is perhaps the analysts' *bastion*, Baranger's (2006) term for a defense of great tenacity behind which sits vulnerability and hopelessness. Analysts' difficulties with self-care may well be a subset of doctors' general and notorious difficulties in being patients but the frequently seen dilemmas in development among mental health workers will also have their own features.

The literary critic Edmund Wilson (1941) drew on a Greek myth to argue that certain writers made art out of wound, drawing on wells of anguish to make exquisite prose, potent stories, and deep truths. The writers he had in mind were Wharton, Dickens, Kipling, and James. The myth he chose was the story of Philoctetes the Archer who was bitten by a snake on the ankle and so long as the wound never healed, his aim was perfect. For analysts, I feel that the term *wounded healers* easily applies. The analytic instrument is made of wound and of skill and of emotion. We heal with contaminated tools.

Many analysts and many of our most venerated leaders – Winnicott, Fairbairn, McLaughlin, Williams, Loewald, and these I name because of the personal stories they have written – were often recruited into caretaking early in their own development. For many in our field, our first patient is likely to have arrived early in our lives, involving us in precociously mature forms of management and functioning. In a collection of essays, *The Mind Object* (Corrigan & Gordon, 1995), a number of authors (Bollas, Phillips, Gorden, Corrigan, Boris) argued that premature precocity created a crisis of containment, often requiring the child to use his or her own mind as a container and his or her own internal experience as transitional space.

This strategy, always only partially successful but often surprisingly tenacious, leaves the person often very saddled with omnipotence, a character structure designed to abolish or evacuate neediness, shame, or vulnerability. We see this in any young children who effectively (though temporarily) abolish awareness of their own needs to manage the anguish and needs of others (siblings, parents, etc.). This is the idea Corrigan and Gordon (1995) and their colleagues pursued. Similarly, Bromberg (1998) sees dissociative mechanisms as one prime manner in which children sequester personal need and remain attuned and parental as a way to remain attached to a damaged or damaging parent. Dissociation is the price tag on attachment. I will address the implications of this process for difficulties in the *analyst*'s tolerance for change.

Where and how does precocious caretaking arise? The answer is quite interesting and somewhat surprising. The attachment theorists have looked at the many inspired patterns children have devised to organize a relational configuration with a parental figure or figures that appear broken or collapsing or dangerous or all three. Lyons-Ruth (1999, 2003) calls an adaptive coping style "tend/befriend," that is the capacity to be parental. She names this as one of the potential strategies of a child in a family or dyadic pattern termed *disorganized*. This kind of apprenticeship whenever it arises carries a significant cost. The analyst must bulwark his or her vulnerability at all costs. Omnipotent defenses silence need or shame or sadness or fear of loss. Need or neediness is evacuated into others. To the degree that this (in some variation) is a path for many healers we may wonder how many of us define ourselves by our healing, a process that has both strengths and weaknesses.

How might this structure in the analyst create conflicts over the course of treatment, particularly when the patient is courting and approaching change? Thinking relationally means that if one part of the system changes, other parts of the system will have to mutate as well. Being an analyst has often meant that one sublimates one's basic needs to cure and repair our own objects. But that can never be perfectly achieved. Can the analyst relinquish the project of caretaking the dying objects in his or her internal world? What does relinquishing the patient to a healthier future open for an analyst at any stage of one's career (Cooper, 2003)? A functional system will be tested in moments of change in the patient. What hopes of the analyst are carried by the patient? But for many analysts, the ability to help a patient change in the light of the impossible task of healing their own objects raises a serious possibility of impasse.

This kind of trouble seems equally likely when the change is seen in positive terms or when the pace or movement of treatment disappoints and fails. The change demanded of the analyst is a shift (partial or general) from melancholy to mourning. But this is a change which many analysts have spent a lifetime defeating. What I mean by that is that our mission to care for and help another is for many people (not solely analysts) built on a powerful structure of omnipotence. We might think of this in the Barangers' terms as a bastion, a defensive structure behind or beneath which lurks great dread of powerlessness and vulnerability. This is an archaic state in any character formation, but it may have special force in a person whose history of caretaking goes back to a very precocious but early place in development.

So for the analyst to accept the patient's changes will require for the analyst some degree of mourning, of accepting the limits of omnipotence, the ultimate and inevitable failure to repair the analyst's own internal dying or injured objects. Mourning in the analyst could be, must be, and perhaps must precede creating space for mourning in the patient (Harris, 2005). It is the paradox that the analyst must watch a patient successfully negotiating the conflict of change aware that he or she has facilitated for another what was impossible for the analyst himself or herself. We endlessly prepare our patients to be able to give up the errand (Apprey, 2015) of repairing their damaged objects. Yet our professional identity carries our hopeless task into the heart of professional competence.

I think of Searles (1959, 1973) in this regard, quite often. Searles was keenly attuned to the complexity of his countertransference and regarded the presence of deep love, often or usually deep erotic love for a patient – man or woman – as a harbinger of change. He is an early proponent of the power of countertransference experience as integral to the patient's change.

An unexamined aspect of analytic work, I believe, is the complex competitions and envies that are part of the analyst's conscious or unconscious involvement with the patients' internal objects, particularly the parental figures who disappoint and injure the patient. Something quite complex may be afoot here. The patient's damaged and damaging objects may stir up identifications and old object ties for the analyst. Score settling, triumph, all overlaid with the veneer of repair and concern, may constitute complex conflicts for the analyst who must relinquish these hidden projects in order to liberate the patient. Inevitably in the resolution of countertransference feelings, the pain of failed repairs in the analyst's history must resurface: the injuries not fixed, the losses unmourned.

Creation, destruction, change, and chaos theory

It is one of the useful and productive paradoxes in certain views of creativity, that making and unmaking, creating and destroying, intertwine. The notion that change proceeds through transformative interweaving of creation and destruction surfaces in an early paper by Sabina Spielrein (1912/1981). In that paper, Spielrein argued that there are potent transformations in which creativity and destruction interweave and work in dialectical tension. Wreckage and anguish are elements in excitement and both building and destroying are inevitable parts of any transformations. She made this argument both in regard to sexuality and in regard to mind and thought.

One can see this developmental process echoing and evolving over the next century of psychoanalytic and psychological theorizing about development and about change. Spielrein has a quite modern model of splits in mental life, a fragmenting of self-states, and the presence of various kinds of otherness in the self, all in dynamic transformative process in the service of change and growth. One sees a similar appreciation of catastrophe and disequilibrium in Bion's theories of change and in chaos theory and in the work of neuroscientists like Walter Freeman (1995, 2001), who draws on chaos theory (non-linear dynamic systems theory) to model developments and transformations in the brain.

Currently this idea is pervasive in many theoretical realms, particularly the relational and the neo-Bionian worlds. From various figures (Bromberg, 1998; Ferro, 2002; Bass, 2007; D. B. Stern, 2009; Peltz & Goldberg, 2013; Ogden, 2014) there is a strong commitment to a way of work, filled with uncertainty and challenge, more organized around experience than understanding. Clinical work in this perspective is risky, unsettling, set up to invite the "unbidden," or, to speak with less contradiction, to be, as best as possible, available to contact with the patient often in experiences of deep anguish and psychic danger.

To be invited or to feel the need to work in this way puts any analyst in a state of conflict. Responsible and free, caretaking and adventurous, careful and carefree, hate-filled and loving (Winnicott, 1994, 1974), the negotiations of contradiction and conflict are daunting.

For all these figures one can trace the emergence of creation and destruction as inherent aspects of growth. As part of the paradox, growth is seen as always emergent in experiences of regression and undoing alongside steps toward integration. Change occurs at a tipping point but often when the outcome is uncertain and where the system is as likely to crash as to re-equilibrate in a new form. There is an interesting modern take on this in the work of the Botellas (2014) on figurability and symbolization. They take up phrases of translation in French that honor a Freudian concept in which regression is not a collapse and disintegration but a form of psychic work and transformation: regrediante, not regression.

Perhaps also in this lineage from Spielrein, we can posit Winnicott's vision of aggression and conflict as a critical aspect of development, a line of thought he developed most particularly in "Hate in the Counter-transference." The child comes to notice the difference between the wish to destroy and the fact of the other's survival. The outcome of that process, Winnicott (1965) thought, was a capacity to apprehend reality and, as Benjamin (1998) and Ghent (2002) add, deepening a capacity for love.

Walter Freeman's (1995, 2001) interest in change and destructiveness arose in the domain of neuroscience. Chaos or complexity theory situates development in a particular moment of useful productive conflict. A system, stable enough to sustain life and some identity, but tipping also toward disequilibrium and destruction, is a system on the edge of chaos and thus potentially on the edge of transformation. This state – the edge of chaos – may be the site of productive change or of disintegration. The conflict that ushers in potential for change is inherently enigmatic, heading for transformation or collapse and fragmentation. The result is always emergent. Change and growth are never, in some purely mechanical way, predicted. Nevertheless change arises through pattern and organization. Conflict may be an entry point for change but may also lead to its derailment.

Bion (1970) spoke of this process in more dramatic less mechanical language, but I think it is helpful to see that he is also describing a non-linear dynamic change process. A patient, a person, feels the imperative and imminence of change and is almost inevitably drawn into a state of anxiety and peril. Change augers separation. It may feel murderous as change entails the burying or at least leave-taking of dying and damaged internal objects. In these ways, change very often feels lonely. How can the old objects be abandoned unhealed and now alone? Rey (1988) tracked this process in patients' determination to cure their objects before changing themselves. Change threatens the integrity and survival of precious objects and necessary, even if unconscious, errands. The internal dialogues and conflict lived as fear, calmed often through dissociation, yanking analyst and analysand in a wild tumbling scene, often both boiling and freezing. Change ushers in inevitable states of conflict in the unpredictable move toward organization with bumps along the way.

If we think of development as always pushed by a hunger for novelty and checked by a comparably deep comfort in reliability, we might see how much change and ongoing conflict fuel growth. Different developmental theories parse these problems in different ways, examining the conflict within stages or positions (Piaget, 1954) or between simultaneous but different levels of experience (Fischer, 1980) or within a process that is inevitably individual and dyadic, cultural and personal (Vygotsky, 1963).

We might also think of the absence of these moments of conflict and disequilibrium as moments of pathology. Craig Piers (2000) has illustrated this in his example of the difficulties inherent on too much stability and regularity, that is, too stable a heart rate. A rigid pendulum, a swinging and oscillating system whether a monotonously regular heart beat or a scripted and repeated marital quarrel, is an unhealthy system. In her model of couples treatment, Goldner (2014) has used the work of Benjamin (2004) on "doer/done to" – the oscillating experiences of projection and counter reaction. The fixed pendulum-like action of move/countermove keeps a couple in a destructive lock-down.

One of the most powerful renderings of conflict is Ferenczi's (1932/1949) "Confusion of Tongues" paper where he argues that the conflict within an abusing adult is unconsciously transmitted to the child and that, therefore, the conflict is always both between and within subjectivities leaving much uncertainty as whose guilt is being felt, whose anxiety, whose desire. We might see Ferenczi's account of these phenomena as lying on the far end of

168 Adrienne Harris

the spectrum of enigmatic but also traumatic seduction and transcription outlined by Laplanche (1999)

Willy Baranger (2009a) writes about what he terms the *dead-alive*. He is concerned with persons in thrall to a figure neither alive nor dead, a feature of a ghost world, perhaps persecutory, perhaps spectral and weakened, but nonetheless tenaciously held by the living survivor. Baranger notes, in clinical examples, the terrible price in ego impoverishment that is entailed in the task of keeping the dead-alive figure in place. Change and growth and any working through is both a threat and a hope. Bion's sense of change as a point of the abyss seems relevant here.

With all these theoretical sources: Bion (1962a, 1962b), Bromberg on dissociation, Rey (1988) on the frozen internal object world, W. Baranger (2009a) on the demands of a dying internal world, change is conflictual, almost unbearable, and actually unbearable in some cases. It is interesting that the field theorist's model of change is less about the lightning strike of good interpretations and more about a gradual spiral (Bleger, 2012) in which motion is always forward and back and in which there is an expansion of mental freedom arising in subtle and almost undiscernible moves. But even in patterns of subtle movement, there is always backward as well as forward motion.

Clinical situations

The conflict inherent in change and mutative action arises in ways both subtle and gross. A patient has finally begun to track the long-term effect of his heavy caretaking role growing up in his family, a caretaking that encompasses several generations. He can also link this historical work to his current professional projects which are mostly experienced in a torturous way as he must always buoy up and support his co-workers. Insight is followed by an expansiveness, a beginning of permission for more pleasure, less ordeal and significantly less masochistic enslavement to the various stand-ins for the original objects. But in the midst of this positive expansion, suddenly there are more and more canceled sessions, lateness, chaos from the patient's work world flowing into the analysis.

What is striking, but I think quite typical, is that it takes many repetitions of this process – expansion followed by rupture and threat to the analytic frame and the relational projects – before the analyst can master surprise and confusion and disappointment. How often the surprise and sense of unbidden rupture occurs even in analyses of long duration. Reflective experience becomes broken and unavailable. Thought has been banished as the patient (and perhaps also the analyst in hidden negative countertransferences) is determined to pull the plug, drown hope, provoking fantasies of scorched earth and death.

It is, of course, a staple of neo-Kleinian and Bionian ideas to notice the attacks on links, on functionality in the analyst as acts of primary destructiveness, but I think these feelings are also joined up with fear, (Harris, 2014; Slade, 2014) with the terror that change will be only destructive and that a fundamental and unalterable contract with dying or damaged objects is being abridged.

Yet as the conflict enters the transference the patient brings a dilemma for the analyst. Growth and change equals abandoning a damaged object. The conflict inherent in this situation is untenable. It is the knot the analysis must untie but the consequences for the patient are, at an unconscious and sometimes conscious level, often untenable. Guilt and terror at abandoning these fragile internal objects often holds a terrible power over patient and analyst.

Baranger (2009a) and others (Bion, Goldberg) make careful distinctions between the developmental levels at which these conflicts are lived and played out. Bion, interestingly, considers that the premature links (what we would also call the work of mourning) done at archaic levels – paranoid-schizoid functioning – are potentially catastrophic. Growth and change are disasters by virtue of an experienced attack on a symbiotically tied although also dying object.

I think one sees and feels these conflicts in treatments where there is a strong element of intergenerational transmission of trauma (Laub, 2013; Apprey, 2015) The imagined abandonment of the lost figures whose legacy is in the unconscious leaks and memory traces that are seamlessly part of the patients' whole mode of functioning pose an intolerable conflict. In thinking of the crisis of change, one encounters and undertakes an important debate on what change is safe enough to pursue, on both sides of the dyad.

Clinical material

A woman in late middle age comes to treatment, a treatment that slowly but surely deepens into an analysis. She has had almost a lifetime of treatment and an unchanging symptom. Despite life events of significance and depth, and even after the victory over terrifying inhibitions to produce creative work, she says, simply and calmly, "I am not real. I don't feel. I can't want." It is actually worse than that, we discover. If she should visibly want and act in the service of any ambition or wish, she lives with the sure and genuine fear that she would be killed. The severity of the fears, the deadening of opportunity, and the bedrock conviction of the deathly fate of action and desiring are very striking. Like Ferenczi's unwanted child, this woman arrived at birth already wrong and bad. No process with anyone significant in her family altered this conviction.

In my years of work with this patient, I never, for a moment, doubted how high the stakes were. I realized that I was afraid for her and sometimes I was afraid of her. Aggression was chillingly flattened in her process and our process together. Yet murderous danger had us both in its grip. Change threatened outbreaks of violence that seemed beyond imagination yet were clearly deeply infusing her imagination and mine. She more explicitly feared death and murder. I feared madness and breakdown.

Any suggestion of aggression or rage or any fury directed at an abusive parent made the patient go blank. In our excavation of history, put together from shards and shattered bits of memory, it was clear that this woman had been genuinely at risk from conception onward. Among the frozen elements in the patient's psychic life, a reverential melancholic pall hung over her memories and narratives about her mother. This mother was fragile, saintly, doing her best, and bedridden. Anger was significantly absent. Any questioning on my part led the patient to an imaginative flight out of the consulting room. Perhaps, she mused, she would shop after her session. The lingerie shop near the office was often the place of reverie and escape. There was one space where fury and aggression surfaced and that was in creative work where murders, smothering, falling, and beheading (pre-ISIS) flourished. I tell her quite often that I think her writing is a site of her sanity.

Our work deepened and intensified. Unsettling feelings surfaced in dreams and in morning reveries. Death was in the air between us. Death and murder. She often wondered why I was not frightened someone would break into the office and kill us. This was delivered in a curious voice. Cool but interested.

In the course of our work, she began to move toward a more public presentation of her work. As everyone around her was encouraging, she became more anxious and unsure. Something terrible would or could happen if she stepped into visibility. It was unthinkable. These acts of assertion of self had been longed for over a lifetime, yet when they arrived they brought the fear of catastrophe. I believe that for this patient change involved the destruction of her mother and the tie to that mother and that act would/could lead to murder. At one level what she could not bear to see was the memory of murderous looks in her mother's face. But in another experience of this conflict it is her own murderousness that is so terrifying.

What is so difficult here is the need to unpack the aggressive wish to kill off and destroy the mother who had so endangered and hated her. The patient lived as if she could only be the recipient of aggression, particularly when she initiated some change, some expansion of visible actions and accomplishments. The object tie is simultaneously fragile and soldered. Change was a catastrophe for the murky tie to a dying but dangerous object.

I am pretty sure that the anxiety in me was tied to fear of an unmanageable catastrophe attendant on change. No doubt this reverberated through her life and mine. Omnipotent defenses in the analyst entrained with omnipotent fantasies in the patient operating over a lifetime. The conflict over change seemed life threatening. Spielrein (1912) might see the transformative power of destructiveness, the radical longings for rebirth, death to bring life. Certainly in chaos theory the radical destabilization of a rigid and pendulum-like system is a necessary move in effecting real change. She was hated. She must remain small. This idea seemed to her not a hypothesis but bedrock. Doubt and uncertainty, the necessary harbingers of movement in analyst and patient, were anticipated as forms of dynamite.

From the perspective of Winnicott and an object relations view of internal phantasy and the imagined fate of a precious object, the patient stayed and wished to stay virtually blind to the conflict that was emerging inside her. She was dimly conscious of conflict but really only as an intellectual construct. A parent who suffered so silently was surely a saint. The truth that this parent had very nearly destroyed her could not be experienced. In that sense there is no conflict, time stands still, and so there is no change.

Treatment and my engagement with the patient unsettle those still waters. Paradoxically, and I think both of us feel this, it is not clear if change will murder or save. The analyst's omnipotence in this regard is not helpful. Bion makes this so clear.

Another patient works this edge of doing and undoing in a more subtle and skillful way. The other significantly older patient functions in relation to change like a rigid 8-year-old. This patient, a young adult, is well along in her analysis, with much insight into her process with husband and family. Fifteen years ago she entered treatment, and in the first session said that her mother's mother had died when this mother was 4 years old. Fifteen years later this sentence has still not been fully unpacked. Deep understanding of the flight of a now aging and compromised parent is stopped short, derailed in repeating moments of adolescent-tinged refusal.

Change threatens too much. The patient will become unrecognizable to herself. She will have to forgive and comprehend, hold the depressive position, and end the endless indictments. It certainly strikes me that the incessant conflict that she conducts in her life and in her analysis is designed to keep at bay the conflictual experience that comes with internal change and with the surfacing of the internal unconscious fantasy of the need to keep a dying figure alive giving way to the depth of various hopes that cannot be relinquished. A scene of repair must occur and if that is not possible (and actually it is not) scorched earth takes its place.

Virtually every facet of this patient's life and functioning would expand and flourish, but the catastrophe she imagines shuts down a process of disequilibrium and destruction at a different order. We both know this and yet any shift undertaken with both our hopes and intelligence engaged runs aground. This happens at a micro level. I have many experience of beginning an hour, hearing something loving and hopeful in the early opening minutes of the session and then, sometimes suddenly, sometimes slowly, but always inexorably, a dark disappointed sometimes hostile note appears. My heart sinks. I ask myself why I am still surprised. I suspect some very subtle process of unconscious force between us where my hopes actually unexpressed but probably palpable in some inchoate but significant way must be canceled out. Change is dangerous. Hope must be snuffed out. It is certainly the case that thinking of the function of projective identification as a communication is greatly of use here. I am treated again and again to the disappointing dashed hopes of the patient, constantly disappointed and psychically dropped by an anxious and disengaging mother.

In thinking of conflict this way, its intersubjective and its intrapsychic forms will always be operating, in tandem or in opposition.

A patient with a long history of treatment and many tools for intro-spection and psychic work remains battered and beleaguered by terrible self-beratement. He and I talk about the origins of these self-attacks, the contemptuous and terrorizing voices that hammer away: ridiculous, stu-pid, empty, useless. Internal dialogues are like acid, toxic leaks pooling in an otherwise attuned and thoughtful mind.

We both notice that these voices wax and wane. His mind expands, he feels the freedom and relief, but this freedom is short-lived. The minute an externally generated critique is silenced, the internal monologues begin. Calm seems too often to lead to depression, to sleeplessness, to despair.

Many treatments ago, this man figured out with his therapist that he was carrying these woes and self-hatreds for the larger family, but carry-ing these woes while the family considered them foolish and unimportant. Without much difficulty, he and I figured out another element in the story: the unmarked and unmourned losses in an earlier generation which had become the patient's inheritance. He had an errand he could not relinquish (Apprey, 2015).

The official story within his family was that all this fuss over loss was just that, fuss. Why bother? Really. I think in such situations, the only change possible is the most feared and resisted. Separate, change, resign your commission. That choice feels like a murder and the enigma of who is being murdered, patient or parent, never really settles. This is a clinical situation encountered very frequently and one that remit and shifts only with very hard and often dangerous work. I want to add to our understand-ing of these moments, moments when melancholy must turn to mourning, that the work of the analyst must include the resolving of conflicts around comparable scenes in the analysts' internal world. How is the analyst who may have made a career of caretaking going to encourage a patient to abandon the task/errand that has defined his or her life. We might be wor-ried in this regard about the analyst's envy of the patient's getting support to change. This is oddly an envy of what the analyst is himself or herself supplying to the patient.

As I began to peruse many different clinical situations over the lifetime of my practice, I see that the struggle against omnipotence, the conflict about vulnerability, the impasse around melancholy is one primary ele-ment in my generic countertransference, that is conflictual experience that seems both characterological and developmental. I have been arguing that this particular conflict is a knot in many analytic instruments. (to mix

174   Adrienne Harris

metaphors). In a sense we ask patients to be able to do what, looked at a certain way, we have great difficulty doing ourselves.

The Barangers (Baranger & Baranger, 2006) proposed that we think of all analyses coming finally down to the basic conflict within what they termed the *bastion* – the line of ultimate defense behind which the painful remnants of dread and helplessness are kept sequestered. It was their brilliant insight (along with Bleger, 2012) that this bastion is a site of conflict in the analyst and so these kinds of conflict remain always within and between persons.

A patient must mourn her mother, a person both hated and feared. Cathleen Adams (personal communication) has been writing about mother-daughter estrangement, about the complex inner conflicts of daughters who have felt the necessity of stopping contact with mothers who are still living. Adams is accurate about the relief this can bring in daily life and the violent remnants of unconscious links and mostly unconscious projects of repair. Paradoxically, for patient and analyst must lose or dismantle fantasies of potency, face the terror of what Bion rightly called "the abyss" and encounter a particular mix of vulnerability and danger. One woman in my practice, struggling to distinguish herself from a vulnerable and depressed mother, fights against change and struggles toward it. "I don't feel viable," she offered, to her surprise and mine. Faced with her own determination to change in the context of the demands of parenting her children, this woman experiences the prospect of change as both the loss of safety and the loss of meaning.

When these particular conflicts around change are engaged with experiences of aggression and destructiveness, the demands for repair of dying objects and the wish to destroy them create very potent demands on treatments. Destructive aggression is toggled always between self-harm and a kind of scorched earth scene with significant others. In a period of expansiveness when the patient was emerging from strict and tight inhibitions around work and relationships, the state of mental freedom that emerged was very quickly prey to potent bouts of mental self-destructiveness. Freedom of thought and affect countered experiences of genuine exploration and the courage to imagine more life and thought for himself. These movements operate as a kind of spiral (Baranger, 2009b).

One potent way to conceptualize these conflicts is to see the individual caught between loyalty to bad objects and something transformative. Fairbairn (1954) was illuminating in this regard. In a modern voice, Maurice Apprey (2015) notes the demands on certain children in certain families to undertake an "errand." That errand may be destructive, self-destructive, or enhancing. But whatever its format or agenda, it cannot be declined in favor of self-actualization. The stakes for change and growth become very high, death-dealing in some cases, crippling and paralyzing in others.

One possible outcome of this focus on change as a site of conflict is that the language and the clinical descriptions can make the process look like an extreme sport. Negotiating conflict is treated as a form of triple black diamond skiing. I want to draw on a recent paper of Rachel Peltz and Peter Goldberg (2013), who are describing a mode of working that is precisely the opposite. Using the work of Bion, Ferro (2002) and Ogden, Peltz and Goldberg make a plea for negative capability, for uncertainty and openness to unexpected experience. Reverie, reflection, a loose attention to experience and sensation, more attunement to body schemes and bodily experience are for these authors a way to get inside psychoanalysis, inside, following John Berger, a "pocket of resistance." This process which in heightened moments of change and transformation will have vulnerability throughout the dyad and the system is challenging precisely because athleticism will not be helpful.

However, this complex moment or moments with patients whether leading to shameful collapse or sturdy reorganization (or some sequence of both) emerge always in a relational context. In being attentive to a variety of theoretical investments in thinking of conflict, I want to stress the tension and contradiction in thinking of conflict as the harbinger of change, its necessary preparatory moment, and also as conflict having the potential to undermine change and growth precisely through the inability to manage the anxiety of change, its catastrophic import. These demands play out on both sides of the analytic dyad.

In an essay on impasse (Harris, 2009), I considered that breaks in impasse, of the sort that will inevitably arise in moments of profound change and transformation, the analyst must mourn. What I increasingly understand about that process is that the omnipotence with all its melancholy suspension of finality and loss must be reduced, resolved, dissolved, mutated to some degree in the analyst in order for that movement to occur in the patient.

I am taking a field theory approach here, seeing that projects of transference and projective identification and omnipotent projects, in both partners in an analytic process, must mutate in some way and to some degree. The patient has to accept the new task of self-care and freedom, the task of separation from internal dying objects. The analyst must bear the ironic and often tragic awareness that the new substitute object (the patient) is more transformable than the analyst's own internal figures. Failure of the archaic task or errand is wound around successful care and transformation of the analysand. All within limits, of course, and always in the context of internal conflicts that are intersubjective and intrapsychic, on both sides of the couch.

Each analyst within each treatment dyad and within his or her own history and context will negotiate this intricately interdependent process. Slavin (2010) describes a moment in a very tumultuous treatment with a suicidal patient whom he felt both deeply worried over and trapped by. At a certain moment and in a spirit he describes as enigmatic and filled with uncertainty, he simply declares that he cannot keep the patient alive. It is a transformative moment and in the context of this essay on conflict one in which the analyst has moved through a piece of his own omnipotence to a place of limit, a place where realities including the reality of limit and death are not under the management of the analyst. It is a moment or moments where the analyst stares into the abyss, both the same and a different one from the patient.

Analysis with all these patients I have thought about in this essay seemed often to take place in a field of land mines, ones set and often detonated by various figures, real and imagined, in analysand and analyst. Relational work on enactment identifies these moments as crucial tipping points, won and lost repeatedly over the time of an analysis.

Among the ways we might think of this is to see how melancholy linked to omnipotent strategies is one response to the demands of change and mutative action. Another aspect of this clinical dilemma is the management (in analysand but particularly in analyst) of destructiveness, a destructiveness that has the potential for transformation and for undoing and thwarting.

Chapter 11

The dialectic of desire

A view of intrapsychic conflict in the work of Jacques Lacan

David Lichtenstein

The divided subject

In Jacques Lacan's view the participants in the psychoanalytic encounter are other than what they appear. The ordinary individual, the everyday self, is based upon an illusion that is sustained more or less in everyday life, but dissolves in effective psychoanalytic work. What takes the place of the person is a radically divided subject who is never wholly present at any single place or time. In order to appreciate Lacan's approach to psychoanalysis, one must first recognize this radical theory of subjectivity.

For Lacan the conscious sense of self is based upon an unavoidable misperception rooted in the inherently defensive structures of the ego. As he put it in one of his earliest papers (on the "mirror stage"),

> Analytic experience . . . teaches us not to regard the ego as centered on the *perception-consciousness system* or as organized by the "reality principle" . . . but, rather, to take as our point of departure the *function of misrecognition* that characterizes the ego.
>
> (Lacan, 2006, p. 80, emphasis in the original)

The function of misrecognition that Lacan refers to in this essay is a false sense of self as whole and complete. It is a necessary fiction and is related to the primal repression that S. Freud (1915b) discusses as growing out of an effort to expel the sources of unpleasurable experience and create a purified pleasure-ego. For Lacan this comes together as an infantile self-image of wholeness and coherence that belies the disorganized and chaotic state of being. This is what is meant by Lacan's notion of the *function of misrecognition* and that he views as inherent to the conscious ego. It is not particular to certain pathological states nor potentially corrected by a True Self. The condition of consciousness is an inevitable state of alienation (Lacan, 2006). This alienated conscious self is divided from unconscious sources of subjective truth and this division, conceived as a result of repression understood largely in the Freudian sense, is the source of an inherent and irredeemable duality in the human character. The division between the unconscious subject and the conscious self of misrecognition has many complex ramifications in Lacan's thought, but it is here in this inherent duality that something akin to intrapsychic conflict can be located in Lacan's thought.

Speaking in the place of this ego of misrecognition is an irrevocably divided subject, partly present in this defensive self, and partly in *an other* place: the Freudian unconscious. This is why we inevitably say more than we intend, why we misconstrue our own actions, and are subverted by our own desires. The function of analysis is not to overcome this irrevocable division, rather to reduce the illusion that it can be overcome, and thereby help people to live more gracefully in their divided state.

Lacan considers his view of the subject to be in keeping with the theory of the subject as established in Freud's early works such as *The Psychopathology of Everyday Life* (1901), where the presumed transparency of consciousness is first put into doubt, but also in later works such as *The Ego and the Id* (1923), where the structural division of the subject is elaborated in new terms. Lacan repeats again and again in his teaching that he is taking Freud seriously and that he means to offer a corrective to a tendency among psychoanalysts to reduce the radical import of Freudian thought.

Thus Lacan is deeply indebted to Freud's statement that, "the ego is not even master in its own house, but must content itself with scanty information of what is going on unconsciously in its mind," (Freud, 1916, p. 285). For Lacan, this definitive and inescapable lack of ego mastery is taken to mean that the integrity of the house itself is in question. The self as a coherent entity can only be a fiction. If that is so, then who or what can speak truthfully from the locus of this fictive self? Either everything that is said in the name of this impostor who claims mastery is fundamentally untrustworthy or there is another source of truth that may speak through this fictive self.

There is an unconscious subject that speaks, using the same mind and body, the same experience and words that are used by the conscious self, but using them in surprising ways that depart from conscious intent. This division in our subjectivity is the first fundamental element for developing an idea of Lacan's theory of conflict. It reflects a return to the earlier Freud of the first topography but with recognition of the later structural theory and, indeed, a sublation of the differences between the two topographies. Lacan's theory of the divided subject represents an effort to create a new model that respects both of Freud's earlier models. In both its conception of subjective division and of subjective structure, I will suggest that Lacan's theory also implicitly reflects a new theory of intrapsychic conflict.

Although Lacan's teaching has been appropriated by schools of criticism and other academic fields beyond psychoanalysis, he was first and foremost a clinical psychoanalyst and he believed that the essential division of the subject and the ensuing dialectic expressing this division was the orienting vector of clinical psychoanalytic work (Lacan, 2006). The analyst's bearings, how to listen and to intervene, come from attention to the division in the speaking subject (Lacan, 2006).

To explore the role of *conflict* in Lacan's work, a term that has no particular currency as such within Lacan's writing and teaching, I will look instead to the idea of subjective *division* and the structure of that division as Lacan sees it. In so doing, I hope to illustrate both what it is in Lacan's work that derives from the classical idea of intrapsychic conflict and what departs from it.

As in S. Freud's (1923) structural model, Lacan's structure of the divided subject entails bodily, cultural, relational, and psychological factors. I intend to discuss Lacan's thought on its own terms and to show how it address the contemporary interest in the intersubjective dimensions of psychoanalysis while retaining fundamental principles of the Freudian perspective regarding the structure of the psyche. To do so it will be necessary to develop some of the other basic concepts of the Lacanian vocabulary.

The function of lack in the formation of the divided subject

> The repressed instinct (drive) never ceases to strive for complete satisfaction, which would consist in the repetition of a primary experience of satisfaction. No substitutive or reactive formations and no sublimations will suffice to remove the repressed instinct's (drive's) persisting tension, and it is the difference in amount between the pleasure of satisfaction that is *demanded* and that which is actually *achieved* that provides the driving factor.
>
> (S. Freud, 1920, p. 36)

180   David Lichtenstein

A fundamental concept in Lacan's theory of the divided subject is that of lack. The word in French, *manqué*, conveys both "loss" and "lack" but also "void" and "emptiness." Lacan viewed the psychic encounter with loss as essential to the formation of the human subject. Indeed, the subject as such comes into being by encountering and representing loss and without it, the formation of the subject does not occur. This is essential in Lacan's theory of the subject. It is rooted in Freud's view of primal repression as expressed earlier in *Beyond the Pleasure Principle* (1920) and takes this process as being essential to the formation of subjectivity *per se*. The "primary experience of satisfaction" that Freud refers to is a mythic point of origin since there is no representation of it and thus no experience of it in the psyche until it is lost. The effort to regain this lost moment is a defining principle of subjectivity. It is rooted in the human capacity for representation and in this sense at the core of this distinctly human function is the principle of lack, that is, of lost satisfaction. There is a dialectic relation in Lacan's thought here that draws upon Freud: the primary repression of the lost satisfaction can occur only once there is a representation to be repressed, but there can only be a representation of it as already lost, that is repression and representation must arise together: the lost object comes into being *as already lost*.

The first cry that is addressed to the mother (primary caregiver) expresses a representation of this lack and is taken as such by the other. For Lacan, this initiates the distinctly human form of the object relation. It is not present innately but formed as the subject is formed through the expression and interpretation of lack. Object relations like all human subjectivity are formed discursively in an intersubjective encounter structured around the expression and interpretation of lack.

That the lack in question is simple hunger does not stop the parent from giving it the significance of a social link, putting words to it, and treating the child's expression of need, the cry, as an expression of longing and desire. The existence of a discursive matrix, a social context maintained through speech and language, means that the infant without words *per se* is already interpellated, called into the social world, as an expressive being. And the first formative interpretation quite rightly is that the infant needs something, that is, that there is a lack.

One consequence of Lacan's placing loss at the core of the subject's being is that it subverts any idea of the infant as a purely natural creature living outside of culture. The idea of an instinctual infant expressing innate patterns of behavior, including attachment patterns, is far from Lacan's idea of the subject as inscribed in culture from the beginning of its existence. That first inscription is always around the act of nurturance, the recognition of lack and the exchange or gift that constitutes the idea of love.

It is, of course, impossible to know anything about the infant's earliest registration or awareness of this exchange and of the meanings it has for the others, but with time, as representations develop and the child shows the earliest signs of awareness, this economy of loss and restoration are clearly central to its being.

Thus S. Freud's (1920) account of his grandson's playing with a spool in his crib has great resonance for Lacan representing the role of lack or loss in the earliest symbolizations of the child.

Lack and desire

The primal representation and interpretation of lack as constitutive of the human subject has implications for how we view language and desire, as well as the subject, in psychoanalysis. To hold that there is no human subject prior to the expression of desire, and, indeed, the expression of desire in language through the interpretations of the (mother) caregiver, is to locate the effects of language and desire within the subject much earlier and more centrally than is generally done in psychoanalytic theory. It means that there is an effect of language on the subject prior to the development of both comprehension and speech.

Indeed, it is a fundamental principle of Lacan's theory that there is no subject outside of language. All non-linguistic dimensions of human subjectivity interact from the start with the linguistic functions of the cultural surround and the subject emerges only as a part of that surround. This is important because of the change implied not only in the linguistic function itself that is present in some significant form from earliest infancy, but also in the representational character of desire, that is, desire is a consequence of representation rather than simply a naturally occurring expression of biological needs.

Theories of conflict in psychoanalysis generally focus on the experience of pleasurable vs. unpleasurable wishes and efforts to resolve the conflicts between the two. Necessarily this implies a theory of "wishing," of motivation, intention, or desire. The latter term, *desire*, and indeed the conceptual relationship between *desire* and *wish*, play fundamental roles in Lacanian thought and thus on the implicit function of intrapsychic conflict within that thought.

As a term, *desire* has deep philosophical roots in the work of Spinoza (1994), Hegel 1976), and Nietzsche (2014) among others. *Wish* has much less history and conceptual affiliations. Using one term or the other, therefore, has at least an effect on the intellectual framework or history of discourse that is put into play. In addition, on semantic grounds, *wish* tends more toward the discreet and the time-bound, whereas *desire* more to the pervasive and enduring; however, that is not an absolute distinction. In English, for instance, one can speak of a "death wish" as an enduring pervasive unconscious desire. The distinction between the terms may seem too subtle to warrant discussion but in fact there are substantive matters at stake.

Concerning translation across languages, the matter becomes more complicated. The French word *désir* is an adequate translation of the German *Wunsch*, the word generally used by Freud and translated as *wish* in English. However, *désir* also renders the German *Begierde* (*Begehren*) which is the word that generally appears in Hegel's texts, a more complex one than *Wunsch*, and one suggesting an intensity beyond that of a wish, that is, passion, greed, or lust. Both Freud's *Wunsch* and Hegel's *Begierde* are connoted by Lacan's *désir* and both could, in fact, be represented in English by the word *desire* but not as well by the English word *wish*. Therefore, in choosing *wish* as the term in English for unconscious strivings, we lose both a richer field of philosophical connotations and a sense of passion that is more readily conveyed by the word *desire*.

As a thought experiment, we can observe the effects that occur when we substitute the word *desire* for *wish* in contemporary psychoanalytic discourse. Consider the following statement by Charles Brenner (2006) regarding the persistence of infantile wishes: "What can be observed in each individual case that can be studied with the help of the psychoanalytic method are that individual's attempts to achieve the pleasurable satisfaction of sexual and aggressive wishes" (p. 136).

If we replace the final words *wishes* with *desire*, the sentence now reads: "What can be observed in each individual case that can be studied with the help of the psychoanalytic method are that individual's attempts to achieve the pleasurable satisfaction of sexual and aggressive desire." What is gained through this change is a sense of a pervasive and ineradicable dimension to the striving. What is lost in the second version as compared to Brenner's original is the sense of discrete and actual moments.

Brenner himself, in fact, addresses this implicit difference between the particular wish and the more general desire. According to Brenner (2006), wishes do not ignore external reality:

> A child of three years or thereabouts wants satisfaction from its parent, i.e., from a particular person, and it wants a particular form of physical contact with that person. It does not want "oral gratification" for example. It wants to suck or swallow a particular person's penis or breast.
>
> (p. 136)

For Lacan, that a child wants to suck the mother's breast or the father's penis would each be linked to a desire that has a broader meaning than the specific wish alone conveys in its particular context. Perhaps not "oral gratification" but a supplemental meaning that has the character of unconscious phantasy, which is thus the proper register of desire. As Lacan (2002) puts it, "This is why human desire is adjusted not to an object, but to a phantasy. It is a fact of experience that analysis has articulated in the course of its experience" (p. 15).

In Brenner's view, the wish to suck the father's penis would presumably be repressed and thus subsequently survive also only as an unconscious phantasy, but it would remain as a discrete repressed phantasy. In Lacan's view, the wish itself is always and already a singular expression of desire, a desire addressed to the father in this instance. From the start, a phantasy regarding desire and, indeed, regarding the father's desire, would already be present in the discreet wish.

Thus in considering the contrasting terms *wish* and *desire*, we encounter differences regarding the function of phantasy and, indeed, the unconscious itself. Brenner's idea that the original wishes are essentially realistic and that only become repressed phantasies out of conflict with more powerful wishes, that is, for avoiding disapproval, and so forth, is entirely different from Lacan's idea of the inception of desire as unconscious phantasy that may then be conveyed by various discreet wishes.

There is more, however, in the distinctly Lacanian use of the concept of desire in psychoanalysis. If desire presumes a phantasy, it does so always in relation to an other who is likewise a desiring subject. The phantasy presumes the other as a desiring subject. This is where the function of

184 David Lichtenstein

language comes into play in relation to the emergence of desire. The other is known to be a desiring subject through her expressive acts and especially through her speech. The mother expresses her desire even as she provides for the infant's needs. Even if she expresses it in language that is not yet known, it is known to be an expression of desire. She expresses her desire and interprets in language the desire of the infant.

Thus the infant's needs are not only met (partially), but they are interpreted. In this way desire is first encountered through the other's speech as a supplement to the fulfillment of needs. An infant cries out and the other responds not only by offering the breast but also by speaking about it. The infant experiences not only the momentary satisfaction of its needs but also an exchange of signs, words, and phrases. When Freud wrote (earlier) about the difference between the pleasure demanded and that received it is the demand that establishes the discursive framework and the ineradicable difference between wish and satisfaction that inscribes that difference as a condition of desire. Lacan joins Freud's notion of the difference in pleasure between what is asked for and what is received to the linguistic context and thus that difference is linked to the speech of the other.

As noted, this desire is different from the discreet wish. The wish can be met or not, but the desire for more than that which is received would remain in effect regardless. It would even be enhanced by the (partial) satisfaction of the wish. Thus Lacan, of course, recognizes wishes, conscious and unconscious, acceptable and unacceptable, but they serve a different function than the pervasive structuring function of desire.

Desire as the distinctly human experience rests upon the symbolic function, the representation of the missing thing, a function that not only structures its expression but is, indeed, the condition for that desire to come into being. The subject is thus both a divided subject and a desiring subject, and these two dimensions are inextricably linked. The desire of the subject as human subject is unlike that of any other being in that it comes into being through the encounter with language, a uniquely human experience. Thus in addition to being a divided and desiring subject, the human subject is one formed by an encounter with the complex figurative effects of speech that are made possible by the structure of language.

Lacan created a portmanteau word for this desiring verbal subject that conveys the sense of a distinct character of being that is brought about through the representation of speech and language: *parlêtre*. As a neologism *parlêtre* cannot be translated without the loss of the poetic effects that go into its creation. That it is made up of the two words *parler* (to speak) and *être* (to be) is obvious. But the effect of combining them and then treating them as a substantive as Lacan does, that is as a noun that refers to the human subject, not only conveys an important meaning that we can render into English as "a being as an effect of speech" but also illustrates the way language works. Meaning effects are created by the combination of words and those effects are both apparent (translatable) and elusive (untranslatable). Hence the *parlêtre* lives both with meaning and with something that escapes meaning. The elusive effects of language are, in turn, linked to the missing part that we were considering in the first place: the lack that forms the desiring subject.

The idea that the subject and subjectivity do not simply exist as givens but must come into being through a particular encounter and engagement with the surrounding world is already a notion found in Freud and elaborated by other psychoanalysts (Mahler, Segal, Winnicott, etc.). In Lacan's estimation, it is essential to understand that the subject comes into being as a subject of desire not a subject of consciousness *per se*. It is not the Cartesian subject of thinking but more the Hegelian (and Spinozan) subject of desiring.

While the idea that this subject of desire is brought about by an encounter with symbolization and is, indeed, an effect of this encounter with speech and language is present for other psychoanalytic theorists, it is particularly developed in Lacan's work. This complex interactive and formative dialectic of subjective lack, speech, and desire plays a fundamental role in Lacan's thought with implications for how he then characterizes both psychoanalytic theory and practice.

Lacan comes to this view from two sides. In terms of clinical phenomena he asks who it is that we find in the psychoanalytic encounter and what takes place in the "talking cure." Then he addresses the idea of the divided subject of desire from a foundation in theory and philosophy, from a close reading of Freud with links to the work of Hegel, Heidegger, Levi-Strauss, and others.

The structuring effects of desire play a fundamental role in the analytic encounter. It is not dissatisfaction and conflict alone that make possible the articulation of specific wishes in psychoanalysis. It is also the implicit belief that the analyst knows the access to the cause of desire, indeed, the cause of desire that supports the analysand's speech. This is the link then between lack, desire, and transference. An analytic transference develops insofar as the analysand imputes to the analyst this knowing about the cause of desire and seeks to gain access to it through the relationship to the analyst.

The clinical presentation of desire

Consider the clinical subject with the familiar subversive effects that are observed in psychoanalytic work: the forgetting, the slips, the misprisions. Consider the subject who is not master in his or her own house, the subject of always-incomplete knowledge regarding the meaning of his or her own utterances. The divided subject requests help from the analyst – the one who is presumed to know what the subject does not, who is presumed to be whole through having access to the cause of desire. The divided subject, and especially the neurotic subject – those who view the analyst as having or knowing what they lack – approach the analyst but not for this knowledge *per se* but for help with their suffering. And while the analysis may result in a reduction of this suffering it won't be due to the analyst giving the help that is requested.

Here, once again, is a division in the subject of analysis: what is asked for is other than what is desired. This can readily be seen in clinical treatment. If initial manifest requests are met, that is, if the analyst immediately gives the patient the help that is asked for, the treatment goes nowhere. The analyst recognizes that regarding requests for advice, or for immediate relief from doubt, or from feelings of failure, all requests that a therapist can certainly try to meet, unless a deferral or frustration of these requests occurs, there will be no psychoanalysis. There will be no analysis because there will be no chance to get to what else is meant by these requests. While the analysand asks for help to reduce painful or unpleasant experiences, the analysis proceeds rather to address what else these requests may mean. To do otherwise, to turn immediately toward an effort to reduce the unpleasure, forecloses the possibility of analysis. The inescapable conclusion is that there is some other wish in this request for help, and perhaps a wish that is oriented around the idea of the all-knowing analyst and in the gifts that the knowing analyst will bestow (i.e., in transference). This other wish reflects the division between the (conscious) request and the (unconscious) desire. All clinical psychoanalytic work occurs on the axis of this division.

In French a request is *une demande*. Hence this division in the subject of psychoanalysis tends to be addressed in the English translations of

Lacanian thought as that between demand and desire. Whether there is a conflict between the two, it is certainly the case in clinical work that there is a difference between them and that the satisfaction of the former tends to preclude the expression of the latter. It is through the expression of the latter, the unconscious desire that is loosely linked to the manifest demand that the real benefit of psychoanalysis occurs.

The distinction between demand and desire is similar to the familiar distinction between manifest and latent content but it is not exactly the same distinction. For Lacan, the manifest content of the demand is less important than its logic. The demand has the logic of an imagined solution to the lack: "If I could have what I want I would be complete." Because the wish when conveyed in this form carries the implication of an imagined wholeness, it is *narcissistic* in form. It presumes an imaginary repair for the imagined injury. That is why it is frustrated in a successful analysis. In frustrating this demand for an imaginary solution, the analyst directs the treatment instead toward the expression of new metaphors of the lack, new expressions of desire. There is a resonance in this view both with Hans Loewald's (1960) notion of the new object in analysis and perhaps with the familiar ego psychological notion about the creation of new compromise formations. The Lacanian view of this new possibility relies upon the essential difference between the structure of desire as an ongoing symbolic expression of inescapable lack and that of demand as a belief in completeness, integration, or healing as a solution to lack.

Although the two intentions are different in their structure and logic, it is impossible to encounter a pure expression of desire except as it is both expressed and hidden in a demand. Desire never appears in a pure declarative form. A request for help, for advice, for affection, for support, for love will necessarily be the vehicle for conveying something beyond that request on the register of unconscious desire. And the occasion for that desire will always occur in the here and now expression of an interpersonal request (demand). Thus, if it makes sense to think of desire and demand as in conflict, it is a dialectical conflict whereby only in taking them together can one find something new. This has clinical significance because if the demand is thought of as only a defense against desire, it is possible that analysts will fail to hear the desire hidden there, that is, the drive derivative represented in the defense, to use more classical terminology.

For example, a patient enters analysis for a persistent agonizing problem related to indecision. Again and again the request [*demande*] is made for relief: *if the analyst would only weigh in on the question at hand the patient would see how it was done, would learn from the analyst's example and do better in the future,* etc. However, not only would the analyst's satisfaction of the request likely fail in the instance – the advice would no doubt either be insufficient or the possibility of following it impossible – but also the act of responding by trying to satisfy the request would undermine movement toward the expression of desire that is linked to it. The desire for a knowing and beneficent authority and even the desire for a certain abjection and abnegation dedicated to the worship of that authority might only be expressed to the extent that the request to actually provide such a figure is denied. Where that desire may lead, what further expressions of it might be possible so as to find the fuller meaning of the patient's loyalty to it, should be the work of the analysis. It is equally true that it is only through the expression of the immediate request and the implication that the analyst should satisfy it that the possible expressions of this desire are put into play.

The psychoanalytic setting makes it possible to focus upon the continuous expression of the dialectical relation between *demande* and *désir*. It is the analyst's function to recognize the distinction so as to frustrate the former and facilitate the latter to be heard. The distinction between them returns us to the original idea of lack. Lacan suggests that the logic of the demand rests on the premise that it is possible for it to be met. Whatever seems to be lacking can be found and wholeness restored. There is something wished for, which if it were given, would result in a true and complete satisfaction. It is possible to get what one wants and to feel complete. However, it is in the very structure of desire that it leads always to another desire and never to a full and complete satisfaction. The satisfaction of desire is inherently fleeting and always points to another object of desire. Thus, it is not in the content of the request but in the character both of its expression and of its satisfaction that the distinction between demand and desire resides.

Lacan (2002) referred to as Imaginary the belief that a request can be fully satisfied and a sense of wholeness thereby restored. He referred to desire and its constant displacement never arriving at the elimination of the lack that set it in motion as Symbolic. In Lacanian terms, the dialectic interplay of demand and desire is also the dialectic of the Imaginary and the Symbolic. The gap between them, the never realized difference between what we ask for and what we desire, is addressed by Lacan's concept of the Real. The interplay among these three registers of being, the Real, the

Intrapsychic conflict in the work of Lacan   189

Symbolic, and the Imaginary, is a metapsychological model in Lacan's work which I can do no more than indicate in the present discussion.

Narcissism and the theory of desire

Lacan first addresses the idea of lack in his essay on what he calls the "mirror stage" (2006) following the work of developmental psychologist Henri Wallon (1934, 1973). He was concerned with how the visual gestalt of the body as a whole is taken to represent the self and the ramifications of that identification. The idea that the ego develops as a projection of the body was also S. Freud's (1923): "The ego is first and foremost a bodily ego; it is not merely a surface entity but is itself the projection of a surface" p. 26).

Lacan proposed a theory of the ego as rooted in the young child's recognition of himself or herself in the mirror. That is, a visual identification of one's personal form (gestalt) is instrumental in the psychic development of the concept of self. Lacan suggested that there are consequences to this process of identification that affect the function of the ego and the concept of the self throughout life, consequences that are relevant to our discussion of the divided subject.

In the identification with the mirror image there is an inherent gap between the seer and the seen. What is seen is a whole intact image, a coherent visual *gestalt*. Indeed, what is seen is not only a whole figure, but also the image of a self as the representation of that wholeness. However, due to the relative immaturity of the young child, the lack of motoric coordination and coherence, there is a disjunction between the image of coherence that is seen and the incoherent self that is doing the seeing. The gap is between the image of wholeness and the subjective experience of relative incoherence, both linked to the self though different representations. There is a sense of perfection and completeness about the mirror image that is not the experience of the seer. Thus the image in the mirror is experienced simultaneously as self and as other. It is thus an occasion for both identification and alienation. This simultaneous creation of identity and of alienation and the dialectic interplay between them haunts the ego for the rest of life.

It is Lacan's approach to the problem of narcissism. There is a contradiction at the core of the narcissistic relation in that the subject occupies two opposing positions simultaneously: the seer and the seen. If the seer identifies fully with the wholeness of the seen, his own being as seer, as experiencing subject, is lost in the image. This, of course, is what happens in the classical tragedy of Narcissus. If the image is instead abandoned as an identification, so as to avoid this danger, the very idea of wholeness and coherence is sacrificed. The structure of narcissism thereby challenges the subject to both maintain and identify with the image of wholeness and to stand apart from this image and to see, or speak, from another place. This is thus another way of characterizing the idea of the divided subject.

It is the division of the subject as approached from what Lacan calls the Imaginary register, called this in part, because narcissism is constituted of the image. In this, Lacan (2006) draws from Hegel and the dialectical constitution of the self through the encounter with the other.

One way to navigate this narcissistic structure without either collapsing into the identification with completeness or sacrificing the ideal entirely in an act of resignation is to represent the gap, the lack that is the basis for the experience of incompleteness. This entails a paradox because what is missing cannot be represented and still experienced as missing, yet it is precisely this paradox that defines the structure of desire. To represent as missing a nothing that never existed. That is to represent an object that only exists as already lost. This again is Lacan's object a, the cause of desire.

If the cause of desire is the experience of lack, the narcissistic solution would be to eliminate the lack through a union or identification with the image of completeness. An alternative to the narcissistic solution is to represent the cause and then pursue those representations with the intent of finding the lost object and gaining satisfaction. Although one never finds the lost original cause, one lives with the possibility of desire rather than the narcissism of completeness. This is Lacan's version of the contrast between object desire and narcissistic desire – that is, between desire and demand.

What interests Lacan is that the pursuit of representations of the original lost object requires a representational capacity and ultimately a system of symbolization. If those representations are to substitute for one another then the system of representations must have the unique character of human language, its capacity for creative substitution through poetic devices like metaphor and metonymy. That one word can stand in for another and that in this substitution new meanings are generated is a human experience that is noted very early in children's speech. They discover that you can call something by another word and delight in the effects of this possibility. This creative substitution can be applied both to the self and to its objects supporting a text of desire that is to be contrasted with the fixed identification with the self as mirror image.

The formation of neurotic symptoms is an instance of this creative substitution. According to this view, neurosis is not seen as a compromise solution to a conflict but rather as the metaphoric representation of a lack. That neurotic symptoms are metaphors is what makes the talking cure possible, because a cure entails the creation of new metaphors. That it is possible to take symptoms instead as fixed images and to identify with them, as in the identification with the image in the mirror, is what resists in psychoanalysis. If there is a theory of conflict in Lacan it is between these two ways of treating the lack, the creative play of symbolic substitution and the fixed identification with images of completeness: the dialectic of desire and demand.

Desire in practice

In successful psychoanalytic work, the speech of the analysand loosens its grip on the certainties of identification. This is the primary purpose of the fundamental rule, the couch, and the other accoutrements of the analytic setting. However, it is equally important that the analyst follow the same path in listening. The idea that there are two tracks in the discourse of the analysand and that they reflect the difference between demand and desire can guide the analyst's listening beyond the frame of the person-to-person demand.

In any given utterance, both tracks are present although not always apparent. It is the analyst's function to listen for the evidence of desire in the ongoing expression of demand. The analysand is divided by these two discourses and the effects are a kind of subversion: *the subversion of the subject and the dialectic of desire* as Lacan (2006) put it. The analyst's role is not to heal or even suture this division, but to listen for it, to make the analysand aware of it, and to indicate that the path through whatever symptomatic impasse that brings the analysand to the analysis is to be found there. It is akin to what Loewald (1978) referred to as the "aware appropriation of the interplay and communication between unconscious and conscious modes of mentation and desire," (pp. 50–51). The key here that links Loewald's view with Lacan is the phrase "modes of mentation." It is not the content that differentiates desire and demand, or even id and ego – it is the mode by which it is represented.

Listening for the expression of desire behind the apparent meaning of the demand suggests that the analyst ought not to focus entirely on understanding but should be listening in another way, listening instead to ways of expression (modes of mentation) that run alongside the manifest meaning, as it were. The question remains whether anything is gained by viewing this process in terms of the dialectic between desire and demand rather than, for example, the more traditional psychoanalytic categories of drive derivatives and defenses. Is there a reliable clinical difference in the sort of analytic listening that is informed by Lacan's ideas about the divided subject and other analytic approaches that in their own way focus on the speech act?

Ideas in themselves guarantee little regarding the variations of analytic practice. Facilitating an awareness of the unconscious processes of defense (P. Gray, 1994), for instance, will function very differently in the hands of different clinicians. Likewise the Lacanian idea of marking the expressions of desire, punctuating the discourse of the analysand in various ways so as to indicate that something else was said beyond the intended discourse, is very sensitive to the particular analyst's way of listening and intervening.

Nevertheless, with that caution in mind, it may be worthwhile to say a few things about clinical technique as informed by these ideas. The expression of desire in speech always partakes of the figurative substitutions and subversions of expected meaning that is made possible by the structure of language. Interpreting *id* as opposed to *ego* contents is not what is at stake in listening to the expression of desire. It is instead listening for the character of the utterance, for its capacity to evoke the over-determined play of meanings, that is a better guide to how the analyst facilitates the subversion of the imaginary certainties. All explanatory interventions, whether they are intended to address defense or drive derivatives, run the risk of grounding the discourse in the certainty of identifications, of an objectification of the subject that blocks the play of meaning that is the calling card of desire.

The analyst's interpretation should function to alert the analysand that another mode of desire (Loewald, 1978) has been expressed. It is not important for the analyst to be the one to make meaning out of that expression of desire. The analysand will generally come to do that on his or her own. If the analyst listens to that other way of speaking, new meanings

Intrapsychic conflict in the work of Lacan 193

will emerge. To return to the analogy with the close analysis of defense (P. Gray, 1994), the idea there is that by understanding the meaning of defensive thoughts they will diminish and the drive derivatives will emerge more freely. Lacan's attention to the character of discourse suggests that rather than focusing on the understanding of meaning, analysis is most effective when it focuses on the poetic effects of the discourse itself, and through that focus a history and its new possibilities will emerge less constrained by identification and imaginary certainties.

A classical clinical illustration of the dialectic of desire and how to listen to the poetic effects of the discourse itself is present in Freud's account of the "Dream of the Butcher's Wife" and in Lacan's (2006) discussion of it. The initial text of the dream is as follows:

> I wanted to give a supper party, but I had nothing in the house but a little smoked salmon. I thought I would go out and buy something, but remembered then that it was Sunday afternoon and all the shops would be shut. Next I tried to ring up some caterers, but the telephone was out of order. So I had to abandon my wish to give a supper party.
> (S. Freud, 1900, p. 180)

According to Freud the patient presented the dream as proof that his theory was false. Since the wish for the supper party is abandoned it does not follow Freud's theory that dreams are the fulfillment of a wish. How could a dream of a wish abandoned also be a wish fulfilled? The patient's expressed request was for Freud to acknowledge that he could be wrong, that he was fallible.

It is through the work of interpretation that the dream reveals itself to be not merely the expression of the wish to prove Freud wrong but of another level of desire hidden in that wish.

Lacan (2006) takes up this dream in his essay: *The direction of the treatment and the principles of its power* (p. 518). There he suggests that Freud hits upon a form of desire that is of a different order than the simple wish. It is the desire to have an unsatisfied desire. The patient in question actually maintains an unsatisfied desire for caviar, that is she continually says she loves it but never wants to have it, and she uses this complex desire to playfully tease her husband about the meaning of satisfaction. In the dream she has smoked salmon in the house but doesn't want to serve it. In not serving it, she puts smoked salmon in the symbolic place of caviar, that is, the object of unsatisfied desire. Smoked salmon in reality is a favorite food of her friend. The dream thus brings her friend into the frame of unsatisfied desire through the substitution of smoked salmon for caviar. The dream is not simply a wish to frustrate a rival but the expression of desire that links the two women in a lover's triangle.

The complex desire expressed by the dream – the desire for an unsatisfied desire – involves the function of desire itself. Remember the dream was created so as to address and refute Freud's theory of wish fulfillment thereby addressing her analyst's desire. However, the dream also expresses how desire structures the dreamer's being in relation to her husband and his desire, her friend as a rival, her friend's desire, and the triangle through which she explores the meaning of her husband's love.

Here we see how the term *wish* falters. Smoked salmon/caviar is not simply the object of a wish. It represents a state of desire and, indeed, a state of desire that is maintained by not being satisfied. This is a state that is fundamental to the formation of the subject, but also to the structure of neurosis, and especially hysteria.

Lacan named the object that in its absence brings desire into being the object "a." It does not exist as a thing in ordinary reality but always as the lost object that is at the root of desire. Desire comes into being through this very process of representation rather than through the experience of pleasurable things *per se*. It is of a different order than that of an organic need but also of a different order than that of a simple wish for one's favorite food. Desire may not always appear as the desire for an unsatisfied desire, but it always refers to that which is beyond satisfaction and always has the effect of bringing the Real into play.

Chapter 12

Forces at play in psychical conflict[*]

Jean Laplanche

Note by the editor of the translation

The editors of this volume have asked me to provide an introduction. Because his work will be unfamiliar to many, I offer "Laplanche standing on one foot" (Laplanche in fewer than 350 words) which gives a simplified account of some – though not all – of his most important contributions. Necessarily simplified, but I hope not simplistic, not so caricatured, that I fail in my aim to set up the paper and to seduce your further interest in Laplanche.

This 1994 paper is typical of Laplanche in at least two ways: it is grounded in close reading of Freud (a return to Freud, if you will) and it aims to be direct and clear. Nevertheless it will not be easy for those unfamiliar with his work. It was written for a conference devoted to a discussion of his work, a group he correctly understood would have read his previous work including what he called the "hinge"[1] of his writings, New Foundations for Psychoanalysis *(1987) his synthesis of his teaching from 1970 to 1984 (which had been published as* Problématiques *I through V) and* The Unfinished Copernican Revolution *(1992) in which he collected his major papers from 1967 to 1992. Most of this work remains untranslated. However, the Unconscious in Translation, with the support of the Institut de France and the Fondation Jean Laplanche, is in the process of translating and publishing all of Laplanche's work in more or less reverse chronological order. The following paper is excerpted from* Between Seduction and Inspiration: Man, *(UIT 2015)*

---

[*] This essay is from Jeffrey Mehlman's translation of Laplanche's *Entre séduction et inspiration: l'homme* which was published in 2014 by Unconscious in Translation (UIT). UIT plans to publish English translations of all of Laplanche's work. UIT's General Editor, Jonathan House, is also the editor of this translation.

196 Jean Laplanche

Laplanche's choice of his major papers from 1992 to 1999. The book is available at ucsintranslation.com.

Laplanche standing on one foot:

(1) From birth infants are dependent on adults in an attachment relationship which centers on communication; for the baby the communication is initially instinctual and conscious/pre-conscious and pre-verbal (but not, therefore, pre-symbolic); for the adult, the communication is not instinctual and is only partly conscious/pre-conscious.

(2) Of course, all attachment communication entails activity – biological, bodily activity – and associated sensations. When activity and sensations are represented mentally by the infant, those representations are exact and logical – exact and logical to the extent and in a form which, at a given stage of development, the infant has the capacity for precise perception and logical thinking.

(3) So initially, for the baby and for the adult, communication – verbal and pre-verbal/gestural – entails logical, secondary process thinking.

(4) However, adults have a sexual unconscious, infants do not. This asymmetry is what Laplanche calls the Fundamental Anthropological Situation.

(5) The adult's sexual unconscious compromises the attachment communications adding an enigmatic dimension – enigmatic both to the child and to the adult.

(6) The child seeks to make sense of the adult's communications, in Laplanche's terms to translate them – including the enigmatic elements. This is the General Theory of Seduction. In other words, the child is stimulated (seduced, inspired) to make meaning out of the adult's communications including the enigmatic meanings which parasitize the adult's conscious message and which are generally outside of the adult's conscious and pre-conscious awareness.

(7) At every stage of development, the child's translation of the adult's communication can never fully succeed, especially for the enigmatic aspects. This partial failure leaves untranslated bits – residues which are de-signified signifiers. These residues constitute the unconscious. This process of partially failed translation is primal repression. Laplanche calls this The Translational Model of Repression.

(8) Humans are a meaning making species. The untranslated bits, the primally repressed, remain a constant source of stimulation to translation, translation which can never succeed, once and for all. These

untranslated bits are also the object of meaning making and thus Laplanche calls them the source/object of the drive.

Jonathan House

FORCES AT PLAY IN PSYCHICAL CONFLICT*

For this clarification concerning neurotic conflict, Freud's two texts of 1924, "Neurosis and Psychosis" and "The Loss of Reality in Neurosis and Psychosis," can serve, if not as a model to be applied, at least as a point of departure. For Freud, it is explicitly a question of inserting conflict into the framework of his new theory of the psychical apparatus. And three peculiarities retain our attention from the outset:

(1) The description of conflict is essentially in terms of the structure of the mental apparatus and yet, curiously, that version of the structural[1] model does not invoke solely the three agencies that have been in place since 1920: ego, id, and superego. Abruptly, a new "agency" appears as an autonomous force: "reality." As a result, the conflict resides in the way in which the ego finds itself caught between two principal forces and is obliged to ally itself with one or the other. In neurosis, it is reality that would win out, at the expense of the id. In psychosis, it would be the reverse.

(2) Concerning the drives, which are classically opposed to each other in the psyche (defense, symptom, compromise, etc.), the new opposition between "life drives" and "death drives"[2] completely fails to find its place. Far from there being a struggle between them, the two great drives are encompassed in the id and share a common fate.

(3) As for the former opposition, that of sexual drives and drives of self-preservation, its absence is not surprising, since it disappeared as a major axis of Freudian thought after 1915, but nevertheless is cruelly felt precisely whenever there is a question of reality.

On reality

On the basis of a robust "realism," Freud always distinguished between two types of reality: material external reality, to which we accede by perception, and psychological reality, corresponding to perceptions of what emanates from within, initially feelings of pleasure-displeasure, then affects, and finally representations, fantasies, logical arguments, and so forth.[3]

It is not a matter of challenging this first opposition, but of establishing distinctions within it, pondering which forces (or "drives") are in play, and also of wondering about the possibility of a third type of reality, transverse to the other two.

Concerning *exterior reality*, it is utterly simplistic to speak of the "real exterior world" without specifying it, and without taking into account the forces that polarize it. To simply say that "for the ego, perception plays the part which in the id falls to [drive]"[4] is to establish a symmetry without rigor by conjuring away the question of force. The exterior world sketches lines of force only through the investment by a living being. One is even justified in supposing that the exterior world quite simply can *be perceived* solely as a function of such an investment. What is indifferent is not noticed by the living creature. The air we breathe irrupts violently only when it becomes suffocating or is lacking.[5]

For a given individual, we can describe in an elementary way the forces that animate reality according to three paired oppositions: sexuality/self-preservation, attraction/repulsion, living (and, more narrowly, human) environment/inanimate environment.

Let us provisionally put aside sexuality in order to concentrate on the domain of *self-preservation* or adaptation. This is the domain which is generally made to coincide with the notion of "reality" in general, "realism" having adopted as guiding maxim "life before all else" (*primum vivere*), before philosophy or even before making love. Following the attraction/repulsion polarity, the realm of self-preservative needs has the contours of an environment (*Umwelt*) composed of poles of attraction (objects of need) and negative poles (dangers). Those needs are inscribed in the individual by way of more or less fixed or adaptable mechanisms, inherited phylogenetically. But it is here that the difference between two types of environment (living/inanimate) intervenes and it is incumbent on us to distinguish clearly between species, depending on whether they are directly plugged into an inanimate environment or whether that insertion occurs through the mediation of another living being. For a certain number of living species, these mechanisms are directly pre-adapted to the object of consumption or the situation to avoid (appetite for a specific source of nourishment, instinctive knowledge of a precise danger). For other species, access to the material object or knowledge of the factual danger are inseparable from the mediation of the "socius." In the case of the human being (which is the only one to concern us here), Freud emphasized forcefully a congenital ignorance of *dangers*; and as for *desires* directly pre-adapted to an object, specifically the desire for nourishment, it appears that they too are inexistent. The baby initially has no "thought" of the milk; it is only by way of the attraction and the proposition of the breast, its warmth, the nesting that it proposes, etc., that the infant accedes to the notorious "food-value."[6] The human world of self-preservation, as opposed to what transpires in the case of numerous animals, is thus from the outset and in its entirety an interactive world, oriented by reciprocal vectors without their being, for all that, uniformly complementary. Fully as much as "self-preservative," this force field, insofar as it is interhuman or interanimal, can be called the field of "tenderness" (Freud) or "attachment" (modern psychology – ethology).

It is paradoxical but true to say that this domain of self-preservation is described here only by way of abstraction with regard to the human being. Present at birth in the form of innate instinctual dispositions, it is quickly *covered over, disqualified*, by another play of forces, those of human sexuality.

But before introducing sexuality, it is indispensable to delineate a third order of reality, not *alongside* material reality and psychological reality, but transverse in relation to them: the reality of the *message*, whose materiality may be characterized as "signifying." This realm of reality is one that Freud intuits occasionally, identifying a "psychical reality" distinct from not only material reality but also merely psychological reality and, so to speak, more indestructible and resistant than it. It is notably the case for what he names "unconscious wishes reduced to their ultimate and truest expression,"[7] or, in accord with our realism of the unconscious, the "de-signified signifiers" ("thing-representations") that populate the unconscious.

The materiality of the message outside of any "psychical" insertion into external reality might be figured as the presence of a tablet of hieroglyphics abandoned in the desert. But the message and the signifier are not, for all that, reducible to verbal language alone: an arrow indicative of direction, drawn on the wall of a cavern, is also a message; as are a smile, a threatening gesture, or even the destruction by an American airplane of an Iraqi missile base. The realm of reality specific to the message includes the following features: (1) the message is not necessarily verbal, nor even integrated into a semiotic system, but it is always inscribed in a (signifying) materiality; (2) the message, before representing something (a signified), always represents an other for someone: it is communication, address; and (3) the message, by virtue of its materiality, is dedicated to polysemy.

It is at this juncture that it is useful to discuss the distinguishing characteristics of the *adult* message addressed to the child. Like any other, this message is open to numerous interpretations. But we say it is "enigmatic" in a very precise sense, exceeding all polysemy. Indeed, the adult message, addressed to the child on the basis of a dialogue, a reciprocal dialogue of self-preservation, turns out to be inhabited, compromised by the unconscious sexuality of the adult. If it appears as enigmatic to the child, it is undoubtedly because it exceeds the nursing infant's possibilities of understanding and mastery, but more fundamentally it is because in its duplicity it remains opaque to the understanding of the very person emitting it. The term *compromised* message refers to an essential notion in psychoanalysis, intended to account for the psychopathology of everyday life, including actions, speech acts, writings, and so forth, all addressed to an other, and all affected by an "interference" from the unconscious of the emitter.

The sexual message thus *inhabits* the self-preservative message. But as opposed to the latter, it does not imply a reciprocity of the request-response sort, and is fundamentally asymmetrical, finding its origin in the (adult) other.

It is here that the theory of propping and generalized seduction becomes necessary. Not being able to take it up in detail, I will limit myself initially to the following diagram (see Figure 12.1) showing how the self-preservative, interactive message of the adult is paired with a unidirectional message of a sexual nature.

We will be alluding to the rest of the process further on. But what is significant here for the *problem of reality* is that – at each of its *stages*, on each of its *levels*, in each of its bodily *locations* – the relation of self-preservation is infested, invaded, and soon completely overwritten by sexual meanings.

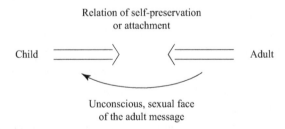

Figure 12.1

What is called "pansexualism" in psychoanalysis is the theory positing that sexuality accounts for the totality of the human being. Yet we are positing that theoretical pansexualism is but the reflection of a *real* pansexualism, that is, of a movement by which sexuality reinvests the entirety of human activities. Sexuality is not everything, but it is everywhere.

At the conclusion of this overview of "reality" and its impact on psychical conflict, we may summarize as follows: exterior reality can intervene as a force only to the extent that it is invested. The investment of self-preservation (needs) in man is entirely mediated by interhuman relations. These, in turn, are totally infested, compromised, on the adult side, by the participation of the adult's sexual unconscious.

Like a neutral country invaded by two foreign armies battling each other, not only to share its territory but also to exercise supremacy with regard to other spoils, such is the situation of the domain of self-preservation in the human being, invaded by sexual conflict. The self-preservative forces remain feeble and incapable of exercising any significant influence. Scarcely capable in themselves of conflict, their fate remains entirely dependent on sexual conflict. It is well-known that the human being, once sexualized, remains inaccessible to purely adaptive concerns. He feeds himself or deprives himself of nourishment "for love of" or "out of hatred against" and not in order to survive. The bizarre impulses and follies of human beings, their destructive or altruistic ideals are not amenable to intimidation. The *compulsion* of love or perversion mocks every interdiction. To that extent, the idea of a "real danger" being the key to repression and neurosis (as it emerges from a certain reading of *The Problem of Anxiety*) does not hold up for a second in the face of experience. Castration was never a "real danger": it intervenes as a psychical force only on the basis of a threat that has been uttered (*Androhung* and not *Drohung*), and the latter, in turn, cannot be separated from the unconscious sexual meanings present in the person uttering it.[8]

The realm of self-preservation is thus not directly party to psychical conflict. It is the field on which psychical conflict is deployed and eventually what is at stake in it. Hysterical blindness[9] is not the result of a conflict between a non-sexual, adaptive visual function and sexual impulses, but it is the consequence, for the visual function, of a conflict between antagonistic sexual forces. It is that particular position of self-preservation that justifies its situation at the borders of psychoanalytic therapy and its "tub."[10]

The apparatus of the soul

Freud asserted on several occasions that the psychical apparatus could be understood only by way of its genesis in the individual. He did not always remain faithful to that perspective, notably by appealing, in his description of the psychical "agencies," to roots or innate cores. This is notably the case for the id, whose conception, alongside a positive intention, conveys the risk of returning to innate instinctual (and no longer drive) forces.[11]

Another risk, which is in no way less significant, consists in believing that what is described by the "metapsychology" is a more refined, precise, and "extensive" version of psychology: the expression "dynamic psychology," which is occasionally employed, serves to promote just such an error. And it is against it that we make use, following Freud, of the slightly outmoded term, *soul-apparatus*, by which we mean, quite precisely, the *sexual* psychical apparatus.

Psychoanalysis undoubtedly exceeds its rights in pretending to supplant cognitive psychology, whose legitimacy remains intact. But there occurs, in the world of "interior" psychological reality, something comparable to the process of "real pansexualism": the sexual apparatus of the soul tends to reclaim as its own, to invade and to appropriate the domain of psychological reality, which is in principle independent but which, in the human being, is independent only in an abstract way.

The Freudian division of the apparatus of the soul into an id, an ego, ideal agencies, and a superego, remains an indispensable guiding thread. Distinctions between an *ego* and a *self*, or between the *ego* and the *I*, are eminently subject to criticism and are rather a response to ideological exigencies: the *self* is a way of giving back to a rational ego some of its alleged autonomy, while neglecting its narcissistic component. Inversely, the introduction of an "I," whatever the pretexts for such a split, leads us back to a philosophy of the "subject" that is not innocent.

But the agencies of the apparatus of the soul can only be conceived by way of their origin: the impact on a developing biological organism of enigmatic messages emanating from the other. If one were obliged to introduce an agency or "instance" other than Freud's classic cases, it would thus not be an "instance of the letter,"[12] an abstract power issuing from structuralist theory but, in fact, an instance of the other.

This priority of the (external) other in the constitution of the soul-apparatus will be duplicated by the instance of the internal other: the id.

Forces at play in psychical conflict   203

For the latter is not there primordially and for all eternity: it is that part of the message emanating from the external other that never succeeded in being completely translated (integrated, metabolized).[13] It is, so to speak, a "quintessence" of otherness.

The constitution of the soul-apparatus, in its topographical aspect as much as in the forces at work (the economic-dynamic aspect), is correlative with the process of repression. The latter, in turn, is to be understood in the framework of the generalized theory of seduction: implantation of the enigmatic signifier, its reactivation *après-coup*, attempts at mastery, and the failure of translation resulting in the deposit of source-objects in the id. I will not return to this sequence, my objective being to arrive at the already constituted soul-apparatus, as it functions in normal/neurotic conflict.

Some supplementary remarks on the structural model

The structural model is a point of view of the ego and in that sense every model of the mind is of the ego: it finds its origin in the ego and reflects the ego's interests. This is in agreement with Freud's intuition: "the psyche is extended, but does not know it." Quite so: the ego is certainly a part of the psyche (the apparatus of the soul), but it is also hegemonic: it lays claim to being the whole and is potentially the whole.[14] That the ego can be described as extended is certainly to be understood in relation to its narcissistic origin. Narcissism, as we know, is not to be conceived as an initial monadic state, but as a libidinal investment "of the ego," or, more precisely, as a libidinal investment which *constitutes* the ego in the image of the other body as a totality (the body of the other – but also my body as other). Narcissism is nothing other than narcissistic identification.

Forces of the drive: binding and unbinding

We come now to the forces involved, concerning which we assert, in direct alignment with the theory of seduction and the pansexualist "invasion," that they are solely of a sexual nature. It is within sexuality that the separation between the sexual forces of unbinding (Freud's death drive) and the sexual forces of binding (Freud's Eros) is produced. It is imperative to understand that it is repression itself that creates the drive forces of unbinding. The threat to the organism bent on self-preservation constituted by the strangeness of the message emanating, from the other (a strangeness grounded in sexuality) ultimately ends up confining that strangeness in the repressed unconscious. The reasons for that unbinding, and for the primary process governing the unconscious contents, are to be sought nowhere else than in repression itself. It acts in a "highly individual manner" (Freud, 1915, p. 150), breaking connections between the elements of the message, and above all disconnecting the link between signifier and signified. The unconscious contents are the residue of that strange metabolism,[15] which "treats" the messages of the other, but fails to "treat" the strangeness itself. It is those "de-signified signifiers" that pursue their existence side by side in the unconscious or contract between them the most absurd alliances (i.e., by displacement-condensation).

The binding forces are no less erotic than those that unbind, and it is quite legitimately that Freud designated them by the name of Eros, which "tends to establish ever larger unities." But the error of the founder was in having wanted to annex the totality of the erotic to Eros, whereas it is only the "bound" aspect.

Eros's center of action is the ego; Eros replenishes itself endlessly with libido invested in *totalities*: in this sense object-libido and ego-libido are strictly correlative: if man lives by love, it is indissociably by love of the ego and love of the (total) object.

In light of all that, should we solidify the conflict as though it were produced between two antagonistic forces defined once and for all as drives that unbind and drives that bind, and annexed to two immutable psychical "instances" or agencies, the id and the ego? It seems not. On the one hand, it is the same sexual force (libido) that is found on both sides, and it would be scarcely conceivable that there not be conversions from one form into the other. We are well aware that an extreme case of the will to bind can result in an extreme bout of unbinding.[16]

Binding and unbinding are thus best conceived as two principles (types of process, modes of functioning) at work at all structural levels. This is tantamount to saying that the structural limits and the economic-dynamic play of forces coincide only in an extremely crude approach to the question: there are both elements that are more unbound and those that are less unbound in the id, and likewise both that are more and less bound in the ego.[17]

Forces at play in psychical conflict   205

We should also guard against the great injustice we would risk committing by purely and simply assimilating binding to the ego, and the ego to narcissism. Maintaining that the starting point, the bud of the ego, is to be situated in a specular identification with the image of a fellow creature should not bring us to neglect the identificatory contributions and successive re-arrangements that come to enrich and dialecticize that "instance" or agency. In correlation with which, the fact that the ego always remains the pole to which *binding* actions are attached does not imply that such actions merely impose rigidity. Even if many neurotic defense mechanisms preferentially appeal to narcissistic rigidity, more supple modes of binding of the drive are commonly in play.

Schematically, we can distinguish two types of binding: binding by means of a *form* imposed from the exterior, as a "container" for aggressive elements of the drive, and binding by way of *symbolization*, that is, by integration into the sequences, networks, and symbolic structures apt to put in order the largest possible share of strangeness of the drives.

Among those "binding" elements, one should rank in first place the great "complexes," Oedipus and Castration, and all the great collective or individual myths, whether archaic or more recent, or even forged, restructured, or reinvigorated by psychoanalysis itself (murder of the father). Far from being primordial elements of the id, Oedipus and Castration are instruments for ordering, in the service of binding. The *castration complex* puts into play not an *anxiety* (without object), but a determinate fear, fixated on an object. Castration is first of all an "infantile sexual theory" which received its canonical form from its co-authors (Hans and Sigmund), and which allows one to translate anxieties and enigmatic messages into masterable form. The fact that there exist less constraining forms of symbolization than the logic of castration is something I have attempted to demonstrate in my book *Castration, symbolisations*.[18]

To return to two aspects of binding, containing and symbolizing, it is important to perceive that they are present *jointly* in every concrete process. Thus no casting of the individual history of the subject into narrative, myth, or novel can be conceived without the intervention of narcissistic elements, which precipitate, coagulate, from their presence in one place or another, into an "ego" or "ideal" in the fantasmatic structure. Inversely, however narcissistic they be, identifications take on a mobility and a dialectic through their insertion into the scenarios, however rudimentary, that every individual forges in order to give form to the enigmatic.

Concerning the opposition between binding and unbinding, let us return for a moment to the primal situations of seduction. For having insisted on the elements of instability, aggression, and unbinding included in the messages emanating from the other, for having declared ironically that the mother, in order to generate the drive in the child, would have to have been "sufficiently bad," we have run the risk of neglecting the fact that the other, whether a parent, also furnishes the child with the essential part of his arsenal for binding: the other's love, care, and "holding" sustain the child's narcissism; in addition, the other brings to the child the (verbal but also extra-verbal) elements indispensable to his self-theorization, conveying to the child, by reorganizing them in its own way, collective myths and scenarios. All this and much more make for the "good enough" parent.[19]

The superego

I am reproached for my silence on the subject of the superego. I can say only a few words on the subject: the question merits being sent back to the workshop. The opposition between a (Kleinian) drive-driven pre-Oedipal superego and a legislating Oedipal superego cannot satisfy us other than as an index of the difficulty of the question. Freud himself advances the most contradictory formulations, which make the superego at times the representative of reality, at others an agency deriving all its force from drives. The primacy of the adult other in the genesis of the world of the drives of the child should at least allow us to take up the exogenous-endogenous question differently. The fact that the superego is discovered (in Freud and in every individual) in the form of pronouncements, messages of either interdiction or command, that those messages are most often immutable in a specific individual (that is, unable to be metabolized) allows us to surmise an origin in parental messages not having been subjected to primal repression. The comparison which I advanced with a "psychotic" enclave is subject to debate and elaboration.

The paradox remains that the superego, even though originally emerging from the unbound, plays an important role in the processes of binding – notably in secondary repression, whose interdictions support and, as it were, *seal* the activation of Oedipal and castratrative structures.

Anxiety and symptoms

To take a stance on the old opposition – debated by Freud in numerous texts without, despite appearances, finding a resolution in *The Problem of Anxiety* – anxiety, in our view, is anxiety of the drive, that is, the manifestation of the most primal affect, in the ego, of an attack by the drive that unbinds.[20] This in no way means a choice to return to the sort of alchemy which Freud renounced, concerning his "first theory" and according to which libido would be "transformed into anxiety." Anxiety, as primal affect and without an object, comes from the libidinal attack of the drive emanating from the id and occurs in the ego, as every affect, moreover, does. The series of negative affects – shame, guilt, fear – should be considered as a negative genealogy, corresponding to different levels of elaboration and binding of anxiety. Real danger, far from being the origin of anxiety, is one way to master and stabilize it as fear. This is notably the case for the fear of castration.

Symptoms, in turn, constitute various means, often quite costly and inappropriate, through which the drive is expressed and bound. Among the symptoms that lead to binding, we may recall acting out, concerning which the expression "criminals out of a feeling of guilt" remains quite eloquent and eminently true. To this I have added the idea that Oedipus himself can be considered as the most illustrious (if not the very first) of those criminals out of guilt. That inverted formulation, willfully provocative of so-called Oedipal guilt, tends to re-situate the myth in its proper place, not as foundational and primordial but as an attempt at binding to be situated as secondary, in the higher layers of the apparatus of the soul.

The forces in play in analytic treatment

It would be simple to say that the forces in play in treatment are the same as those that confront each other in the soul-apparatus in the course of everyday life. "Simple," but allowing little hope for genuine change. In our view, therapy is one of the rare situations[21] and assuredly the privileged situation for calling into question the Ptolemaic enclosure of the soul-apparatus. Transference[22] is to be considered as the possibility of reopening that apparatus, renewing and prioritizing the enigmatic address emanating from the other, instigating and even generating a neo-genesis of libidinal energy. The renewal, *mutatis mutandis*, of the primal situation of seduction may, indeed, place a check on the "constancy" principle concerning the sum total of psychical energies.

Notes

1 [Editor's note: In English psychoanalytic texts, Freud first model of mind – Ucs/Pcs/Cs – is usually called the "topographic" model and his second model – Ego/Superego/Id – is usually called the "structural" model. This may suggest that one is more descriptive and less structural than the other. In French, each of Freud's models of the mind is referred to as a "*topique*": the first "*topique*" and the second "*topique*." This permits, as in this sentence, a model of the mind which is close to but not identical with the structural model also to be called a topography. JH]

2 Whatever the meaning one is inclined to attribute to them. [See "The So-called Death Drive: A Sexual Drive" by Jean Laplanche in Between Seduction and Inspiration: Man (New York: The Unconscious in Translation, 2015)].

3 Psychological reality is not specific to the human being. It develops in every living creature, growing in complication with the complexity of the central nervous system.

4 *The Ego and the Id*, SE, XIX. [Editor's note: here and elsewhere, when necessary, we have modified the Standard Edition to be consistent with Laplanche's thinking and to retain the clarity of Laplanche's translation of Freud. Modifications are indicated by square brackets.]

5 See D. Lagache, "In their behavior, living organisms deal with positive and negative values, or with object-values, and not with objects, in the sense that common or scientific knowledge attributes to that term" ("Le psychologue et le criminal," *Oeuvres* II (Paris: PUF, 1979), p. 192.

6 A term employed by Lagache to emphasize the fact that the environment is not neutral, but oriented by values, which are so many vectors of force. But precisely, the vector of nourishment as a relation to the inanimate is not a primal vector for the infant, as it is for the paramecium or newly hatched salmon attached to its yolk sac.

7 See *Traumdeutung* in GW, II–III, p. 265.

8 The threat of castration is itself seduction in the broad sense in which we define it. As for the "theory of castration," its metapsychological status is quite different.

9 "The Psychoanalytic View of Psychogenetic Disturbance of Vision" in *SE*, XI, pp. 209–218. See also the first chapter of *The Problem of Anxiety*, concerning inhibition, *SE*.

10 See *Problématiques IV: L'Inconscient et le ça* (Paris: PUF, 1981), pp. 207ff, *Problématiques V: Le baquet. Transcendance du transfert* (Paris: PUF. 1987), for example, pp. 81, 156, 181, 211. The discourse of self-preservation can be "heard" in analytic treatment only insofar as it evokes, triggers, and even generates sexuality.

11 See *Le fourvoiement biologisant de la sexualité* (Paris: Synthélabo, 1993) and *Problématiques IV: L'inconscient et le ça* (Paris: PUF, 1981); the problematic of the id. Freud's return to instinct (*Instinkt*) is emphatic in his final texts, for example, *Moses and Monotheism*.

12 Lacan, "L'Instance de la lettre . . .," in *Ecrits* (Paris: Seuil, 1966).

13 See *New Foundations for Psychoanalysis*, op. cit., Part II, and *La révolution copernicienne inachevée*, "Punctuation."

14 At the risk, when it is that whole, of no longer having any power: in the dream, the ego, fixated on the wish to sleep, is dilated to the point of again coinciding with the limits of the ego-body; but it allows far greater play to the primary process.

Forces at play in psychical conflict   209

15 On the subject of the metabolic, see *Problématiques IV: L'inconscient et le ça* (Paris: PUF, 1981), pp. 135ff.

16 See the analysis by Jacques André of the Terror during the Revolution in *La révolution fratricide* (Paris: PUF, 1993).

17 Freud, in his *New Introductory Lectures*, proposed a comparison with a country whose various populations are divided *grosso modo* solely according to geographical criteria: the Germans, who raise livestock, in the hills; the Magyars, who grow crops, on the plain; and the Slovaks, who fish, on the shores of the lakes. The terrible current situation of the Yugoslavian conflict may allow us to give some currency to the comparison. The level of physical geography (plains, mountains, lakes, etc.) is but a ground which does not allow for an understanding of the conflict; compare it, in the individual, to the level of self-preservation, the terrain but also one of the stakes in the conflict. The political level of the state, with its borders, would correspond to the psychical topography; finally, the ethnic-ideologic-cultural forces present correspond to the psychical conflict in its reality. It is useless to try to contain the actual conflict within borders that it essentially overflows. Ethnic cleansing (creating borders corresponding to pure ethnic divisions) is a point of view . . . of the ego. But fortunately, the ego can also have more flexible points of view: assimilation, intermarriage, co-existence.

18 *Problématiques II* (Paris: PUF, 1980).

19 I thank Silvia Bleichmar for having insisted on the parental contribution of elements that bind, restoring to the tableau of the adult-child relation its indispensable equilibrium.

20 See *Problématiques I: L'angoisse* (Paris: PUF, 1980) and "Une métapsychologie à l'épreuve de l'angoisse" in *La révolution copernicienne inachevée* (Paris: Aubier, 1992), pp. 143–158.

21 Alongside certain "cultural" constellations.

22 See "Transference: its Provocation by the Analyst" in Laplanche, *Essays on Otherness*, pp. 214–233.

Chapter 13

On conflict in attachment theory and research

Howard Steele and Miriam Steele

John Bowlby had a keen clinical understanding of the troublesome role unconscious conflict may cause in parent-child and, indeed, all relationships (Bowlby, 1979). Yet this clinical understanding played, at best, a limited role in attachment research until the 1980s, when a number of attachment research instruments were developed that reliably identify unconscious conflict. It was in the late 1980s when we began a longitudinal attachment research project in London that began with Adult Attachment Interviews administered to 100 expectant mothers and their partners, 100 expectant fathers; we then followed these families through infancy (Fonagy et al., 1991; Steele et al., 1996) and on through the teenage years of their first offspring; notably, when it came to summarizing the findings of our intergenerational study, most relevant to this chapter, we fastened on the title "understanding and resolving emotional conflict" (Steele & Steele, 2005). This chapter broadly summarizes the history of attachment theory and research as it concerns the construct of conflict, before concluding with four discrete findings from our longitudinal study that sharpen the focus on conflict and how it is understood from an attachment perspective, pointing to the immense clinical relevance of attachment research.

Introduction: the difference the 1980s made

To understand how conflict has been understood and researched from the perspective of attachment theory, the early 1980s demand one's attention. It was in 1980 when Bowlby published the third volume of his trilogy, *Loss* (1980), preceded by *Attachment* (1969) and *Separation* (1973). *Loss* built on the previous two volumes but also anchored attachment theory in cognitive science of the day as concerns defensive exclusion (or defense mechanisms) and the complicated strategies the mind deploys to contain, avoid, or otherwise distract itself from the pain of reality. In other words, conflicts within the mind of the individual were described and explained at length in *Loss*, with a sustained focus on the mind of the bereaved or the trauma survivor. Conflict was seen primarily as originating in interactions (involving separation or loss) with others in the external world. The functioning of the internal world, for Bowlby, was governed by the individual's internal working model of self and other(s), and like all psychic structures, was assumed to be formed early in life and thereafter to be resistant to change, as these models guide expectations and play a role in shaping interactions. But, interactions with others, when conflicting with expectation, can modify the internal world. When functioning well, in response to good enough experiences, the internal working model is thought to be a tolerably accurate reflection of the external world. However, when experiences not only conflict with expectations but are overwhelming, adverse, or traumatic, the internal working model may be compelled to deploy a range of defensive measures leading to internal fragmentation. Bowlby's sense of the fragmented internal world resembles S. Freud's (1900) topographical model where internal representations of threatening experiences are stored deep in the mind (excluded from conscious awareness). At this deep core place in the mind, traumatic memories are held together with associated (overwhelming) feelings of extreme distress. In contrast, at a conscious level one may hold to a more sanitized (idealized) view of the self and others in order to keep painful thoughts and feelings at bay and function without breaking down. But, of course, such functioning is maintained at a cost as efforts must be continually allocated to contain the traumatic memories and feelings that can break through at times of stress with unsettling consequences for the individual. For Bowlby (1988), the task of the therapist, after establishing a relationship of trust, is to explore with the patient his or her internal working models of current experience, and then move to exploring internal working models of prior (childhood) experiences, revealing links between the past and the present of which the patient remains unaware, and finally help the patient to update current models so that the past and present are better integrated, and the future is approached with greater spontaneity, enthusiasm, and less conflict (among inner models), permitting more satisfying resolutions of conflict with others in the lived external world.

As will be clear from this chapter, a core assumption of attachment theory concerns the range of interactions with others in the external world, including experiences of loss and trauma, as these directly impact the internal world, which, in turn, influence future interactions with others and, correspondingly, one's mental health. The 1980s are notable not only because of Bowlby having completed his trilogy with *Loss*, but later in the decade saw the appearance of a breakthrough publication for the attachment field. This was the paper that introduced the Adult Attachment Interview (AAI) bearing a title that included the memorable words *a move to the level of representation* (Main et al., 1985). This catapulted attachment research from a focus on the behavior of infants to the diversity of language used by their parents to describe and evaluate their attachment histories, including loss and trauma. Thus the AAI vastly extended the reach of attachment research making its relevance to clinical work plain to see. Two more publications from this period that helped to define attachment theory, and its clinical relevance, came from John Bowlby's publications of his lectures given from the 1950s through the early 1980s. In these two works, Bowlby outlined his approach to clinical problems: (1) *The Making and Breaking of Affectional Bonds* (Bowlby, 1979) and (2) *A Secure Base: Clinical Applications of Attachment Theory* (Bowlby, 1988).

The book on the "making and breaking of affectional bonds" included talks and publications of Bowlby from the 1950s through the 1970s, the formative time for attachment theory, leading off with "Psychoanalysis and Child Care" based on a lecture he gave in 1956 to the British Psychoanalytic Society on the 100th anniversary of Sigmund Freud's birth (Bowlby, 1979). We have elsewhere written about the immense significance of this 1956 lecture in respect of the relevant and enduring advice he offered to parents regarding their own, and their children's, inevitable ongoing conflict between love and hate, what he still called (in 1956) libidinal and aggressive drives (Steele, 2010). By 1988, Bowlby could confidently summarize the powerful contributions of attachment research to the understanding of personality development from childhood evident from the observation of behavior under stress and upon reunion with the caregiver (Ainsworth et al., 1978), and on through adulthood via the close study of language used to describe and evaluate one's attachment history (Main et al., 1985). Thus, it may be seen that the 1980s set in motion a clear shift, if not a seismic evolution, in attachment theory and research moving the discipline beyond an exclusive focus on observed parental and infant behavior to much broader and detailed focus on language used by older children and adults to present or represent their thinking and feeling about attachment relationships and the self, and a corresponding enlargement of the understanding of intrapersonal conflict (Steele et al., 1999; Emde et al., 2003; Steele & Steele, 2008).

Interpersonal conflict and intrapersonal conflict

Conflict in attachment theory and research has moved over the decades from an initial position of regarding conflict as arising primarily *between* people, essential to the formulation of the theory, to a more balanced view of how conflict arises both *within* and *between* people. The initial focus on conflict between people was tied in with a well-known disagreement between John Bowlby and Melanie Klein, as Klein and her followers (including Bowlby's training analyst, Joan Riverre) paid little or no attention to the external world inhabited by the child, and attended instead to the child's inner conflicts, fantasies, and instinctual drives operating largely outside of consciousness. Already in the 1930s, before he completed his analytic training, Bowlby was certain of the need for psychoanalytic theory to account for the child's family environment as the primary influence upon his or her immediate and long-term mental health. This was a strong conviction for Bowlby rooted in S. Freud's (1900) own thinking prior to his book on dreams when Freud greatly modified his affect-trauma theory (Sandler et al., 1971), and it remains the primary scientific claim of attachment theory, one for which robust supporting evidence exists (Grossmann et al., 2005; Sroufe, 2005). But at this formative stage of attachment theory in the 1930s, Bowlby had not yet embraced the ethological and evolutionary thinking that would inform his articulation of a motivational system (displacing Freudian drive theory) underpinning human behavior, namely "the attachment behavioral system" with precise activating and terminating conditions. Bowlby would later deliver that theory in a three-volume work. Attachment research developed in parallel with Bowlby's writings on the attachment behavioral system, with a strong focus on interpersonal conflict, but since 1985 when Mary Main and her colleagues introduced the Adult Attachment Interview (Main et al., 1985), a needed corrective in attachment theory and research was achieved with conflict coming to be seen as both interpersonal and intrapersonal, titrating one way and then the other. Across the decades, attachment theory and research has remained consistent in its focus on love, loss, trauma, and grief responses, assuming that the fundamental anxiety in human life is activated in response to loss of the loved one, or fear of loss of the loved one, that is, fear of separation and fear of abandonment – an admittedly selective reading of *Inhibitions, Symptoms and Anxiety* (S. Freud, 1926a) but one that has garnered much empirical evidence (Main & Hesse, 1990; Main & Solomon, 1990; Grossmann et al., 2005; Sroufe, 2005), and elaboration in writings about clinical process and technique (e.g., Slade, 1999, 2008; Eagle, 2013).

Attachment theory as an affect-trauma model of the mind, with a twist

If one searches for the word *conflict* in John Bowlby's monumental trilogy, *Attachment* (1969), *Separation* (1973), and *Loss* (1980), which has been cited more than 30,000 times in the scientific literature, with 500 additional references appearing every month, it is only the words *conflict behavior* that is indexed in respect of Volume 1, *Attachment*. The "conflict behavior" Bowlby wrote about typically concerned ethological observations of weaning conflicts and other conflicts that originate *between* rather than *within* people. And this is the central assumption of attachment theory, that is, that anxiety and conflict arise because of the frustrations, distress, and trauma imposed on the individual child by the outside world. Freud advanced this model of the mind according to his first model of personality, namely the "affect-trauma" frame of reference cogently described, and contrasted with Freud's later frames of reference by Sandler et al. (1971, 1973). For Bowlby, Freud made a wrong turn with his dream book and the departure into psychosexual theory. And, while Bowlby adhered closely to Freud's affect-trauma frame of reference, Bowlby did borrow heavily and selectively from S. Freud's (1926a) *Inhibitions, Symptoms and Anxiety*. Namely, it was here from this 1926 work of Freud's that Bowlby would find what he regarded as the fundamental anxiety in human (and other animal) life. For Freud, anxiety may be signaled in the ego by all ranges of internal and external sources, including envy and aggression, castration anxiety (in line with his psychosexual theory), or annihilation anxiety (self-destructive urges or fear of being overwhelmed and eliminated by a powerful other), and anxiety in response to loss of a loved one, or fear of loss of a loved one (S. Freud, 1926a). Yet it would be these last two points on to which Bowlby fastened and made central in the theory he would advance. That is the conviction that the primary anxiety in human and other animal life is not the fear of being alone or the fear of one's personal death, but the fear of being bereft of the loved one or without confidence in the return of the loved one, most acutely felt in the fear of abandonment. This is the revolutionary idea at the heart of Bowlby's theory of attachment, an appropriation from Freud that he would acknowledge, yet also a rejection of Freudian drive theory in favor of an unwavering focus on the importance of interactions with the external world, and the corresponding quality of relationships one knows as most familiar, very definitely early in life when an infant is vulnerable and needs the more-or-less continuous attention of one or more attachment figures, but also across the life span and into old age as we grow best and thrive most in the context of support from others. Conflict arises, then, when we feel deprived of the support we need, and conflict diminishes when the support we need is available, with a resulting confidence in our capacity to provide support to loved ones and others.

There are longstanding questions about the place of the self, aggression, and sexuality in attachment theory. These are questions well answered by others (e.g., Fonagy, 2001; Eagle, 2013). Both clinical and developmental observations of typical or healthy development confirm that the picture involves the regulation of feelings and conflicts, a supply of good self-feelings, the control of aggression and the satisfaction (in healthy ways) of the sexual drive, and productivity in the place of work or study – phenomena that are more common among children and adults with secure attachment histories (Steele & Steele, 1998; Grossmann et al., 2005). In other words, when the fear of loss, or loss of the loved one, is acknowledged, understood, and contained, the individual is at once more healthy in his own mind, and comfortable in his interactions with others. Clinically, we might see the patient, who is deeply unsettled with regard to the primary (and other) anxieties in human life, and is all too aware of pressing mental and emotional conflicts, often impelling the individual toward self- or other-directed violence *because* this is the familiar history of the individual and there appears to be little possibility of change.

Mary Ainsworth's influence on attachment theory and her identification of defensive behaviors in infants

Attachment theory would have remained a clinical theory in the tradition of British independent analysts (together with Balint, Winnicott, and others) but for one important difference, that is, a relationship – namely, the collegial professional relationship between John Bowlby and Mary Ainsworth, who pioneered attachment research and contributed in vital ways to the theory of attachment (Ainsworth, 1967; Ainsworth et al., 1978 – reissued in 2015 in paperback). Ainsworth and her students observed many thousands of hours of interaction between infants and their caregivers over the first year of life giving rise to the measurable construct of maternal sensitivity (the focus of a recent special issue of the journal, *Attachment & Human Development*, on the 100th anniversary of Ainsworth's birth, in 2013). After developing rating scales for assessing maternal sensitivity that remain in wide use, Ainsworth developed a 20-minute laboratory- or clinic-based procedure for observing the 12–20-month-old child's attachment to caregivers, that is, the Strange Situation Procedure (SSP). The SSP presents the 1-year-old child with a dilemma. That is, how to divide attention, and emotional investment, between exploration of the stimulating playroom (novel toys) on the one hand and attachment, paying attention to mother's availability, and relying on her, to help assuage the unsettling feelings to which separation gives rise. Quite literally, the conflict is whether to explore the play objects or seek out the primary object (attachment) figure. Children with an insecure avoidant attachment favor investment in play, do not cry on separation (despite being physically distressed by the parent's absence), and on reunion move away or keep distant from the parent maintaining a defensive pretense of being more interested in the play objects. Children with an insecure resistant attachment often fail to explore the play objects effectively, cry on separation, and remain inconsolable (angry or passive/ helpless) upon reunion. Children with secure attachments show the least defensive response playing well prior to separation, crying freely on separation and in any case showing diminished play, but then happy to see the parent upon reunion, settle promptly if crying, and return quickly to play. A fourth type of response, known as disorganized since it was first noted in the late 1980s (Main & Solomon, 1990), includes a range of behaviors that suggest deep conflict within the child when displayed in the presence of the parent. Disorganized behaviors include interrupted, anomalous postures, freezing, crying uncontrollably, hiding the face, going prone/prostrate, walking backward in the presence of the parent, and hiding from the parent. As the latter words suggest, these are all behaviors that reveal a profound fear felt in response to the parent, the very person the child most depends on in the world. Correspondingly, Main and Solomon (1990) referred to the position of the child with a disorganized/disoriented attachment to the caregiver as being trapped in a "conflict without a solution."

The words *disorganized/disoriented* come from Bowlby's (1980) account of the normative response to significant loss or trauma experiences. That is, in the moment of seeing or hearing that a significant loss or trauma event has occurred, or is occurring, we cannot help but become disorganized (unsure of where and who we are – threatened to our ontological core) and disoriented (unsure of the direction to follow with a usual epistemological sense). This is a universal response to loss or trauma, one that we typically recover from or later become reorganized but this is a process that unfolds in fits and starts, often with one or two steps backward, just as there are one or two steps forward. Across cultures, the normative period of mourning is typically 6–9 months.

Mary Main and the "move the level of representation" that illuminated the inner conflicts that characterize the adult, especially one with loss or trauma experiences that preoccupy the mind

The most striking characteristic of the Adult Attachment Interview's 20 questions (George et al., 1985) is their reliable capacity to identify adults who are beset with deep unconscious conflicts arising from past loss or trauma. In the nomenclature of the AAI rating and classification system (Main et al., 2008), the detailed questions around loss and abuse reveal the speaker who is unresolved with respect to past loss or trauma, evident via lapses in the monitoring of speech or reason, often with excessive attention to detail (absorption/guilt). A lapse in the monitoring of speech is when a "slip of the tongue" goes uncorrected and presumably unnoticed (e.g., "I died when my father died"). A lapse in the monitoring of reason is evident when a speaker refers to a dead person as if he or she were alive (e.g., "My [dead] mother can run down to the corner store faster than I can") or refers to an abusive figure as having behaved appropriately, while assuming responsibility (e.g., "He taught me a lesson, and I deserved the punishment" or "I was asking for it") – normal perhaps for a child who is being abused and coerced – but not for an adult. And while there is some overlap between Unresolved responses to the AAI and independent measures of dissociation (Hesse & van IJzendoorn, 1999), PTSD (Stovall-McClough et al., 2008), and heightened levels of adverse childhood experiences (Murphy et al., 2014), the consequences of Unresolved AAI responses extend across generations to the infants of these parents with unresolved mourning regarding past loss or trauma. Their infants are significantly likely to show disorganized/disoriented behavior toward the parent in the Strange Situation (Lyons-Ruth & Jacbovitz, 2008). In other words, the ghost in the nursery (after Fraiberg et al., 1975) is the parent with unresolved mourning regarding past loss or trauma – a troubling web of internal conflict.

The Adult Attachment Interview (George et al., 1985) and accompanying ratings and classification system (Main et al., 2008) moved attachment theory out of the domain of infancy research and into the clinical domain of the consulting room with adults. From the early 1990s, almost commensurate time with Bowlby's death, psychoanalytic societies on both sides of the Atlantic were routinely inviting attachment researchers to give lectures on attachment theory and research, especially the insights to be gained from the Adult Attachment Interview. Of course, there is a paradox here as these societies that now welcomed attachment researchers were the same institutions that made Bowlby himself feel so unwelcomed in the 1960s. On Bowlby's part, he reacted by refraining from attending scientific meetings at the British Psychoanalytic Society from the early 1960s onward but never relinquished his membership or identity as a psychoanalyst. He lived long enough to see the pendulum beginning to swing away from a reductionist behaviorist definition being assigned to his work toward a view that more fully appreciated the clinical relevance of attachment theory. Thus, he included an account of the Adult Attachment Interview in his 1988 book A *Secure Base: Clinical Applications of Attachment Theory*. A leading interpreter of how the AAI may inform the understanding of the individual adult in psychotherapy has been Arietta Slade in her important chapters in the first and second editions of the *Handbook of Attachment* (Slade, 1999; 2008) with a third edition published July 2016. In these writings, Slade has shown that typical (neurotic) responses to the Adult Attachment Interview are well-known to the clinician. These typical insecurities take the form of dismissing or preoccupying responses to the AAI. In the former case, the dismissing speaker claims that he or she has no conflicts, insists that his or her parents behaved in an idealized or good enough way, beyond question, and yet a core unhappiness or lack of fulfillment in relationships is palpable. The task for the clinician with the dismissing individual is to gently query his or her relationship status in the present (and in the past), proceeding cautiously so as not to upset what may be rigid or strong defenses against acknowledging psychic pain. With respect to the adult with a preoccupying stance toward attachment, conflict is all too evident. The speaker has complaints about present relationships that meld together with complaints about the past in an involving angry way or a passive needy way. The clinical task with such an individual beset by conflict is to introduce a safe place to slow down, to be heard, and to co-create a sense of understanding of the role of themselves and the other in their interpersonal struggles. But this is an over-simplification because many responses to the AAI, especially those from clinical samples, which can include both dismissing and preoccupying elements, are assigned the *Can't Classify* rating, signifying the speaker's reliance on a blending of conflicting strategies to make sense of their inner world. In other words, conflict exists in the mind at many different levels, such that the belief in a conflict-free mind is illusory.

The myth of a conflict-free mind

Perhaps because of the American belief in the right to the pursuit of happiness, there is an expectation of many in the US that life or many parts of life should be unremittingly joyful. And so we have parenting advocates advancing the idea that "attachment parenting" is about doing everything with a sense of joyfulness. This may be appealing but it is, of course, unrealistic. As all too often we are not full of joy, but rather fatigue, or fears about the future, regrets about the past, sadness or anger that does not easily dissipate. Acknowledging and understanding such negative feelings will be very difficult if we believe that all our actions should be undertaken with joy, or lead to joy.

Attachment theory is consonant with traditional and contemporary (relational) psychoanalysis in urging acknowledgement and acceptance of a certain inevitability regarding psychic conflict. Charles Brenner's classic ego psychology book, *The Mind In Conflict* (1982b), leaves one to wonder "when is the mind not in conflict?" And the rupture-repair model advanced by Tronick (1989) based on observations of infants, and skillfully applied to the psychotherapeutic consulting room by Safran et al. (1990), offers both an empirical basis for understanding conflict, and a hopeful way forward, that is, conflict may be ever-present, but so is the possibility of resolution or repair and the joy that brings.

On the understanding of conflict and the inevitability of mixed feelings

When we are asked to summarize the more than 12 years of longitudinal research that began with our doctoral research (in the late 1980s) for an edited book on the "major longitudinal attachment studies" (Grossmann et al., 2005), we quickly settled on the following title: "Understanding and Resolving Emotional Conflict: The London Parent-Child Project." We chose this title because of a powerful finding that emerged from our six-year follow-up of the children (and parents). We observed that an understanding of mixed emotions, or the possibility of having different feelings in response to a given dilemma, or situation, was linked (backward) to security of attachment to mother (in infancy) and to having a mother who provided a secure-autonomous response to the AAI when still pregnant with this first child (Steele et al., 1999). Prior to that finding being published the developmental literature suggested that it is not until 11 years of age that children show a capacity to understand ambivalence (Harter & Buddin, 1987). We showed that security of attachment makes such understanding of mixed feelings appear earlier than expected. The value of this understanding is evident as when one is faced with frustration or distress, it enables the sufferer to acknowledge the distress and readily imagine relief through a way forward. In early childhood, relief typically arrives through the physical presence of the caregiver. By the onset of the school years (ages 5–7) it is adaptive to be able to self-generate a feeling of security within (from representations of self with mother, with father, or with others) that enables one to face, acknowledge, and know distress that arises, while also to imagine a safe way out.

Distinctive influence of early experiences with mother, father and others

Regarding which inner representations (of self with mother, with father, or with others) that are influential at any one point in time, attachment research offers some clues as to the typical influences, and just how early infants become differentially responsive to caregiving figures (Steele et al., 1996). In our longitudinal work documenting the independence of infant-mother and infant-father attachment relationships (Steele et al., 1996), it was demonstrated not only that an infant behaves differently with mother than she or he does with father, but also that this difference is systematically linked to individual differences in mothers' and fathers' responses to the AAI. In other words, by the end of the first year of life if not well before, an infant knows what it feels like to be with mother (largely determined by the extent to which *she* has resolved childhood attachment conflicts) and, independently, what it feels like to be with father (largely determined by the extent to which *he* has resolved childhood attachment conflicts). Extensive longitudinal research findings show that the infant-mother attachment relationship influences the child's later relationships (with peers, teachers, and eventual romantic partners) as well as the child's later understanding of emotion and his or her capacity to resolve emotional dilemmas or conflicts across childhood and into adolescence (Steele & Steele, 2005). This paternal line of influence, confirmed by a number of independent longitudinal studies, is typically in the domain of social conflicts, peer relations, and mental health (Suess et al., 1992; Steele & Steele, 2005).

We do not assume that these long-term influences of early experience stem from internalized experiences from the first year of life alone, but rather, it is most likely that infant-parent relationship qualities are markers of types of parenting strategies that are likely to be stable across the childhood and adolescent years. These "types" are well captured by the Adult Attachment Interview and the extent to which the adult can speak coherently about past emotional conflicts. When a speaker is coherent in the interview such that his or her responses are categorized "free-autonomous" then such an adult, despite having talked about past and/or current conflicts, is likely to be in a positive and energetic mood (Steele & Steele, 2005). Showing convincingly that an individual possesses a coherent valuing of attachment leaves one feeling good and confident that conflicts can be acknowledged and, at least partially, resolved so that one may be resilient in the face of future conflicts, under no illusion that they can be avoided.

The need to state explicitly both sides of a conflict

In working with school-age children, adolescents, or adults, there is an imperative to be ever-mindful of the fact that the patient or client needs to know that you believe she or he is capable of change. For example, in respect of an adult with unresolved mourning regarding past loss, the clinician may best connect with the patient, by NOT saying "you seem to believe your dead father is still alive by how you speak of him in the present tense" and instead saying "on the one hand, you know your father died seven years ago and yet, on the other hand, you wish and believe at times that he was still here." This mode of intervention is strongly supported by attachment theory and research insofar as mixed feelings, including wishes for things to stay as they are, and co-existing wishes for things to change, are the natural backdrop to the flow of interpersonal and intrapersonal life.

Conclusion

This chapter has addressed the topic of conflict from an attachment perspective, where conflict is seen as an expression of the primary anxiety in human (and other animal life), that is, the fear of loss of the loved one, or the fear of loss of love, with the normative response to actual loss being disorganization and disorientation (Bowlby, 1980). Typically, after 6–9 months, if not sooner, the grieving individual charts a pathway to resolution of loss, via understanding of the conflicts engendered by it, and becoming reorganized with a focus on living loved ones and study or work that is a source of satisfaction. Chronic mental health troubles are to be understood, from this perspective, as stemming from ongoing unresolved conflicts regarding past loss (of a loved one) or trauma (especially when perpetrated by a loved one). Finally, a strategy to help individuals with loss or trauma has been advanced, on the assumption that some measure of interpersonal and intrapersonal conflict is an inevitable part of a meaningful life.

Chapter 14

Addressing defenses against painful emotions

Modern conflict theory in psychotherapeutic approaches with children

Leon Hoffman, Timothy R. Rice, and Tracy A. Prout

Child and adolescent concepts

In 1913, Ferenczi (1952) first reported on his meeting with 5-year old Árpád who wanted to watch roosters being slaughtered. Ferenczi noted the boy's immediate interest in roosters, both through his drawings and interest in a small bronze rooster that was in the office. Despite the patient's apparent appropriateness for treatment, Ferenczi noted that the boy was bored and only wanted to get back to his toys:

> Direct psycho-analytic investigation was therefore impossible, and I had to confine myself to getting the lady who was interested in the case and, being a neighbour and friend of the family, could watch him for hours at a time, to note down his curious remarks and gestures.
>
> (p. 244)

This inauspicious response to a little boy's play appears to be all too common, even among contemporary mental health professionals who do not have intimate clinical contact with children. In other words, for too many mental health practitioners, like Ferenczi, playing with and observing a child is an activity not worthy of an analyst's time. In a field which privileges the spoken word, play, activity, action, and a variety of non-verbal communications are often ignored. These non-verbal behaviors may be considered to be signs of immaturity, developmental regression, or even psychopathology. Only recently, in tandem with contemporary neuroscience data, has psychoanalysis truly begun to recognize that non-verbal interactions may very well be the "real" mutative agents in a psychotherapy or psychoanalysis (Pally, 2001).

In psychotherapy sessions, young children play with toys and interact with the clinician. School-age children (latency-age children) play structured games and talk about their work in school. Adolescents may regale the clinician with tales of their victories and defeats in their relationships and want to discuss all of their current involvements with the popular cultural activities of the day. Or the child or adolescent may remain silent. Is the child withdrawing or giving the clinician the silent treatment? Clinicians with limited experience working with children and adolescents may have difficulty addressing these types of interactions and may see them as distractions from the "real" therapeutic work of psychotherapy or psychoanalysis. Some providers may feel helpless in the face of challenging interactions and confrontations. Clinicians working with children for the first time may have difficulty appreciating that a child does not verbally free associate like an adult. In fact, such clinicians may not appreciate that play and activity serves a comparable function to verbalization (Sandler & Freud, 1981). Like Ferenczi, some non-child clinicians have come to believe that because of a lack of direct verbalization, a direct psychodynamic investigation of a child's mental life is nearly impossible. These difficulties are a defined clinical problem in the practice of both psychoanalysis as well as family systems therapy (Wachtel, 1994).

Freud understood the importance of understanding the nature of the actions between patient and analyst, especially in the development of the concept of transference as first explicated in the "Postscript to Dora" (S. Freud, 1905) where he conjectures that it would have been valuable for him to address with Dora any actual physical similarities between Herr K and himself. Or when S. Freud (1914a) states that "The patient does not say that he remembers that he used to be defiant and critical towards his parents' authority; instead, he behaves in that way to the doctor" (p. 150); or when he (Freud, 1926b) says that what the patient is "showing us is the kernel of his intimate life history: *he is reproducing it tangibly, as though it were actually happening, instead of remembering it*" (italics in the original, p. 226).

This, of course, is what children and adolescents do with a clinician all the time. They show and act and interact (even when they are using words). They play out the important themes of their lives without consciously appreciating the connections to their current real-life concerns or the connection to unremitting concerns from past events. In contrast to Ferenczi's failed first session the first person to understand this was Hermine von Hug-Hellmuth (L. Hoffman, 1995). Just a few years after Ferenczi's case report, von Hug-Hellmuth (1921), in a still-relevant passage, wrote,

The first hour in treatment is of the utmost importance; it is the opportunity for establishing a *rapport* with the young creature, and for "breaking the ice." It causes much strain and stress . . . even to the experienced analyst. . . . But no rules and no programme can be laid down.

(p. 293)

In most psychoanalytic and psychotherapeutic quarters, understanding the nature of the interaction between clinician and patient (and the shift from the so-called "one-person" to the "two-person" psychology) is au courant. One such relevant concept is the concept of enactment, which is reviewed by Auchincloss and Samberg (2012). They state that the term *enactment* originally referred in the psychoanalytic literature "to the general human tendency to symbolically enact unconscious fantasies" (p. 76) and later, enactment referred to the mutual influences between patient and analyst. In their play and activities, children re-create their unconscious conflicted fantasies, conscious fantasies, memories, as well as their real-life experiences. Ferenczi did not seem to appreciate that in the very first session, Árpád's interest in the bronze sculpture was an *action* containing a displaced, important communication about his real-life concerns.

Despite the prominence of the seminal works of Anna Freud and Melanie Klein in the world of psychoanalysis, it is striking how the insights derived from child psychoanalysis and psychodynamic therapy are so often missing from the psychoanalytic debates about the nature of the interaction between analyst and patient, theoretical and technical (L. Hoffman, 2000). There does not seem to be a full appreciation that the debates in the 1920s between Melanie Klein and Anna Freud seemed to be a historical forerunner of contemporary "one-person" versus "two-person" issue. In fact, in a so-called "classic" child and adolescent psychoanalytic education at the New York Psychoanalytic Society and Institute, Ted Becker, the teacher for many contemporary child and adolescent psychoanalysts, noted in his ongoing teachings that it mattered less exactly how one acted with a child in a session but rather the focus should be on the meaning of the action to the child. Certainly, on face value, there seems to be a difference between such an approach (trying to understand the meaning of the interaction between patient and clinician to one of the parties, the patient) and one in which the clinician believes that the meaning of the transference/countertransference is co-constructed by the contributions from both participants.

Exploring the differences between those two conceptions is beyond the scope of this chapter.

However, in a recent study consisting of in-depth interviews of 20 child and adolescent analysts throughout the country, we found that these analysts felt that their child and adolescent education helped them understand the complexities in their work with adults, such as enactments (Derish et al., 2014). In fact, Jacobs (1996), one of the important contributors to the literature on enactments, noted, "Adult analysts have been slow to incorporate into their treatment . . . notions derived from understanding development and child analytic technique about the flexible – and creative – use of analytic technique" (p. 233).

In this chapter we discuss the added value of ideas derived from modern conflict theory, particularly the concept of interpreting defenses against unpleasant emotions, as applied to child and adolescent dynamic and psychoanalytic treatments. The added value afforded by this perspective includes the specialized relatedness gained from firsthand experience of infant, toddler, child, and adolescent development. This includes the importance of play, parent-child interactions, peer interactions and school activities, the impact of siblings, trauma (including that experienced as a result of learning and other cognitive difficulties), and the interdependence of cognitive and emotional development. It is our contention that without firsthand observation of and work with children, adolescents, and their parents, clinicians do not experience the full benefits of this perspective and may struggle with the developmental components of psychodynamic theories. Without firsthand knowledge of children, a clinician may think of developmental constructs abstractly, without considering how such constructs may be inconsistent with real-life development, biologic or interactional. This includes, for example, an attribution of cognitive activities to a young child prior to his or her actual development or failure to modify a theory which is not based on actual observation of children. For example, recently Stapert and Smeekens (2011) propose that a re-conceptualization of psychoanalytic theories of the superego should be considered as a result of the observation of very young children with good conscience.

In the chapter, our aim is to apply a developmental perspective to the construct of "conflict and compromise formation" (Brenner, 1994) and to show its value in the treatment of children and adolescents in a psychotherapeutic session. We will proceed by presenting the conception of conflict and compromise formation by emphasizing the relevance of the basic concepts of defense mechanisms first systematized by Anna Freud (1936), explicated by Sandler and A. Freud (1985), and elaborated by Berta Bornstein with her concept of *addressing defenses against painful emotions* (1945, 1949, 1951). This technique (*an experience-near technique* which does not require *experience-distant* "guesses" or conjectures of inferred unconscious motivators) is the central technique utilized when working in a psychodynamic manner with children.[1]

It is important to note that in the adult literature there are very few references that describe how and when to address affect in the clinical situation (Lotterman, 2012). Lotterman (2012) notes that, in contrast to ideas and fantasies, affect

> is an especially good marker of the workable psychic surface. Affect is part of a very early signaling system that alerts the individual and others about the status of the self. It is a rapid response and a largely automatic reaction that is only partially controlled by the ego and its defenses. Affects by their very presence mark the fact that a certain mental element has become significant to the self; therefore, affect can be a particularly consistent and helpful barometer of what is currently on the patient's mind.
>
> (p. 330)

We present one case example of a child with internalizing symptoms and another with externalizing symptoms in order to illustrate some of these ideas.

Conflict and compromise formation

Ernst Kris (1947), cited by Brenner, 1992) described psychoanalysis as a way to view the mind from the perspective of conflict. This idea was developed and expanded over time by Charles Brenner (1982b) and came to be called modern conflict theory. Conflict and compromise formation theory is a useful way of organizing the sources of a patient's psychological dysfunctions as they are expressed in the consulting room. Compromise formations are the ideational, affective, and behavioral resultants of attempts at solution of conflict among the psychic agencies (abstractly called id, ego, and superego) and the outside world. As Brenner (2003) states: "When a pleasure-seeking wish is associated with unpleasure, the mind is in conflict. What one observes in thought and behavior in situations of conflict is compromise formation" (p. 1095). There are adaptive and maladaptive compromise formations. In the consulting room, we, of course, try to understand the sources of maladaptive (pathological) compromise formations.

Problems in children and adults may be broadly categorized as *externalizing* or *internalizing* (Achenbach & Edelbrock, 1978; PDM Task Force, 2006). *Internalizing* problems include behaviors which the child himself or herself experiences as problematic, that is, problematic emotions that from the child's perspective come from within. In contrast, *externalizing* behaviors refer to those situations in which the child expresses or reacts behaviorally to his or her conflicts or feelings instead of describing problematic feelings as emanating from within. Among externalizing disorders are those that can be globally categorized as disruptive disorders (DD). The rationale for this broad categorization is that in empirical studies, there is a great deal of comorbidity within both internalizing problems (anxiety and depression) and externalizing problems (oppositional defiant disorder [ODD], conduct disorder [CD], and attention deficit hyperactivity disorder [ADHD]). More recently, children who can be categorized with the new category of disruptive mood dysregulation disorder (DMDD) also exhibit many externalizing behaviors. At the internalizing end of the spectrum we include children with the large variety of emotional disorders with dysphoric affects with a great deal of overt self-recriminations, guilt and/or shame. At the externalizing end of the spectrum, one tends to observe a seeming "lack of insight" into personal responsibility.

By conceptualizing both internalizing and externalizing disturbances as compromise formations, that is, pathological compromise formations, the clinician is able to try to understand the *meaning* of the child's symptomatic behavior. This conceptualization allows the clinician to try to understand the meaning of the patient's verbal and non-verbal communications. The clinician can then communicate his or her understanding to the patient in order to broaden the child's view of himself or herself. During this process, rather than gratifying or rejecting the patient, the clinician examines the nature of the patient's conscious and unconscious desires, defenses, and moral demands as they may be reproduced in the relationship to the clinician/analyst. The clinician communicates this understanding, or interprets, to the child.

For example, a child who has not developed the usual kinds of social behaviors such as the capacity for sharing or controlling asocial impulses may be considered to have developed a maladaptive compromise formation (an *externalizing* behavior). One can infer that in this child's development, he or she did not inhibit greedy wishes (id) and did not learn the moral principle of sharing or behaving in a socially appropriate manner (superego and ego). In contrast, another child with severe inhibitions may have developed a pathological compromise formation by relinquishing all or most of his or her desires and inhibiting all aggression toward the rival (*internalizing* behavior). Such a child would literally "be afraid of his shadow" and, in fact, may easily be taken advantage of by other children.

Although Charles Brenner published *The Mind in Conflict* in 1982, few psychoanalysts of any theoretical orientation have appreciated, or understood fully, the clinical and theoretical implications of Brenner's discussion of drive derivative (see L. Hoffman, 1999, for a full discussion). Brenner distinguished the concept of drive (an abstract concept) from that of drive derivative. When one listens to patients, particularly using the psychoanalytic method, one can observe or infer a patient's conscious and unconscious *wishes*. These wishes are called *drive derivatives*. Thus as one listens to a child or observes a child's play and activity one can perceive that the child is expressing or inhibiting a particular wish and, most important, its connection to other people, his parents, siblings, teachers, and in the therapeutic relationship, toward his clinician (transference). As Brenner describes: "A drive derivative is unique to a particular individual and is connected to particular people in that person's life" (Brenner, 1982b, pp. 25–26).

The concept is not a reified static concrete entity. There are two broad categories of drive derivatives and drives: the sexual or libidinal and the aggressive, which evolve during development.

Defenses and defense mechanisms[2]

The construct of *defense* is central to the concept of Conflict and Compromise Formation. Both in health and mental dysfunction, defenses play a prominent role allowing the development of a balance between full expression of one's desires (regardless of their consequences) and a control of those desires as a result of conflict. This delicate balancing act results in what is called a compromise formation.

Sigmund Freud

From the beginning of his career Sigmund Freud (1892b) was aware of the centrality of defense in mental life. Yet in his early formulations defense and pathology were equivalent. At first, Freud maintained that in order to bring about therapeutic change, the analyst's job was to attempt to forcibly overcome the patient's defenses (or what has been called resistance to uncovering unconscious material) in order to allow for free awareness and expression of unconscious wishes. For example, S. Freud's (1893b) early approach to addressing resistances seemed to be equivalent to a battle with a pathological force, where Freud described "the important part played by the figure of the physician in creating motives *to defeat* the psychical force of resistance" (p. 301) [italics added].

S. Freud's (1923, 1926a) central change in technique involved understanding the inevitable defensive responses that arise in treatment. Freud came to appreciate that these resistances to uncovering (i.e., defensive reactions) were automatically expressed by the patient and were unconscious themselves. He came to see that these defenses had to be respected and addressed in analysis rather than forcibly overcome.

Anna Freud's ego and the mechanisms of defense

Although Sigmund Freud was acutely aware by 1926a that to help a patient, one needed to address and discuss defenses and not attempt to overcome them forcibly, it was Anna Freud (1936) who began the first systematic study of defenses and defense mechanisms. In that volume, she discusses defense mechanisms, such as repression (already discussed in depth by Sigmund Freud), regression, reaction formation, isolation, undoing, projection, identification, sublimation, displacement, transformation into the opposite, and turning against one's self. In addition there were three other defenses: *denial in fantasy, denial in word and act,* and *identification with the aggressor.* These three defenses are active in children with externalizing behaviors (Hoffman et al., 2016).

Over a period of a year in 1972–1973, Anna Freud with Joseph Sandler and others at the Hampstead Clinic (later, the Anna Freud Center) (Sandler & Freud, 1985) studied Anna Freud's (1936) original volume. This helped the spread and development of Anna Freud's ideas.

Development of the technique of interpretation of defenses against unwelcome affects

A key question in the development of technique in child analysis was the question of the role of external environment and relationships (especially parents). Although in the 1920s, Anna Freud (A. Freud, 1926) observed that children generally did not develop a transference neurosis, she later argued,

> Even if one part of the child's neurosis is transformed into a transference neurosis as it happens in adult analysis, another part of the child's neurotic behavior remains grouped around the parents who are the original objects of his pathogenic past.
>
> (A. Freud, 1945, p. 130)

Thus, she concluded, it was important that the analyst consider the child patient's environment and relationships and, in particular, to form an alliance with both the child and his or her parents. Melanie Klein, 1927, on the other hand, maintained that early failure to demonstrate a transference neurosis merely reflected the preparatory phase (where the analyst acted in an exaggeratedly benign and giving way). In analytic work with children, she stated, the analyst should not be concerned with the child's relationship to the outside world. Rather, reality issues and work with the parents were unnecessary, corrupting a child's analysis by interfering with the development of a transference neurosis.

One resolution to the conflicting approaches between the Kleinian view and Anna Freud's view was accomplished with the development of defense analysis with children. This technique may be an unacknowledged forerunner of Paul Gray's (2005) conceptualizations about the lag in the utilization of defense analysis with adults (L. Hoffman, 2000).

Anna Freud (1966b) explained how alteration of classical techniques were made necessary by the child's inability to use "free association, by the immaturity of his ego, the dependency of his superego, and by his resultant incapacity to deal unaided with pressures from the id" (p. 9). She adds, "We were impressed by the strength of the child's defenses and resistances and by the difficulty of interpreting transference, the impurity of which we ascribed to the use of a nonanalytic introductory period" (p. 9).

In her classic paper, Berta Bornstein (1945) described in great detail a technique for interpreting defenses against painful feelings in children, using a clinical example to demonstrate how this can be done without inflicting painful narcissistic injury. She suggested addressing the child's defenses against painful emotions instead of directly confronting the child's unwelcome thoughts and fantasies. This, she posited, would allow the therapist to connect with the child in a much more sensitive and, thus, effective way.

Bornstein's ideas form the basis of the contemporary approach to addressing a patient's defenses, whether the child experiences an *internalizing* disorder or an *externalizing* disorder.

The first step in any therapeutic endeavor, of course, is engaging the patient. Without such an engagement treatment is not possible. We are suggesting that there is a fundamental technical approach to a child's introduction to treatment (or, any patient's, for that matter): understanding, addressing, and interpreting the patient's defenses against unwelcome affects. An inability to regulate affective responses to negative stimuli is a key feature in children with both internalizing and externalizing disorders. In Rice and L. Hoffman (2014), we discuss the modern neurocognitive concept of emotion regulation (ER) (both explicit and implicit) and its similarity to the psychoanalytic concepts of coping mechanisms and defense mechanisms. Explicit ER processes are more similar to conscious coping mechanisms than to unconscious defense mechanisms. These explicit processes entail an emotional adaptation that allows one to work consciously toward achieving an emotional goal.

In the neuroscience literature implicit emotion regulation has been defined as "any process that operates without the need for conscious supervision or explicit intentions, and which is aimed at modifying the quality, intensity, or duration of an emotional response" (p. 701). This description is similar to the definition of defense mechanisms ("automatic psychological processes that protect the individual against anxiety and from the awareness of internal or external dangers or stressors" (*DSM-IV* definition cited by Rice & L. Hoffman, 2014, p. 696).[3]

Historically, analysts have made a distinction between clarification and interpretation. From Bibring's classical analytic perspective (Bibring, 1954), clarifications refer to *experience-near interventions*, "which assist the patient to reach a higher degree of self-awareness, clarity and differentiation of self-observation which makes adequate verbalization possible"

(p. 755) whereas for Bibring, interpretation refers to an evolving, *experience-distant* process wherein the analyst presents "hypothetical constructions and reconstructions of unconscious processes which are assumed to determine [the patient's] behavior" (p. 758).

From our perspective, interpretation is considered to include clarification which is built upon. When addressing a child's defenses against awareness of unpleasant affects, the clinician must not stray very far from the surface and ***should not*** transgress the clinical data (Bibring's idea of an interpretation, 1954) but rather stay as experience-near as possible.

This preferential focus on the process of defense against disturbing affects includes the caution not to focus prematurely on a patient's unconscious libidinal or aggressive wishes or, in fact, defenses about which the patient has no awareness at all. The clinician should try to avoid "guessing" what is on the patient's mind, although inevitably a certain amount of guessing always takes place. The ideas are consistent with Sugarman's (1994, 2003) application of Paul Gray's technique with children. In Sugarman's (1994) words, the child is helped to expand "the control of the conscious ego over other structures of the psyche" (p. 329).

With this approach, from the very beginning of the therapeutic work, the clinician first tries to understand, then judiciously explore, and eventually describe the child's current mental state in terms of the defenses against a conscious awareness of the emotional pain that the child seems to be experiencing. As the clinician understands how the child is hiding the emotional pain from him or herself (consciously or unconsciously keeping bad feelings out of awareness, avoiding direct verbalization, or disavowing the painful feeling states), the clinician needs to discern ways of addressing such defenses. When the clinician understands how the child is protecting himself or herself from painful feelings, the clinician can try to communicate this understanding verbally or non-verbally to the child.

The child's defensive maneuvers are explored and eventually interpreted to the child in a careful, respectful, and developmentally appropriate way. This ideally leads to a situation in which the child feels less threatened by the painful feeling states. This allows the child to share the feelings with another person in a more direct or more elaborated (though disguised) way. The child then feels in greater control of himself or herself, leading to greater mastery of affects and more adaptive interactions with the environment. In some children, over time, there may be greater verbal elaboration

234   Leon Hoffman et al.

of feelings and fantasies and exploration of the origins of the painful feelings, while for other children, mastery of feelings and diminishment of maladaptive defenses is achieved without touching upon the origins of the overwhelming states.

Clinical illustration: internalizing disorders

The following example illustrates the clinical value of the conflict and compromise formation theory derived from the inference that there may be an unconscious connection between two seemingly disparate communications.

A depressed 8-year-old boy, Jimmy, came to the clinician's office because of withdrawal in school. He had no trouble separating from his mother. His understanding of the reason for his visit with the clinician was that he was having stomachaches and headaches when he read at home and during school. (They played catch while they chatted.) He said he was nervous about school and reading in general and book reports and homework in particular. He preferred earlier grades because there was less writing and reading and he liked it better when "you could play." Later, he expressed intense guilt and responsibility when he said that he feels very bad when he gets angry at his little brother; he feels sorry for him and has to make up with him. He denied feeling sad.

In this first session one can conjecture that for some reason, the child developed a pathological compromise formation in which autonomous assertive acts such as doing his work were inhibited because they were infused with forbidden aggression.

In the second session, he reported a dream wherein a dinosaur approached him and his family at a baseball game and ate his brother. He was very upset about that, and he called out to his favorite player to try to help him. The player did not hear him and turned away from him. The parents reported his extreme compliance occasionally marred by minimal complaints that the brother got more than he did. The clinician was struck by the virtual absence of overt negative thoughts about the brother in the session. The boy reported that he always did what the brother wanted.

In this session we see the expression of a pervasive pathological compromise formation, manifested by a very strong defense against hostile wishes toward the younger brother. In other words, his hostile wishes caused such unpleasure that he always had to avoid the awareness of those wishes by instituting strong mental activities such as inhibiting his own desires, submitting to his brother's wishes, avoiding direct reports of anger at his brother, and withdrawing from activity in school. His developmental progress was impaired. The aggression could only emerge in the dream (in displaced form), which was in contrast to the real-life compliance and withdrawal.

Further evidence for this formulation was seen at the end of one session when he said that he felt bad for the Mazda (a car with which he did not play), he felt bad for others (like the brother) even if they were not alive, even more than for himself. The clinician noted that it was difficult for him to have bad feelings toward someone else. *This comment addressed the boy's defensive avoidance of an unpleasant emotion, that is, aggression. The clinician **did not** address the content, that the feared aggression was directed at his brother.* The child responded that he didn't think of this as a problem. Comments, such as this one, addressing his defenses against overt expression of aggression, were repeated over time. He began to play out aggressive themes involving his brother; for example, while two children were walking near a lake, a little boy who tried to take their toys away fell into the lake and was eaten by crocodiles.

After a period of several weekly sessions, the mother reported that Jimmy was much better at school and seemed much happier. In addition, and very significantly, for the first time he fought a tremendous amount with the brother. The mother observed that "he seemed freed up to fight with him." Prior to the sessions, he always gave in. He became much freer in school and the new teacher said that she would not have guessed that there were problems. In other words, the therapy situation, *systematically addressing his defenses against his feared emotion, overt expression of aggression toward his brother*, enabled the boy to express aggressive wishes to the brother which were previously forbidden. The parents understood that the misbehavior at home was indicative of progress for this inhibited boy and not a regression.

There were two kinds of interventions in this brief therapy that were helpful: the creation of an atmosphere which allowed free expression of his fantasies and feelings and second, addressing the child's need to defend against negative feelings toward another person.

Interpretation of defenses against painful affects: a dynamic approach to children with externalizing behaviors[4]

In the case of the depressed child, Jimmy, whom we describe earlier, it is clear that he experiences internalized symptoms, that is, the child constructs inhibitions and thus prevents expressions of feelings which he considers forbidden. He does not perceive his problems as originating from others in his life. Such children are in psychological pain and want to be helped. Dynamic psychotherapy is often very effective for these children, as the clinician addresses the defenses the child utilizes to prevent forbidden feelings and fantasies from emerging into consciousness. At the other end of the spectrum are children who exhibit externalizing symptoms and behaviors. In short these children blame the environment for their problems; they do not think that issues within themselves are the causes of the problems.

Children with disruptive symptoms often blame the environment for their problems, insisting that if the environment changed, their maladaptive behaviors would change. Attempts at modifying their surroundings often have minimal effects. The underlying principle in working dynamically with children who disrupt is to consider the disruptive behavior as a way to defensively protect themselves from unbearable emotions.

The avoidance of such painful feelings can be conceptualized to be similar to avoidance of external phobic situations (McCullough et al., 2003). Similar to the response-prevention component of exposure, response prevention (ERP), the child is prevented from engaging in avoidance mechanisms, or established "responses." The clinician achieves this through recognizing and commenting on the avoidance (defense) and thus disempowering their function. The emphasis remains on observed behaviors and emotions within the clinical encounter; naming of inferred instinctual drives and intellectualized "deep" interpretations are avoided. It is important to stress that this technique is an "experience-near" treatment whereby the clinician mainly speaks with the child about the "in-the-moment" interaction between child and clinician and minimizes discussion of what he or she heard from the parents and/or school. This technique allows the clinician to help the child observe and discuss the inevitable repetitions in the sessions of the maladaptive problematic externalizing behaviors. In addition, since this technique does not require the clinician to infer the children's motivations which are not observable, it is a technique which allows for ease of replicability and facilitates capability for empiric studies of treatment efficacy. The following is a case example addressing the defensive meaning of externalizing behaviors.

Jonah, a 7-year-old, very bright boy, exhibited a variety of behavioral disruptions in the classroom since nursery school; he could not sleep alone. In this example, one source of his externalizing behaviors was illustrated at the end of the first session.

When the clinician realized they had only a few minutes left in the session, she said, "Jonah, we are almost out of time. We will have to say goodbye soon and meet again next week." Jonah replied, "But where will all the animals sleep when it is nighttime in the dollhouse?" The clinician said, "Why don't you show me where they sleep." As if a switch had been flipped, Jonah became frenetic and the dollhouse erupted in chaos as he shoved every animal and action figure he could grasp into one bedroom. He became tearful, whining, "They sleep together! They always sleep in the big bed." Addressing the animals he said, "I won't make you leave!"

In this moment, Jonah allowed the clinician to see how intensely dysregulated he could become around separations – both the end of the session and separation from his parents at bedtime. When told that the session would be ending, Jonah put himself in the role of the clinician revealing both that he felt the clinician was making him leave and that he would never be so cruel himself. In this moment, the feelings of rejection and perhaps even terror were tangibly reproduced as though the experience were happening in the present moment.

The clinician simply said to Jonah that she saw how hard it was to say goodbye to her but they would meet next week. *With this remark, and without making a correct direct connection to the play, or to his problems at home, the clinician addressed his difficulty leaving as a defense against the painful feelings accompanying separation. His wish to be close to the clinician was thwarted, provoking painful emotions, which he protected himself from experiencing by becoming dysregulated.*

Several sessions later, Jonah explained that the baby animals had to sleep in the parents' room to "keep an eye on things" and "keep everyone safe." *Although this may have been a veiled reference to the primal scene and his concern about it, it was too experience-distant to address it as a conjecture.*

Many themes were addressed with Jonah during the course of therapy, including the anxiety about separation at nighttime and its connection to his externalizing behaviors, as well his experience of his intelligence which was not challenged at school. For example, in his play, Jonah described how monsters scared children in order to compensate for their loneliness and lack of agency. This tension between overt problematic actions and inner distress was difficult for Jonah and his family to navigate and, thus, they sought treatment, which included helping the parents navigate Jonah's anxiety without simply treating it as if it were "bad" behavior.

Since Jonah was clearly of superior intelligence, the clinician recommended an educational evaluation to assess the appropriate level of instruction. Throughout the process of the evaluation, Jonah asked the clinician why he had not been given the tests earlier. He was coming closer to expressing anger at his teachers and even his parents for labeling him a difficult child and not rewarding his giftedness. In one session, Jonah became very angry over the selection of board games in the clinician's office. He yelled, "I hate it here! This is a place for babies!" The clinician affirmed that the games were not at Jonah's level, empathizing with his frustration and adding, "It must make you angry when we underestimate you. It is easier to get angry than to worry about your mind." *This is one example of the clinician addressing the defensive nature of his externalizing behavior (avoiding consciously accentuating worries about himself).*

The clinician empathized with Jonah's hurt feelings about his sense of self because the important people in his life underestimated his capacity and *addressed his defensive (protective) response of aggression to ward off the hurt feelings.* Jonah then began playing; a story unfolded of a duck whose teacher could not tolerate all the tricks he did during swimming lessons in the pond. The duck eventually swam away from the group and did tricks on his own, even though he knew it would get him in trouble. The duck yelled at his parents, "Tell her! Tell her! I don't want to be on my own with my tricks!" Although the individualized education plan had been in place for several weeks, it was the clinician's addressing the defensive nature of his expressed anger that precipitated a radical improvement in Jonah's classroom behavior. While meeting his educational needs was an essential part of the solution, his ability to understand the defensive meaning of his disruptive behavior was ultimately the turning point. *With this play he utilized higher level defenses than he used in the beginning of the treatment. Playing out his conflict about being thwarted from his wishes to be close to the parents (clinician) he used displacement to the play as well as greater sublimatory-like activity. In contrast, earlier he utilized many more action-level lower level defenses.*

Manual of Regulation-Focused Psychotherapy for Children (RFP-C) with Externalizing Behaviors: a Psychodynamic Approach

In contrast to behavioral approaches, in a psychodynamic treatment for children with externalizing behaviors (like with children with internalizing symptoms) the clinician tries to understand the meaning of the child's maladaptive disruptive behavior. The clinician does not try to teach the child how to behave properly nor try to teach parents management techniques. Instead the clinician communicates to the child that there is meaning to the behavior and that it is safer to act up than feel painful emotions, such as sadness, shame, or other negative affect. Child treatments have to include an active parent component. In our manual, we describe how to help parents understand the meaning of their children's behavior and how to approach their children in a more effective way, understanding the working of their child, his or her own individual needs, worries, and responses to stress.

In short, we (L. Hoffman et al., 2016) describe how to systematically apply this technique, its clinical and theoretical roots, and how it is derived from the psychoanalytic concept of defense mechanisms. This work is consistent with modern neurocognitive concepts of emotional regulation, particularly implicit emotion regulation and consistent with the new National Institute of Mental Health (NIMH) RDoC system (Research Domain Criteria). As a result there can be a systematic integration of clinical findings with neurocognitive function.

As described in our manual:

> With Regulation Focused Psychotherapy for Externalizing Behaviors (RFP-C), the focus of the treatment is not to promote cognitive or intellectual change in the child, referred to as classical insight, as in,
>
> "Oh, now I understand" but to promote implicit awareness that:
>
> (1) The emotional state that is feared or is seen as overwhelming by the child is not as overwhelming as he/she thinks it is and that it will not destroy him/her;
> (2) There are better ways to manage those emotions than to fight;
> (3) The clinician will not be hurt by those feelings and then the child will feel that those feelings will not destroy him or her;

(4) The clinician, by understanding that the behavior has meaning, is always implicitly communicating that to the child and communicating that the child is not bad.

(p. 218)

With many dysregulated children, participating in a course of RFP-C will result in symptomatic improvement as they become more tolerant of painful emotions and develop an awareness that they do not have to be so vigorously warded off. The child reaches this implicit awareness within the relationship with the clinician and can then expand it to his or her life situations in home and at school.

In other words, painful emotions can be mastered more effectively and the child's use of aggression as his or her main coping device is diminished. As a result of Regulation-Focused Psychotherapy the child can master painful emotions more effectively and has less need for the use of maladaptive protective devices such as fighting.

Conclusion

In this chapter we have highlighted the historical roots and the principles developed when addressing children via the lens of modern conflict theory, particularly utilizing the technique of interpretation of defenses against painful emotions. It is important to stress that the technique involves experience-near interventions which can be utilized in short-term therapies as well as in longer term analytic treatments. Throughout the treatment the clinician has to be aware that there is meaning to the child's non-verbal and verbal communications and that the child's direct expression of emotions, needs, anxieties, as well as passionate desires are often masked by actions.

Notes

1 Although addressing children's reactions to unpleasant affects is the core technique which we describe, there are situations, especially in long-term intensive treatments, when the clinician addresses genetic (in the psychoanalytic sense) connections. However, even in those situations, it is valuable that the interpretation be as experience-near as possible.
2 Many of the ideas discussing defenses are directly derived from or reprinted from Hoffman, Rice, with Prout (*Manual of Regulation-Focused Psychotherapy for Children (RFP-C) with Externalizing Behaviors: A Psychodynamic Approach*, 2016).

3 Therefore, for our manualized psychodynamic treatment, we have chosen the term *regulation-focused* instead of *defense-focused* because the term *regulation* is more descriptive and theory-neutral than the term *defense*.
4 Readers interested in a practical application of the ideas spelled out in this chapter with regard to externalizing disorder may find our treatment manual, *Manual of Regulation-Focused Psychotherapy for Children (RFP-C) with Externalizing Behaviors: A Psychodynamic Approach* (L. Hoffman et al., 2016) useful.

Chapter 15

Implicit attitudes, unconscious fantasy, and conflict

Benjamin A. Saunders and Philip S. Wong

Psychoanalysis is a theory of mind based on conflict. There is a critical need for research that emerges from outside of the consulting room based on data independent of the clinical process. In this chapter, we discuss whether a particular kind of conflict – between implicit and explicit attitudes – may serve as a useful contrast to psychoanalytic perspectives on unconscious fantasy and conflict. In the social cognition literature, an upsurge of interest in mental processes outside awareness has developed, centered on a methodology called the Implicit Association Test (IAT). We report on selected aspects of IAT research (especially on racial stereotypes), and examine the conceptual convergence and divergence of this research with psychoanalytic perspectives on unconscious conflict.

Although psychoanalysis is a theory of mind based on conflict, the exact nature of conflict varies depending on the theoretical branch of psychoanalysis to which one ascribes. The importance of conflict between systems of the mind-Unconscious and Pre-conscious-Conscious (Ucs. and Pcs.-Cs.)– was a core feature of Freud's topographical model (S. Freud, 1915e). The well-known shift to the structural model was spurred on by clinical observation that there are aspects of mental activity, such as defense or moral prohibitions, which are unconscious in the same sense as the instinctual impulses of the system Ucs. (S, Freud, 1923). In subsequent theoretical revisions, Arlow and Brenner (1964) and Brenner (1982b) attempted to reconcile the differences between Freud's topographical model with its focus on systemic differences between Pcs.-Cs. and Ucs., and the structural model with its focus on a descriptive and dynamic unconscious (Arlow & Brenner, 1964). In these theoretical revisions, a consistent theme of conflict is identified (Brenner, 1982b). Conflict, and most especially conflict that stems from or involves significant activity outside awareness, that is, unconscious conflict, is key. The concept of unconscious conflict brings together central elements of the topographical and structural models and is one of several unifying concepts in psychoanalysis.

Considering another feature of modern classical theory – unconscious fantasy (Arlow, 1969; Abend, 2008) – can help elucidate what is unconscious and what specifically is in conflict. These fantasies are what Freud (1926a) described as the danger situations, or calamities of childhood (Brenner, 1979a), and are based on instinctual (libidinal and aggressive) wishes met with childhood experiences (loss of love, loss of object, bodily harm/castration, punishment), resulting in fantasy that is ultimately – and at times only distantly – related to elements of these childhood experiences. These fantasies, involving instinctual wishes and real or imagined reactions to them (the basis of conflict), are expressed through compromises or "compromise formations" (Brenner, 1982b) that emerge in awareness in different guises shaped by primary process activity.

Unconscious fantasy is manifest in symptoms, dreams, and parapraxes through a permeable and malleable boundary between awareness and unawareness. The interaction between unconscious fantasy and conscious experience is complex, and depends on the perceived content, the importance of the content (the level of activation or cathexis), and the general state of the person's functioning, including reality-testing and defensive structure (Arlow, 1969). Unconscious fantasies and their derivatives can emerge into awareness at different times; a sharp distinction between conscious and unconscious is unnecessary (Arlow, 1969; Abend, 2008). In fact, Arlow (1969) clearly states that a sharp distinction between conscious and unconscious limits our understanding of the dynamics of childhood fantasies. These fantasies are expressed variably in relation to awareness and depend highly on the context.

Experimental literature

Although unconscious conflict and fantasy are central elements of clinical theory and practice for those adhering to modern psychoanalytic structural (or conflict) theory, much of the data and conclusions have been drawn from the consulting room. While the clinical situation is rich with meaning and nuance, there is a critical need for research that emerges from outside the consulting room based on data independent of clinical process (e.g., Shevrin, 1995). Psychoanalytic theory, and any theory for that matter, makes assumptions upon which different elements of the theory are tested and revised. However, independent examination of a theory's assumptions is necessary for robust development and evolution of a theory. For psychoanalysis, two of these assumptions are the concept of a psychological unconscious and conflict that ensues between instinctual wishes and gratification of these wishes (unconscious fantasy).

The experimental literature on conscious and unconscious processes has a lengthy and involved history in different areas of psychology. The clinical literature contains investigations of hypnosis and subliminal perception (see Shevrin & Dickman, 1980). The experimental literature includes investigations of divided attention, implicit and explicit memory, and automatic processes (see Bargh & Chartrand, 1999). There are also a few interdisciplinary approaches aimed at integrating cognitive-experimental methods with psychoanalytic ideas (e.g., Shevrin et al., 1996; Wong, 1999).

In the social and social cognitive literature, an upsurge of interest in mental processes outside awareness has developed, centered on a methodology called the Implicit Association Test (IAT). As will be described, the IAT has been used to investigate implicit psychological processes – those processes that occur either without perceptual awareness of the object in question (the stimulus) or without awareness of the effects of the object in question. The IAT is based on an associationist view of the mind which posits that items (objects, images, thoughts, feelings) that are linked in time or behavior (via association) are likely related in important ways. A relevant feature of the IAT for our purposes is that we can examine the nature of conflict, operationalized by the difference or disparity between explicit and implicit associations.

The psychoanalytic view of unconscious fantasy and conflict holds that there are identifiable "unconscious fantasies" or what in social cognitive terms could be called "organized implicit associations" that shape what happens in awareness or in behavior. In what follows, we will first describe the IAT and its research, focusing in particular on racial stereotyping (an emotionally-charged topic that involves reaction to difference). We will describe the basics of the IAT and then identify areas in the literature that shed light on how we might understand conflict. In particular, we will examine the question of how conflict between implicit and explicit associations may serve as a useful contrast to psychoanalytic perspectives on unconscious fantasy and conflict.

Implicit attitudes

Since before the birth of psychology as a field, scientists have known that things outside of one's awareness can affect behavior (Suslowa, 1863). Indeed, not long after S. Freud (1910a) developed psychoanalysis and quite some time before his work rose to prominence in the United States, two researchers at the University of Würzburg reported the first experimental evidence of "imageless thought," or thought in the absence – generally – of specific conscious representations (Mayer & Orth, 1901; see Mandler, 2011 for a review). They discovered these so-called imageless thoughts by examining participants' thought processes, with a particular focus on what happened between participants' exposure to a stimulus word and their reaction to that word. What Mayer and Orth observed was that although participants were able to report a conscious experience that was neither an image nor an act of volition (i.e., a choice, a series of physical movements), participants themselves were unable to elaborate on these imageless thoughts any further. Not knowing how to study a phenomenon for which their participants had no words, they introduced a new theoretical term for them – *bewusstseinslagen* (i.e., dispositions of consciousness). But Mayer, Orth, and their Würzburg contemporaries received considerable backlash from Wilhelm Wundt (1907), Edward Titchener (1909) and others for their interest in "high psychical processes" that Wundt believed were not applicable to experimental analysis (Mandler, 2011). The empirical study of unconscious thoughts, therefore, failed to reach the mainstream for another several decades. The idea that a person could have thoughts or attitudes outside awareness has drawn intense experimental scrutiny only recently in mainstream psychology. It has only been in the last 25 years that implicit social cognition (i.e., the thoughts that we may have about our social world that are outside of our awareness) emerged as an earnest scientific endeavor. The proverbial crown jewel of implicit social cognition is the *implicit attitude*, which Greenwald and Banaji (1995) defined as a trace of some previous experience to which people do not have conscious access that affects our thoughts, emotions, or actions toward social objects (i.e., people, places, ideas or policies). Implicit and explicit attitudes differ in several ways. Although the measurement of explicit attitudes typically involves self-report (i.e., pencil-and-paper) measures, the measurement of implicit attitudes is much more sophisticated and quite often (but not always) involves the use of personal computers. These measures collectively differ from explicit measures in that they do not involve introspection on the part of the participant. Instead of reporting feelings or evaluations about a particular idea, group of people, and so forth, participants completing implicit measures are typically asked to make decisions under time constraints, and these constraints are important because the speed with which people make these decisions is a strong indicator of how they feel about the attitudinal object under investigation (Fazio, 2000).

Our general knowledge to date suggests that explicit and implicit attitudes are distinct-but-related attitudes (Nosek, 2007). In one of the more robust tests of this argument, Nosek (2005) used the correlational method to examine the relationship between explicit and implicit attitudes. Positive correlations, moreover, would suggest that participants who explicitly reported preferring one concept to another tended to show a similar preference on the implicit level. Participants were randomly assigned to complete implicit and explicit measures of the same topic across 50 different issues. Some participants reported their attitudes on social issues, like whether they were *pro-choice* or *pro-life* with respect to abortion. Other participants completed the same task although with more trivial issues, including their preferences for talk show hosts Jay Leno or David Letterman, short people or tall people, or summer versus winter. The correlation between explicit and implicit attitudes ranged from below .20 to above .75, and the study produced a median correlation of .48 (Nosek, 2005). Overall, then, among many attitudes, there appears to be a moderate positive correlation between implicit and explicit measures. What this finding suggests is that even though people tend not to be aware of their implicit attitudes, these attitudes often – but not always – correlate with their explicit attitudes. For our purposes, however, we are interested in the phenomena in which explicit and implicit attitudes do not correlate. As described in the following, we will operationalize this as implicit-explicit discrepancy and take this discrepancy as an index of conflict. Since a substantial amount of the attitude literature discusses and, perhaps more important, uses one particular measure of implicit attitudes, we will discuss that measure in some detail next.

The implicit association test

The Implicit Association Test (IAT; Greenwald et al., 1998) is by far the most popular measure of implicit, evaluative associations in psychology (Oswald et al., 2013), having been administered well over 14 million times, across 39 different nations, and in 25 languages (Banaji & Greenwald, 2013). The IAT measures implicit attitudes by assessing the speed with which people respond to concepts, where these concepts largely, if not entirely, consist of words and images (Nosek et al., 2007). The logic of the IAT is that this sorting task should be easier (and responses given more quickly) when a stimulus and category are strongly associated than when they are weakly associated.

Although numerous IATs have been designed to measure evaluative associations toward a range of attitudinal objects, the preponderance of research, attention, and controversy surrounds the race IAT (Greenwald et al., 1998), which assesses the degree to which people hold implicit racial preferences for White Americans over Black Americans, or vice versa. As with most IATs, the race IAT is publicly available online at Project Implicit (https://implicit.harvard.edu/implicit/) and various other secondary websites that administer IAT tests. Upon initiating the race IAT, people view words and images, one at a time, on a computer screen, and categorize these stimuli by pressing one of two keys (see Figure 15.1 for a schematic

Block	Left Key Assignment	Right Key Assignment
1	Black American faces	White American faces
2	Pleasant words	Unpleasant words
3	Black American faces + Pleasant words	White American faces + Unpleasant Words
4	Black American faces + Pleasant words	White American faces + Unpleasant Words
5	White American faces	Black American faces
6	White American faces + Pleasant words	Black American faces + Unpleasant words
7	White American faces + Pleasant words	Black American faces + Unpleasant words

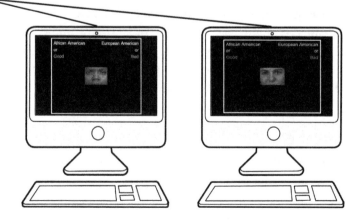

Figure 15.1 Schematic Overview of the Race IAT

overview). For example, one key refers to the category *White* or *pleasant* and the other key refers to the category *Black* or *unpleasant*. If the stimulus presented on the computer screen is either a picture of a White face or a pleasant word, then participants press the key specified for that pairing. If the stimulus presented is either a picture of a Black face or an unpleasant word, then participants press the key specified for this alternate pairing. The race IAT records the time it takes people to classify each word-image pairing, and this response time is the basic unit of analysis. The aforementioned sequence of the race IAT is often referred to as the *compatible judgment* to denote that it should be relatively easy for someone who prefers White people to Black people. Participants perform this sequence multiple times with different stimuli centered on the same idea. Another sequence of the race IAT instructs participants to classify words or pictures in the same fashion, except one of the keys is associated with the category *White* or *unpleasant* and the other with the category *Black* or *pleasant*. This sequence is referred to as the *incompatible judgment* to denote that it should be relatively difficult for someone who prefers White people to Black people; participants also perform this sequence multiple times across numerous stimuli. Preference for one group over the other is determined by computing the "IAT effect" – the mean response time for the incompatible trials minus the mean response time for the compatible trials (after certain transformations of the measures have been applied). People who perform compatible judgments faster than incompatible judgments show an automatic preference for White people, and those who perform the incompatible judgment faster than the compatible judgment show an automatic preference for Black people. On the basis of the size of the difference between the two response latencies, respondents are told they possess either a "slight," a "moderate," or a "strong" preference, and the race IAT findings reliably show that the majority of Americans (~73%) show an automatic preference for White people (Dasgupta et al., 2000; Blanton & Jaccard, 2006; Banaji & Greenwald, 2013).

Predicting behavior

In recent years, the idea that implicit attitudes as measured by the IAT predict a range of psychologically meaningful behaviors has received considerable empirical support. In particular, participants' scores on a racial stereotype version of the IAT predicted how they viewed a target's ambiguous behavior (Rudman & Lee, 2002). Specifically, when the target had a name typically more associated with Black Americans (e.g., Kareem), participants with higher racial stereotype IAT scores judged the target's behavior as being more hostile and sexist than when the target had a name typically more associated with White Americans (e.g., Donald).

Ultimately, however, measures of prejudice are only considered valuable when they go beyond predicting how people *interpret* ambiguous behavior and allow researchers to predict how people will actually *behave*. With that particular goal in mind, McConnell and Leibold (2001) tested whether the race IAT would predict non-verbal behavior during interactions with a Black or White experimentalist. In their study, participants, believing that they were to complete a study on "word perception," were videotaped as they completed an interview with a White female experimentalist. In their interview, participants answered questions about their experiences in psychology. They subsequently completed a questionnaire booklet that contained several explicit measures of prejudice before completing the race IAT. After participants completed the IAT, they were greeted by a Black female experimentalist who asked them questions about the study. Following this task, participants were thanked and debriefed. What participants did not know until the debriefing session, however, was that their behavior had been recorded by video cameras and that the experimentalists rated each participant on how friendly they had acted toward the experimentalists. Trained judges rated participants' videotaped behavior, and they examined, among other things, participants' speaking time, how much they smiled, the number of speech errors and speech hesitations committed as well as the number of social comments that participants made to the experimentalists. The results revealed that both explicit and implicit measures of prejudice predicted how the experimentalists perceived the participants. That is, as participants' preferences for White people over Black people tended to increase on both the race IAT and on explicit measures of prejudice, they also tended to be perceived as more positive by the White experimentalist than by the Black experimentalist. However, only the race IAT predicted participants' non-verbal behavior toward the experimentalists. Specifically, favorable bias toward White people on the IAT predicted less speaking time, less smiling, fewer social comments, more speech errors, and more speech hesitations in interactions with the Black (compared to the White) experimentalist. Thus, in predicting non-verbal behaviors related to prejudice, the race IAT was able to predict a range of behaviors that explicit measures of prejudice were not able to account for.

The race IAT also predicts peoples' perceptions of the hostility of Black faces in a task where two-dimensional faces morph to express anger and happiness. Participants with higher race IAT scores took longer to notice when Black faces changed from being angry to being happy than it took them to do the same for White faces. However, when Black faces were initially happy, participants with higher race IAT scores were quicker to notice their facial expressions as having changed from happy to angry than they were able to do for White faces (Hugenberg & Bodenhausen, 2003). A follow-up study revealed that participants with higher race IAT scores judged faces designed to be racially ambiguous as being Black when the facial expressions were angry but not when they were happy (Hugenberg & Bodenhausen, 2004).

The race IAT is also associated with brain activity and self-regulatory resources. In one study, Richeson and Shelton (2003) instructed participants who had taken the race IAT to complete the Stroop (1935) task, wherein participants report the color of stimulus words on successive trials. On control trials, the color of the word matches the semantic meaning of the word. But on incompatible trials, the semantic meaning of the stimulus word does not match the color in which the word is presented (e.g., the word *red* might be presented with a green font color). The speed with which participants accurately respond to control trials is then subtracted from their response latencies to incompatible trials to produce a measure of Stroop interference, and this interference varies as a function of attentional capacity (Macleod, 1991; Engle, 2002). What they found is that White participants with anti-Black IAT scores suffered from greater loss of attentional capacity, as measured by the Stroop test, after interacting with a Black (but not White) actor (Richeson & Shelton, 2003). Moreover, the IAT predicted greater activation of the amygdala, an area of the brain associated with fear responses, when participants viewed unfamiliar Black faces compared to unfamiliar White faces (Cunningham et al., 2003). Importantly, anti-Black implicit attitudes may have real life-or-death consequences in the hospital, as physicians with such attitudes were less likely to recommend thrombolysis therapy for myocardial infarction to Black patients and more likely to recommend thrombolysis therapy for comparably-diagnosed White patients (Green et al., 2007).

The IAT is the most widely known and used measure of implicit, evaluative associations in psychology. The race version of the IAT predicts a multitude of meaningful psychological behaviors, including the degree to which Black targets are viewed as hostile or sexist; the expression of averse non-verbal behavior to Black targets; the construal of racially ambiguous faces as being Black when they were paired with angry (but not happy) facial expressions; the depletion of cognitive resources; the activation of a brain region associated with fear when viewing unfamiliar Black faces; and the likelihood of recommending thrombolysis therapy for Black versus White patients. One prevailing, but erroneous, assumption about implicit attitudes, however, is that they are incapable of changing. Fortunately, just like explicit attitudes, implicit ones are, in fact, malleable, and recent research suggests that their change often depends on the social context in which one lives.

Malleability of implicit attitudes

What we know from social cognitive research is that implicit attitudes can shift depending on their social context. In the first demonstration of this effect, Dasgupta and Greenwald (2001) recruited participants for an experiment that involved two sessions. During the first session, participants completed a race IAT in addition to what they were told was a "general knowledge" task but was in actuality one of three experimental conditions. In one condition, participants viewed images of – according to Dasgupta and Greenwald – admired Black individuals (e.g., Martin Luther King, Jr., Michael Jordan, Denzel Washington) and disliked White individuals (e.g., Jeffrey Dahmer, Timothy McVeigh, Ted Bundy). In another condition, participants viewed images of disliked Black individuals (e.g., O. J. Simpson, Marion Barry, Louis Farrakhan) and admired White individuals (e.g., Tom Hanks, John F. Kennedy, Jay Leno). Participants in these two conditions were ultimately compared to control participants who viewed non-racial stimuli (e.g., flowers and insects). Next, participants completed the race IAT and explicit measures of prejudice and returned to the laboratory 24 hours later to complete the race IAT and explicit measures of prejudice a second time. Their results showed that participants who were exposed to pro-Black media (admired people who were Black and disliked people who were White), compared to participants in the pro-White media exposure and control conditions, demonstrated a reduction in their level of implicit bias for people who were White as measured by the IAT. This reduction in bias occurred only on participants' implicit measures – no pattern of reduction emerged on explicit measures of prejudice. The reduction, moreover, was persistent for at least 24 hours, as participants completed a second race IAT the following day and the results were concordant with their first tests. Taken together, this study revealed that our implicit attitudes are malleable and subject to shifts according to minor cues in our social context.

More recent research further extends Dasgupta and Greenwald's (2001) findings in two important ways. First, in addition to reducing bias, social context may affect self-concept by altering one's perceptions of abilities and skills. Second, changes in implicit attitudes may persist for well over 24 hours, as the following longitudinal study yielded changes in implicit attitudes over the course of an academic semester.

The potential for something as subtle as social context to alter self-perceptions has far-reaching implications. For example, women who pursue education or careers in science, technology, engineering, and mathematics (STEM) fields, may be affected by widely known cultural stereotypes that women are less skilled in these areas, ultimately discouraging women from pursuing STEM aspirations (Dasgupta, 2011). Stout et al. (2011) examined how exposure to positive, same-gender instructors influenced the performance of female students in a STEM calculus course. In a longitudinal and quasi-experimental design, Stout and colleagues tracked the academic progress of groups of students across multiple sections of the same calculus course while also sampling students' implicit attitudes toward mathematics compared to humanities, implicit identification with math compared to the humanities, and explicit confidence in their math abilities (as measured by their expected performance in their calculus class) at the beginning and end of the term. They found that although the gender of the instructor did not affect male students' implicit attitudes, identification, and self-efficacy in math, contact with female instructors increased female students' implicit attitudes toward math, their implicit identification with the field of mathematics, and their explicit self-efficacy in math. In other words, the presence of positive female role models in a traditionally stigmatized domain enhanced female students' implicit self-perceptions. Taken with the results of the earlier study, these results suggest that social context influences not only one's implicit biases toward others, but one's implicit self-perceptions as well.

Conflict

The idea that matters of the heart and mind often conflict, producing an array of unpleasant results, is not only well-known, but has also guided many of the world's classic literary works – like Homer's *The Odyssey* to contemporary works alike, as in Collins's *The Hunger Games*. But conflict in the social cognitive sense has important implications for how people make sense of the social world, those who reside in it, and people themselves. For our current purposes, we define conflict as the discrepancy between implicit and explicit attitudes.

When people hold implicit-explicit attitudinal discrepancies (IEDs), they tend to process discrepancy-relevant information more carefully (Briñol et al., 2006). For example, when people show a discrepancy between explicit measures of something relevant to the self-concept and implicit measures of the same construct (as measured by the IAT), they pay more attention to the quality of arguments when being persuaded in a subsequent task. Briñol et al. (2006) asked psychology majors to complete an IAT that assessed participants' levels of implicit shyness. Participants next completed an explicit measure of shyness, and then read a persuasive message containing weak or strong arguments (the experimental manipulation) on the benefits of being shy for psychologists. Finally, participants rated the degree to which they themselves believed that shyness was a positive trait for psychologists. The results revealed that participants' degree of discrepancy predicted how carefully they reviewed the persuasive message on shyness. That is, the magnitude of participants' IEDs predicted how much their final rating of shyness as being a positive trait for psychologists was influenced by whether the persuasive message about shyness was weak or strong.

The fact that people who hold implicit-explicit attitudinal discrepancies think about things more carefully does not mean that they will ultimately hold stronger attitudes. In fact, recent research suggests that the converse is more likely to be true. People with greater implicit-explicit attitudinal discrepancies about exercising reported more changes in their subsequent attitudes about exercising (after being persuaded that they were more or less into exercising than they thought) than people with fewer discrepancies (Karpen et al., 2012). Thus, although implicit-explicit attitudinal discrepancies predict enhanced information processing, this additional processing does not lead to stronger attitudes. In fact, some purport that the added information processing serves to reduce feelings of implicit self-doubt (Briñol et al., 2003, as cited in Briñol et al., 2006; Petty & Briñol, 2009). Next we will discuss how IEDs may affect one's self-concept and the way that they interact with others – aside from information processing.

Conflict and the self-concept

In addition to feelings of implicit self-doubt and information processing, IEDs also predict feelings of increased discomfort, operationalized as speech interruptions in observations of verbal behavior and as self-touching in observations of non-verbal behavior (Olson & Fazio, 2007). In one experiment, White participants completed a measure of implicit prejudice and subsequently evaluated a Black target individual on two explicit measures: a self-report questionnaire and a videotaped presentation. The degree to which their implicit and explicit evaluations diverged positively predicted their degree of speech interruptions and self-touching during the videotaped presentation. Importantly, the direction of participants' discrepancy did not qualify the pattern of their behavior. In other words, having favorable implicit attitudes toward Black people and unfavorable explicit attitudes toward the Black target individual was associated with the same level of discomfort as when the pattern of the discrepancy was reversed.

Not only do IEDs about social groups give rise to personal feelings of discomfort, but discordant self-esteem predicts defensive behavior (Jordan et al., 2003). In his now classic work, Leon Festinger (1957) showed that people experience a particular kind of stress, which he termed *cognitive dissonance*, upon realizing that they hold: (a) two opposing beliefs or values, or (b) a belief or value that conflicts with their behavior. When people experience cognitive dissonance, then, they are motivated to reduce it (Festinger, 1957). Jordan et al. (2003) show that people with high IEDs with regard to self-esteem engaged in greater efforts to reduce dissonance (through rationalization) than their low IED peers. Implicit-explicit discrepant self-esteem not only leads to defensive behaviors but is also associated with negative health outcomes. Schröder-Abé et al. (2007) found that participants reported higher levels of anger suppression and depressive attributions, and lower levels of mental (as measured by the nervousness subscale of the Trier Personality Inventory [Becker, 1989]) and physical health (as measured by the degree to which participants reported the number of days that they had been ill enough to stay in bed, had not felt well, and had experienced bad mood) when their implicit and explicit self-esteem were in conflict than when they were congruent.

Taken together, these findings suggest that IEDs, whether the discrepancies emerge between external attitudinal objects or emerge among aspects of the self-concept, lead to feelings of discomfort and defensive behaviors. To put this another way, conflict between implicit and explicit attitudes has consequences for self- and affect regulation.

Conflict and interpersonal relations

The potential discrepancy between implicit and explicit attitudes, and the implications that such a discrepancy could have for social relations, have comprised an area of inquiry in social psychology prior to the arrival of procedures designed to measure implicit attitudes. Gaertner and Dovidio (1986) coined the term *aversive racism* to describe people who consciously identify as non-prejudiced but appear to carry unconscious prejudices. In one study designed to test the aversive racism theory, non-Asian participants with low levels of explicit prejudice completed a measure of implicit prejudice and were identified as either truly low in prejudice or in possession of implicit attitudes consistent with aversive racism (Son Hing et al., 2005). Compared to participants who were truly low in prejudice, those whose attitudes were consistent with aversive racism discriminated more against a relevant out-group by disproportionately cutting that group's student association budget. Consistent with this idea, another study showed that after receiving negative performance feedback White and Asian participants with high explicit self-esteem and low implicit self-esteem tended to recommend more severe punishment for a Native American target individual (i.e., John Proudfoot) who had started a fistfight than they recommended for a similarly behaving White target individual (i.e., John Pride; Jordan et al., 2005). Participants with congruent implicit and explicit self-esteem did not show the same pattern of results and were more equivalent in their recommendations. Thus, participants with low implicit but high explicit self-esteem felt compelled to derogate an out-group member as a means of maintaining a positive self-view. What these findings suggest is that, consistent with their disruption to self-regulation and affective processes, IEDs may lead to discrimination or out-group derogation when one's self-image is threatened.

Implicit associations, unconscious conflict, and psychoanalytic theory

We now turn to a discussion in which we address the following question: To what extent do elements of psychoanalytic conflict theory converge or diverge with results from research on implicit attitudes and associations (i.e., the IAT)? Before beginning this discussion, a few cautions about terminology are in order. In the IAT, "implicit" and "explicit" refers loosely to a person's awareness of an association between two objects. More specifically, an implicit association is one in which a person is not asked directly about the relationship between two objects which are visible in awareness; rather, the relationship is assessed in indirect ways such as with reaction time. An explicit association is one in which a person is asked directly about the relationship between two objects and responds verbally. In psychoanalysis, use of conscious and unconscious is only partly related to the implicit-explicit distinction. Descriptively, a patient is aware (conscious) of a thought, idea, or feeling in clinical process, as articulated through language. This descriptive use is similar to the experimental approach of asking for a research participant's explicit association. In clinical process, however, unconscious fantasies are reflected in myriad ways that can include behaviors (e.g., enactments) but also other subtle modes of expression. For current purposes, we will adhere to the descriptive use of the conscious-unconscious distinction (as opposed to the topographic model's systemic use of this distinction).

Areas of convergence

Conflict between implicit and explicit attitudes has consequences for self- and affect regulation

There are three relevant considerations here. First, research on the implicit-explicit discrepancy (IED) suggests that greater discrepancy leads to a manifest experience of discomfort (increased self-touching and speech interruptions). Although self-touching/discomfort or speech interruptions do not approach the intensity of a clinical symptom, this IED finding is consistent with the psychoanalytic clinical observation that unconscious conflict can result in peremptory (immediate) and automatic (uncontrollable) behavior. In the example of self-touching, the behavior also coincides with an experience of discomfort. This finding and the process it reveals is notably similar to psychoanalytic formulations of symptom formation in that a symptom is often peremptory, uncontrollable, and involves discomfort.

Second, the IED finding above also highlights how unconscious conflict can be expressed in behavior. While this behavior (self-touching, speech interruptions) was not understood as clinically problematic, it is plausible that such behaviors, which are thought to be expressions of unconscious conflict, could be woven into pathological clinical (behavioral) enactments.

And third, when explicit and implicit self-esteem are in conflict, there are higher levels of anger suppression and depressive attributions, and lower levels of mental and physical health. Discrepant self-esteem also leads to defensive behaviors such as increased rationalization. A disparity between explicit self-esteem (high) and implicit self-esteem (low) is consistent with what has been observed clinically with narcissistic disturbances.

Conflict between implicit and explicit attitudes leads to increased derogation of others

When one's self-image is threatened, IEDs lead to increased discrimination and marginalization of the out-group. This dynamic process is, again, consistent with what has been observed with narcissistic disturbances: negative attitudes are expressed toward others in order to maintain a fragile self.

Malleability of implicit attitudes

There is increasing evidence suggesting that social context influences not only one's implicit biases toward others but also one's implicit self-perception as well. These findings indicate that the boundary between implicit associations and explicit attitudes or behavior can be fluid. Similarly, in psychoanalysis, unconscious fantasy and conflict related to the fantasy can emerge in awareness in many different forms, depending on the context. Data from experimental work appear to support the common clinical observation that context matters.

Areas of divergence

In order to maintain close experimental control over variables, the IAT and other research on implicit attitudes examine constructs in a way that does not (and probably cannot) approximate the complexity of the clinical situation. Methodologically, the IAT relies on data about the associative strength between two items. Conceptually, the IAT presents a focused model of implicit and explicit associative networks, including observations of interactions between the networks. The theory is, in most respects, guided by the data.

In contrast, psychoanalytic theory provides a comprehensive, sweeping model of the mind that includes, among many other things, developmental hypotheses, a distinction between conscious and unconscious, and a distinction between forms of thought. The theory includes the idea that unconscious fantasy is expressed in a variety of ways reflecting different sides of a conflict. The ultimate developmental source of conflict can be traced to early instinctual needs and psychic trauma that has universal salience (loss of love, loss of object, bodily harm/castration). These core conflicts are enduring aspects of personality, and when they are intense (i.e., not resolved in typical fashion), they can lead to troubles in living. Research on implicit attitudes and associations, which we view as conceptually similar to the psychoanalytic view of unconscious fantasy, does not have these theoretical assumptions connected to its model. For example, it is not posited at this point that implicit associations are developmentally established or have enduring salience regarding one's overall life experience. Not surprisingly, then, there is no IAT data as yet investigating implicit associations that approximate the complex unconscious fantasies that may have origins in early childhood struggles. Instead, current IAT studies investigate simple implicit associational strength between two items while observing the effects of these associations in awareness or in behavior.

Similarly, the IAT does not address the possibility of alternate modes of thought such as primary and secondary process. In psychoanalysis, the structure of unconscious fantasy is based largely on primary process mental activity whereas implicit associations are structured on secondary process mental activity. The approach to implicit associations is, thus far, bound to evaluative attitudes (whether something is good or bad, positive or negative) and not variations in meaning. Symbolic meaning and different levels of meaning, which are important features of unconscious fantasy, are not part of the IAT paradigm as it is currently configured.

Conclusion

Our examination of areas of convergence and divergence between the psychoanalytic view of unconscious conflict and fantasy, and the social cognitive view of implicit-explicit association and discrepancy, suggests that there are several areas for future development. Further investigation of the role of conflict/IED in symptom formation, behavioral enactments, and narcissistic disturbances can lead to increased understanding of the nature of unconscious fantasy and conflict.

In our quest to understand the human mind, these manifestly separate but related disciplines – psychoanalysis and social cognition – can each benefit from the other's perspectives and findings. Both disciplines examine closely how context matters. Social cognition tends to highlight the current social and interpersonal context in understanding what emerges in behavior from a network of implicit (unconscious) cognitive and affective associations. Psychoanalysis tends to highlight unconscious (implicit) cognitive, affective, *and* motivational associations and their impact on behavior. Context in psychoanalysis also includes a strong emphasis on early developmental experiences and on different modes of thought and association. Social cognitive research could benefit from increased attention to developmental and motivational complexities in implicit processes and behavior. Psychoanalytic research could benefit from increased attention to operationalizing complex contextual information in order to understand further the nature of unconscious processes and behavior. Implicit associations, unconscious fantasy, and the conflicts that arise among these associations and fantasies constitute one potentially fruitful area of investigation involving social cognition and psychoanalysis.

Chapter 16

Neural basis of intrapsychic and unconscious conflict and repetition compulsion

Heather A. Berlin and John Montgomery

Recently, psychologists, psychiatrists, and neuroscientists have shown interest in scientific data relevant to analytic theory (Bilder & LeFever, 1998; Westen, 1999; Solms & Turnball, 2002) and in the reformulation of its concepts using advances in cognitive science (Erdelyi, 1985; Kihlstrom, 1987; Horowitz, 1988; D. Stein, 1992, 1997; D. Stein et al., 2006; Turnbull & Solms, 2007; Berlin, 2011). Psychodynamic theories emphasize unconscious dynamic processes and contents that are defensively removed from consciousness as a result of conflicting attitudes. Empirical studies in normative and clinical populations are beginning to elucidate the neural basis of some psychodynamic concepts like repression, suppression, dissociation, and repetition compulsion.

The neural underpinnings of conflict

Repression

S. Freud (1892a) wrote that human behavior is influenced by unconscious processes, which work defensively to manage socially unacceptable ideas, motives, desires, and memories which might otherwise cause distress. He argued (1915d) that repression works defensively to conceal these "unacceptable" mental contents and their accompanying distress, but that the concealed thoughts, emotions, or memories may still influence conscious thoughts and feelings as well as behavior. Mental illness arises when these unconscious contents are in conflict with each other.

Research suggests a link between physical illness and people with repressive personality style (usually measured by questionnaires and/or psychological tests), who tend to avoid feeling emotions and defensively renounce their affects, particularly anger (Jensen, 1987; Schwartz, 1990;

Weinberger, 1992, 1995). The inhibition of conscious access to emotions puts the body, especially the heart and immune system, under significant stress (Westen, 1998). These memories and emotions continue to influence behavior, for example, when a person with repressed memories of childhood abuse later has difficulty forming relationships. Repressed contents may leak into consciousness via a Freudian slip (accidentally revealing a hidden motive), free association, or dreams, or they may be expressed through symptoms (e.g., a repressed sexual desire may resurface as a nervous cough [Breuer & Freud, 1895]).

Studies show that while people who repress report healthy coping and adaptation, objective physiological or cognitive measures indicate that they are hypersensitive to anxiety-provoking information, especially when it is personally relevant (Furnham et al., 2003). For example, in one study (Adams et al., 1996), homophobia was associated with homosexual arousal. Heterosexual men in the study exhibited increases in penile circumference when exposed to both heterosexual and female homosexual videos. However, among those men who identified as heterosexual, only those who also endorsed homophobic ideas showed an increase when exposed to male homosexual stimuli. Homophobia may thus be a response to a threat to an individual's own homosexual impulses causing repression, denial, or reaction formation to such impulses (West, 1977).

The neural mechanisms underlying repression are unknown; however, some studies have revealed neural activity associated with it. People with a repressive personality style have been found to have smaller evoked potentials to subliminal stimuli and to give significantly fewer verbal associations to the stimuli (Shevrin et al., 1969, 1970; Shevrin, 1973). Repressiveness was also related to the presence of unconscious conflict reflected in differential brain responses to subliminal and supraliminal conflict-related words (Shevrin et al., 1996). There is also evidence that subliminal conflicts are resolved without a significant contribution from the anterior cingulate cortex, which is normally active during conscious conflict monitoring tasks (Dehaene et al., 2003).

In a study of memory repression Kikuchi et al. (2010) investigated the neural activity associated with memory retrieval in two dissociative amnesia patients using fMRI. Their findings suggest that the dorsolateral PFC plays an important role in inhibiting the activity of the hippocampus during repression of unwanted memories (Figure 16.1).

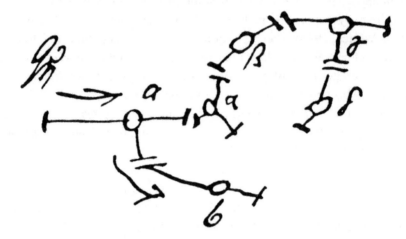

Figure 16.1 Freud's (1895) own sketch of neurons and the flow of neural energy, illustrating his concept of diversion of neural energy via a "side-cathexis." The normal flow of energy (arrow on left labeled $Q'\eta$) is from neuron "a" to "b." Freud proposed that a side-cathexis of neuron "α" would attract the $Q'\eta$ and divert the flow from neuron "b." He believed this postsynaptic attraction of energy or side-cathexis was the neuronal mechanism underlying repression of forbidden wishes in both waking and dreaming (from McCarley, 1998).

Note: Portions of this chapter were extracted from Berlin, H.A. (2011). The neural basis of the dynamic unconscious. *Neuropsychoanalysis*, 13(1): 5–31.

Acknowledgments: Rachel Turetzky, BA, MA helped assemble the bibliography.

Although some have technical objections to his account (e.g., Koch, 2004), Libet (1966, 1973, 1978, et al., 1964) found that a critical time period for neural activation is needed for a stimulus to become conscious. During neurosurgical treatment for dyskinesias, the patient's primary somatosensory cortex was stimulated with an electrode, eliciting a sensation in a portion of the contralateral hand, wrist or forearm. A train of repetitive 0.5-ms pulses of liminal intensity had to persist for about 500 ms to elicit a sensation. This was known as the minimum "utilization train duration" (UTD). UTD values varied little over time within subjects but varied between subjects from 200–750 ms. Those with a longer UTD exhibited a greater tendency to repression, as measured by a battery of psychological tests (Shevrin et al., 2002). It may be that, just as people with high intelligence may be prone to develop intellectualization as a defense against unacceptable unconscious wishes, people who need a longer time period of neural activation in order to develop a conscious experience of a stimulus may be prone to utilize repression.

Using a clever paradigm and technique called "continuous flash suppression" (Tsuchiya & Koch, 2005; Tsuchiya et al., 2006), Jiang and He (2006) demonstrated that interocularly suppressed ("invisible") images of naked men and women, that do not enter the subjects' consciousness, can attract or repel subjects' spatial attention based on their gender and sexual orientation. Despite being unaware of the suppressed images, heterosexual males' attention was attracted to invisible female nudes, heterosexual females' and homosexual males' attention was attracted to invisible male nudes, and homosexual/bisexual females performed in-between heterosexual males and females. What was particularly interesting was that *heterosexual* males were actually *repelled* by pictures of naked men in that their attention was diverted away from areas of their visual field where invisible naked men were presented. None of the other groups showed this repulsion effect. This appears to be an example of the Freudian concept of repression, that is, the unconscious prevention of anxiety-provoking thoughts or desires (in this case, perhaps latent homosexual desires in heterosexual men) from entering consciousness. Another controversial implication of this experiment is that it suggests that an individuals' sexual orientation can be statistically inferred from their unconscious attentional biases (Koch, 2008). Although these results are only behavioral and do not uncover the neural pathways that enable such unconscious attentional modulation, the authors suggest that because the stimuli were arousing erotic images, the amygdala is likely to play a critical role.

Despite the evidence described earlier, the existence of repression remains contentious, due in part to its association with trauma and the practical and ethical problems of studying it in controlled animal and human experiments. Therefore, creative paradigms with which to study the mechanism underlying repression in the laboratory are needed.

Suppression

Suppression, the voluntary form of repression proposed by S. Freud (1892a), is the *conscious* process of pushing unwanted information (thoughts, emotions) out of awareness and is thus more amenable to controlled experiments than repression. While some claim that memory repression or suppression is a clinical myth with no scientific support (Kihlstrom, 2002), others have provided evidence for memory suppression (Anderson & Green, 2001; Anderson et al., 2004; Anderson & Hanslmayr, 2014). Memory suppression requires people to override or stop the retrieval process of an unwanted memory, and this impairs its later retention (Anderson & Green, 2001). Executive control processes can be recruited to prevent unwanted declarative memories (provoked by cues) from entering awareness, and this cognitive operation makes later recall of the rejected memory harder (Anderson & Green, 2001). If suppression by executive control processes becomes habitual over time, inhibition may be maintained without any intention of avoiding the unwanted memory, evolving from an intentional to an unintentional process (i.e., repression).

Anderson et al. (2004) used a "think/no-think paradigm" where participants first learned word pairs (e.g., ordeal-roach), and then, during fMRI, were shown one member of a pair (e.g., ordeal) and told to recall and think about the associated response (e.g., roach) (respond condition) or to prevent the associated word from entering consciousness for the entire 4-second stimulus presentation (suppression condition). Suppression impaired memory. After scanning, cued recall for Suppression items, when given the originally trained cue, was inferior to recall of Baseline items that did not appear during scanning. So suppression during scanning made subjects unable to recollect memories that had been formed pre-scanning, and this memory deficit was beyond what was measured for simple forgetting over time. Further, controlling unwanted memories (suppression) was associated with increased dorsolateral PFC activation and reduced hippocampal activation. The magnitude of forgetting was predicted by both PFC and right hippocampal activations. These results establish a neurobiological model for guiding research on motivated forgetting (suppression) and integrate it with widely accepted mechanisms of behavior control.

Depue et al. (2007) employed Anderson's (Anderson & Green, 2001; Anderson et al., 2004) think/no-think paradigm but instead used neutral faces as cues and negative pictures as targets. The behavioral evidence showed that subjects effectively suppressed memory. Using fMRI, they found that emotional memories are suppressed by two neural mechanisms: (1) initial suppression by the right inferior frontal gyrus over areas that support sensory elements of the memory representation (e.g., thalamus, visual cortex), proceeded by (2) right medial frontal gyrus control over areas that support emotional and multimodal elements of the memory representation (e.g., amygdala, hippocampus), both of which are influenced by fronto-polar areas. This implies that memory suppression does, in fact, occur and is under the control of prefrontal regions, at least in healthy populations.

In a comprehensive review, Anderson and Hanslmayr (2014) summarize neuroimaging and behavioral evidence that suggests that inhibitory control processes mediated by the lateral PFC are responsible for suppressing awareness of unpleasant memories at the level of encoding or retrieval. These lateral PFC mechanisms interact with brain structures that encode memories, like the hippocampus, and disrupt memory traces and retention.

Dissociation

The concept of "dissociation" was originally put forth by the French psychiatrist Pierre Janet (1859–1947) to describe the "dual consciousness" characteristic of hysteria (Ellenberger, 1970). Dissociation is a psychological state in which certain thoughts, emotions, sensations, or memories are separated from the rest of the psyche (APA, 2013). Dissociation is not inherently pathological but it is more prevalent in people with mental illness. The *Diagnostic and Statistical Manual of Mental Disorders-V* (APA, 2013) describes dissociative disorders as "a disruption of and/or discontinuity in the normal integration of consciousness, memory, identity, emotion, perception, body representation, motor control, and behavior" and specifies five dissociative disorders: dissociative identity disorder (DID), dissociative amnesia, depersonalization/ derealization disorder (DPD; Simeon & Abugel, 2006), other specified dissociative disorder, and unspecified dissociative disorder (Kihlstrom, 2005). Dissociation may also present as a symptom in other psychiatric disorders (Sar & Ross, 2006). We will discuss studies in patients with DPD and DID in particular that give us some insight into the neural mechanisms involved in dissociation.

Depersonalization disorder

DPD is a dissociative disorder characterized by a persistent or recurrent feeling of being detached from one's mental processes or body, accompanied by a sense of unfamiliarity/unreality and hypoemotionality, but with intact reality-testing (APA, 2013). People with DPD have difficulties with information processing in relation to the dissociative detachment feature of depersonalization, especially in early perceptual and attentional processes, and with effortful control of the focus of attention (Guralnik et al., 2000, 2007; D. Stein & Simeon, 2009). They have also been shown to have attenuated emotional perception, disrupted emotional memory, and a difficulty in identifying feelings (Medford et al., 2006; Montagne et al., 2007; Simeon et al., 2009).

Sierra and Berrios (1998) put forward a "corticolimbic disconnection hypothesis," which is supported by functional neuroimaging and psychophysiological studies. This hypothesis suggests that depersonalization occurs via a fronto-limbic suppressive mechanism which is mediated by attention and generates a state of subjective emotional numbing and disables the process by which perception (including that of one's own body) and cognition become emotionally colored. This emotional "decoloring" results in a qualitative change of conscious awareness and feelings of "unreality" or detachment, which becomes persistent and dysfunctional in people with DPD (Sierra & Berrios, 1998; Sierra, 2009). More specifically, they suggest that hyperactivity of the right PFC (in particular the right dorsolateral PFC) increases alertness, while left PFC activation inhibits the amygdala and other limbic structures (in particular the anterior insula), causing chronic hypoemotionality in DPD (Sierra & Berrios, 1998; Phillips & Sierra, 2003; Sierra, 2009). Understanding the neural basis of consciousness requires an account of the neurocognitive and neurobiological mechanisms that underlie distortions of self-perception such as those seen in the context DPD.

Dissociative identity disorder

DID is a complex, chronic, and severe dissociative disorder, and it also presents as a symptom in the other dissociative disorders. Challenging the notion of a unitary self-consciousness, DID is characterized by identity fragmentation, rather than proliferation, and is usually associated with a history of severe childhood trauma (Putnam, 1997). DID involves the presence of two or more distinct dissociative identity states, characterized by different emotional responses, cognitions, moods, and perceived self-images that recurrently and alternately take control of one's behavior and consciousness. Clinical data suggest the "traumatic identity state" (TIS) has access to traumatic autobiographical memories and intense emotional responses to them. But when in the "neutral identity states" (NIS), patients claim amnesia for traumatic memories (coinciding with the notion of suppression) too extensive to be explained by normal forgetfulness. In the NIS they appear to inhibit access and responses to traumatic memories, processing and responding to trauma-related information as if it pertains to neutral and/or non-autobiographical information, thus enabling daily life function.

Neurobiological studies support the validity of the diagnosis of DID and provide clues to the neural basis of dissociation. In the first controlled structural MRI study of DID, Vermetten et al. (2006) found that compared to healthy controls, DID patients had 19.2% smaller hippocampal and 31.6% smaller amygdalar volumes. Ehling et al. (2008) also found that DID patients had smaller hippocampal (25%–26%) and amygdala (10%–12%) volumes than healthy controls, and those who recovered from DID had more hippocampal volume than those who did not. Stress acting via N-methyl-D-aspartic acid (NMDA) receptors in the hippocampus may mediate symptoms of dissociation (Chambers et al., 1999). Early life exposure to elevated glucocorticoid levels, released during stress, may result in progressive hippocampal (a target for glucocorticoids) atrophy (M. B. Stein et al., 1997; Bremner et al., 2003). However, stress may not cause hippocampus damage; rather, those born with a small hippocampus and/ or amygdala, perhaps owing to genetics, may be at greater risk for DID. In fact, abused subjects without DID had larger hippocampal and amygdalar volumes than non-abused subjects without DID (Vermetten et al., 2006), perhaps helping protect against sequelae of early trauma. Psycho- and/ or pharmacotherapy for dissociative disorders may increase hippocampal volume (Vermetten et al., 2003), but longitudinal studies are needed.

Interestingly, electrical stimulation of the hippocampus in epilepsy patients resulted in dissociative-like symptoms, including feelings of déjà vu, depersonalization, derealization, and memory alterations (Penfield & Perot, 1963; Halgren et al., 1978). And ketamine, an NMDA receptor (concentrated in the hippocampus) antagonist, resulted in dissociative symptoms in healthy subjects, including feelings of being out of body, of time standing still, perceptions of body distortions, and amnesia (Krystal et al., 1994).

In relation to an orbitofrontal hypothesis of DID (Forrest, 2001), using SPECT, Sar et al. (2001, 2007) found that compared to healthy controls, DID patients had decreased perfusion (regional cerebral blood flow [rCBF] ratio) in the orbitofrontal cortex bilaterally, and increased perfusion in median and superior frontal and occipital regions bilaterally, and in the left lateral temporal region. Dysfunctional interaction between anterior and posterior brain areas may contribute to the neurophysiology of dissociation. Reinders et al. (2003) found specific changes in localized brain activity (via positron emission tomography [PET]) consistent with DID patients' ability to generate at least two distinct mental states of self-awareness, each with its own access to trauma-related memories.

The rCBF patterns showed involvement of medial PFC and posterior associative cortices (including parietal areas) in the representation of the different states of consciousness. Based on findings with other "disorders" of consciousness (e.g., Laureys, Goldmen et al., 1999; Laureys, Lemaire et al., 1999; Laureys et al., 2000, 2004; Laureys, 2005), these highly connected areas have been suggested to be part of the neural network for consciousness.

Data suggest that one brain can generate at least two distinct states of self-awareness, each with its own pattern of perception, reaction, and cognition (Dorahy, 2001; Nijenhuis et al., 2002) and displaying different psychobiological traits that are generally not reproducible in DID-simulating controls (e.g., S. Miller & Triggiano, 1992; Putnam, 1997). Differential responses in DID patients have been reported in electrodermal activity (Ludwig et al., 1972; Larmore et al., 1977), autonomic nervous system variables, arousal (Putnam et al., 1990), EEG (Mesulam, 1981; Coons et al., 1982; Hughes et al., 1990; Putnam, 1993), visual evoked potentials (Putnam, 1992), and rCBF (Mathew et al., 1985; Saxe et al., 1992; Tsai et al., 1999). Brain areas directly or indirectly involved in emotional and memory processing are most consistently reported as being affected in DID (Dorahy, 2001; Nijenhuis et al., 2002).

Physiologic differences across identity states in DID also include differences in dominant handedness (which may indicate opposing hemispheric control of different identity states), response to the same medication, allergic sensitivities, endocrine function, and optical variables like variability in visual acuity, refraction, oculomotor status, visual field, color vision, corneal curvature, pupil size, and intraocular pressure in the various DID identity states, compared to healthy controls (Birnbaum & Thomann, 1996). One patient (BT) with DID in response to trauma gradually regained sight during psychotherapy after 15 years of diagnosed cortical blindness by neuro-ophthalmic examination (Waldvogel et al., 2007). Initially only a few personality states regained vision, while others remained blind. Amazingly, visual evoked potentials were absent in the blind personality states but normal and stable in the sighted ones. This case shows that, in response to personality changes, the brain has the ability to prevent early visual processing and consequently obstruct conscious visual processing at the cortical level. The neural basis of this ability is being explored (Strasburger et al., 2010). Top-down modulation/suppression of activity in the early stages of visual processing, perhaps at the level of the thalamus or primary visual cortex, may be the neural basis of psychogenic blindness (Berlin & Koch, 2009).

Reinders et al. (2006) were the first to compare the response to trauma-related stimuli in the same DID patients in different dissociative identity states. Differences were found between the NIS and TIS, in response to a trauma-related vs. neutral memory, in subjective reactions (emotional and sensorimotor ratings), cardiovascular responses (heart rate, blood pressure, heart rate variability) and cerebral activation patterns (rCBF via PET). When exposed to identical trauma-related stimuli, the two dissociative identity states exhibited different autonomic and subjective reactions and rCBF patterns implicating different neural networks. This extends findings in healthy subjects (Anderson et al., 2004) that memory suppression can be transferred to unrelated memories, which Reinders et al. (2006) suggest may result in psychopathology.

Neural basis of dissociation

Evidence suggests there is "splitting" of consciousness in DID patients. But how does this relate to the neural correlates of consciousness? By what mechanism can multiple selves co-exist or alternate in the same brain? There is remarkable similarity between psychiatric and neurological dissociation syndromes, but the main difference is that the former are conceived as a disconnection between psychic functions like seeing and acting, while the latter are defined in terms of physical disconnection between specialized brain regions like vision and motor areas. But both types of disorders can be considered disorders of integration, the former because of a "functional" or dynamic impairment of connectivity and the latter because of a neuroanatomical lesion.

Thus, what appears to be altered in both neurological disconnection syndromes and dissociative disorders is not so much the degree of *activity* of a brain area or psychic function, but the degree of *interactivity* between such areas or functions. Integration of various cortical and subcortical areas appears to be necessary for cohesive conscious experience (Laureys, Goldmen et al., 1999; Laureys, Lemaire et al., 1999; Laureys et al., 2000; Tononi, 2004, 2005). Dissociation may involve disruption of cortico-, thalamo-, amygdalo- or hippocampo-cortical connectivity (Krystal et al., 1998). Many of these connections are excitatory NMDA receptor-mediated and are blocked by the NMDA antagonist ketamine, which results in dissociative symptoms in healthy subjects. Psychopathologies, like dissociative disorders, that defy the apparent unity of the self, may be failures of coordination or integration of the distributed neural circuitry that represents subjective self-awareness (Kinsbourne, 1998).

Hysteria and hypnosis

The French neurologist Jean-Martin Charcot (1825–1893) believed that the transient effects of hypnosis and the inexplicable neurological symptoms of "hysteria," currently known as "dissociative (conversion) disorder," involved similar brain mechanisms. In line with this, recent studies in cognitive neuroscience reveal that the brain processes involved in symptoms of "hysteria" are, in fact, similar to those seen in hypnotic phenomena (Bell et al., 2011). Studies also indicate that hypnotizability is associated with a tendency to develop dissociative symptoms, particularly in the area of sensorimotor function, and that suggestions in highly hypnotizable people can replicate dissociative symptoms (Bell et al., 2011). Interestingly, converging evidence indicates that dissociative symptoms, whether simulated through hypnosis or diagnosed clinically, are linked to increased PFC activation. This implies that interference by the prefrontal/executive system in voluntary and automatic cognitive processes is a shared neural feature of both dissociation and hypnosis. However, systematic, well-controlled, and well-designed experiments investigating the neurocognitive basis of dissociation and hypnosis are needed.

The repetition compulsion

The repetition compulsion – the behavioral compulsion expressed by many people to repeat or re-experience certain painful, traumatic experiences from the past – is one of Freud's most seminal and important ideas and is a primary tenet and guiding force of current psychodynamic counseling approaches (Corradi, 2006). Freud's idea of the repetition compulsion was most fully elaborated in *Beyond the Pleasure Principle*, where he described the paradoxical phenomenon of people being "fixated" to specific past traumas that "include no possibility of pleasure" (S. Freud, 1920, p. 21). Freud concluded that "there really does exist in the mind a compulsion to repeat which overrides the pleasure principle" (S. Freud, 1920, p. 24) and noted that the "manifestations of a compulsion to repeat . . . give the appearance of some 'daemonic' force at work" (S. Freud, 1920, p. 41).

Post-traumatic stress disorder and the repetition compulsion

Perhaps the clearest examples of a repetition compulsion are cases arising from traumas during warfare or from other severe traumas such as sexual abuse. Freud began to more deeply explore the concept of the repetition compulsion after the conclusion of World War I, when he met and treated many soldiers who were experiencing what Freud called a "war neurosis," with symptoms that included repetitive dreams during which the soldiers relived and re-experienced devastating traumatic experiences, such as witnessing close friends being blown apart by grenades or artillery. Such patients – who would now be diagnosed as having post-traumatic stress disorder, or PTSD – were "obliged," Freud said, to compulsively re-experience their trauma rather than "remembering it as something belonging to the past" (S. Freud, 1920, p. 19).

In 1987, Van der Kolk and M. Greenberg made the provocative suggestion that PTSD may be driven by an "addiction to trauma" that is very similar to an addiction to alcohol or addictive drugs. Studies have shown that when old traumas are re-experienced in PTSD, the stress response is activated at very high levels (Newport & Nemeroff, 2000; Liberzon et al., 2007), and several lines of evidence suggest that the stress hormones released by the stress response may become reinforcing in the brain under certain conditions (Piazza & Le Maol, 1997; Montgomery & Ritchey, 2008). The stress response is highly conserved evolutionarily and is extremely similar in all mammals (Nicolaides et al., 2015). Studies have shown that rats in the laboratory will do work, such as pressing a lever, to receive intravenous injections of stress hormones, much as rats will work to receive other reinforcers such as food or addictive drugs (Piazza & Le Maol, 1997). There is also extensive evidence in both humans and experimental animals that stress hormones and addictive drugs such as cocaine or methamphetamine "cross-sensitize" – that is, a chronically hyperactive stress response, which typically produces chronically high levels of stress hormones, makes a person or non-human animal far more likely to develop an addiction to drugs such as methamphetamine, and developing a drug addiction makes it far more likely that a person or animal will develop a chronically hyperactivated stress response (Yavich & Tiihonen, 2000; Wand et al., 2007; Kippin et al., 2008). In further support of the idea that stress hormones and addictive drugs often have very similar effects in the brain, it has been found (Saal et al., 2003; Ungless et al., 2003) that stress and various addictive drugs, including cocaine, morphine, and nicotine, produce nearly identical modifications in excitatory synapses in the ventral tegmental area (VTA), a brain reward area known to be critical for the development and maintenance of drug addiction.

Part of the normal stress response is the release of β-endorphin – an endogenous opioid closely related to morphine, heroin, and other opiates – which, when released in the brain, has been shown to be associated with pleasure, euphoria, and the reduction of physical or emotional pain (Kelley & Berridge, 2002; Nicolaides et al., 2015). Dopamine, which along with β-endorphin has been shown to be a critical neurotransmitter involved in drug addiction and alcoholism, is also released at very high levels as a consequence of the stress response in reward areas of the brain, such as the nucleus accumbens or ventral tegmental area, that are known to be critically involved in drug addiction and alcoholism (Lekners & Tracey, 2008). Thus, as originally suggested by Van der Kolk and M. Greenberg (1987), it is possible that when an old trauma is reactivated, the release of high levels of dopamine and β-endorphin, and perhaps other stress hormones such as cortisol, acts as the equivalent of a drug exposure, thus reinforcing the pattern of repeatedly re-experiencing the old trauma much as a drug addiction is reinforced by repeatedly taking addictive drugs. Furthermore, much as substance abusers repeatedly and compulsively continue to self-administer drugs despite negative consequences, people with PTSD repeatedly re-experience and re-engage in distressing and painful traumas.

Physical and emotional self-harm

Drug addiction and the repetition compulsion are widely considered to be destructive and maladaptive behavior patterns (Nielsen & Germain, 2000; Paulus, 2007), and thus may be closely related to what are perhaps the clearest examples of maladaptive behavior – overt patterns of self-harm, such as with "cutters" who compulsively and repeatedly make painful cuts to themselves on various parts of their bodies (Strong, 1998; Klonsky, 2007). Other common types of self-harm include head banging, skin picking, interfering with wound healing (dermatillomania), and hair pulling (trichotillomania) (Laye-Gindhu & Schonert-Reichl, 2005). Self-harming behavior involves self-administered pain, and various types of physical pain, including sustained pain in a jaw muscle (Zubieta et al., 2001) and burns and electrical shocks (Becerra et al., 2001; Schmidt et al., 2002), have been shown to strongly activate the stress response and to release high levels of dopamine and β-endorphin into reward areas of the brain. The cuts made by a cutter have also been shown to release large amounts of β-endorphin (Sandman et al., 1997; Sher & Stanley, 2008; Bresin & Gordon, 2013). Sandman et al.

Conflict and repetition compulsion   273

(1999) found that administering μ-opioid receptor blockers that interfere with the activity of endogenous opioids such as β-endorphin, significantly reduces the amount of self-harm in patients, suggesting that at least part of the underlying behavioral reinforcement for self-harming acts may result from β-endorphin release within the brain during those acts. In further support of a possible relationship between self-harming behaviors, addiction, and PTSD, Pitman et al. (1990) found that Vietnam veterans who were triggered into old war traumas by watching videos of dramatized combat released large amounts of β-endorphin while at the same time experiencing pain reduction. Pain reduction was found to be absent with the administration of naloxone, a blocker of the μ-opioid receptor, suggesting that the pain-reduction effect was a direct consequence of β-endorphin release in the brain (Nicolaides et al., 2015).

Emotional pain appears to activate many of the same pathways in the brain as physical pain (Eisenberger & Lieberman, 2004), and studies have shown that emotional pain, which is typically triggered by and re-experienced in any repetition compulsion, can also release significant amounts of endorphin in the brain. Brain imaging studies using PET found that when people with major depressive disorder (Kennedy et al., 2006) or borderline personality disorder (Prossin et al., 2010) were told to think of sad or painful thoughts from their past – such as a painful romantic breakup – significant amounts of β-endorphin were released in their brains as a direct and immediate consequence of the painful thought.

Depression is typically a prominent feature of PTSD, and clinical depression, similar to PTSD, often involves repeatedly revisiting or ruminating about painful events from the past (Beck, 2006) – a compulsive thought pattern that appears to qualify as a repetition compulsion. An apparent neural correlate of anhedonia, another major feature of depression, is hypoactivation in reward areas such as the ventral striatum, which, in clinically depressed patients, has been shown to be hypoactivated in response to positive words (Epstein et al., 2006) and happy autobiographical or facial-expression stimuli (Keedwell et al., 2005). These studies, combined with PET studies showing that β-endorphin is released in response to sad or painful thoughts in people with clinical depression (Kennedy et al., 2006), suggest that people with clinical depression not only have a reward deficit in receiving healthy rewards but also, perhaps as a compensation, may compulsively recall and ruminate about painful memories, which then release β-endorphin in their brains. Thus similar to cutters who self-administer physically-painful cuts, people with clinical depression may unconsciously, in effect, "self-administer" emotional pain that, by releasing β-endorphin and perhaps other stress hormones in the brain, reinforces the ruminative thought pattern (Montgomery & Ritchey, 2008).

Evolutionary mismatch, homeostasis, and addictive patterns

Montgomery and Ritchey (2008, 2010) have proposed that nearly all psychological disorders, including clinical depression and anxiety disorders, are driven by literal biochemical addictions to exaggerated and inappropriate negative emotional states, such as fear, anxiety, or emotional pain, that are compulsively re-experienced in a repetition compulsion. The model further proposes that the dysfunctional thought and behavior patterns that are associated with maladaptive emotional responses are set up by "evolutionary mismatch" effects that are generated whenever human beings or animals live in environments, such as modern cities or cages, for which they are not biologically or evolutionarily adapted (Glantz & Pearce, 1989; A. Stevens & Price, 1996; Montgomery & Ritchey, 2008).

Overt behavioral or psychological dysfunctions have only rarely been observed, for example, in wild chimpanzees. However, when chimpanzees are placed in environments, such as cages, that differ significantly from their environment of evolutionary adaptedness, psychopathologies that are very similar to human psychopathologies tend to arise at high frequencies (Brüne et al., 2006). Hence cage-living chimpanzees, particularly when individually housed, frequently demonstrate abnormal, often overtly self-harming, behavior patterns such as head banging, compulsive rocking, self-mutilation, and urine drinking. Although dysfunctional behavior patterns such as these are very common in captive chimpanzees, most of these patterns have never been observed in wild populations of chimpanzees.

Humans appear to exhibit psychological evolutionary mismatch effects that are very similar to the evolutionary mismatch effects observed in non-human primates. While rates of clinical depression, for example, in modern, industrialized cultures such as the United States are roughly 10%–20% (Blazer et al., 1994; Ilardi, 2009), clinical depression may be relatively rare in contemporary hunter-gatherer cultures, whose lifestyles appear to be broadly similar to those of our evolutionary ancestors (Lieberman, 2013). An extensive study of the Kaluli hunter-gatherers of the New

Guinea highlands, for example, found that of over 2,000 of these hunter-gatherers who were interviewed in detail, only one person was found to exhibit symptoms indicative of possible clinical depression – a rate of less than 0.05% (Schieffelin, 1985). Other cross-cultural studies strongly support evolutionary mismatch effects in the etiology of depression, generally showing that the more industrialized, or "modern," a culture or society is, the higher its rate of depression will typically be (Ilardi, 2009). Rates of anxiety and depression, for example, have been shown to be far higher in fully industrialized cultures than in pre-industrial cultures or than in, for example, Amish cultures, which maintain many elements of a traditional, 18th-century lifestyle (K. Miller et al., 2007). One could argue that some of these studies may be biased because Western diagnostic criteria have been applied to non-Western cultures, where the social and cultural expression of psychological disorders may differ from Western models. However, this potential bias does not appear to apply to the Amish, who, although only semi-industrialized, are completely Western, and whose rates of anxiety and depression are about half of those found in the surrounding, fully industrialized Western culture (K. Miller et al., 2007). This possible bias also does not account for studies showing that rates of anxiety and depression, as well as rates of psychopathologies such as schizophrenia, are significantly higher in urban areas compared to rural areas within the same Western culture (Lederbogen et al., 2011). All of these data taken together appear to support the existence of significant evolutionary mismatch effects in the etiology of various psychological disorders.

The dysfunctional thought and behavior patterns that are part of any specific repetition compulsion, and that may, in turn, be strongly associated with states of evolutionary mismatch, consistently and maladaptively drive a person out of equilibrium, or homeostasis. Paulus (2007) proposed that psychiatric disorders, such as drug addiction, are associated with "altered homeostatic processing" that may lead to non-homeostatic decisions, such as compulsively taking addictive drugs. Similarly, Montgomery and Ritchey (2008) proposed that nearly all psychological disorders – including the repetition compulsion and associated states of chronic anxiety or depression – are generated by a "non-homeostatic drive" that consistently acts to throw a person, both physically and emotionally, out of homeostasis. This non-homeostatic drive may be generated because the stress response, which is intimately associated with any non-homeostatic state, releases neurochemicals such as β-endorphin that may be rewarding to the brain and thus may reinforce the thought and behavior patterns that generate the maladaptive states of non-homeostasis. These rewards, however, may often be unconscious and not associated with overt states of "pleasure" (Montgomery & Ritchey, 2010). Studies have indicated, for example, that low concentrations of ingested methamphetamine, though not consciously perceived as being rewarding, may influence behavioral decisions (Hart et al., 2001).

This proposed non-homeostatic, or "addictive," drive that leads to maladaptive states of stress and disequilibrium, frequently conflicts with and directly opposes the functional, adaptive "homeostatic drive," which is biologically and evolutionarily designed to keep humans and other animals in states of homeostasis whenever possible (Montgomery & Ritchey, 2008; Craig, 2009). The importance of the general maintenance of homeostasis to any organism, and particularly to mammals, is a fundamental principle of modern biology (Cooper, 2008). Craig (2003) has suggested that pain is a "homeostatic" emotion that is at once a subjective feeling but that is also biologically or evolutionarily designed to create a behavioral drive state intended to re-establish a state of homeostasis. The maintenance of synaptic homeostasis in the brain is also seen as being critical for adaptive neural functioning (O'Leary et al., 2014; Wang et al., 2014). The non-homeostatic drive, however, is proposed (Montgomery & Ritchey, 2010) to consistently generate inappropriate states of non-homeostasis, particularly emotional pain and distress, that serve no functional purpose, but that are instead dysfunctionally and unconsciously reinforced by the release of neurochemicals such as β-endorphin during the stress response. In this view, the dysfunctional and maladaptive non-homeostatic drive – enabled by evolutionary mismatch effects and reinforced by rewarding neurochemicals released by the stress response – consistently opposes the healthy, functional homeostatic drive, and may represent the unconscious "daemonic force" that Freud long ago observed as being an essential part of the repetition compulsion.

Conclusion

Freud had the foresight to look to the brain for answers (Figure 16.1), but his efforts were limited by the mechanistic understanding and technologies available at the time. New advances in neuroscience and technology are now enabling the neurobiology of the dynamic unconscious that

Freud envisioned to come to fruition (e.g., Solms, 1995; Ramachandran, 1996; Vuilleumier et al., 2001, 2003; Vuilleumier, 2004, 2005; Berti et al., 2005; de Gelder et al., 2005). In the process, a good deal of what Freud originally put forth based solely on clinical observations has been revised, refined, and enhanced (Guterl, 2002). But this is to be expected as the initial insights of every discipline in its early stages requires modification over time (Turnbull & Solms, 2007). Only by studying precisely how the human brain processes information will we fully comprehend the true nature of the dynamic unconscious (Tallis, 2002). Devising novel ways, using modern technology, to empirically test dynamic unconscious processes will help unveil their neural basis and ultimately lead to more effective treatment options for psychiatric patients, completing the task that Freud began over a century ago.

References

Abend, S. M. (2008). Unconscious fantasy and modern conflict theory. *Psychoanalytic Inquiry, 28*, 117.

Abraham, K. (1911). *Notes on the psychoanalytical investigation and treatment of manic-depressive insanity and allied conditions in selected papers on psycho-analysis.* London: Hogarth Press, 1927.

Achenbach, T. M., & Edelbrock, C. S. (1978). The classification of child psychopathology: A review and analysis of empirical efforts. *Psychological Bulletin, 85*(6), 1275–1301.

Adams, H. E., Wright, L. W. Jr., & Lohr, B. A. (1996). Is homophobia associated with homosexual arousal? *Journal of Abnormal Psychology, 105*(3), 440–445.

Ainsworth, M. D. S. (1967). *Infancy in Uganda: Infant care and the growth of love.* Baltimore: Johns Hopkins University Press.

Ainsworth, M. D. S., Blehar, M. C., Waters, E., & Wall, S. (1978). *Patterns of attachment: A psychological study of the strange situation.* Hillsdale, NJ: Erlbaum.

Aisenstein, M. (2007). On therapeutic action. *The Psychoanalytic Quarterly, 76S*, 1443–1461.

Akhtar, S. (1999). The distinction between needs and wishes. *Journal of the American Psychoanalytic Association, 47*, 113–151.

Akthar, S. (2009). Comprehensive Dictionary of Psychoanalysis. London: Karnac.

Alexander, F. (1950). *Psychosomatic medicine.* New York: Norton.

Alexander, F., & French, T. M. (1946). *Psychoanalytic therapy: Principles and application.* New York: Ronald Press.

American Psychiatric Association. (2013). *Diagnostic and statistical manual of mental disorders* (5th ed.). Washington, DC: Author.

Anderson, M. C., & Green, C. (2001). Suppressing unwanted memories by executive control. *Nature, 410*, 366–369.

Anderson, M. C., & Hanslmayr, S. (2014). Neural mechanisms of motivated forgetting. *Trends in Cognitive Science, 18*(6), 279–292.

Anderson, M. C., Ochsner, K. N., Kuhl, B., Cooper, J., Robertson, E., Gabrieli, S. W., . . . Gabrieli, J. D. (2004). Neural systems underlying the suppression of unwanted memories. *Science, 303*, 232–235.

Apfelbaum, B. (1966). On ego psychology: A critique of the structural approach to psychoanalytic theory. *The International Journal of Psychoanalysis, 47*, 451–475.

Apprey, M. (2015). The pluperfect errand: A turbulent return to beginnings in the transgenerational transmission of destructive aggression. *Free Associations: Psychoanalysis and Culture, Media, Groups, Politics, 77*, 15–28.

280 References

Arlow, J. A. (1969). Unconscious fantasy and disturbances of conscious experience. *The Psychoanalytic Quarterly, 38*, 61–73.

Arlow, J. A. (1979). The genesis of interpretation. *Journal of the American Psychoanalytic Association, 27S*, 193–206.

Arlow, J. A. (1995). Stilted listening: Psychoanalysis as discourse. *The Psychoanalytic Quarterly, 64*, 215–233.

Arlow, J. A. (2002, circa). Some notes on intersubjectivity. *International Psychoanalysis*, http://internationalpsychoanalysis.net/2011/11/09/some-notes-on-intersubjectivity-by-jacob-arlow/

Arlow, J., & Brenner, C. (1964). *Psychoanalytic Concepts and the Structural Theory*. New York: International Universities Press.

Armstrong-Perlman, E. M. (1994). The allure of the bad object. In J. S. Grotstein & D. B. Rinsley (Eds.), *Fairbairn and the origin of object relations*. New York: Guilford Press, pp. 222–235.

Aron, L. (1991). The Analysand's experience of the analyst's subjectivity. *Psychoanalytic Dialogues, 1*, 29–51.

Atwood, G., & Stolorow, R. (1984). *Structures in subjectivity*. Hillsdale, NJ: The Analytic Press.

Atwood, G., & Stolorow, R. (1997). Defects in the self: Liberating concept or imprisoning metaphor? *Psychoanalytic Dialogues, 7*, 517–522.

Auchincloss, E., & Samberg, E. (2012). *Psychoanalytic terms & concepts*. New Haven, CT: Yale University Press.

Bacal, H. (1985). Optimal responsiveness and the therapeutic process. In A. Goldberg (Ed.), *Progress in self psychology, Vol. 1*. New York: Guilford Press, pp. 202–227.

Bacal, H. (1998a). Introduction: Relational self psychology. In A. Goldberg (Ed.), *Progress in self psychology, Vol. 14*. Hillsdale, NJ: The Analytic Press, pp. xiii–xviii.

Bacal, H. (1998b). *Optimal responsiveness: How therapists heal their patients*. Northvale, NJ: Jason Aronson Inc.

Bacal, H., & Carlton, L. (2011). *The power of specificity in psychotherapy: When therapy works and when it doesn't*. Lanham, MD: Aronson.

Bach, S. (1994). *The language of perversion and the language of love*. Northvale, NJ: Jason Aronson.

Balint, M. (1937). Early developmental states of the ego. In M. Balint (Ed.), *Primary love and psychoanalytic technique*. London: Karnac Books, 1965, pp. 74–90.

Balint, M. (1958). The three areas of mind – Theoretical considerations. *International Journal of Psychoanalysis, 39*, 328–340.

Balint, M. (1968). *The basic fault: Therapeutic aspects of regression*. New York: Brunner/Mazel.

Banaji, M. R., & Greenwald, A. G. (2013). *Blindspot: Hidden biases of good people*. New York, NY: Delacorte Press.

Baranger, W. (2009a). The dead-alive: Object structure in mourning and depressive states. In L. G. Fortini (Ed.), *The work of confluence: Listening and interpreting in the psycho-analytic field*. London: Karnac, pp. 203–216.

Baranger, W. (2009b). Spiral process and the dynamic field. In In L. G. Fortini (Ed.), *The work of confluence: Listening and interpreting in the psychoanalytic field*. London: Karnac, pp. 45–62.

Baranger, W., & Baranger, M. (2006). The analytic situation as a dynamic field. *The International Journal of Psychoanalysis, 89*, 795–826.

References 281

Bargh, J. A., & Chartrand, T. L. (1999). The unbearable automaticity of being. *American Psychologist, 54*, 462–479.

Basch, M. F. (1981). Psychoanalytic interpretation and cognitive transformation. *International Journal of Psycho-Analysis, 62*, 151–175.

Bass, A. (1997). The problem of "concreteness". *The Psychoanalytic Quarterly, 66*, 642–682.

Bass, A. (2007). When the frame doesn't fit the picture. *Psychoanalytic Dialogues, 17*, 1–27.

Becerra, L., Breiter, H. C., Wise, R., Gonzalez, R. G., & Borsook, D. (2001). Reward circuitry activation by noxious thermal stimuli. *Neuron, 32*, 927–946.

Beck, A. T. (2006). How an anomalous finding led to a new system of psychotherapy. *Nature Medicine, 12*(10), 1139–1141.

Becker, P. (1989). *Trierer Perso¨nlichkeitsfragebogen* (TPF) [*Trier personality inventory*]. Göttingen: Hogrefe.

Beebe, B., & Lachmann, F. (2002). *Infant research and adult treatment: Co-constructing interactions*. Hillsdale, NJ: The Analytic Press.

Bell, V., Oakley, D. A., Halligan, P. W., & Deeley, Q. (2011). Dissociation in hysteria and hypnosis: evidence from cognitive neuroscience. *Journal of Neurology, Neurosurgery, and Psychiatry, 82*(3), 332–339.

Benedek, T. F. (1956). Toward the biology of the depressive constellation. *Journal of the American Psychoanalytic Association, 4*, 389–427.

Benjamin, J. (1988). *The bonds of love: Psychoanalysis, feminism, & the problem of domination*. New York: Pantheon.

Benjamin, J. (1998). *The shadow of the other: Intersubjectivity and gender in psychoanalysis*. New York: Routledge.

Benjamin, J. (2004). Beyond doer and done to: An intersubjective view of thirdness. *The Psychoanalytic Quarterly, 73*, 5–46.

Benjamin, J. (2005). Creating an intersubjective reality. *Psychoanalytic Dialogues, 15*, 447–457.

Benjamin, J. (2010). Where' s the gap and what' s the difference?: The relational view of intersubjectivity, multiple selves, and enactments. *Contemporary Psychoanalysis, 46*, 112–119.

Bergmann, M. S. (1997). The historical roots of psychoanalytic orthodoxy. *Journal of the International Psychoanalytical Association, 78*, 69–86.

Bergmann, M. S. (2001). Life goals and psychoanalytic goals from a historical perspective. *The Psychoanalytic Quarterly, 70*, 15–34.

Berlin, H. A. (2011). The neural basis of the dynamic unconscious. *Neuropsychoanalysis, 13*(1), 5–31.

Berlin, H. A., & Koch, C. (2009). Neuroscience meets psychoanalysis. *Scientific American Mind, 20*(2), 16–19.

Berti, A., Bottini, G., Gandola, M., Pia, L., Smania, N., Stracciari, A., & Paulesu, E. (2005). Shared cortical anatomy for motor awareness and motor control. *Science, 309*, 488–491.

Bibring, E. (1953). The mechanism of depression. In P. Greenacre (Ed.), *Affective disorders*. New York: International Universities Press, pp. 13–48.

Bibring, E. (1954). Psychoanalysis and the dynamic psychotherapies. *Journal of the American Psychoanalytic Association, 2*(4), 745–770.

Bilder, R. M., & LeFever, F. F. (Eds.). (1998). Neuroscience of the mind on the centennial of Freud's project for a scientific psychology [theme issue]. *Annals of the New York Academy of Sciences, 843*, 1–185.

282 References

Bion, W. R. (1956). Development of schizophrenic thought. In W. R. Bion (Ed.), *Second thoughts: Selected papers on psychoanalysis*. London: Heinemann, 1967, pp. 36–42.

Bion, W. R. (1957a). On arrogance. In W. R. Bion (Ed.), *Second thoughts: Selected papers on psychoanalysis*. London: Heinemann, 1967, pp. 86–92.

Bion, W. R. (1957b). Differentiating of the psychotic from the non-psychotic personalities. In W. R. Bion (Ed.), *Second thoughts: Selected papers on psychoanalysis*. London: Heinemann, 1967, pp. 43–64.

Bion, W. R. (1959). Attacks on linking. In W. R. Bion (Ed.), *Second thoughts: Selected papers on psychoanalysis*. London: Heinemann, 1967, pp. 93–109.

Bion, W. R. (1962a). A theory of thinking. In W. R. Bion (Ed.), *Second thoughts: Selected papers on psychoanalysis*. London: Heinemann, 1967, pp. 110–119.

Bion, W. R. (1962b). *Learning from experience*. London: Karnac.

Bion, W. R. (1963). *Elements of psycho-analysis*. London: Heinemann.

Bion, W. R. (1965). *Transformations*. London: Karnac.

Bion, W. R. (1967a). Notes on memory and desire. In W. R. Bion (Ed.), *Cogitations*. London: Karnac, pp. 380–385.

Bion, W. R. (1967b). *Second thoughts: Selected papers on psychoanalysis*. New York: Jason Aronson.

Bion, W. R. (1970). *Attention and interpretation*. London: Karnac.

Bion, W. R. (1977). *Two papers: The grid and caesura*. Rio de Janeiro: Imago Editora Ltada.

Birksted-Breen, D. (2012). Taking time: The tempo of psychoanalysis. *The International Journal of Psychoanalysis, 93*, 819–835.

Birnbaum, M. H., & Thomann, K. (1996). Visual function in multiple personality disorder. *Journal of the American Optomological Association, 67*, 327–334.

Blanton, H., & Jaccard, J. (2006). Arbitrary metrics in psychology. *American Psychologist, 61*, 27–41. doi:10.1037/0003–066X.61.1.27

Blass, R. B. (2010). Affirming that's not psycho-analysis! On the value of the politically incorrect act of attempting to define the limits of our field. *International Journal of Psychoanalysis, 91*(1), 81–99.

Blass, R. B. (2011). On the immediacy of unconscious truth: Understanding Betty Joseph's 'here and now' through comparison with alternative views of it outside and within Kleinian thinking. *The International Journal of Psychoanalysis, 92*, 1137–1157.

Blazer, D. G., Kessler, R. C., McGonagle, K. A., & Swartz, M. S. (1994). The prevalence and distribution of major depression in a national community sample: The National Comorbidity Survey. *American Journal of Psychiatry, 151*(7), 979–986.

Bleger, J. (2012). *Symbiosis and ambiguity*. London: New Library of Psychoanalysis, Routledge.

Boesky, D. (1994). Discussion of "The Mind as conflict and compromise formation," by C. Brenner. *Journal of Clinical Psychoanalysis, 3*, 509–522.

Bollas, C. (1989). *Forces of destiny: Psychoanalysis and human idiom*. London: Free Association Books.

Bolognini, S. (1997). Empathy and 'empathism'. *International Journal of Psychoanalysis, 78*, 279–293.

Bornstein, B. (1945). Clinical notes on child analysis. *Psychoanalytic Study of the Child, 1*, 151–166.

Bornstein, B. (1949). The analysis of a phobic child-some problems of theory and technique in child analysis. *Psychoanalytic Study of the Child, 3*, 181–226.

References 283

Bornstein, B. (1951). On latency. *Psychoanalytic Study of the Child, 6,* 279–285.

Boston Change Process Study Group. (2008). Forms of relational meaning: Issues in the relations between the implicit and reflective-verbal domains. *Psychoanalytic Dialogues, 18*(2), 125–148.

Botella, C. (2014). On remembering: The notion of memory without recollection. *The International Journal of Psychoanalysis, 95,* 911–936.

Bowlby, J. (1960). Grief and mourning in infancy and early childhood. *Psychoanalytic Study of the Child, 15,* 9–52.

Bowlby, J. (1969). *Attachment and loss.* New York: Basic Books.

Bowlby, J. (1973). *Attachment and loss (vol. 2). Separation: Anxiety and anger.* New York: Basic Books.

Bowlby, J. (1979). *The making and breaking of affectional bonds.* London: Tavistock Publications.

Bowlby, J. (1980). *Attachment and loss (vol. 3). Loss: Sadness and depression.* New York: Basic Books.

Bowlby, J. (1988). *A secure base: Clinical applications of attachment theory.* London: Routledge.

Brandchaft, B. (1994). To free the spirit from its cell. In A. Goldberg (Ed.), *The widening scope of self psychology, progress in self psychology, Vol. 9.* Hillsdale, NJ: The Analytic Press, pp. 209–230.

Brandchaft, B., Doctors, S., & Sorter, D. (2010). *Toward an emancipatory psychoanalysis.* New York: Routledge.

Brandt, L. W. (1961). Some notes on English Freudian terminology. *Journal of the American Psychoanalytic Association, 9*(2), 331–339.

Bremner, J. D., Vythilingam, M., Vermetten, E., Southwick, S. M., McGlashan, T., Nazeer, A., & Charney, D. S. (2003). MRI and PET study of deficits in hippocampal structure and function in women with childhood sexual abuse and posttraumatic stress disorder. *American Journal of Psychiatry, 160,* 924–932.

Brenner, C. (1959). The masochistic character: Genesis and treatment. *Journal of the American Psychoanalytic Association, 7,* 197–226.

Brenner, C. (1974). Depression, anxiety and affect theory. *The International Journal of Psychoanalysis, 55,* 25–32.

Brenner, C. (1975). Affects and psychic conflict. *The Psychoanalytic Quarterly, 44,* 5–28.

Brenner, C. (1976). *Psychoanalytic technique and psychic conflict.* New York: International Universities Press.

Brenner, C. (1979a). Depressive affect, anxiety, and psychic conflict in the phallic-oedipal phase. *The Psychoanalytic Quarterly, 48,* 177–197.

Brenner, C. (1979b). Working alliance, therapeutic alliance, and transference. *Journal of the American Psychoanalytic Association, 27,* 137–158.

Brenner, C. (1982a). The concept of the superego: A reformulation. *The Psychoanalytic Quarterly, 51*(4), 501–525.

Brenner, C. (1982b). *The mind in conflict.* Madison, CT: International University Press.

Brenner, C. (1985). Countertransference as compromise formation. *The Psychoanalytic Quarterly, 54,* 155–163.

Brenner, C. (1988). Interview with Frank Parcells at the Michigan Psychoanalytic Society. Retrieved from http://internationalpsychoanalysis.net/conf-av/

Brenner, C. (1992). The structural theory and clinical practice. *Journal of Clinical Psychoanalysis, 1,* 369–380.

284   References

Brenner, C. (1994). The mind as conflict and compromise formation. *Journal of Clinical Psychoanalysis*, *3*(4), 473–488.

Brenner, C. (2003). Is the structural model still useful? *The International Journal of Psychoanalysis*, *84*, 1093–1096.

Brenner, C. (2006). *Psychoanalysis or mind and meaning*. New York: The Psychoanalytic Quarterly, Inc.

Brenner, C. (2008). Aspects of psychoanalytic theory: Drives, defense, and the pleasure-unpleasure principle. *The Psychoanalytic Quarterly*, *77*, 707–717.

Brenner, C. (2009). Memoir. *The Psychoanalytic Quarterly*, *78*(3), 637–673.

Bresin, K., & Gordon, K. H. (2013). Endogenous opioids and nonsuicidal self-injury: A mechanism of affect regulation. *Neuroscience and Biobehavioral Reviews*, *37*, 374–383.

Breuer, J., & Freud, S. (1893). On the psychical mechanism of hysterical phenomena: Preliminary communication. In J. Strachey (Ed.), *The standard edition of the complete psychological works of Sigmund Freud, Vol. 2*. London: Hogarth Press, 1955, pp. 3–17.

Breuer, J., & Freud, S. (1895). Studies on hysteria. In J. Strachey (Ed.), *The standard edition of the complete psychological works of Sigmund Freud, Vol. 2*. London: Hogarth Press, 1955, pp. 1–319.

Briñol, P., Petty, R. E., & Wheeler, S. (2006). Discrepancies between explicit and implicit self-concepts: Consequences for information processing. *Journal of Personality and Social Psychology*, *91*, 154–170. doi:10.1037/0022-3514.91.1.154

Britton, R. (1989). The missing link: Parental sexuality in the Oedipus complex. In J. Steiner (Ed.), *The Oedipus complex today: Clinical implications*. London: Karnac, pp. 83–101.

Brodsky, B. (1967). Working through: Its widening scope and some aspects of its metapsychology. *The Psychoanalytic Quarterly*, *36*, 485–496.

Bromberg, P. M. (1996). Standing in the spaces: The multiplicity of self and the psychoanalytic relationship. *Contemporary Psychoanalysis*, *32*(4), 509–535.

Bromberg, P. M. (1998). *Standing in the spaces: Essays on clinical process, trauma and dissociation*. Hillsdale, NJ: The Analytic Press.

Bromberg, P. M. (2003). Something wicked this way comes: Trauma, dissociation, and conflict: The space where psychoanalysis, cognitive science, and neuroscience overlap. *Psychoanalytic Psychology*, *20*(3), 558.

Bromberg, P. M. (2004). More than meets the eye. *Psychoanalytic Inquiry*, *24*, 558–575.

Bromberg, P. M. (2008). Grown-up words: An interpersonal/relational perspective on unconscious fantasy. *Psychoanalytic Inquiry*, *28*, 131–150.

Brothers, D. (2008). *Toward a psychology of uncertainty: Trauma centered psychoanalysis*. New York: Francis and Taylor Group, Routledge.

Brüne, M., Brüne-Cohrs, U., McGrew, W. C., & Preuschoft, S. (2006). Psychopathology in great apes: Concepts, treatment options and possible homologies to human psychiatric disorders. *Neuroscience and Biobehavioral Reviews*, *30*, 1246–1259.

Bruner, J. S. (1986). *Actual minds, possible worlds*. Cambridge, MA: Harvard Universities Press.

Bruner, J. S. (1990). *Acts of meaning*. New York: Basic Books.

Bruner, J. S. (2002). *Making stories, law, literature, life*. New York: Farrar Strauss.

Busch, F. (1992). Recurring thoughts on the unconscious ego resistances. *Journal of the American Psychoanalytic Association*, *40*, 1089–1115.

Busch, F. (1993). In the neighborhood: Aspects of a good interpretation and a "developmental lag" in ego psychology. *Journal of the American Psychoanalytic Association*, *41*, 151–176.

References 285

Busch, F. (1995). Beginning a psychoanalytic treatment: Establishing an analytic frame. *Journal of the American Psychoanalytic Association, 43*, 449–468.

Busch, F. (2005). Conflict theory/trauma theory. *The Psychoanalytic Quarterly, 74*, 27–45.

Busch, F. (2007). 'I noticed': The emergence of self-observation in relationship to pathological attractor sites. *International Journal of Psycho-Analysis, 88*, 423–441.

Busch, F. (2009). On creating a psychoanalytic mind: Psychoanalytic knowledge as a process. *Scandinavian Psychoanalytic Review, 32*, 85–92.

Busch, F. (2011). The workable here and now and the why of the there and then. *The International Journal of Psychoanalysis, 92*, 1159–1181.

Busch, F. (2013). *Creating a psychoanalytic mind: A method and theory of treatment.* London: Routledge.

Cassirer, B. (1923). Translated as *the philosophy symbolic forms. Volume one: Language.* New Haven: Yale University Press, 1955.

Cassirer, B. (1925). Translated as *The philosophy of symbolic forms. Volume two: Language.* New Haven: Yale University Press, 1955.

Chambers, R. A., Bremner, J. D., Moghaddam, B., Southwick, S. M., Charney, D. S., & Krystal, J. H. (1999). Glutamate and post-traumatic stress disorder: Toward a psychobiology of dissociation. *Seminars in Clinical Neuropsychiatry, 4*, 274–281.

Charcot, J. M. (1885). Lecons sur les maladies du syteme nerveux. *Oeuvres Completes, VII*, 335–337.

Chefetz, R. A. (2004). The paradox of "detachment disorders": Binding-disruptions of dissociative process. *Psychiatry: Interpersonal and Biological Processes, 67*(3), 246–255.

Coburn, W. (2014). *Psychoanalytic complexity: Clinical attitudes for therapeutic change.* New York: Taylor and Francis Group, Routledge.

Coons, P. M., Milstein, V., & Marley, C. (1982). EEG studies of two multiple personalities and a control. *Archives of General Psychiatry, 39*, 823–825.

Cooper, S. J. (2003). You say oedipal, I say post oedipal: Considerations of desire and hostility in the analytic relationship. *Psychoanalytic Dialogues, 13*, 41–63.

Cooper, S. J. (2008). From Claude Bernard to Walter Cannon: Emergence of the concept of homeostasis. *Appetite, 51*, 419–427.

Corradi, R. B. (2006). Psychodynamic psychotherapy: A core conceptual model and its application. *Journal of the American Academy of Psychoanalysis and Dynamic Psychiatry, 34*(1), 93–116.

Corrigan, E., & Gordon, P. E. (1995). *The mind-object: Precocity and the pathology of self-sufficiency.* New York: Jason Aronson.

Craig, A. D. (2003). A new view of pain as a homeostatic emotion. *Trends in Neurosciences, 26*(6), 303–307.

Craig, A. D. (2009). How do you feel – Now? The anterior insula and human awareness. *Nature Reviews Neuroscience, 10*, 59–70.

Cunningham, W. A., Johnson, M. K., Gatenby, J., Gore, J. C., & Banaji, M. R. (2003). Neural components of social evaluation. *Journal of Personality and Social Psychology, 85*, 639–649. doi:10.1037/0022–3514.85.4.639

Dasgupta, N. (2011). Ingroup experts and peers as social vaccines who inoculate the self-concept: The stereotype inoculation model. *Psychological Inquiry, 22*, 231–246.

Dasgupta, N., & Greenwald, A. G. (2001). On the malleability of automatic attitudes: Combating automatic prejudice with images of admired and disliked individuals. *Journal of Personality and Social Psychology, 81*, 800–814.

286 References

Dasgupta, N., McGhee, D. E., Greenwald, A. G., & Banaji, M. R. (2000). Automatic preference for White Americans: Eliminating the familiarity explanation. *Journal of Experimental Social Psychology, 36*, 316–328.

Davies, J., & Frawley, M. G. (1994). *Treating the adult survivor of childhood sexual abuse: A psychoanalytic perspective*. New York: Basic Books.

de Gelder, B., Morris, J. S., & Dolan, R. J. (2005). Unconscious fear influences emotional awareness of faces and voices. *Proceedings of the National Academy of Sciences of the United States of America, 102*, 18682–18687.

Dehaene, S., Artiges, E., Naccache, L., Martelli, C., Viard, A., Schürhoff, F., & Martinot, J. L. (2003). Conscious and subliminal conflicts in normal subjects and patients with schizophrenia: The role of the anterior cingulate. *Proceedings of the National Academy of Sciences of the United States of America, 100*(23), 13722–13727.

Dent, L., & Christian, C. (2014). *The rise and fall of psychic conflict: A Corpus-based exploratory study of psychoanalytic literature*. Poster presented at 2014 Spring Meeting of the Division 39, April 23–27, New York, NY.

Depue, B. E., Curran, T., & Banich, M. T. (2007). Prefrontal regions orchestrate suppression of emotional memories via a two-phase process. *Science, 317*(5835), 215–219.

Derish, N., Rice, T., Merchant, A., Maskit, B., Bucci, W., & Hoffman, L. (2014). *The professional impact of child and adolescent psychoanalytic education: A systematic analysis utilizing grounded theory*. XVI World Congress of Psychiatry, September 17th, 2014, Madrid, Spain.

Descartes, R. (1989). *Meditations* (J. Cottingham, R. Stoothof, D. Murdoch, & A. Kenny, Eds. & Trans). Buffalo, NY: Prometheus Books. (Original work published 1641)

DiAmbrosio, P. (2006). Weeble wobbles: Resilience within the psychoanalytic situation. *International Journal of Psychoanalytic Self Psychology, 1*, 263–284.

Dollard, J., & Miller, N. E. (1950). *Personality and psychotherapy*. New York: McGraw-Hill.

Dorahy, M. J. (2001). Dissociative identity disorder and memory dysfunction: The current state of experimental research and its future directions. *Current Psychiatry Reports, 21*, 771–795.

Eagle, M. N. (in press). Core Psychoanalytic Concepts: Evidence and Conceptual Critique (2 volumes). London: Routledge.

Eagle, M. N. (1984). *Recent developments in psychoanalysis: A critical evaluation*. New York: McGraw-Hill.

Eagle, M. N. (2000). Repression. *Psychoanalytic Review, 87*(1,2), 1–38; 161–189.

Eagle, M. N. (2003). The postmodern turn in psychoanalysis. *Psychoanalytic Psychology, 20*, 411–424.

Eagle, M. N. (2007). Attachment and sexuality. In D. Diamond, S. J. Blatt, & J. D. Lichtenstein (Eds.), *Attachment and sexuality*. New York: The Analytic Press, pp. 27–50.

Eagle, M. N. (2011). *From classical to contemporary psychoanalysis: A critique and integration*. Florence, KY: Routledge.

Eagle, M. N. (2013). *Attachment and psychoanalysis: Theory, research, and clinical implications*. New York: Guilford Press.

Eagle, M. N., & Wolitzky, D. L. (2011). Systematic empirical research versus clinical case studies: A valid Antagonism? *Journal of the American Psychoanalytic Association, 59*, 791–818.

Eagle, M. N., Wolitzky, D. L., & Wakefield, J. C. (2001). The analyst's knowledge and authority. *Journal of the American Psychoanalytic Association, 49*, 457–488.

Edelman, G. M. (1987). *Neural Darwinism*. New York: Basic Books.

Edelman, G. M. (1989). *The remembered present: A biological theory of consciousness*. New York: Basic Books.

References 287

Edelman, G. M. (1992). *Bright air, brilliant fire: On the matter of the mind.* New York: Basic Books.

Ehling, T., Nijenhuis, E. R., & Krikke, A. P. (2008). Volume of discrete brain structures in complex dissociative disorders: Preliminary findings. *Progress in Brain Research, 167,* 307–310.

Eisenberger, N. I., & Lieberman, M. D. (2004). Why rejection hurts: A common neural alarm system for physical and social pain. *Trends in Cognitive Sciences, 8*(7), 294–300.

Ellenberger, H. F. (1970). *The discovery of the unconscious: The history and evolution of dynamic psychiatry.* New York: Basic Books.

Ellman, S. J. (1991). *Freud's technique papers: A contemporary perspective.* Northvale, NJ: Jason Aronson.

Ellman, S. J. (1997). An analyst at work. In J. Reppen (Ed.), *More analysts at work.* Northvale, NJ: Jason Aronson, pp. 91–115.

Ellman, S. J. (2010a). Discussion of the Oedipal conference. *Psychoanalytic Inquiry, 30,* 563–578.

Ellman, S. J. (2010b). *When theories touch: A historical and theoretical integration of psychoanalytic thought.* London: Karnac.

Ellman, S. J., & Moskowitz, M. (2008). A study of the Boston Change Process Study Group. *Psychoanalytic Dialogues, 18,* 812–837.

Emde, R. N., Wolf, D. P., & Oppenheim, D. (2003). *Revealing the inner worlds of young children: The MacArthur story stem battery.* Oxford: Oxford University Press.

Engle, R. W. (2002). Working memory capacity as executive attention. *Current Directions in Psychological Science, 11,* 19–23. doi:10.1111/1467–8721.00160

Epstein, J., Pan, H., Kocsis, J. H., Yang, Y., Butler, T., Chusid, J., & Silbersweig, D. A. (2006). Lack of ventral striatal response to positive stimuli in depressed versus normal subjects. *American Journal of Psychiatry, 163*(10), 1784–1790.

Erdelyi, M. H. (1985). *Psychoanalysis: Freud's cognitive psychology.* New York: WH Freeman.

Fairbairn, W. D. (1952). *An object relations theory of the personality.* New York: Basic Books.

Fairbairn, W. D. (1954). Observations on the nature of hysterical states. *British Journal of Medical Psychology, 27,* 105–125.

Fairbairn, W. D. (1958). On the nature and aims of psychoanalytic treatment. *International Journal of Psychoanalysis, 39,* 374–385.

Fajardo, B. (1991). Analyzability and resilience in development. In J. A. Winer (Ed.), *The annual of psychoanalysis, Volume XIX.* Hillsdale, NJ: The Analytic Press, pp. 107–126.

Fazio, R. H. (2000). Accessible attitudes as tools for object appraisal: Their costs and benefits. In G. Maio & J. Olson (Eds.), *Why we evaluate: Functions of attitudes.* Mahwah, NJ: Erlbaum, pp. 1–36.

Fenichel, O. (1938). Problems of Psychoanalytic Technique. Psychoanal. Q., 7:421–442.

Ferenczi, S. (1932/1949). Confusion of tongues between the adults and the child. *The International Journal of Psychoanalysis, 30,* 225–230.

Ferenczi, S. (1933). Confusion of tongues between adults and the child. In M. Balint (Ed.), *Final contributions to the problems and methods of psycho-analysis.* London: Karnac Books, 1980, pp. 156–167.

Ferenczi, S. (1952). A little chanticleer. In E. Jones (Ed.), *First contributions to psychoanalysis: The international psycho-analytical library, 45:1–33.* London, UK: Hogarth Press and the Institute of Psychoanalysis, pp. 240–252.

Ferro, A. (2002). *Seeds of illness, seeds of recovery: The genesis of suffering and the role of psychoanalysis.* London: Karnac.

288 References

Ferro, A. (2009). *Mind works: Technique and creativity in psychoanalysis*. London: Routledge.

Festinger, L. (1957). *A theory of cognitive dissonance*. Stanford, CA: Stanford University Press.

Finnegan, P. (1993). *On multiple personality*. Paper given to Toronto Psychoanalytic Society, May 14, 1993.

Fischer, K. (1980). A theory of cognitive development: The control and construction of hierarchies of skills. *Psychological Review, 87*, 477–531.

Fiss, H. (1989). An experimental self psychology of dreaming: Clinical and theoretical applications. In A. Goldberg (Ed.), *Dimensions of self experience, progress in self psychology, Vol. 5*. Hillsdale, NJ: Analytic Press, pp. 13–24.

Fiss, H. (1990). Experimental strategies for the study of the function of dreaming. In S. Ellman (Ed.), *The mind in sleep: Psychology and psychophysiology*. New York: John Wiley and Sons, pp. 308–326.

Fonagy, P. (2001). *Attachment theory and psychoanalysis*. New York: Other Press.

Fonagy, P., Gergely, G., Jurist, E. L., & Target, M. (2001). *Affect regulation, mentalization, and the development of the self*. New York: Other Press.

Fonagy, P., Steele, H., & Steele, M. (1991). Maternal representations of attachment during pregnancy predict the organization of infant-mother attachment at one year of age. *Child Development, 62*, 891–905.

Forrest, K. A. (2001). Toward an etiology of dissociative identity disorder: A neurodevelopmental approach. *Consciousness and Cognition, 10*, 259–293.

Fosshage, J. (1983). The psychological function of dreams: A revised psychoanalytic perspective. *Psychoanalysis and Contemporary Thought, 6*(4), 641–669. Also in M. Lansky (Ed., 1992) *Essential Papers on Dreams*, New York: New York University Press.

Fosshage, J. (1992). Self psychology: The self and its vicissitudes within a relational matrix. In N. Skolnick & S. Warshaw (Eds.), *Relational perspectives*. Hillsdale, NJ: Analytic Press, pp. 21–42.

Fosshage, J. (1994). Toward reconceptualizing transference: Theoretical and clinical considerations. *The International Journal of Psychoanalysis, 75*(2), 265–280.

Fosshage, J. (1995). Interaction in psychoanalysis: A broadening horizon. *Psychoanalytic Dialogues, 5*(3), 459–478.

Fosshage, J. (1997a). The organizing functions of dreams. *Contemporary Psychoanalysis, 33*(3), 429–458.

Fosshage, J. (1997b). Listening/experiencing perspectives and the quest for a facilitative responsiveness. In A. Goldberg (Ed.), *Conversations in self psychology, progress in self psychology, Vol. 13*. Hillsdale, NJ: The Analytic Press, pp. 33–55.

Fosshage, J. (1999). *Different forms of intimacy: The case of Samantha*. Presented at the 22nd Annual International Conference on the Psychology of the Self, Toronto, Canada.

Fosshage, J. (2003a). Contextualizing self psychology and relational psychoanalysis: Bidirectional influence and proposed syntheses. *Contemporary Psychoanalysis, 39*(3), 411–448.

Fosshage, J. (2003b). Fundamental pathways to change: Illuminating old and creating new relational experience. *International Forum of Psychoanalysis, 12*, 244–251.

Fosshage, J. (2005). The explicit and implicit domains in psychoanalytic change. *Psychoanalytic Inquiry, 25*(4), 516–539.

Fosshage, J. (2007). The organizing functions of dreaming: Pivotal issues in understanding and working with dreams. *International Forum of Psychoanalysis, 16*, 213–221.

References 289

Fosshage, J. (2011a). Development of individuality within a systems world. In W. Coburn & R. Frie (Eds.), *Persons in context: The challenge of individuality in theory and practice*. New York: Routledge, Taylor and Francis Group, pp. 89–105.

Fosshage, J. (2011b). How do we "know" what we "know?" And change what we "know?" *Psychoanalytic Dialogues, 21*(1), 55–74.

Fosshage, J. (2011c). The use and impact of the analyst's subjectivity with empathic and other listening/experiencing perspectives. *The Psychoanalytic Quarterly, LXXX*(1), 139–160.

Fosshage, J. (2013). Forming and transforming self-experience. *International Journal of Psychoanalytic Self Psychology, 8*(4), 437–451.

Fraiberg, S., Adelson, E., & Shapiro, V. (1975). Ghosts in the nursery. *Journal of the American Academy of Child Psychiatry, 14*, 387–421.

Freeman, W. (1995). *Societies of brains: A study in the neuroscience of love and hate*. New York: Psychology Press.

Freeman, W. (2001). *How brains make up their minds*. New York: Columbia University Press.

Freud, A. (1926). An hysterical symptom in a child of two years and three months old. *International Journal of Psychoanalysis, 7*, 227–228.

Freud, A. (1936). *The ego and the mechanisms of defense*. New York: International Universities Press, 1946.

Freud, A. (1945). Indications for child analysis. *The Psychoanalytic Study of the Child, 1*, 127–149.

Freud, A. (1965). *Normality and pathology in childhood: Assessments of development: The writings of Anna Freud, Vol. 6*. New York: International Universities Press.

Freud, A. (1966a). *The ego and the mechanisms of defense*. New York: International Universities Press.

Freud, A. (1966b). A short history of child analysis. *The Psychoanalytic Study of the Child, 21*, 7–14.

Freud, S. (1892a). A case of successful treatment by hypnotism. In J. Strachey (Ed.), *The standard edition of the complete psychological works of Sigmund Freud, Vol. 1*. London: Hogarth, 1966, pp. 117–128.

Freud, S. (1892b). Draft K the neuroses of defense from extracts from the files papers: (A Christmas Fairy Tale). In J. Strachey (Ed.), *The standard edition of the complete psychological works of Sigmund Freud, Vol. 1 (1886–1899): Pre-psycho-analytic publications and unpublished drafts*. London: Hogarth, pp. 220–229.

Freud, S. (1893a). On the psychical mechanism of hysterical phenomena. In J. Strachey (Ed.), *The standard edition of the complete psychological works of Sigmund Freud, Vol. 3*. London: Hogarth, 1962, pp. 25–39.

Freud, S. (1893b). The psychotherapy of hysteria from studies on hysteria. In J. Strachey (Ed.), *The standard edition of the complete psychological works of Sigmund Freud, Vol. 2 (1893–1895): Studies on hysteria*. London: Hogarth, pp. 253–306.

Freud, S. (1894). The neuro-psychoses of defence. In J. Strachey (Ed.), *The standard edition of the complete psychological works of Sigmund Freud, Vol. 3*. London: Hogarth, 1962, pp. 45–61.

Freud, S. (1895). Project for a scientific psychology. In J. Strachey (Ed.), *The standard edition of the complete psychological works of Sigmund Freud, Vol. 1*. London: Hogarth Press, 1966, pp. 294–397.

Freud, S. (1896). Further remarks on the neuropsychoses of defense. In J. Strachey (Ed.), *The standard edition of the complete psychological works of Sigmund Freud, Vol. 3*. London: Hogarth, 1962, pp. 141–158.

290 References

Freud, S. (1897). *The complete letters of Sigmund Freud to Wilhelm Fliess, 1887–1904*. Cambridge, MA: Harvard University Press.

Freud, S. (1898). Sexuality in the etiology of the neuroses. In J. Strachey (Ed.), *The standard edition of the complete psychological works of Sigmund Freud, Vol. 3*. London: Hogarth, 1962, pp. 259–285.

Freud, S. (1900). The interpretation of dreams. In J. Strachey (Ed.), *The standard edition of the complete psychological works of Sigmund Freud, Volume 4/5*. London: Hogarth.

Freud, S. (1901). *The standard edition of the complete psychological works of Sigmund Freud, Volume 6 (1901): The psychopathology of everyday life*. London: Hogarth.

Freud, S. (1905). Fragment of an analysis of a case of hysteria (1905 [1901]). In J. Strachey (Ed.), *The standard edition of the complete psychological works of Sigmund Freud, Vol. 7 (1901–1905): A case of hysteria, three essays on sexuality and other works*. London: Hogarth, pp. 1–122.

Freud, S. (1909). Notes upon a case of obsessional neurosis. In J. Strachey (Ed.), *The standard edition of the complete psychological works of Sigmund Freud, Vol. 10*. London: Hogarth Press, 1955, pp. 153–318.

Freud, S. (1910a). The origin and development of psychoanalysis. *The American Journal of Psychology, 21*, 181–218. doi:10.2307/1413001

Freud, S. (1910b). The psychoanalytic view of the psychogenic disturbance of vision. In J. Strachey (Ed.), *The standard edition of the complete psychological works of Sigmund Freud, Vol. 11*. London: Hogarth, 1957, pp. 209–218.

Freud, S. (1911). Formulations on the two principles of mental functioning. In J. Strachey (Ed.), *The standard edition of the complete psychological works of Sigmund Freud, Vol. 12 (1911–1913): The Case of Schreber, Papers on Technique and Other Works*, London: Hogarth, pp. 213–226.

Freud, S. (1912a). The dynamics of transference. In J. Strachey (Ed.), *The standard edition of the complete psychological works of Sigmund Freud, Vol. 12*. London: Hogarth, pp. 97–108.

Freud, S. (1912b). Recommendations to physicians practicing psycho-analysis. In J. Strachey (Ed.), *The standard edition of the complete psychological works of Sigmund Freud, Vol. 12*. London: Hogarth, pp. 111–120.

Freud, S. (1912c). Types of onset of neurosis. In J. Strachey (Ed.), *The standard edition of the complete psychological works of Sigmund Freud, Vol. 12*. London: Hogarth, 1958, pp. 227–238.

Freud, S. (1912d). On the universal tendency to debasement in the sphere of love (Contributions to the Psychology of Love II). In J. Strachey (Ed.), *The standard edition of the complete psychological works of Sigmund Freud, Vol. 11 (1910): Five lectures on psycho-analysis, Leonardo da Vinci and other works*. London: Hogarth, pp. 177–190.

Freud, S. (1914a). Remembering, repeating and working through. In J. Strachey (Ed.), *The standard edition of the complete psychological works of Sigmund Freud, Vol. 12*. London: Hogarth, pp. 145–156.

Freud, S. (1914b). On the history of the psycho-analytic movement. In J. Strachey (Ed.), *The standard edition of the complete psychological works of Sigmund Freud, Vol. 14 (1914–1916): On the history of the psycho-analytic movement, papers on metapsychology and other works*. London: Hogarth, pp. 1–66.

Freud, S. (1915). Repression. *The Standard Edition of the Complete Psychological Works of Sigmund Freud, Volume XIV (1914–1916): On the History of the Psycho-Analytic Movement, Papers on Metapsychology and Other Works*, 141–158.

References 291

Freud, S. (1915a). Instincts and their vicissitudes. In J. Strachey (Ed.), *The standard edition of the complete psychological works of Sigmund Freud, Vol. 14.* London: Hogarth, pp. 105–146.

Freud, S. (1915b). Papers on metapsychology. In J. Strachey (Ed.), *The standard edition of the complete psychological works of Sigmund Freud, Vol. 14.* London: Hogarth, pp. 159–215.

Freud, S. (1915c). Repression. In J. Strachey (Ed.), *The standard edition of the complete psychological works of Sigmund Freud, Vol. 14.* London: Hogarth Press, 1966, pp. 214–243.

Freud, S. (1915d). Repression. In J. Strachey (Ed.), *The standard edition of the complete psychological works of Sigmund Freud, Vol. 14.* London: Hogarth, pp. 143–158.

Freud, S. (1915e). The unconscious. In J. Strachey (Ed.), *The standard edition of the complete psychological works of Sigmund Freud, Vol. 14.* London: Hogarth, pp. 161–215.

Freud, S. (1916). Introductory lectures on psychoanalysis. In J. Strachey (Ed.), *The standard edition of the complete psychological works of Sigmund Freud, Vol. 15.* London: Hogarth, pp. 243–263.

Freud, S. (1917). Mourning and Melancholia. *The Standard Edition of the Complete Psychological Works of Sigmund Freud, Volume XIV (1914–1916): On the History of the Psycho-Analytic Movement, Papers on Metapsychology and Other Works,* 237–258

Freud, S. (1918). From the History of an Infantile Neurosis. In J. Strachey (Ed.), *The standard edition of the complete psychological works of Sigmund Freud, Vol. 17.* London: Hogarth Press, pp. 1–122.

Freud, S. (1919). Introduction to psycho-analysis and the war neuroses. In J. Strachey (Ed.), *The standard edition of the complete psychological works of Sigmund Freud, Vol. 17 (1917–1919): An infantile neurosis and other works.* London: Hogarth, pp. 205–216.

Freud, S. (1920). Beyond the pleasure principle. In J. Strachey (Ed.), *The standard edition of the complete psychological works of Sigmund Freud, Vol. 18.* London: Hogarth, pp. 1–64.

Freud, S. (1923). The ego and the id. In J. Strachey (Ed.), *The standard edition of the complete psychological works of Sigmund Freud, Vol. 19.* London: Hogarth, pp. 3–68.

Freud, S. (1924). The economic problem of masochism. In J. Strachey (Ed.), *The standard edition of the complete psychological works of Sigmund Freud, Vol. 19.* London: Hogarth, 1964, pp. 155–170.

Freud, S. (1925). An autobiographical study. In J. Strachey (Ed.), *The standard edition of the complete psychological works of Sigmund Freud, Vol. 20.* London: Hogarth, 1964, pp. 1–74.

Freud, S. (1926a). Inhibitions, symptoms and anxiety. In J. Strachey (Ed.), *The standard edition of the complete psychological works of Sigmund Freud, Vol. 20.* London: Hogarth, 1978, pp. 75–176.

Freud, S. (1926b). The question of lay analysis. In J. Strachey (Ed.), *The standard edition of the complete psychological works of Sigmund Freud, Vol. 20.* London: Hogarth, 1978, pp. 177–258.

Freud, S. (1930). Civilization and its discontents. In J. Strachey (Ed.), *The standard edition of the complete psychological works of Sigmund Freud, Vol. 21 (1927–1931): The future of an illusion, civilization and its discontents, and other works.* London: Hogarth, pp. 57–146.

Freud, S. (1933). New introductory lectures on psycho-analysis. In J. Strachey (Ed.), *The standard edition of the complete psychological works of Sigmund Freud, Vol. 22.* London: Hogarth, 1964, pp. 1–182.

Freud, S. (1937). Analysis terminable and interminable. In J. Strachey (Ed.), *The standard edition of the complete psychological works of Sigmund Freud, Vol. 23.* London: Hogarth, 1964, pp. 209–253.

292 References

Freud, S. (1939). Moses and monotheism: Three essays. In J. Strachey (Ed.), *The standard edition of the complete psychological works of Sigmund Freud, Vol. 23*. (Original work published 1934–1938). London: Hogarth, 1964, pp. 1–137.

Freud, S. (1940–41). Sketches for the 'preliminary communication' of 1893. In J. Strachey (Ed.), *The standard edition of the complete psychological works of Sigmund Freud, Vol. 1*. (Original work published 1892). London: Hogarth, 1966, pp. 145–154.

Freud, S. (1940a). An outline of psycho-analysis. In J. Strachey (Ed.), *The complete psychological works of Sigmund Freud, Vol. 23*. London: Hogarth, pp. 138–207.

Freud, S. (1940b). Splitting of the ego in the process of defense. In J. Strachey (Ed.), *The standard edition of the complete psychological works* of *Sigmund Freud, Vol. 23*. (Original work published 1923). London: Hogarth, pp. 271–278.

Friedman, L. (2007). Respecting the unity of mind: Waelder's 1936 multiple function paper. *The Psychoanalytic Quarterly, 76*, 119–148.

Friedman, L. (2011). Charles Brenner: A practitioner's theorist. *Journal of the American Psychoanalytic Association, 59*, 679–700.

Frosch, A. (1995). The preconceptual organization of emotion. *Journal of the American Psychoanalytic Association, 43*, 423–447.

Furnham, A., Petrides, K. V., Sisterson, G., & Baluch, B. (2003). Repressive coping style and positive self-presentation. *British Journal of Health Psychology, 8*(Part 2), 223–249.

Gaertner, S. L., & Dovidio, J. F. (1986). The aversive form of racism. In J. F. Dovidio & S. L. Gaertner (Eds.), *Prejudice, discrimination, and racism*. Orlando: Academic Press, pp. 61–86.

George, C., Kaplan, N., & Main, M. (1985). *Adult attachment interview*. Unpublished manuscript, Berkeley, CA: University of California at Berkley.

Ghent, E. (2002). Wish, need, drive: Motive in the light of dynamic systems theory and Edelman's selectionist theory. *Psychoanalytic Dialogues, 12*(5), 763–808.

Gill, M. M. (1976). Metapsychology is not psychology. In M. Gill & P. S. Holzman (Eds.), *Psychology versus metapsychology: Psychoanalytic essays in memory of George S. Klein*. New York: International Universities Press, pp. 71–105.

Gill, M. M. (1977). Psychic energy reconsidered: Discussion. *Journal of the American Psychoanalytic Association, 25*, 581–597.

Gitelson, M. (1963). On the problem of character neurosis. *Journal of the Hillside Hospital, 12*, 3–17.

Glantz, K., & Pearce, J. K. (1989). *Exiles from Eden: Psychotherapy from an evolutionary perspective*. New York: W. W. Norton.

Goldberg, P. (2008). *Catastrophic change, communal dreaming and the counter-catastrophic personality*. Paper read at 4th EBOR Conference, November 1, 2008, Seattle, WA.

Goldner, V. (2014). Romantic bonds, binds, and ruptures: Couples on the brink, *Psychoanalytic Dialogues, 24*, 402–418.

Gray, P. (1964). The ego and the analysis of defense. New York: Jason Aronson.

Gray, P. (1982). "Developmental lag" in the evolution of technique for psychoanalysis of neurotic conflict. *Journal of the American Psychoanalytic Association, 30*, 621–655.

Gray, P. (1994). *The ego and analysis of defense*. New York: Jason Aronson.

Gray, P. (2005). *The ego and the analysis of defense* (2nd ed.). Northvale, NJ: Jason Aronson.

Gray, S. H. (1986). Bulletin of the Menninger clinic. XLVII, 1983. *The Psychoanalytic Quarterly, 55*, 201.

Green, A. (1975). The analyst, symbolization and absence in the analytic setting (On changes in analytic practice and analytic experience): In memory of D. W. Winnicott. *International Journal of Psychoanalysis*, *56*, 1–22.

Green, A. R., Carney, D. R., Pallin, D. J., Ngo, L. H., Raymond, K. L., Iezzoni, L., . . . Banaji, M. R. (2007). Implicit bias among physicians and its prediction of thrombolysis decisions for black and white patients. *Journal of General Internal Medicine*, *22*, 1231–1238.

Greenberg, J. (1991). *Oedipus and beyond: A clinical theory*. Cambridge, MA: Harvard University Press.

Greenberg, J. (1993). *Oedipus and beyond: A clinical theory*. Cambridge, MA: Harvard Press.

Greenberg, J., & Mitchell, S. (1983). *Object relations in psychoanalytic theory*. Cambridge, MA: Harvard University Press.

Greenberg, R. (1987). The dream problem and problems in dreams. In M. Glucksman & S. Warner (Eds.), *Dreams in new perspective*. New York: Human Sciences Press, pp. 45–58.

Greenson, R. R. (1965). The working alliance and the transference neurosis. *The Psychoanalytic Quarterly*, *34*, 155–181.

Greenwald, A. G., & Banaji, M. R. (1995). Implicit social cognition: Attitudes, self-esteem, and stereotypes. *Psychological Review*, *102*, 4–27. doi:10.1037/0033-295X.102.1.4

Greenwald, A. G., McGhee, D. E., & Schwartz, J. K. (1998). Measuring individual differences in implicit cognition: The implicit association test. *Journal of Personality and Social Psychology*, *74*, 1464–1480. doi:10.1037/0022-3514.74.6.1464

Griesinger, W. (1845). *Mental pathology and therapeutics*. London: New Sydenham Society, 1867.

Grossmann, K., Grossmann, K., & Waters, E. (2005). *Attachment from infancy to adulthood: The major longitudinal studies*. New York: Guilford Press.

Grotstein, J. (2004). The seventh servant: The implications of a truth drive in Bion's theory of O. *International Journal of Psychoanalysis*, *85*(5), 1081–1101.

Grotstein, J. (2007). *A beam of intense darkness: Wilfred Bion's legacy to psychoanalysis*. London: Karnac.

Guntrip, H. (1969). *Schizoid phenomena, object-relations, and the self*. Madison, CT: International Universities Press.

Guralnik, O., Giesbrecht, T., Knutelska, M., Sirroff, B., & Simeon, D. (2007). Cognitive functioning in depersonalization disorder. *The Journal of Nervous and Mental Disease*, *195*, 983–988.

Guralnik, O., Schmeidler, J., & Simeon, D. (2000). Feeling unreal: Cognitive processes in depersonalization. *American Journal of Psychiatry*, *157*, 103–109.

Guterl, F. (2002). What Freud got right. *Newsweek*, Nov. 11, 62–63.

Halgren, E., Walter, R. D., Cherlow, D. G., & Crandall, P. H. (1978). Mental phenomena evoked by electrical stimulation of the human hippocampal formation and amygdala. *Brain*, *101*, 83–117.

Harris, A. (2005). Conflict in relational treatments. *The Psychoanalytic Quarterly*, *74*(1), 267–293.

Harris, A. (2009). You must remember this. *Psychoanalytic Dialogues*, *19*(1), 2–21.

Harris, A. (2010). *The analyst's omnipotence and the analyst's melancholy*. Unpublished paper, BIPSE.

Harris, A. (2014). Discussion of Arietta Slade. *Psychoanalytic Dialogues*, *24*, 267–276.

Hart, C. L., Ward, A. S., Haney, M., Foltin, R. W., & Fischman, M. W. (2001). Methamphetamine self-administration by humans. *Psychopharmacology*, *157*, 75–81.

294 References

Harter, S., & Buddin, B. J. (1987). Children's understanding of the simultaneity of two emotions: A five-stage developmental acquisition sequence. *Developmental Psychology*, *23*, 388–399.

Hartmann, E. (1998). *Dreams and nightmares*. Cambridge, MA: Perseus Books.

Hartmann, H. (1939*). Ego psychology and the problem of adaptation*. New York: International University Press.

Hegel, G. W. F. (1976). *Phenomenology of spirit* (A. V. Miller, Trans.). London: Oxford University Press.

Heidegger, M. (1962). *Being and time* (J. Macquarrie & E. Robinson, Trans.). New York: Harper & Row. (Original work published 1927)

Hermann, I. (1933). Zum triebleben der primaten [On the instinctual life of primates]. *Imago*, *19*, 113–125.

Hermann, I. (1976). Clinging – Going-in-search – A contrasting pair of instincts and their relation to sadism and masochism. *The Psychoanalytic Quarterly*, *45*, 5–36.

Hesse, E., & Van Ijzendoorn, M. (1999). Propensities towards absorption are related to lapses in the monitoring of reasoning or discourse during the adult attachment interview: A preliminary investigation. *Attachment and Human Development*, *1*, 67–91.

Hilgard, E. R. (1991). A neodissociation interpretation of hypnosis. In S. J. Lynn & J. W. Rhue (Eds.), *Theories of hypnosis: Current models and perspectives*. New York, Guilford Press, pp. 83–104.

Hobson, J. A. (1999). The new neuropsychology of sleep: Implications for psychoanalysis. *Neuro-Psychoanalysis*, *1*(2), 157–182.

Hobson, A. (2013). ERGO SUM ERGO: Toward a psychodynamic neurology. *Contemporary Psychoanalysis*, *49*(2), 142–164.

Hoffman, I. (2009). Therapeutic passion in the countertransference. *Psychoanalytic Dialogues*, *19*, 617–637.

Hoffman, L. (1995). *Hermine Hug-Hellmuth: Her life and work*: By George MacLean and Ulrich Rappen. New York/London: Routledge, 1991. 305 pp. [Book review]. *The Psychoanalytic Quarterly*, *64*, 600–603.

Hoffman, L. (1999). Passions in girls and women. *Journal of the American Psychoanalytic Association*, *47*, 1145–1168.

Hoffman, L. (2000). Letter: The exclusion of child psychoanalysis. *Journal of the American Psychoanalytic Association*, *48*, 1617–1618.

Hoffman, L. (2008). Oedipus and autonomy assertion, aggression, and the idealized father. *The Annual of Psychoanalysis*, *35*, 85–100.

Hoffman, L. (2015). Berta Bornstein's Frankie: The contemporary relevance of a classic to the treatment of children with disruptive symptoms. *The Psychoanalytic Study of the Child*, *68*, 152–176.

Hoffman, L., Rice, T., & Prout, T. (2015). *Manual for regulation-focused psychotherapy for children with externalizing behaviors (RFP-C): A psychodynamic approach*. New York: Routledge.

Hoffman, M. T., & Hoffman, L. W. (2014). In G. S. Clarke & D. E. Scharff (Eds.), *Fairbairn and the object relations tradition*. London: Karnac, pp. 69–85.

Holt, R. (1976). Drive or wish? A reconsideration of the psychoanalytic theory of motivation. In M. Gill & P. S. Holzman (Eds.), *Psychology versus metapsychology: Psychoanalytic essays in memory of George S. Klein*. New York: International Universities Press, pp. 158–197.

Horney, K. (1946). *Our inner conflicts*. New York: Norton.

References 295

Horowitz, M. J. (1988). *Psychodynamics and cognition*. Chicago, IL: University of Chicago Press.

Hugenberg, K., & Bodenhausen, G. V. (2003). Facing prejudice: Implicit prejudice and the perception of facial threat. *Psychological Science, 14*, 640–643. doi:10.1046/j.0956–7976.2003. psci_1478.x

Hugenberg, K., & Bodenhausen, G. V. (2004). Ambiguity in social categorization: The role of prejudice and facial affect in race categorization. *Psychological Science, 15*, 342–345. doi:10.1111/j.0956–7976.2004.00680.x

Hug-Hellmuth, H. (1921). On the technique of child-analysis. *International Journal of Psychoanalysis, 2*, 287–305.

Hughes, J. R., Kuhlman, D. T., Fichtner, C. G., & Gruenfeld, M. J. (1990). Brain mapping in a case of multiple personality. *Cognition and Emotion, 21*, 200–209.

Ilardi, S. S. (2009). *The depression cure*. Cambridge, MA: Da Capo Press.

Jacobs, T. J. (1986). On countertransference enactments. *Journal of the American Psychoanalytic Association, 34*, 289–307.

Jacobs, T. (1996). On therapeutic interventions in the analysis of certain "unanalyzable" patients – lessons from child and adolescent technique. *Contemporary Psychoanalysis, 32*, 215–235.

Jaenicke, C. (2008). *The risk of relatedness: Intersubjectivity theory in clinical practice*. New York: Aronson.

Jaenicke, C. (2011). *Change in psychoanalysis: An analyst's reflections on the therapeutic relationship*. New York: Routledge.

Jaenicke, C. (2014). *The search for a relational home: An intersubjective-systems view of therapeutic action*. New York/London: Routledge.

Janet, P. (1889). *L'automatisme psychologique*. Paris: Felix Alcan (Reprint, Société Pierre Janet, Paris, 1973).

Janet, P. (1907). *The major symptoms of hysteria*. New York: Macmillan.

Janov, A. (1970). *The primal scream*. New York: Putnam.

Jensen, M. R. (1987). Psychobiological factors predicting the course of breast cancer. *Journal of Personality, 55*, 317–342.

Jiang, Y., & He, S. (2006). Cortical responses to invisible faces: Dissociating subsystems for facial-information processing, *Current Biology, 16*, 2023–2029.

Jordan, C. H., Spencer, S. J., & Zanna, M. P. (2005). Types of high self-esteem and prejudice: How implicit self-esteem relates to ethnic discrimination among high explicit self-esteem individuals. *Personality and Social Psychology Bulletin, 31*, 693–702. doi:10.1177/0146167204271580

Jordan, C. H., Spencer, S. J., Zanna, M. P., Hoshino-Browne, E., & Correll, J. (2003). Secure and defensive high self-esteem. *Journal of Personality and Social Psychology, 85*, 969–978.

Joseph, B. (1983). On understanding and not understanding: Some technical issues. *International Journal of Psychoanalysis, 64*(3), 291–298.

Jung, C. G. (1953). *Two essays on analytical psychology*. New York: Pantheon Books.

Karpen, S. L., Jia, L., & Rydell, R. J. (2012). Discrepancies between implicit and explicit attitude measures as an indicator of attitude strength. *European Journal of Social Psychology, 42*, 24–29.

Keedwell, P. A., Andrew, C., Williams, S. C. R., Brammer, M. J., & Phillips, M. L. (2005). The neural correlates of anhedonia in major depressive disorder. *Biological Psychiatry, 58*, 843–853.

296 References

Keiser, S. (1969). Psychoanalysis – Taught, learned, and experienced. *Journal of the American Psychoanalytic Association, 17*, 238–267.

Kelley, A. E., & Berridge, K. C. (2002). The neuroscience of natural rewards: Relevance to addictive drugs. *The Journal of Neuroscience, 22*(9), 3306–3311.

Kennedy, S. E., Koeppe, R. A., Young, E. A., & Zubieta, J.-K. (2006). Dysregulation of endogenous opioid emotion regulation circuitry in major depression in women. *Archives of General Psychiatry, 63*, 1199–1208.

Kernberg, O. (1967). Borderline personality organization. *Journal of the American Psychoanalytic Association, 15*(3), 641–685.

Kernberg, O. (1995). *Object-relations theory and clinical psychoanalysis*. New York: Jason Aronson.

Kierkegaard, S. (1847). *Purity of heart is to will one thing*. New York: Harper and Row. (English translation, 1956).

Kihlstrom, J. F. (1987). The cognitive unconscious. *Science, 237*, 1145–1152.

Kihlstrom, J. F. (1992a). Dissociative and conversion disorders. In D. J. Stein & J. Young (Eds.), *Cognitive science and clinical disorders*. San Diego: Academic, pp. 247–270.

Kihlstrom, J. F. (1992b). Dissociation and dissociations: A comment on consciousness and cognition. *Consciousness & Cognition, 1*, 47–53.

Kihlstrom, J. F. (2002). No need for repression. *Trends in Cognitive Sciences, 6*(12), 502.

Kihlstrom, J. F. (2005). Dissociative disorders. *Annual Review of Clinical Psychology, 1*, 227–253.

Kikuchi, H., Fujii, T., Abe, N., Suzuki, M., Takagi, M., Mugikura, S., & Mori, E. (2010). Memory repression: Brain mechanisms underlying dissociative amnesia. *Journal of Cognitive Neuroscience, 22*(3), 602–613.

Kinsbourne, M. (1998). Taking the *project* seriously: The unconscious in neuroscience perspective. *Annals of the New York Academy of Sciences, 843*, 111–115.

Kippin, T. E., Szumlinski, K. K., Kapasova, Z., Rezner, B., & See, R. E. (2008). Prenatal stress enhances responsiveness to cocaine. *Neuropsychopharmacology, 33*, 769–782.

Klein, G. S. (1973). Two theories or one? *Bulletin of the Menninger Clinic, 37*, 102–132.

Klein, G. S. (1976). *Psychoanalytic theory*. New York: International Universities Press.

Klein, M. (1921). Development of a child. In R. Money-Kyrle (Ed.), *The writings of Melanie Klein, Vol. 1: Love, guilt, and reparation and other works 1921–1945*. New York: The Free Press, 1984, pp. 1–53.

Klein, M. (1927). Symposium on child-analysis. *International Journal of Psychoanalysis, 8*, 339–370.

Klein, M. (1928). Early stages in the Oedipus conflict. In R. Money-Kyrle (Ed.), *The writings of Melanie Klein, Vol. 1: Love, guilt, and reparation and other works 1921–1945*. New York: The Free Press, 1984, pp. 186–198.

Klein, M. (1929). Personification in the play of children. In R. Money-Kyrle (Ed.), *The writings of Melanie Klein, Vol. 1: Love, guilt, and reparation and other works 1921–1945*. New York: The Free Press, 1984, pp. 199–209.

Klein, M. (1932). *The psychoanalysis of children*. New York: The Free Press, 1984.

Klein, M. (1933). Development of conscience in the child. In R. Money-Kyrle (Ed.), *The writings of Melanie Klein, Vol. 1: Love, guilt, and reparation and other works 1921–1945*. New York: The Free Press, 1984, pp. 248–257.

Klein, M. (1935a). The contribution to the psychogenesis of manic-depressive states. In *Contributions to psychoanalysis, 1921–1945*. New York: McGraw-Hill, 1964.

References 297

Klein, M. (1935b). The psychogenesis of manic-depressive states. In R. Money-Kyrle (Ed.), *The writings of Melanie Klein, Vol. 1: Love, guilt, and reparation and other works 1921–1945.* New York: The Free Press, 1984, pp. 262–289.

Klein, M. (1940). Mourning and its relation to manic-depressive states. In R. Money-Kyrle (Ed.), *The writings of Melanie Klein, Vol. 1: Love, guilt, and reparation and other works 1921–1945.* New York: The Free Press, 1984, pp. 344–369.

Klein, M. (1975). Envy and Gratitude and Other Works 1946–1963. *Int. Psycho-Anal. Lib.,* 104:1–346. London: The Hogarth Press and the Institute of Psycho-Analysis.

Klonsky, E. D. (2007). The functions of deliberate self-injury: A review of the evidence. *Clinical Psychology Review, 27*(2), 226–239.

Koch, C. (2004). *The quest for consciousness: A neurobiological approach.* Englewood, CO: Roberts and Company Publishers.

Koch, C. (2008). Consciousness redux: Rendering the visible invisible. *Scientific American Mind, 19,* 18–19.

Kohut, H. (1971). *The analysis of the self.* New York: International Universities Press.

Kohut, H. (1972). Thoughts on narcissism and narcissistic rage. *Psychoanalytic Study of the Child, 27,* 360–400.

Kohut, H. (1977). *The restoration of the self.* New York: International Universities Press.

Kohut, H. (1982). Introspection, empathy, and the semicircle of mental health. *International Journal of Psycho-Analysis, 63,* 395–408.

Kohut, H. (1984). *How does analysis cure?* Chicago: University of Chicago Press.

Kramer, M. (1993). The selective mood regulatory function of dreaming: An update and revision. In A. Moffit, M. Kramer, & R. Hoffman (Eds.), *The functions of dreaming.* Albany, NY: State University of New York Press, pp. 223–230.

Kris, A. O. (1976). On wanting too much: The 'exceptions' revisited. *International Journal of Psychoanalysis, 57,* 85–95.

Kris, A. O. (1977). Either-or dilemmas. *Psychoanalytic Study of the Child, 32,* 91–117.

Kris, A. O. (1982). *Free association: Method and process.* New Haven/London: Yale University Press.

Kris, A. O. (1983). Determinants of free association in narcissistic phenomena. *Psychoanalytic Study of the Child, 38,* 439–457.

Kris, A. O. (1984). The conflicts of ambivalence. Psychoanalytic Study of the Child, *39,* 213–234.

Kris, A. O. (1985). Resistance in convergent and in divergent conflicts. *The Psychoanalytic Quarterly, 54,* 537–568.

Kris, A. O. (1987). Fixation and regression in relation to convergent and divergent conflicts. *Bulletin of the Anna Freud Centre, 10,* 99–117.

Kris, A. O. (1988). Some clinical applications of the distinction between divergent and convergent conflicts. *International Journal of Psychoanalysis, 69,* 431–441.

Kris, A. O. (1990a). Helping patients by analyzing self-criticism. *Journal of the American Psychoanalytic Association, 38,* 605–636.

Kris, A. O. (1990b). The analyst's stance and the method of free association. *Psychoanalytic Study of the Child, 45,* 25–41.

Kris, A. O. (1992). Interpretation and the method of free association. *Psychoanalytic Inquiry, 12,* 208–224.

Kris, A. O. (1994). Freud's treatment of a narcissistic patient. *International Journal of Psychoanalysis, 75,* 649–664.

Kris, A. O. (2013). Unlearning and learning psychoanalysis. *American Imago, 70,* 341–355.

298 References

Kris, E. (1947). The nature of psychoanalytic propositions and their validation. In L. Newman (Ed.), *The selected papers of Ernst Kris*. New Haven, CT: Yale University Press, 1975, pp. 3–23.

Krystal, J. H., Bremner, D. J., Southwick, S. M., & Charney, D. S. (1998). The emerging neurobiology of dissociation: Implications for treatment of posttraumatic stress disorder. In J. D. Bremner & C. R. Marmar (Eds.), *Trauma, memory & dissociation*. Washington, DC: American Psychiatric Publishing, Inc.

Krystal, J. H., Karper, L. P., Seibyl, J. P., Freeman, G. K., Delaney, R., Bremner, J. D., & Charney, D. S. (1994). Subanesthetic effects of the noncompetitive NMDA antagonist, ketamine, in humans: Psychotomimetic, perceptual, cognitive, and neuroendocrine responses. *Archives of General Psychiatry, 51*, 199–214.

Lacan, J. (2002). *The seminar of Jacques Lacan VI: Desire and its interpretation* (C. Gallagher, Trans.), from unedited manuscripts.

Lacan, J. (2006). *Ecrits* (B. Fink, Trans.). New York: Norton.

Lachmann, F. M. (1986). Interpretation of psychic conflict and adversarial relationships: A self-psychological perspective. *Psychoanalytic Psychology, 3*, 341–355.

Lachmann, F. (2008). *Transforming narcissism: Reflections on empathy, humor, and expectations*. New York: The Analytic Press.

Langer, S. (1942). *Philosophy in a new key: A study in the symbolism of reason, rite and art*. Cambridge, MA: Harvard University Press.

Laplanche, J. (1999). *Essays on otherness*. Routledge: London.

Larmore, K., Ludwig, A. M., & Cain, R. L. (1977). Multiple personality – An objective case study. *British Journal of Psychiatry, 131*, 35–40.

Lau, D. C. (1979). *Confucius: The analects*. Harmondsworth, UK: Penguin.

Laub, D. (2013). On leaving home and the flight from trauma. *Psychoanalytic Dialogues, 23*, 568–580.

Laureys, S. (2005). The neural correlate of (un)awareness: Lessons from the vegetative state. *Trends in Cognitive Science, 9*(12), 556–559.

Laureys, S., Faymonville, M. E., Luxen, A., Lamy, M., Franck, G., & Maquet, P. (2000). Restoration of thalamocortical connectivity after recovery from persistent vegetative state. *The Lancet, 355*, 1790–1791.

Laureys, S., Goldman, S., Phillips, C., Van Bogaert, P., Aerts, J., Luxen, A., & Maquet, P. (1999). Impaired effective cortical connectivity in vegetative state: Preliminary investigation using PET. *Neuroimage, 9*, 377–382.

Laureys, S., Lemaire, C., Maquet, P., Phillips, C., & Franck, G. (1999). Cerebral metabolism during vegetative state and after recovery to consciousness. *Journal of Neurology, Neurosurgery, and Psychiatry, 67*, 121.

Laureys, S., Owen, A. M., & Schiff, N. D. (2004). Brain function in coma, vegetative state, and related disorders. *The Lancet Neurology, 3*(9), 537–546.

Laye-Gindhu, A., & Schonert-Reichl, K. A. (2005). Nonsuicidal self-harm among community adolescents: Understanding the 'whats' and 'whys' of self-harm. *Journal of Youth and Adolescence, 34*(5), 447–457.

Lecours, S. (2007). Supportive interventions and nonsymbolic mental functioning. *International Journal of Psychoanalysis, 88*(4), 895–915.

Lederbogen, F., Kirsch, P., Haddad, L., Streit, F., Tost, H., Schuch, P., & Meyer-Lindenberg, A. (2011). City living and urban upbringing affect neural social stress processing in humans. *Nature, 474*, 498–501.

Lekners, S., & Tracey, I. (2008). A common neurobiology for pain and pleasure. *Nature Reviews Neuroscience, 9*, 314–320.

References   299

Levenson, E. (1983). *The ambiguity of change*. New York: Basic Books.

Levenson, E. (1988). Real frogs in imaginary gardens: Facts and fantasies in psychoanalysis. *Psychoanalytic Inquiry, 8*, 552–567.

Levithan, D. (2014). What can literature teach us about love? *N.Y. Times Book Review*, Feb. 9, p. 18.

Liberzon, I., King, A. P., Britton, J. C., Phan, K. L., Abelson, J. L., & Taylor, S. F. (2007). Paralimbic and medial prefrontal cortical involvement in neuroendocrine responses to traumatic stimuli. *American Journal of Psychiatry, 164*(8), 1250–1258.

Libet, B. (1966). Brain stimulation and the threshold of conscious experience. In J. C. Eccles (Ed.), *Brain and conscious experience*. New York: Springer-Verlag.

Libet, B. (1973). Electrical stimulation of cortex in human subjects and conscious sensory aspects. In A. Iggo (Ed.), *Handbook of sensory physiology*. New York: Springer-Verlag, pp. 743–790.

Libet, B. (1978). Neuronal vs. subjective timing for a conscious sensory experience. In P. A. Buser & A. Rougeul-Buser (Eds.), *Cerebral correlates of conscious experience*. Amsterdam: Elsevier.

Libet, B., Alberts, W. W., Wright, E. W., Delattre, L. D., Levin, G., & Feinstein, B. (1964). Production of threshold levels of conscious sensation by electrical stimulation of human somatosensory cortex. *Journal of Neurophysiology, 27*, 546–578.

Lichtenberg, J. (1989). *Psychoanalysis and motivation*. Hillsdale, NJ: The Analytic Press.

Lichtenberg, J. (1991). What is a selfobject? *Psychoanalytic Dialogues, 1*, 455–479.

Lichtenberg, J. (1998). Experience as a guide to theory and practice. *Journal of the American Psychoanalytic Association, 46*, 17–36.

Lichtenberg, J. (2002). Values, consciousness and language. *Psychoanalytic Inquiry, 22*(5), 841–856.

Lichtenberg, J., Lachmann, F., & Fosshage, J. (1992). *Self and motivational systems: Toward a theory of technique*. Hillsdale, NJ: The Analytic Press.

Lichtenberg, J., Lachmann, F., & Fosshage, J. (1996). *The clinical exchange: Technique from the standpoint of self and motivational systems*. Hillsdale, NJ: The Analytic Press.

Lichtenberg, J., Lachmann, F., & Fosshage, J. (2002). *A spirit of inquiry: Communication in psychoanalysis*. Hillsdale, NJ: The Analytic Press.

Lichtenberg, J., Lachmann, F., & Fosshage, J. (2011). *Psychoanalysis and motivation systems: A new look*. New York: The Analytic Press.

Lichtenberg, J., Lachmann, F., & Fosshage, J. (2015). *Enlivening the self: The first year, critical enrichment, and the wandering mind*. New York: Taylor and Francis Group, Routledge.

Lieberman, D. E. (2013). *The story of the human body*. New York: Pantheon.

Likierman, M. (2001). *Melanie Klein: Her work in context*. London: Continuum.

Loewald, H. (1960). On the therapeutic action of psychoanalysis. *International Journal of Psychoanalysis, 43*, 16–33.

Loewald, H. (1978). *Psychoanalysis and the history of the individual (Freud Lectures at Yale Series)*. New Haven: Yale University Press.

Lotterman, A. C. (2012). Affect as a marker of the psychic surface. *The Psychoanalytic Quarterly, 81*(2), 305–333.

Low, B. (1920). *Psychoanalysis*. London: Hogarth.

Ludwig, A. M., Brandsma, J. M., Wilbur, C. B., Bendfeldt, F., & Jameson, D. H. (1972). The objective study of a multiple personality: Or, are four heads better than one? *Archives of General Psychiatry, 26*, 298–310.

300 References

Lyons-Ruth, K. (1999). The two-person unconscious: Intersubjective dialogue, enactive relational representation and the emergence of new forms of relational organization. *Psychoanalytic Inquiry, 19*, 576–617.

Lyons-Ruth, K. (2003). Dissociation and the parent-infant dialogue: A longitudinal perspective. *Journal of the American Psychoanalytic Association, 51*, 883–911.

Lyons-Ruth, K., & Jacbovitz, D. (2008). Attachment disorganization: Genetic factors, parenting contexts, and developmental transformation from infancy to adulthood. In J. Cassidy and P. Shaver (Eds.), *Handbook of attachment: Theory, research, and clinical applications* (2nd ed.). New York: Guilford Press, pp. 666–697.

Macleod, C. M. (1991). Half a century of research on the Stroop effect: An integrative review. *Psychological Bulletin, 109*, 163–203.

Mahler, M. (1968). *On human symbiosis and the vicissitudes of individuation*. New York: International University Press.

Mahler, M. S. (1974). Symbiosis and individuation – The psychological birth of the human infant. *Psychoanalytic Study of the Child, 29*, 89–106.

Mahler, M., Pine, F., & Bergman, A. (1975). *The psychological birth of the human infant*. New York: Basic Books.

Main, M., & Hesse, E. (1990). Parents' unresolved traumatic experiences are related to infant disorganized attachment status: Is frightened/frightening parental behavior the linking mechanism? In M. Greenberg, D. Cicchetti, & M. Cummings (Eds.), *Attachment in the preschool years*. Chicago: University of Chicago Press, pp. 161–182.

Main, M., Hesse, E., & Goldwyn, R. (2008). Studying differences in language use in recounting attachment history. In H. Steele & M. Steele (Eds.), *Clinical applications of the adult attachment interview*. New York: Guilford Press, pp. 31–68.

Main, M., Kaplan, N., & Cassidy, J. (1985). Security in infancy, childhood, and adulthood: A move to the level of representation. *Monographs of the Society for Research in Child Development, 50*(1–2), 66–104. Chicago: University of Chicago Press.

Main, M., & Solomon, J. (1990). Procedures for identifying disorganized/disoriented infants during the Ainsworth Strange Situation. In M. Greenberg, D. Cicchetti, & M. Cummings (Eds.), *Attachment in the preschool years*. Chicago: University of Chicago Press, pp. 121–160.

Mandler, G. (2011). *A history of modern experimental psychology: From James and Wundt to cognitive science*. Cambridge, MA: MIT Press.

Márquez, G. G. (1985). *Love in the time of cholera* (Edith Grossman, Trans.). New York: Alfred A. Knopf.

Maslow, A. (2011). *A psychology of being* (3rd ed.). New York: Wiley, 1968.

Mathew, R. J., Jack, R. A., & West, W. S. (1985). Regional cerebral blood flow in a patient with multiple personality. *The American Journal of Psychiatry, 142*, 504–505.

Mayer, A., & Orth, J. (1901). Zur qualitativen untersuchung der association. *Zeitschrift für Psychologie, 26*, 1–13.

McCarley, R. W. (1998). Dreams: Disguise of forbidden wishes or transparent reflections of a distinct brain state? *Annals of the New York Academy of Sciences, 843*, 116–133.

McConnell, A. R., & Leibold, J. M. (2001). Relations among the implicit association test, discriminatory behavior, and explicit measures of racial attitudes. *Journal of Experimental Social Psychology, 37*, 435–442. doi:10.1006/jesp.2000.1470

McCullough, L., Kuhn, N., Andrews, S., Kaplan, A., Wolf, J., & Hurley, C. L. (2003). *Treating affect phobia: A manual for short-term dynamic psychotherapy*. New York: Guilford Press.

References 301

Medford, N., Brierley, B., Brammer, M., Bullmore, E. T., David, A. S., & Phillips, M. L. (2006). Emotional memory in depersonalization disorder: A functional MRI study. *Psychiatry Research, 148,* 93–102.

Meltzoff, A. N. (1995). Understanding the intentions of others: Re-enactment of intended acts by eighteen month-old children. *Developmental Psychology, 3,* 838–850.

Mesulam, M. M. (1981). Dissociative states with abnormal temporal lobe EEG: Multiple personality and the illusion of possession. *Archives of Neurology, 38,* 176–181.

Miller, J. (1985). How Kohut actually worked. In A. Goldberg (Ed.), *Progress in self psychology, Vol. 1.* New York: Guilford Press, pp. 13–30.

Miller, K., Yost, B., Flaherty, S., Hillemeier, M. H., Chase, G. A., Weisman, C. S., & Dyer, C. M. (2007). Health status, health conditions, and health behaviors among Amish women: Results from the Central Pennsylvania Women's Health Study (CePAWHS). *Women's Health Issues, 17,* 162–171.

Miller, S. D., & Triggiano, P. J. (1992). The psychophysiological investigation of multiple personality disorder: Review and update. *American Journal of Clinical Hypnosis, 35,* 47–61.

Mitchell, S. A. (1988). *Relational concepts in psychoanalysis.* Cambridge, MA/London, UK: Harvard University Press.

Mitchell, S. A. (1998). The analyst's knowledge and authority. *The Psychoanalytic Quarterly, 67,* 1–31.

Montagne, B., Sierra, M., Medford, N., Hunter, E., Baker, D., Kessels, R. P., . . . David, A. S. (2007). Emotional memory and perception of emotional faces in patients suffering from depersonalization disorder. *British Journal of Psychology, 98,* 517–527.

Montgomery, J., & Ritchey, T. (2008). *The answer model theory.* Santa Monica, CA: TAM Books.

Montgomery, J., & Ritchey, T. (2010). *The answer model: A new path to healing.* Santa Monica, CA: TAM Books.

Moskowitz, M. (1996). The end of analyzability. In R. Pérez Foster, M. Moskowitz, & R. A. Javier (Eds.), *Reaching across boundaries of culture and class: Widening the scope of psychotherapy.* Lanham, MD: Jason Aronson, pp. 179–193.

Murphy, A., Steele, M., Dube, S., Bate, J., Bonuck, K., Meissner, P., & Steele, H. (2014). Adverse Childhood Experiences (ACEs) Questionnaire and Adult Attachment Interview (AAI): Implications for parent child relationships. *Child Abuse & Neglect, 38*(2), 224–233.

Newport, D. J., & Nemeroff, C. B. (2000). Neurobiology of posttraumatic stress disorder. *Current Opinion in Neurobiology, 10,* 211–218.

Nicolaides, N. C., Kyratzi, E., Lamprokostopoulou, A., Chrousos, G. P., & Charmandari, E. (2015). Stress, the stress system and the role of glucocorticoids. *Neuroimmunomodulation, 22,* 6–19.

Nielsen, T. A., & Germain, A. (2000). Post-traumatic nightmares as a dysfunctional state. *Behavioral and Brain Sciences, 23*(6), 978–979.

Nietzsche, F. (2014). *The complete works of Friedrich Nietzsche, Vol. 8 (Beyond good and evil/on the genealogy of morality)* (A. Del Caro, Trans.). Palo Alto: Stanford University Press.

Nijenhuis, E. R. S., van der Hart, O., & Steele, K. (2002). The emerging psychobiology of trauma-related dissociation and dissociative disorders. In H. A. H. D'haenen, J. A. Den Boer, & P. Willner (Eds.), *Biological psychiatry, Volume 2.* West Sussex: Wiley & Sons, LTD, pp. 1079–1098.

302   References

Nosek, B. A. (2005). Moderators of the relationship between implicit and explicit evaluation. *Journal of Experimental Psychology: General, 134,* 565–584. doi:10.1037/0096-3445.134.4.565

Nosek, B. A. (2007). Implicit-explicit relations. *Current Directions in Psychological Science, 16,* 65–69. doi:10.1111/j.1467-8721.2007.00477.x

Nosek, B. A., Greenwald, A. G., & Banaji, M. R. (2007). The implicit association test at age 7: A methodological and conceptual review. In J. A. Bargh (Ed.), *Social psychology and the unconscious: The automaticity of higher mental processes.* New York: Psychology Press, pp. 265–292.

Ogden, T. H. (1983). The concept of internal object relations. *International Journal of Psychoanalysis, 64,* 227–241.

Ogden, T. H. (1997). *Reverie and interpretation: Sensing something human.* Northvale, NJ: Aronson.

Ogden, T. H. (2002). A new reading of the origins of object-relations theory. *International Journal of Psychoanalysis, 83,* 767–782.

Ogden, T. H. (2014). Fear of breakdown and the unlived life. *International Journal of Psychoanalysis, 95,* 205–223.

O'Leary, T., Williams, A. H., Franci, A., & Marder, E. (2014). Cell types, network homeostasis, and pathological compensation from a biologically plausible ion channel expression model. *Neuron, 82,* 809–821.

Olson, M. A., & Fazio, R. H. (2007). Discordant evaluations of Blacks affect nonverbal behavior. *Personality and Social Psychology Bulletin, 33,* 1214–1224.

Orange, D. (2011). *The suffering stranger: Hermeneutics for everyday clinical practice.* New York: Taylor & Francis Group, Routledge.

Orange, D., Atwood, G., & Stolorow, R. (1997). *Working intersubjectively.* Hillsdale, NJ: The Analytic Press.

Ornstein, A. (1974). The dread to repeat and the new beginning. *Annual of Psychanalysis, 2,* 231–248. New York: International Universities Press.

O'Shaughnessy, E. (2005). Who's Bion? *International Journal of Psychoanalysis, 86*(6), 1523–1528.

Oswald, F. L., Mitchell, G., Blanton, H., Jaccard, J., & Tetlock, P. E. (2013). Predicting ethnic and racial discrimination: A meta-analysis of IAT criterion studies. *Journal of Personality and Social Psychology, 105,* 171–192. doi:10.1037/a0032734

Pally, R. (2001). A primary role for nonverbal communication in psychoanalysis. *Psychoanalytic Inquiry, 21*(1), 71–93.

Palombo, S. (1978). *Dreaming and memory.* New York: Basis Books.

Panksepp, J. (1998). *Affective neuroscience: The foundations of human and animal emotions.* New York: Oxford University Press.

Paskauskas, R.A. (Ed.), (1993). Glossary to The Complete Correspondence of Sigmund Freud and Ernest Jones 1908-1939. In *The Complete Correspondence of Sigmund Freud and Ernest Jones 1908-1939,* 821–822.

Paulus, M. P. (2007). Decision-making dysfunctions in psychiatry – Altered homeostatic processing? *Science, 318,* 602–606.

PDM Task Force. (2006). *Psychodynamic diagnostic manual.* Silver Spring, MD: Alliance of Psychoanalytic Organizations.

Peltz, R., & Goldberg, P. (2013). Field conditions: Discussion of Donnel B. Stern's field theory in psychoanalysis. *Psychoanalytic Dialogues, 23,* 660–666.

References 303

Penfield, W., & Perot, P. (1963). The brain's record of auditory and visual experience: A final summary and discussion. *Brain, 86,* 595–696.

Petty, R. E., & Briñol, P. (2009). Implicit ambivalence: A meta-cognitive approach. In R. E. Petty, R. H. Fazio, & P. Briñol (Eds.), *Attitudes: Insights from the new implicit measures.* New York: Psychology Press, pp. 119–161.

Phillips, M. L., & Sierra, M. (2003). Depersonalization disorder: A functional neuroanatomical perspective. *Stress, 6*(3), 157–165.

Piaget, J. (1954). *The construction of reality in the child.* New York: Basic Books.

Piaget, J. (1976). *The grasp of consciousness: Action and concept in the young child.* (Trans by S. Wedgwood). Oxford: Harvard University Press.

Piazza, P. V., & Le Maol, M. (1997). Glucocorticoids as a biological substrate of reward: Physiological and pathophysiological implications. *Brain Research Reviews, 25,* 359–372.

Piers, C. (2000). Character as self organizing complexity. *Psychoanalysis and Contemporary Thought, 23,* 3–34.

Pitman, R. K., van der Kolk, B. A., Orr, S. P., & Greenberg, M. S. (1990). Naloxone-reversible analgesic response to combat-related stimuli in posttraumatic stress disorder: A pilot study. *Arch Gen Psychiatry, 47*(6), 541–544.

Prince, M. (1906). *The dissociation of a personality.* New York: Longmans, Green, & Co.

Prossin, A. R., Love, T. M., Koeppe, R. A., Zubieta, J.-K., & Silk, K. R. (2010). Dysregulation of regional endogenous opioid function in borderline personality disorder. *The American Journal of Psychiatry, 167*(8), 925–933.

Putnam, F. W. (1992). Multiple personality disorder. *The British Journal of Psychiatry, 161,* 415–416.

Putnam, F. W. (1993). Dissociative disorders in children: Behavioral profiles and problems. *Child Abuse & Neglect, 17,* 39–45.

Putnam, F. W. (1997). *Dissociation in children and adolescents: A developmental perspective.* New York: Guilford Press.

Putnam, F. W., Zahn, T. P., & Post, R. M. (1990). Differential autonomic nervous system activity in multiple personality disorder. *Psychological Review, 31,* 251–260.

Ramachandran, V. S. (1996). The evolutionary biology of self-deception, laughter, dreaming and depression: Some clues from anosognosia. *Medical Hypotheses, 47,* 347–362.

Rangell, L. (1963a). The scope of intrapsychic conflict. *Psychoanalytic Study of the Child, 18,* 75–102.

Rangell, L. (1963b). Structural problems in intrapsychic conflict. *Psychoanalytic Study of the Child, 18,* 103–138.

Rangell, L. (2004). *My life in theory.* New York: Other Press.

Reinders, A. A., Nijenhuis, E. R., Paans, A. M., Korf, J., Willemsen, A. T., & den Boer, J. A. (2003). One brain, two selves. *Neuroimage, 20*(4), 2119–2125.

Reinders, A. A., Nijenhuis, E. R., Quak, J., Korf, J., Haaksma, J., Paans, A. M., . . . den Boer, J. A. (2006). Psychobiological characteristics of dissociative identity disorder: A symptom provocation study. *Biological Psychiatry, 60*(7), 730–740.

Renik, O. (1993). Analytic interaction: Conceptualizing technique in light of the analyst's irreducible subjectivity. *The Psychoanalytic Quarterly, 62,* 553–571.

Renik, O. (2006). *Practical psychoanalysis for therapist and analysand.* New York: Other Press.

Rey, J. H. (1988). That which patients bring to analysis. *International Journal of Psychoanalysis, 69,* 457–470.

304 References

Ribble, M. (1943). *The rights of infants*. New York: Columbia University Press.

Rice, T. R., & Hoffman, L. (2014). Defense mechanisms and implicit emotion regulation: A comparison of a psychodynamic construct with one from contemporary neuroscience. *Journal of the American Psychoanalytic Association, 62*(4), 693–708. doi:10.1177/0003065114546746

Richards, A. D. (1998). Politics and paradigms. *Journal of the American Psychoanalytic Association, 46*, 357–360.

Richeson, J. A., & Shelton, J. (2003). When prejudice does not pay: Effects of interracial contact on executive function. *Psychological Science, 14*, 287–290. doi:10.1111/1467-9280.03437

Rothstein, A. (2005). Compromise formation theory: An intersubjective dimension. *Psychoanalytic Dialogue, 15*, 415–431.

Rubens, R. L. (1994). Fairbairn's structural theory. In J. S. Grotstein & D. B. Rinsley (Eds.), *Fairbairn and the origins of object relations*. New York: Guilford Press, pp. 151–173.

Rudman, L. A., & Lee, M. R. (2002). Implicit and explicit consequences of exposure to violent and misogynous rap music. *Group Processes & Intergroup Relations, 5*, 133–150. doi:10.1177/1368430202005002541

Saal, D., Dong, Y., Bonci, A., & Malenka, R. C. (2003). Drugs of abuse and stress trigger a common synaptic adaptation in dopamine neurons. *Neuron, 37*, 577–582.

Safran, J. D., Croker, P., McMain, S., & Murray, P. (1990). Therapeutic alliance rupture as therapy event for empirical investigation. *Psychotherapy, 27*, 154–165.

Sandler, J., Dare, C., & Holder, A. (1971). Basic psychoanalytic concepts: X. Interpretations and other interventions. *The British Journal of Psychiatry, 118*(542), 53–59.

Sandler, J., Dare, C., & Holder, A. (1973). *The patient and the analyst: The basis of the psychoanalytic process*. London: Allen & Unwin.

Sandler, J., & Freud, A. (1981). Discussions in the Hampstead index on 'The Ego and the mechanisms of defense': III. The Ego's defensive operations considered as an object of analysis. *Bulletin of the Anna Freud Centre, 4*, 119–141.

Sandler, J., & Freud, A. (1985). *The analysis of defense: The ego & the mechanisms of defense revisited*. New York: International University Press.

Sandman, C. A., Hetrick, W., Taylor, D. V., & Chicz-DeMet, A. (1997). Dissociation of POMC peptides after self-injury predicts responses to centrally acting opiate blockers. *American Journal on Mental Retardation, 102*(2), 182–199.

Sandman, C. A., Touchette, P. E., Marion, S. D., & Chicz-Demet, A. (1999). Proopiomelanocortin (POMC) dysregulation and response to opiate blockers. *Mental Retardation and Developmental Disabilities Research Reviews, 5*, 314–321.

Sar, V., & Ross, C. A. (2006). Dissociative disorders as a confounding factor in psychiatric research. *Psychiatric Clinics of North America, 29*, 129–144.

Sar, V., Unal, S. N., Kiziltan, E., Kundakci, T., & Ozturk, E. (2001). HMPAO SPECT study of regional cerebral perfusion in dissociative identity disorder, *Journal of Trauma and Dissociation, 2*(2), 5–25.

Sar, V., Unal, S. N., & Ozturk, E. (2007). Frontal and occipital perfusion changes in dissociative identity disorder. *Psychiatry Research, 156*(3), 217–223.

Saxe, G. N., Vasile, R. G., Hill, T. C., Bloomingdale, K., & Van der Kolk, B. A. (1992). SPECT imaging and multiple personality disorder. *The Journal of Nervous and Mental Disease, 180*, 662–663.

Schafer, R. (1968). *Aspects of internalization*. New York: International Universities Press.

Schafer, R. (1973). Action. *Annual of Psychoanalysis, 1*, 159–195.

References 305

Schafer, R. (1997). *The contemporary Kleinians of London.* New York: International Universities Press.

Schieffelin, E. L. (1985). The cultural analysis of depressive affect: An example from New Guinea. In A. Kleinman & B. Good (Eds.), *Culture and depression.* Berkeley, CA: University of California Press, pp. 101–133.

Schmidt, B. L., Tambeli, C. H., Barletta, J., Luo, L., Green, P., Levine, J. D., & Gear, R. W. (2002). Altered nucleus accumbens circuitry mediates pain-induced antinociception in morphine-tolerant rats. *The Journal of Neuroscience, 22*(15), 6773–6780.

Schmidt-Hellerau, C. (2005). We are driven. *The Psychoanalytic Quarterly, 74,* 989–1028.

Schröder-Abé, M., Rudolph, A., & Schütz, A. (2007). High implicit self-esteem is not necessarily advantageous: Discrepancies between explicit and implicit self-esteem and their relationship with anger expression and psychological health. *European Journal of Personality, 21,* 319–339.

Schur, M. (1966). *The Id and the regulatory principles of mental functioning.* New York: International Universities Press, Inc., pp. 1–220.

Schwaber, E. A. (1992). Countertransference: The analyst's retreat from the analysand's vantage point. *International Journal of Psychoanalysis, 73,* 349–361.

Schwartz, G. E. (1990). Psychobiology of repression and health: A systems perspective. In J. L. Singer (Ed.), *Repression and dissociation: Defense mechanisms and personality styles: Current theory and research.* Chicago: University of Chicago Press, pp. 405–434.

Searles, H. (1959). Oedipal love in the counter transference. *International Journal of Psychoanalysis, 40,* 180–190.

Searles, H. (1973). Concerning therapeutic symbiosis. *Annuals of Psychoanalysis, 1,* 247–262.

Segal, H. (1979). *Melanie Klein.* New York: The Viking Press, 1980.

Shane, M., Shane, E., & Gales, M. (1998). *Intimate attachments: Toward a new self psychology.* New York: Guilford Press.

Sher, L., & Stanley, B. H. (2008). The role of endogenous opioids in the pathophysiology of self-injurious and suicidal behavior. *Archives of Suicide Research, 12,* 299–308.

Shevrin, H. (1973). Brain wave correlates of subliminal stimulation, unconscious attention, primary and secondary-process thinking and repressiveness [Monograph 30]. *Psychological Issues, 8*(2), 56–87.

Shevrin, H. (1995). Is psychoanalysis one science, two sciences, or no science at all? A discourse among friendly antagonists. *Journal of the American Psychoanalytic Association, 43,* 963.

Shevrin, H., Bond, J. A., Brakel, L., Hertel, R. K., & Williams, W. J. (1996). *Conscious and unconscious processes: Psychodynamic, cognitive, and neurophysiological convergences.* New York: Guilford Press.

Shevrin, H., & Dickman, S. (1980). The psychological unconscious: A necessary assumption for all psychological theory? *American Psychologist, 35,* 421–434.

Shevrin, H., Ghannam, J. H., & Libet, B. (2002). A neural correlate of consciousness related to repression. *Consciousness and Cognition, 11*(2), 334–341.

Shevrin, H., Smith, W. H., & Fritzler, D. (1969). Repressiveness as a factor in the subliminal activation of brain and verbal responses. *Journal of Nervous and Mental Disease, 149,* 261–269.

Shevrin, H., Smith, W. H., & Fritzler, D. (1970). Subliminally stimulated brain and verbal responses of twins differing in repressiveness. *Journal of Abnormal Psychology, 76,* 39–46.

306 References

Sierra, M. (2009). *Depersonalization: A new look at a neglected syndrome*. Cambridge, UK: Cambridge University Press.

Sierra, M., & Berrios, G. E. (1998). Depersonalization: Neurobiological perspectives. *Biological Psychiatry, 44*, 898–908.

Siggins, L. D. (1966). Mourning: A critical survey of the literature. *International Journal of Psychoanalysis, 47*, 14–25.

Simeon, D., & Abugel, J. (2006). *Feeling unreal: Depersonalization and the loss of the self*. New York: Oxford University Press.

Simeon, D., Giesbrecht, T., Knutelska, M., Smith, R. J., & Smith, L. M. (2009). Alexithymia, absorption, and cognitive failures in depersonalization disorder a comparison to posttraumatic stress disorder and healthy volunteers. *The Journal of Nervous and Mental Disease, 197*, 492–498.

Slade, A. (1999). Attachment theory and research: Implications for the theory and practice of individual psychotherapy with adults. In J. Cassidy & P. Shaver (Eds.), *The handbook of attachment theory and research*. New York: Guilford Press, pp. 575–594.

Slade, A. (2008). The move from categories to process: Attachment phenomena and clinical evaluation. *Attachment: New Directions in Psychotherapy and Relational Psychoanalysis, 2*, 89–105.

Slade, A. (2014). Fear and the attachment system. *Psychoanalytic Dialogues, 24*(3), 253–266.

Slavin, M. O. (2010). On recognizing the psychoanalytic perspective of the other: A discussion of "recognition as: Intersubjective vulnerability in the psychoanalytic dialogue" by Donna Orange (International journal or psychoanalytic self psychology), *5*, 274–292.

Slavin, M., & Kriegman, D. (1992). *The adaptive design of the human psyche*. New York: Guilford Press.

Smith, H. F. (2003). Conceptions of conflict in psychoanalytic theory and practice. *The Psychoanalytic Quarterly, 72*, 49–96.

Smith, H. F. (2007). Voices that changed psychoanalysis in unpredictable ways. *The Psychoanalytic Quarterly, 76*, 1049–1063.

Socarides, D., & Stolorow, R. (1984). Affects and selfobjects. *The Annual of Psychoanalysis, 12*, 105–119.

Solms, M. (1995). New findings on the neurological organization of dreaming: Implications for psychoanalysis. *Psychoanalytic Quarterly, 64*, 43–67.

Solms, M., & Turnball, O. (2002). *The brain and the inner world*. New York: Other Press.

Son Hing, L. S., Chung-Yan, G. A., Grunfeld, R., Robichaud, L. K., & Zanna, M. P. (2005). Exploring the discrepancy between implicit and explicit prejudice: A test of aversive racism theory. In J. P. Forgas, K. P. Williams, & S. M. Laham (Eds.), *Social motivation: Conscious and unconscious processes*. Cambridge, UK: Cambridge University Press, pp. 274–293.

Spielrein, S. (1912/1981). Destruction as a cause of coming into being. *Journal of Analytical Psychology, 39*, 155–186.

Spillius, E. B. (Ed.) (1988). *Melanie Klein today: Development in theory and practice, Vols. 1 & 2*. London: Routledge.

Spinoza, B. (1994). *A Spinoza reader: The ethics and other works* (E. M. Curley, Trans.). Princeton: Princeton University Press.

Spitz, R. A. (1945). Hospitalism: An inquiry into the genesis of psychiatric conditions in early childhood. *Psychoanalytic Study of the Child, 1*, 53–74.

Spitz, R. A. (1946). Anaclitic depression. *Psychoanalytic Study of the Child, 2*, 113–117.

Sroufe, L. A. (2005). Attachment and development: A prospective, longitudinal study from birth to adulthood. *Attachment & human development, 7*(4), 349–367.

Stapert, W., & Smeekens, S. (2011). Five year olds with good conscience development. *Psychoanalytic Study of the Child, 65*, 215–244.

Steele, H. (2010). Test of time: On re-reading "psychoanalysis and child care", John Bowlby's lecture delivered in 1956 on the centenary of Sigmund Freud's birth. *Clinical Child Psychology and Psychiatry, 15*, 453–458.

Steele, H., & Steele, M. (1998). Attachment and psychoanalysis: Time for a reunion. *Social Development, 7*(1), 92–119.

Steele, H., & Steele, M. (2005). The construct of coherence as an indicator of attachment security in middle childhood: The friends and family interview. In K. Kerns & R. Richardson (Eds.), *Attachment in middle childhood*. New York: Guilford Press, pp. 137–160.

Steele, H., & Steele, M. (2008). *Clinical applications of the adult attachment interview*. New York: Guildford Press.

Steele, H., Steele, M., Croft, C., & Fonagy, P. (1999). Infant-mother attachment at one year predicts children's understanding of mixed emotions at six years. *Social Development, 8*, 161–178.

Steele, H., Steele, M., & Fonagy, P. (1996). Associations among attachment classifications of mothers, fathers, and their infants. *Child Development, 67*, 541–555.

Stein, D. J. (1992). Psychoanalysis and cognitive science: Contrasting models of the mind. *Journal of the American Academy of Psychoanalysis, 20*, 543–559.

Stein, D. J. (1992). Psychoanalysis and Cognitive Science. *J. Am. Acad. Psychoanal. Dyn. Psychiatr., 20*, 543–559.

Stein, D. J. (1997). *Cognitive science and the unconscious*. Washington, DC: American Psychiatric Press.

Stein, D. J., & Simeon, D. (2009). Cognitive-affective neuroscience of depersonalization. *CNS Spectrums, 14*(9), 467–471.

Stein, D. J., Solms, M., & van Honk, J. (2006). The cognitive-affective neuroscience of the unconscious. *CNS Spectrums, 11*(8), 580–583.

Stein, M. B., Koverola, C., Hanna, C., Torchia, M. G., & McClarty, B. (1997). Hippocampal volume in women victimized by childhood sexual abuse. *Psychological Medicine, 27*, 951–959.

Stein, M. H. (1981). The unobjectionable part of the transference. *Journal of the American Psychoanalytic Association, 29*, 869–892.

Steiner, J. (1987). The interplay between pathological organizations and the paranoid-schizoid and depressive positions. *International Journal of Psychoanalysis, 68*(1), 69–80.

Stern, D. B. (2009). Partners in thought: A clinical process theory of narrative. *Psychoanalytic Quaterly, 78*, 701–731.

Stern, D. N., Sander, L., Nahum, J., Harrison, A., Lyons-Ruth, K., Morgan, A., . . . Tronick, E. (1998). Non-interpretive mechanisms in psychoanalytic therapy: The "something more" than interpretation. *International Journal of Psychoanalysis, 79*, 903–921.

Stevens, A., & Price, J. (1996). *Evolutionary psychiatry: A new beginning*. New York: Routledge.

Stevens, V. (2010). Bion, Freud and Klein. In S. J. Ellman (Ed.), *When theories touch: A historical and theoretical integration of psychoanalytic thought*. London: Karnac, pp. 521–539.

308 References

Stolorow, R. D. (1978). The concept of psychic structure: Its metapsychological and clinical psychoanalytic meanings. *International Journal of Psychoanalysis, 5*, 313–320.

Stolorow, R. D. (1985). Toward a pure psychology of inner conflict. In A. Goldberg (ed.), *Progress in self psychology, Vol. 1*. New York: Guilford Press, pp. 194–201.

Stolorow, R. D. (2006). The relevance of Freud's concept of danger-situation for an inter-subjective-systems perspective. *Psychoanalytic Psychology, 23*(2), 417–419.

Stolorow, R. D. (2007). *Trauma and human existence: Autobiographical, psychoanalytic, and philosophical reflections*. New York: The Analytic Press.

Stolorow, R. D. (2013). Intersubjective-systems theory: A phenomenological-contextualist psychoanalytic perspective. *Psychoanalytic Dialogues, 23*, 383–389.

Stolorow, R., & Atwood, G. (1992). *Contexts of being: The intersubjective foundations of psychological life*. Hillsdale, NJ: The Analytic Press.

Stolorow, R., & Brandchaft, B. (1987). Developmental failure and psychic. *Psychoanalytic Psychology, 4*, 241–253.

Stolorow, R., Brandchaft, B., & Atwood, G. (1987). *Psychoanalytic treatment: An inter-subjective approach*. Hillsdale, NJ: Analytic Press.

Stolorow, R. D., & Lachmann, F. M. (1980). *Psychoanalysis of developmental arrest: Theory and treatment*. New York: International Universities Press.

Stolorow, R., & Lachmann, F. (1984/85). Transference: The future of an illusion. *The Annual of Psychoanalysis, 12/13*, 19–37.

Stone, A. A. (1997, January-February). Where will psychoanalysis survive? *Harvard Magazine*, 35–29.

Stone, L. (1954). The widening scope of indications for psychoanalysis. *Journal of the American Psychoanalytic Association, 2*, 567–594.

Stone, L. (1961). *The psychoanalytic situation: An examination of its development and essential nature*. New York: International Universities Press.

Stout, J. G., Dasgupta, N., Hunsinger, M., & McManus, M. A. (2011). STEMing the tide: Using ingroup experts to inoculate women's self-concept in science, technology, engineering, and mathematics (STEM). *Journal of Personality and Social Psychology, 100*, 255–270.

Stovall-McClough, K. C., Cloitre, M., & McClough, J. F. (2008). Adult attachment and posttraumatic stress disorder in women with histories of childhood abuse. In Steele, H. & Steele, M. (Eds.), *Clinical applications of the adult attachment interview*, pp. 320–340. New York: Guilford Press.

Strachey, J. (1955). Editor's introduction to Studies on Hysteria. *The standard edition of the complete psychological works of Sigmund Freud, Volume 2 (1893–1895): Studies on Hysteria*, ix–xxviii.

Strasburger, H., Waldvogel, B., Mattler, U., Poggel, D. A., Baudewig, J., Dechent, P., & Wustenberg, T. (2010). *Suppression of afferent visual information in a patient with dissociative identity disorder and state-dependent blindness. Abstract*. 33rd Annual European Conference on Visual Perception, Lausanne, Switzerland.

Strong, M. (1998). *A bright red scream: Self-mutilation and the language of pain*. New York: Penguin.

Stroop, J. R. (1935). Studies of interference in serial verbal reactions. *Journal of Experimental Psychology, 18*, 643–662.

Suess, G., Grossman, K., & Sroufe, L. A. (1992). Effects of infant attachment to mother and father on quality of adaptation in preschool: From dyadic to individual organization of self. *International Journal of Behavioral Development, 15*(1), 43–65.

References 309

Sugarman, A. (1994). Toward helping child analysands observe mental functioning. *Psychoanalytic Psychology, 11*(3), 329–339.

Sugarman, A. (1995). Psychoanalysis: Treatment of conflict or deficit. *Psychoanalytic Psychology, 12*, 55–70.

Sugarman, A. (2003). Dimensions of the child analyst's role as a developmental object: Affect regulation and limit setting. *The Psychoanalytic Study of the Child, 58*, 189–213.

Sullivan, H. S. (1955). *The interpersonal theory of psychiatry*. London: Tavistock Publications Limited.

Summers, F. (2011). Kohut's vision and the nuclear program of the self. *International Journal of Psychoanalytic Self Psychology, 6*(3), 289–306.

Suslowa, M. (1863). Veranderungen der hautgefule unter dem einflusse electrischer reizung. *Zeitschrift fur Rationelle Medicin, 18*, 155–160.

Suttie, I. D. (1935). *The origins of love and hate*. London: Routledge, Trench, Trubner & Co., Ltd.

Tallis, F. (2002). *Hidden minds: A history of the unconscious*. New York: Archade Publishing.

Teicholz, J. (1999). *Kohut, Loewald, and the postmoderns*. Hillsdale, NJ: The Analytic Press.

Thelen, E., & Smith, L. (1994). *A dynamic systems approach to the development of cognition and action*. Cambridge, MA: MIT Press.

Titchener, E. (1909). *Lectures on the experimental psychology of the thought-processes*. New York: MacMillan Co., doi:10.1037/10877-000.

Tolpin, M. (2002). Chapter 11: doing psychoanalysis of normal development: forward edge transferences. *Progress in Self Psychology, 18*, 167–190.

Tononi, G. (2004). An information integration theory of consciousness. *BMC Neuroscience, 5*(1), 42.

Tononi, G. (2005). Consciousness, information integration, and the brain. *Progress in Brain Research, 150*, 109–126.

Tronick, E. Z. (1989). Emotions and emotional communication in infants. *American Psychologist, 44*, 112–119.

Tsai, G. E., Condie, D., Wu, M. T., & Chang, I. W. (1999). Functional magnetic resonance imaging of personality switches in a woman with dissociative identity disorder. *Harvard Review of Psychiatry, 7*, 119–122.

Tsuchiya, N., & Koch, C. (2005). Continuous flash suppression reduces negative afterimages. *Nature Neuroscience, 8*(8), 1096–1101.

Tsuchiya, N., Koch, C., Gilroy, L. A., & Blake, R. (2006). Depth of interocular suppression associated with continuous flash suppression, flash suppression, and binocular rivalry. *Journal of Vision, 6*(10), 1068–1078.

Turnbull, O. H., & Solms, M. (2007). Awareness, desire, and false beliefs: Freud in the light of modern neuropsychology. *Cortex, 43*(8), 1083–1090.

Ungless, M. A., Singh, V., Crowder, T. L., Yaka, R., Ron, D., & Bonci, A. (2003). Corticotropin-releasing factor requires CRF binding protein to potentiate NMDA receptors via CRF receptor 2 in dopamine neurons. *Neuron, 39*, 401–407.

Van der Kolk, B. A., & Greenberg, M. S. (1987). The psychobiology of the trauma response: Hyperarousal, constriction, and addiction to traumatic reexposure. In B. A. van der Kolk (Ed.), *Psychological trauma*. Washington, DC: American Psychiatric Press.

Vermetten, E., Schmahl, C., Lindner, S., Loewenstein, R. J., & Bremner, J. D. (2006). Hippocampal and amygdalar volumes in DID. *The American Journal of Psychiatry, 163*(4), 630–636.

310 References

Vermetten, E., Vythilingam, M., Southwick, S. M., Charney, D. S., & Bremner, J. D. (2003). Long-term treatment with paroxetine increases verbal declarative memory and hippocampal volume in posttraumatic stress disorder. *Biological Psychiatry*, *54*(7), 693–702.

Vuilleumier, P. (2004). Anosognosia: The neurology of beliefs and uncertainties. *Cortex*, *40*, 9–17.

Vuilleumier, P. (2005). Hysterical conversion and brain function. *Progress in Brain Research*, *150*, 309–329.

Vuilleumier, P., Mohr, C., Valenza, N., Wetzel, C., & Landis, T. (2003). Hyperfamiliarity for unknown faces after left lateral temporo-occipital venous infarction: A double dissociation with prosopagnosia. *Brain*, *126*, 889–907.

Vuilleumier, P., Sagiv, N., Hazeltine, E., Poldrack, R. A., Swick, D., Rafal, R. D., & Gabrieli, J. D. (2001). Neural fate of seen and unseen faces in visuospatial neglect: A combined event-related functional MRI and event-related potential study. *Proceedings of the National Academy of Sciences of the United States of America*, *98*, 3495–3500.

Vygotsky, L. (1963). *Thought and language*. Cambridge, MA: MIT Press.

Wachtel, E. (1994). *Treating troubled children and their families*. New York: Guilford Press.

Wachtel, P. L. (1980). Transference, schema and assimilation: The relevance of Piaget to the psychoanalytic theory of transference. *The Annual of Psychoanalysis*, *8*, 59–76.

Wachtel, P. L. (2008). *Relational theory and the practice of psychotherapy*. New York: Guilford Press.

Waelder, R. (1936). The principle of multiple function: Observations on over-determination. *The Psychoanalytic Quarterly*, *5*(1), 45–62.

Waldvogel, B., Ullrich, A., & Strasburger, H. (2007). Sighted and blind in one person: A case report and conclusions on the psychoneurobiology of vision. *Nervenarzt*, *78*(11), 1303–1309.

Wallerstein, R. (1984). Anna Freud: Radical innovator and staunch conservative. *Psychoanalytic Study of the Child*, *39*, 65–80.

Wallon, H. (1934, 1973). *Les origines du caractère chez l'enfant. Les préludes du sentiment de pesonnalité*. Paris: Boisvin, PUF.

Wand, G. S., Oswald, L. M., McCaul, M. E., Wong, D. F., Johnson, E., Zhou, Y., . . . Kumar, A.(2007). Association of amphetamine-induced striatal dopamine release and cortisol responses to psychological stress. *Neuropsychopharmacology*, *32*, 2310–2320.

Wang, T., Hauswirth, A. G., Tong, A., Dickman, D. K., & Davis, G. W. (2014). Endostatin is a trans-synaptic signal for homeostatic synaptic plasticity. *Neuron*, *83*, 616–629.

Weinberger, D. (1992, August). *Not worrying yourself sick: The health consequences of repressive coping*. Paper presented at the 100th Annual Convention of the American Psychological Association, Washington, DC.

Weinberger, D. (1995). The construct validity of the repressive coping style. In J. Singer (Ed.), *Repression and dissociation*. Chicago: University of Chicago Press, pp. 337–386.

Weinshel, E. M. (1984). Some observations on the psychoanalytic process. *The Psychoanalytic Quarterly*, *53*, 63–92.

West, D. J. (1977). *Homosexuality re-examined*. Minneapolis: University of Minnesota Press.

Westen, D. (1998). The scientific legacy of Sigmund Freud: Toward a psychodynamically informed psychological science. *Psychological Bulletin*, *124*, 333–371.

Westen, D. (1999). The scientific status of unconscious processes: Is Freud really dead? *Journal of the American Psychoanalytic Association*, *47*, 1061–1106.

References 311

Westen, D. (2006). Implications of research in cognitive neuroscience for psychodynamic psychotherapy. In G. O. Gabbard, J. S. Beck, & J. Holmes (Eds.), *Oxford textbook of psychotherapy*. Oxford, NY: Oxford Universities Press. pp. 443–448.

Westen, D., & Gabbard, G. O. (2002). Developments in cognitive neuroscience: I. Conflict, compromise, and connectionism. *Journal of the American Psychoanalytic Association*, *50*(1), 53–98.

White, R. W. (1959). Motivation reconsidered: The concept of competence. *Psychological Review*, *66*, 297–333.

Widlöcher, D. (2002a). Presidential address: 42nd congress of the International Psychoanalytical Association. *The International Journal of Psychoanalysis*, *83*, 205–210.

Widlöcher, D. (2002b). Primary love and infantile sexuality: An eternal debate. In D. Widlöccher (Ed.), *Infantile sexuality and attachment*. New York: Other Press, pp. 1–35.

Wilson, E. (1941). *The wound and the bow*. New York: Houghton Mifflin and Company.

Winnicott, D. W. (1938). Shyness and nervous disorders in children. In D. W. Winnicott, *The child and the outside world: Studies in developing relationships, 1957*. London: Tavistock Publications Limited, pp. 35–39.

Winnicott, D. W. (1960a). Ego distortion in terms of true and false self. In: *The maturational processes and the facilitating environment*. London: Hogarth Press, 1965, pp. 56–63.

Winnicott, D. W. (1960b). The theory of the parent–infant relationship. In D. W. Winnicott, *The maturational processes and the facilitating environment*. New York: International Universities Press, pp. 37–55.

Winnicott, D. W. (1965). *The maturational processes and the facilitating environment: Studies in the theory of emotional development*. New York: International Universities Press.

Winnicott, D. W. (1967). The location of cultural experience. *The International Journal of Psychoanalysis, 48*, 368–372.

Winnicott, D. W. (1974). The fear of breakdown. *The International Journal of Psychoanalysis, 1*, 103–117.

Winnicott, D. W. (1994). Hate in the countertransference. *The Journal of Psychotherapy Practice and Research, 3*, 348–356.

Winson, J. (1985). *Brain and psyche*. Garden City, NY: Anchor Press/Doubleday.

Wong, P. S. (1999). Anxiety, signal anxiety and unconscious anticipation: Neuroscientific evidence for an unconscious signal function in humans. *Journal of the American Psychoanalytic Association, 47*, 817–841.

Wundt, W. (1907). Über Ausfrage experimente und über die methoden zur psychologie des denkens. *Psychologische Studien, 3*, 301–360.

Yavich, L., & Tiihonen, J. (2000). Ethanol modulates evoked dopamine release in mouse nucleus accumbens: Dependence on social stress and dose. *European Journal of Pharmacology, 401*, 365–373.

Young-Bruehl, E. (2002). Review of the book *Anna Freud: A view of development, disturbance and therapeutic techniques*. *Psychoanalytic Review, 89*, 757–760.

Zetzel, E. R. (1956). Current concepts of transference. *International Journal of Psychoanalysis, 37*, 369–376.

Zetzel, E. R. (1971). A developmental approach to the borderline patient. *American Journal of Psychiatry, 4*, 149–155.

Zubieta, J.-K., Smith, Y. R., Bueller, J. A., Kilbourn, M. R., Jewett, D. M., Meyer, C. R., . . . Stohler, C. S. (2001). Regional mu opioid receptor regulation of sensory affective dimensions of pain. *Science, 293*, 311–315.

Index

AAI *see* Adult Attachment Interview (AAI)
Abraham, K. 26
abreaction 12
active assimilation into ego 23
Adams, C. 174
adaptation 198
addictive patterns 275–6
addressing defenses against painful emotions technique (Bornstein) 227
Adult Attachment Interview (AAI) 210, 212, 213; Can't Classify rating 219; infant-mother/father attachment relationships and 220–1; rating/classification system 217–19; Unresolved responses 217–18
adversarial self-object 130
affect integration, failure of 150–1
affects, defined 26
affect-trauma model, attachment theory as 214–15
affirmative analytic stance 59–60
"Affirming 'That's not Psycho-Analysis!' On the Value of the Politically Incorrect Act of Attempting to Define the Limits of Our Field" (Blass) 49
aggression, Klein and importance of 92–3
Ainsworth, M. 215–17
Aisenstein, M. 40
Alexander, F. xviii
ambivalence 54
American Psychoanalytic Association 107, 127
American Psychological Association xvi
analysis of defense 25
analyst, modern conflict theory and 32–3, 35–7
analytic pair, truly separate 110

analytic trust 106–26; Bion and 112–15; clinical examples of 115–24; conflict and 109–10; described 106–7; establishment of 110–12; examples of pathways to 111–12; historical review of 107–10; overview of 106–7; termination phase of analysis and 124; transference and 108, 111; truly separate analytic pair and 110; unconscious fantasy and 108–9
analyzability of patients 107
Anderson, M. C. 264, 265
anxiety: defined 26; psychical conflict and 207
Apfelbaum, B. 13–14, 15
Apprey, M. 162, 174–5
Arlow, J. A. 32–3, 36, 242, 243
Armstrong-Perlman, E. M. 78–9
Aron, L. 31
arrest experience, devitalizing attitudes and 135–6
Attachment (Bowlby) 210, 214
attachment theory and research 210–22; AAI rating/classification system and 217–19; as affect-trauma model of mind 214–15; Ainsworth's influence on 215–17; Bowlby and 210–12; conflict-free mind and 219; conflict understanding and 220; core assumption of 211–12; early experiences and, influence of 220–1; interpersonal/intrapersonal conflict and 213–14; in 1980s 210–13; overview of 210; stating both sides of conflict 221–2
attractor state 155
Atwood, G. 31
Auchincloss, E. 225
autonomous ego concept 24
average expectable environment 24
aversive racism 255

bad object situation 77, 82, 85–6, 87, 88
Balint, M. 106, 114
Balints, A. 65
Balints, M. 65
Banaji, M. R. 245, 251–2
Baranger, M. 174
Baranger, W. 161, 162, 168, 169, 174
bastion 174
Becker, T. 225
Benedek, T. F. 65
Benjamin, J. 31, 33, 166
Berger, J. 175
Bergmann, M. 48
Berrios, G. E. 266
beta elements concept 112–13
Between Seduction and Inspiration: Man (UIT) 195
bewusssteinslagen 245
Beyond the Pleasure Principle (Freud) 2–3, 180, 270
Bibring, E. 60, 232–3
binding drives of psychical conflict 203–6
Bion, W. R. 48, 91, 161, 167, 168, 169, 175; analytic trust and 112–15; beta elements concept 112–13; containment concept of 97–101
Birksted-Breen, D. 124–5
Blass, R. B. 49, 124
Boesky, D. 29, 30–1
Bolognini, S. 40, 42
Bornstein, B. 227, 232
Boston Group 137
Botella, C. 166
Bowlby, J. 66, 210–11, 212; conflict behavior and 214; disorganized/disoriented behaviors and 217; interpersonal conflict and 213–14
Brandchaft, B. 132, 139
Brenner, C. xviii–xix, 21, 25, 219, 229, 242; analyst/patient irrationality and 33; childhood wishes and 33–4; compromise formation theory and 227–8; countertransference and 31–2; infantile wishes and 182–3; mechanisms of defense and 27–8; multiple function concept and 28–9; normal behaviors and 28; signal anxiety and 26–7; structural theory and 29–31; transference and 108, 111
Breuer, J. 1, 2
Briñol, P. 253
British Psychoanalytic Society 212, 218

Britton, R. 102–3
Bromberg, P. M. 73, 163, 168; unconscious fantasy interpretation of 108–9
Busch, F. 124, 125

Cassirer, B. 114
Castration, symbolisations (House) 205
Castration complex: attachment theory and 214; binding and 205–6, 207; danger situation and 152, 153, 201; Freud and 15–16; signal anxiety and 26; unconscious fantasy and 258
change, conflict and 160–76; analysts as caretakers and 163–4; analysts as wounded healers and 162–3; chaos theory and 165–8; clinical material 169–76; clinical situations 168–9; countertransference feelings and 164–5; creation/destruction and 165–6; overview of 160–1; relational perspective of 161–2; Rey and 161–2
chaos theory 165–8
Charcot, J. M. 3, 4, 72–3, 270
Chefetz, R. A. 73
children's therapy, conflict theory in 223–40; child/adolescent concepts 223–6; compromise formation theory 227–9; defenses/defense mechanisms 229–30; externalizing symptoms, dynamic psychotherapy approach to 236–8; internalizing symptoms clinical illustration 234–5; overview of 226–7; psychodynamic treatment for 239–40; technique of interpretation, development of 231–4
clarifications, defined 232, 233
cognitive dissonance 254
compatible judgment 248
compromised message 200
compromise formations: components of 30; defined 229; unconscious fantasy and 243
conflict: compromise formation and 227–9; defined 253; elements of 128–9; fate of (*see* conflict, fate of); free association and (*see* conflict, free association and); implicit-explicit attitudes and 253–4; interpersonal relations and 255; in intersubjective-systems theory 147–52; psychoanalysis and xvi; role of xvi–xvii; self-concept and 254–5; in social cognitive sense 253–8; stating both

314 Index

sides of 221–2; understanding of, mixed feelings and 220

conflict, change and 160–76; analysts as caretakers and 163–4; analysts as wounded healers and 162–3; chaos theory and 165–8; clinical material 169–76; clinical situations 168–9; countertransference feelings and 164–5; creation/destruction and 165–6; overview of 160–1; relational perspective of 161–2; Rey and 161–2

conflict, fate of 38–49; metapsychology debates and 39; narcissistic slights and 47–8; new theories and 38–9; overview of 38–9; psychoanalytic technique and 39–42; re-defining psychoanalysis and 45–6; unconscious fantasies role in 42–5

conflict, free association and 51–61; divergences and 52–53; formulation of 51–3; mourning example of 54–8; overview of 51–2; self-criticism example of 58–60; termination of psychoanalysis example of 61

conflict, self psychology model and 127–44; clinical illustration of 141–3; development of 129–33; elements of 128–9; experience and, organization of 133–7; motivation and 137–9; overview of 127–8; theory of therapeutic action and 139–41

conflict and compromise formation 227–9; defenses/defense mechanisms and 229–30; described 227–8; drive derivative concept and 229; internalizing/externalizing disorders and 228–9

conflict-free mind 219

conflict-free sphere concept 24, 28

Confucius 16

"Confusion of Tongues" (Ferenczi) 167–8

constancy principle 2–3, 5–6; mental apparatus and 8–10

containment concept 97–101

continuous flash suppression 263

convergent conflicts 54; self-criticism and 58–60

Corrigan, E. 163

corticolimbic disconnection hypothesis 266

countertransference 31–2

Craig, A. D. 276

danger situation concept 152–5

Dasgupta, N. 251–2

dead-alive 168

defense: compromise formation and 229–30; Freud, A. and 230; Freud, S. and 230; interpretation of, against unwelcome affects 231–4; mechanisms 230, 232

defense mechanisms, defined 232

defenses against unpleasant emotions, interpreting child and adolescent 231–4; overview of 236

defensive self-ideal, development of 150

denial in fantasy, as defense mechanism 230

denial in word and act, as defense mechanism 230

depersonalization disorder (DPD) 265–6

depressive affects, defined 26

depressive position: Klein and 94–7; Likierman and 97

depth psychology 25

Depue, B. E. 264

Descartes, R. 152

desire theory 177–94; clinical presentation of 186–9; divided subject and 177–9; lack and 179–86; narcissism and 189–91; in practice 191–4

developmental arrest 17–18

developmental motivation 138, 143

developmental tilt toward non-conflictual, pre-Oedipal issues 148

"Development of a Child" (Klein) 92

Diagnostic and Statistical Manual of Mental Disorders-V (APA) 265

disorganized behaviors 216

displacement, as defense mechanism 230

disruptive disorders (DD) 228

disruptive mood dysregulation disorder (DMDD) 228

dissociation 265–70; depersonalization disorder 265–6; described 265; dissociative identity disorder 266–9; neural basis of 269; repression and 72–7

dissociative (conversion) disorder 270

dissociative identity disorder (DID) 266–9

divergent conflicts 53–4

divided subject 177–9; lack and formation of 179–81

Dovidio, J. F. 255

"Dream of the Butcher's Wife" (Freud) 193

drive derivatives 229; categories of 229

drives, categories of 229

drive theory 4–5

dual instinct theory 94–7; Klein use of 94–7

Eagle, M. N. 38, 146–7, 153–4
edge of chaos 166
Ego and the Id, The (Freud) 21, 23, 55, 178
Ego and the Mechanisms of Defense, The (Freud) 24–5, 27–8
ego psychology 25; history of 21–2
Ego Psychology and the Problem of Adaptation (Hartmann) 25
Ehling, T. 267
either-or dilemmas 52
emotion regulation (ER) 232
empathic failures 139
enactment, concept of 225
endopsychic structure, Fairbairn's theory of: clinical phenomena 78–84; conflict in 77–8; described 69; dissociation, repression and 72–7; internal object 70–2; in and out program 84–5; splitting of ego and object 68–70; treatment goals 85–9
Eros and destructiveness, conflict between 8–10
evacuation concept 113
evolutionary mismatch 274–5
experience, organization of 133–7; arrest experience, devitalizing attitudes and 135–6; dream research and 133–4; learning and 133, 134–5; memory processes and 133
experience-near technique 227
explicit attitudes: defined 256; implicit attitudes and 246; measurement of 245
explicit emotion regulation 232
explicit self-esteem 257
exterior reality 198
externalizing disorders 228–9; case example of 237–8; described 236–7

Fairbairn, W. D. 10, 63–89, 174
Fairbairn theory of object relations 65–8; conflict in 77–8; described 67–8; influences on 66–7; precursors to 65–7
family systems therapy 224
Fenichel, O. 25
Ferenczi, S. 65, 167–8, 223, 224, 225
Ferro, A. 175
Festinger, L. 254
Fondation Jean Laplanche 195
free association 261
Freeman, W. 165, 166
Freud, A. 5, 6, 14, 76, 225; defense mechanisms systematized by 226–7,

230; mechanisms of defense and 24–5, 27–8; regression and 57–8; transference neurosis in children and 231
Freud, S. xvii, xviii, 1, 2, 38, 76, 113, 177, 179, 181; affect-trauma model 214–15; criteria for analyzability 107, 108; danger situation concept 152–5; defense and 230; developmental arrest illness comparison 17–18; dual instinct theory 94–7; final view 8–10; hypnosis and 12; id-ego relationship and 5, 14–15; inner conflict theory of 1–19; internal representations and 211; mourning and 54–7; Nirvana principle and 9; object relations theory 63–5; repetition compulsion and 270; repression and 52–3, 260; signal anxiety concept 22–3; splitting of consciousness 72; superego concept of 66–7; suppression and 263; transference concept 224; tripartite model 127; unconscious conflict and 41–2; unconscious fantasies and 243; war neurosis and 270–1; working through concept of 12–13
Freudian slip 261
Freudian theory of object relations 63–5; components of 63–4; inner conflict and 64–5; object defined 63; social reality and 65
Friedman, L. 24, 34

Gaertner, S. L. 255
Genesis of an Interpretation, The (Arlow) 36–7
Ghent, E. 161, 166
Goldberg, P. 175
Goldner, V. 167
Gordon, P. E. 163
Gray, P. 42, 231, 233
Green, A. 41
Greenberg, J. 11, 45
Greenberg, M. 271, 272
Greenson, R. R. 107
Greenwald, A. G. 245, 251–2
Griesinger, W. 52
Grotstein, J. 98
Guntrip, H. 71, 84, 85

Hafter-Gray (1986) 31
Hampstead Clinic 230
Handbook of Attachment (Slade) 218
Hanslmayr, S. 265

316 Index

Hartmann, H. 24, 25, 127; normal functioning and 28
"Hate in the Counter-transference" (Winnicott) 166
He, S. 263
Hegel, G. W. F. 182
Heidegger, M. 152
here and now interventions 124
Hermann, I. 65
Hilgard, E. R. 73
Hoffman, L. 31, 232
homeostasis 275–6
homophobia 261
Horney, K. 10
Hunger Games, The (Collins) 253
hysteria: dual consciousness characteristic of 265; hypnosis and 270
hysterical symptoms: inner conflict and 1–2; repression and 2; splitting of consciousness characteristic of 2

id analysis 25
id-ego relationship 5, 14–15
identification: as defense mechanism 230; Fairbairn and 72
identification with the aggressor, as defense mechanism 230
imageless thought 245
Imaginary, Lacan and 188, 190
Implicit Association Test (IAT) 242, 246–52; areas of divergence in 257–8; features of 244, 246–7; implicit attitudes and 245–6, 251–2; logic of 247; predicting behaviors with 248–51; race 247–8; uses for 244
implicit attitudes 245–6; defined 245, 256; explicit attitudes and 246; Implicit Association Test and 246–52; malleability of 251–2, 257; measurement of 245–6
implicit emotion regulation 232
implicit-explicit attitudinal discrepancies (IEDs) 253–4; areas of convergence in 256–7; conflict between 256–7; interpersonal relations and 255; self-concept and 254–5
implicit self-esteem 257
implicit social cognition 245
in and out program 84–5
incompatible judgment 248
infant-father attachment relationships 220–1

infant-mother attachment relationships 220–1
Inhibitions, Symptoms and Anxiety (Freud) 22, 23, 24, 214
inner conflict in Freudian theory 1–19; cases of 1; constancy principle and 2–3, 5–6, 8–10; drive theory and 4–5; epilogue 16–19; between Eros and destructiveness 8–10; forms of 7–10; hysteria and, development of 1–2; between id and ego 5, 14–15; between individual and social reality 6–7; origins and nature of 15–16; between pleasure and reality principles 6; post-Freudian conceptions of 10–11; psychoanalytic treatment and 11–16; repression and 2–4, 11–13; traumatic ideas and 4
Institut de France 195
intentions, defined 137
intention unfolding process, tracking 137
internalizing disorders 228–9; clinical illustration of 234–5
internal object of endopsychic structure 70–2
interpersonal conflict, attachment theory and 213–14
interpretation, defined 233
Interpretation of Dreams, The (Freud) 21, 23, 52
intersubjective awareness 97
intersubjective-systems theory 146–59; case illustration of 156–8; conflict in 147–52; danger situation concept and 152–5; overview of 146–7
intersubjectivity concept 31
intrapersonal conflict, attachment theory and 213–14
intrasystemic conflict 53
isolation, as defense mechanism 230

Jacobs, T. 226
Jacobs, T. J. 32
Janet, P. 2, 3, 4, 72–3, 75, 265
Jiang, Y. 263
Jones, E. 67, 78
Jordan, C. H. 254
Joseph, B. 100
Journal of the American Psychoanalytic Association 37

Kernberg, O. 73
Kierkegaard, S. 16

Kihlstrom, J. F. 73
Kikuchi, H. 261–2
Klein, G. 65, 153
Klein, M. 27, 57, 91–105, 213, 225, 231; aggression in children and 92–3; Britton and 102–3; conflict, contemporary views of 101–3; containment concept and 97–101; depressive position and 94–7; dual instinct theory and 94–7; evacuation concept 113; overview of 91–2; superego and 94
Kohut, H. 17, 45, 59, 89; conflict and, elements of 128–9; development of the self and 129–33; motivation and 137–8; program of action 138; self-selfobject (relational) matrix 127–8; theory of therapeutic action 139–41
Kriegman, D. 130–1
Kris, A. 46
Kris, E. xvi, 1, 21, 91, 227

Lacan, L. 177–94; function of misrecognition and 177–8; *see also* desire theory
Lachmann, F. M. 130
lack: desire and 181–6; function of, in divided subject formation 179–81; wish and 181–2
Langer, S. K. 114
Laplanche, J. 168, 195–6
"Laplanche standing on one foot" (Laplanche) 195–6
Lecours, S. 41
Leibold, J. M. 249
Levenson, E. 45
Levithan, D. 84
Libet, B. 262
Lichtenberg, J. 39, 132–3, 137
Likierman, M. 97
Loewald, H. 187, 191–2
Loss (Bowlby) 210–11, 214
"Loss of Reality in Neurosis and Psychosis, The" (Freud) 197
Lotterman, A. C. 227
Love in the Time of Cholera (Márquez) 84
Low, B. 9
Lyons-Ruth, K. 163

Mahler, M. 11
Main, M. 213, 216, 217–19
Making and Breaking of Affectional Bonds, The (Bowlby) 212
manqué 180

Márquez, G. G. 84
Mayer, A. 245
McConnell, A. R. 249
mechanisms of defense: Brenner and 27–8; in children's therapy 229–30; defined 232; denial in fantasy as 230; denial in word and act as 230; displacement as 230; Freud, A. and 24–5, 27–8; identification as 230; identification with the aggressor as 230; isolation as 230; modern conflict theory and 27–8; projection as 230; reaction formation as 230; regression as 230; sublimation as 230; transformation into the opposite as 230; turning against one's self as 230; undoing as 230
memory repression 261–2
metapsychology 202
Mind in Conflict, The (Brenner) 219, 229
Mind Object, The (Corrigan & Gordon) 163
"mirror stage" (Lacan) 189
misrecognition, function of 177–8
"Missing Link: Parental Sexuality in the Oedipus Complex, The" (Britton) 102
Mitchell, S. 45
Mitchell, S. A. 11, 31, 33, 70, 148, 159
modern conflict theory 227; analyst and 32–3, 35–7; Brenner and 21, 25–9; childhood wishes and 33–4; evolution of 21–37; Fenichel and 25; Freud, A. and 24–5; Freud, S. and 21–3; Hartmann and 24, 28; mechanisms of defense and 27–8; multiple function concept and 23, 28–9; normal functioning and 28; overview of 21; publications critical to development of 21–5; relational turn in psychoanalysis and 31–7; signal anxiety and 26–7; structural theory and 29–31; Waelder and 23–4, 28–9
modes of mentation 191–2
Montgomery, J. 274, 275–6
motivation, self psychology model and 137–9
motives, defined 137
mourning: acknowledgment and 55; convergent conflicts and 54–8; divergent conflicts and 56–7; Freud, A. and 57–8; Freud, S. and 54–7; interrupted 55–6; Ogden and 54
Mourning and Melancholia (Freud) xx, 54–5, 66
multiple function concept 23

narcissism 58–9; desire theory and 189–91
narcissistic slights, conflict and 47–8
National Institute of Mental Health
(NIMH) 239
neural basis of conflict 260–77; addictive
patterns and 275–6; depersonalization
disorder and 265–6; dissociation and
265–70; dissociative identity disorder
and 266–9; evolutionary mismatch and
274–5; homeostasis and 275–6; hysteria,
hypnosis and 270; overview of 260;
PTSD and 270–2; repetition compulsion
and 270–6; repression and 260–3; self-
harm and 272–4; suppression and 263–5
neural basis of dissociation 269
"Neurosis and Psychosis" (Freud) 197
neutral identity states (NIS) 266
neutralization process 24
neutralized energy concept 24
New Foundations for Psychoanalysis
(Laplanche) 195
New York Psychoanalytic Society and
Institute 225
Nietzsche, F. 182
Nirvana principle 9
non-verbal interactions as child therapy
technique 223–4
normal functioning, modern conflict theory
and 28
Nosek, B. A. 246
not me concept 77

object relations, Fairbairn theory of 65–8;
conflict in 77–8; described 67–8; influences on 66–7; precursors to 65–7
object relations, Freudian theory of 63–5;
components of 63–4; inner conflict and
64–5; object defined 63; social reality
and 65
Odyssey, The (Homer) 253
Oedipus complex 13; binding and 205,
207; Britton use of 102; formulation
of, theory 13; Klein use of 93–4;
Kohut exception to 127; termination of
psychoanalysis and 61
Ogden, T. H. xx, 54, 66, 85, 175
omnipotence 163
"one-person" to "two-person" psychology,
shift from 225
"On Understanding and Not
Understanding" (Joseph) 100
Orange, D. 31

organized implicit associations 244
Orth, J. 245
otherness of oneself 16

pansexualism 201–2
parlêtre 184–5
passive object love 65
Paulus, M. P. 275
Peltz, R. 175
Piaget, J. 71
Piers, C. 167
Pitman, R. K. 273
pleasure principle: characteristic of 6;
reality principle and, conflict between 6
post-partum symbiosis 65
"Postscript to Dora" (Freud) 224
post-traumatic stress disorder (PTSD)
270–2
Pre-conscious-Conscious (Pcs.-Cs.) system
of mind 242
primal superego 94
primary identification 84
primary object relation 65
primary process 22
Prince, M. 72
principle of multiple function 28–9
Principle of Multiple Function
(Waelder) 24
Problem of Anxiety, The (Freud) 207
projection, as defense mechanism 230
projective identification 112, 115
psychical conflict, forces at play in 195–207;
in analytic treatment 207; anxiety and
207; binding/unbinding drives as 203–6;
introduction to 195–6; overview of 197;
reality and 197–201; soul and 202–3;
structural model and 203; superego and
206; symptoms and 207
psychical reality 199–201
psychoanalysis: birth of 1; conflict
and xvi; defined 91; described 242;
from id analysis to ego psychology
25; intersubjectivity concept in 31;
re-defining 45–6; relational turn in,
modern conflict theory and 31–7
"Psychoanalysis and Child Care"
(Bowlby) 212
psychoanalytic mind, creating 40
psychoanalytic technique, conflict and
39–42
psychoanalytic treatment, inner conflict
and 11–16

"Psychogenesis of Manic-Depressive States, The" (Klein) 95
psychopathology, conceptions of 17
Psychopathology of Everyday Life, The (Freud) 178
PTSD *see* post-traumatic stress disorder (PTSD)
pull-component of repression 52–3
punitive, unconscious self-criticism 60
push-component of repression 52–3

race Implicit Association Test (IAT) 247–8; brain activity/self-regulatory resources and 250–1; predicting behaviors with 248–51
reaction formation 52; as defense mechanism 230
Real concept, Lacan and 188
reality: exterior 198; psychical 199–201
reality principle: characteristic of 6; pleasure principle and, conflict between 6
regression, as defense mechanism 230
Regulation Focused Psychotherapy for Externalizing Behaviors (RFP-C) 239–40
Reinders, A. A. 267, 269
relational/conflictual model 11
relational experience 128
relational self psychology 128
Renik, O. 32
renunciation 13–14
repetition compulsion 270–6; described 270; PTSD and 270–2; self-harm and 272–4
repression 260–3; as conflict 52; inner conflict and 2–4, 11–13; push/pull-components of 52–4
resilience 130
Rey, J. H. 161, 167, 168
Ribble, M. 65–6
Rice, T. R. 232
Richeson, J. A. 250
Ritchey, T. 274, 275–6
Rothstein, A. 33
Rubens, R. L. 81
rupture-repair model 219

Safran, J. D. 219
Samberg, E. 225
Sandler, J. 214, 227, 230
Sandman, C. A. 272–3

Sar, V. 267
Schafer, R. 30, 70, 100, 105
Schröder-Abé, M. 254–5
Schur, M. 30
Schwaber, E. A. 32
Searles, H. 164
secondary process 22
Secure Base: Clinical Applications of Attachment Theory, A (Bowlby) 212, 218
Segal, H. 57
the self: adversity and 130; defined 129; development of, within self-selfobject matrix 129–33; relationships and 129–30
self-criticism, convergent conflicts and 58–60
self-harm 272–4; emotional 273–4; physical 272–3; types of 272
selfobject: adversarial 130; defined 129; dimension of relationships 132; experience 132; needs 130, 131–2; redefining 132; ruptures 139; transferences 131; trauma and 130–1
self-preservation 198, 200–1
self-preservative message 200
self psychology model, conflict and 127–44; clinical illustration of 141–3; development of 129–33; elements of 128–9; experience and, organization of 133–7; motivation and 137–9; overview of 127–8; theory of therapeutic action and 139–41
self-selfobject matrix: development of self within 129–33; Kohut and 127–8
sense of self 132
Separation (Bowlby) 210, 214
sexual message 200
sexual psychical apparatus 202
Shelton, J. 250
Sierra, M. 266
signal anxiety 22–3; modern conflict theory and 26–7
Slade, A. 218
Slavin, M. 130–1, 176
Smeekens, S. 226
Smith, H. F. 29
Solomon, J. 216
"Some Notes on Intersubjectivity" (Arlow) 33
soul-apparatus 202–3
Spielrein, S. 165, 166, 171
Spillius, E. B. 113, 124
Spinoza, B. 182
Spitz, R. A. 38

320 Index

"Splitting of the Ego in the Process of Defense" (Freud) 74, 86
Stapert, W. 226
Stein, M. H. 108
Steiner, J. 100
Stevens, V. 112–13, 114
Stolorow, R. 31, 132, 139, 146, 150, 152, 154
Stone, A. 16
Stone, L. 106, 107–8
Stout, J. G. 252
Strachey, J. 2
Strange Situation Procedure (SSP) 216
Stroop task 250
structural theory: of the mind 21, 22; modern conflict theory and 29–31
sublimation 13; as defense mechanism 230
Sugarman, A. 45, 233
Sullivan, H. S. 77
superego, psychical conflict and 206
suppression 263–5
Suttie, I. D. 66
Symbolic, Lacan and 188
symptoms, psychical conflict and 207

"That which Patients Bring to Analysis" (Rey) 161–2
theory of practice 25
theory of therapeutic action 139–41; rupture/repair cycles 139
"Relevance of Freud's Concept of Danger-Situations for an Intersubjective-Systems Perspective, The" (Stolorow) 146
think/no-think paradigm 264
Titchener, E. 245
topographic model of the mind 21–2
transformation into the opposite, as defense mechanism 230
trauma: Freud definition of 4; unconscious self-criticism 60
traumatic identity state (TIS) 266
triangular space 102–3
Tronick, E. Z. 219
truth drive 98
turning against one's self, as defense mechanism 230

twinship selfobject needs 130
two-person psychology 31

unbinding drives of psychical conflict 203–6
unconscious conflict 242–3; experimental literature on 243–4
unconscious fantasy 242–59; compromise formations and 243; conflict and 42–5, 109–10, 253–8; described 243; experimental literature on 243–4; future research for 258–9; Implicit Association Test and 246–52; implicit attitudes and 245–6; interpretation of 108–9; overview of 242–3
Unconscious in Translation (UIT) 195
unconscious mentation 41
unconscious self-criticism 60
Unconscious (Ucs.) system of mind 242
"Understanding and Resolving Emotional Conflict: The London Parent-Child Project" (Steele et al.) 220
undoing, as defense mechanism 230
Unfinished Copernican Revolution, The (Laplanche) 195
utilization train duration (UTD) 262

Van der Kolk, B. A. 271, 272
Vermetten, E. 267
von Hug-Hellmuth, H. 224–5

Waelder, R. 23–4; principle of multiple function 28–9
Wallerstein, R. 25
Wallon, H. 189
Weinshel, E. 53
Westen, D. 133
Widlöcher, D. 11
Wilson, E. 162
Winnicott, D. W. 66, 106, 113, 114, 136, 166, 171
Wundt, W. 245

Young-Bruehl, E. 24–5

Zetzel, E. R. 106, 107